THE PHILOSOPHY OF TAXATION AND PUBLIC FINANCE

The Philosophy of Taxation and Public Finance

Robert W. McGee
JD, PhD, CPA, CMA, CIA, CBA
Andreas School of Business
Barry University
Miami Shores, Florida
USA

Kluwer Academic Publishers
Boston/Dordrecht/London

Distributors for North, Central and South America:
Kluwer Academic Publishers
101 Philip Drive
Assinippi Park
Norwell, Massachusetts 02061 USA
Telephone (781) 871-6600
Fax (781) 681-9045
E-Mail <kluwer@wkap.com>
Distributors for all other countries:
Kluwer Academic Publishers Group
Post Office Box 17
3300 AH Dordrecht, THE NETHERLANDS
Tel: +31 (0) 78 657 60 00
Fax: +31 (0) 78 657 64 74

E-Mail <services@wkap.nl>

Electronic Services <http://www.wkap.nl>

The philosophy of taxation and public finance / Robert W. McGee
p.cm.
Includes bibliographical references and index.
ISBN 1-4020-7716-5

Printed on acid-free paper.
Printed in the United States of America

TABLE OF CONTENTS

PART FIVE: THE TAX SYSTEM OF A FREE SOCIETY

PREFACE

Although I had heard of taxation as a child, I didn't take much notice of it until I read Sammy Davis Junior's autobiography as a teenager in the 1960s. His book mentioned the tax audit he was subjected to and the fact that he had to pay more than 90 percent of his income to the federal government. I was shocked that my government -- in the land of the free and the home of the brave -- could get away with that. It seemed grossly unfair that people like Sammy could do all the work and take all the risks and then have to hand over practically all of their earnings to some government. A few years later I read that the Beatles had to pay a similar percentage to the British government and that Michael Caine left England because of its high taxes under Harold Wilson.

My interest in taxation was piqued when I received my first paycheck. I wondered what happened to a large chunk of the money I earned because it was not there. It had vanished before I could see it because the withholding tax rules that President Roosevelt signed into law forced my employer to take out a portion of what I earned and send it to Washington. It made me start to wonder whether FDR was as great a president as my father said he was.

In a sense, the research for this book began in the early 1970s, when I first started working as an accountant while studying economics in graduate school at night. While working as a bank auditor I learned how people set up trusts to minimize the amount of their life savings that would be confiscated by the government when they died. Through my economics study and extracurricular reading I learned how the tax system was used not only to raise funds for government but also to encourage certain activities while discouraging others. I learned how government at all levels wasted billions of dollars doing unproductive things and things it shouldn't be doing at all. My parents and their friends were complaining about property taxes and the fact that they didn't really own their own homes because they had to pay rent to the government in the form of property taxes in order to keep them. I read that some elderly people in California had to sell their homes because they could no longer pay the property taxes the government demanded.

I decided to specialize in taxation, not so much because of the good career path that such a specialty provided but because I wanted to help people to keep as large a portion of the money they earned as possible. I worked in corporate tax and had a small individual tax practice on the side. I went to law school and also earned a master's degree in taxation. I wanted to learn as much as I could about taxation so that I could do the best possible job for my employers and clients.

As I got older my interests shifted more into economic philosophy and public finance, although I maintained my interest in taxation. This book is the culmination of my years of study, practice and reflection. I hope you enjoy reading it as much as I enjoyed writing it.

Robert W. McGee
September 2003

About the author:

Robert W. McGee is a professor in the Andreas School of Business at Barry University in Miami. He has published more than 40 books and more than 300 scholarly papers in the fields of accounting, taxation, economics, law and philosophy. He is a certified public accountant (CPA) and attorney, has taught both public finance and taxation and has doctorates in accounting, taxation, economics, law and philosophy, which makes him uniquely qualified to write this book. Professor McGee was a tax practitioner for many years before becoming an academic and continues to act as a consultant. One of his clients was the United States Agency for International Development (USAID), which sent him to Armenia, Bosnia and Russia to consult on economic reform. He has also served as a nonresident consultant to the USAID economic reform projects in Georgia and Kazakhstan and has done a major study on reforming the Latvian public finance system for the Latvian Finance Ministry.

PART ONE

INTRODUCTION AND OVERVIEW

Chapter 1

WHAT SHOULD GOVERNMENT DO?

One of the threshold questions one must ask when discussing the role of taxation and public finance is: "What should government do?" This question is important because anything that government does must be paid for by someone. The more things that government does, the more things that people must pay for.

Getting back to the question, what should government do, the easy (and wrong) answer is that government should do things that individuals cannot do for themselves. Some people think that government should take care of the young, the old, the infirm, the insane, the unemployed, single parents, people who don't have health insurance, etc., because these groups are unable to take care of themselves. Government should also operate a police force to protect people from murder, rape, robbery and other crimes. Government should maintain an army to protect against invasion or attack by foreigners. It should maintain some kind of court system to settle disputes. It should build and maintain roads. This argument is basic and pervasive within any society. The problems is that all of these things cost money.

The philosophical problem with this line of argument is that it is a non sequitur. In its generic form, the argument runs something like this: There is an unmet need, therefore the government has to provide for the need. When put in this form, the weakness of this line of reasoning becomes more apparent.

A better question would be: Should someone do something to alleviate this perceived problem, and if so, who should do it, the government, the private, profit making sector or the voluntary, nonprofit sector? There are really at least three possibilities. The government solution is only one of at least three options. Actually, there is a fourth option -- do nothing. This option is the best one when doing anything will make the situation worse.

Free trade is one example. Free trade is the best policy; therefore, any other policy is not the best policy. Any policy that restricts free trade causes more harm than good. From a utilitarian standpoint, there are more losers than winners. From the rights standpoint, any restriction on free trade violates someone's rights. So the best solution is not to regulate trade between or among consenting adults under any circumstances. We will not go into a full discussion of the free trade argument here, since doing so would take us too far afield of the main topic, which has to do with taxation and public finance and the place of government. Besides, the free trade argument has been covered elsewhere.[1] But the free trade question is a good illustration of the various options.

There is nothing moral about forcing taxpayers to fund programs that transfer money from the people who have earned it to people who have not earned it. People who receive such government handouts are receiving stolen property. Private charity is better, not only because it is more efficient than government welfare but also because it is based on voluntarism rather than coercion. Voluntary charity is the only moral way to help people who need help.[2]

THE PRIVATIZATION SOLUTION

Getting back to the main argument, if something needs to be done, and if doing nothing is not the best solution, which of the three action-based options is the best -- government, the profit sector or the nonprofit sector? The evidence is clear that the private sector can do just about anything better and cheaper than the government. Hundreds of studies have been done on privatizing government services and the evidence that the private sector can do a better job than government is overwhelming.

One think tank that has done a lot of research in this area is the Reason Public Policy Institute. It has a privatization website that provides a wealth of information about recent privation projects in numerous areas.[3]

The post office is one of the easiest targets. Numerous studies in various countries have advocated all kinds of ways to deliver the mail privately.[4] Where private letter delivery has been tried, it has been found to be faster, more efficient and cheaper. The problem with private delivery is that the government of the United States arrests anyone who tries to compete against its first class mail delivery service monopoly by offering better service at lower cost.

Although the post office is one of the favorite targets for privatization, it is not the only one. Just about everything that government does can be and has been privatized somewhere. In some cases, the private sector has totally taken over the function. In other cases, private firms contract with some government to do the job, which means that tax money is still being used to pay for the service but private firms are doing the actual work, usually better and cheaper. Some examples of functions that have been privatized include professional sports facilities,[5] railroads,[6] highways,[7] public lands,[8] wildlife,[9] prisons,[10] unemployment insurance,[11] public education,[12] medicaid,[13] airports,[14] bus service,[15] infrastructure,[16] solid waste management,[17] housing,[18] roads,[19] bridges,[20] air traffic control,[21] ambulance service,[22] dispute resolution,[23] street lighting, electricity supply,[24] engineering services, utility billing, animal control, water supply, mapping, payroll, street construction, hospitals, cemeteries, assessing, public relations, tax collection, mental health, medical services,[25] sewage disposal,[26] libraries, zoning, treasury functions, fire services, mosquito control, museums, alcoholic rehabilitation, records maintenance, election administration, police communications, inspections, crime laboratories, traffic control and a plethora of other services.[27]

Some Nobel Prize winners[28] and others[29] have even discussed the possibility of privatizing money. After all, if money is a government monopoly, it will behave like any other monopoly, meaning that its quality will be lower and its price higher than would be the case in a competitive market. Competition in money would likely result in lower inflation, and since inflation is a form of taxation, that means that privatizing money would result in lower taxes.

Federal government projects are notorious for waste and inefficiency.[30] Table 1 shows some examples of how privatization could serve to improve quality and/or reduce costs in the oil tanker maintenance and repair business. These figures are based on a U.S. General Accounting Office study[31] of various oil tanker maintenance and repair costs and compared the cost the Navy incurred to the cost that would have been incurred in the private sector.

Table 1
Comparison of Selected Maintenance and Repair Costs for Similar Equipment Items on Navy Oilers and Commercial Tankers

Equipment Item	Naval Oilers Cost	Commercial Tankers Cost	Naval/ Commercial Ratio
Boiler refractory	$40,270	$2,860	14:1
Pumps, main feed	32,035	618	52:1
Pumps, cargo	80,381	3,328	24:1
Pumps, fire and flush	25,922	1,221	21:1
Propeller shaft, bearings	36,830	2,745	13:1
Turbines, nonengine	20,823	6,349	3:1
Turbines, service generator	66,111	4,044	16:1
Valves, safety	3,620	288	13:1

As can be seen, it is much cheaper to let the private sector perform maintenance and repair work on Navy ships. The private sector can repair 14 boiler refractories for what it would cost the government to repair just one. These ratios are a little bit extreme, but they serve to prove a point. Numerous studies have shown that privatizing the various services listed above can save between 20% and 60% or more, with some savings going even higher.[32] That being the case, a very strong case can be made that all of the tasks governments do, with perhaps certain limited exceptions, should be transferred to the private sector. What are those limited exceptions? It is difficult to say, since some government, somewhere has successfully privatized just about every function that government performs.

HOW MUCH GOVERNMENT DO WE NEED?

Since the private sector -- either the profit or nonprofit segment -- can do just about anything better than government, the question then becomes what do we need government for? Do we really need it at all, or would we be better off without it? Whole volumes have been written on this question and the authors of the various treatises cannot agree. Some argue for more government that works more efficiently, while others argue for less government that works more efficiently. A third group takes the position that government can never work as efficiently as the private sector and that we should do away with it, either all of it or most of it.

Think of government as an onion. The more government does, the more layers the onion has. Some people want to peel back just a few layers of government. Others want to peel back more layers. Others would peel and peel and peel until there is nothing left to peel. A fourth group does not think the onion of government needs to be peeled at all, and might prefer even more layers than we now have.

Even if we can agree with a list of things that government should do, the problem has not been solved. We still must decide which government should do it. Let's take the structure of the government of the United States as an example. There are basically three levels of government -- federal state and local. The farther you get from the people, the less control there is over spending and the less efficiently the government works. Local governments are better at providing local services than the other two levels of government. Local governments can also do the job at lower cost than either of the other two levels of government. The federal government is the least efficient and most expensive level of government.

That being the case, one might argue that the federal government should not do anything at all, since it is the least efficient and most expensive level of government. Those who oppose this view would argue that the federal government should take care of national defense, interstate crime and things that are not suited for lower levels of government. Certainly, the federal government of the United States is more able to wage aggressive offensive war than are the states or local communities.

It is probably fair to say that none of the foreign adventures the United States has engaged in would have been possible if national defense were left up to the local communities, or even the states. It is unthinkable that Rhode Island would declare war on Iraq. Any Rhode Island politician who seriously advocated such a thing would be run out of office, or perhaps even placed in personal physical jeopardy.

There is no need to have American troops stationed in more than 100 countries around the world. We could cut the defense budget by more than 50 percent if we quit being the world's policeman and brought the troops home. There is no need for any American soldier to be stationed outside the United States, with the possible exception of a few soldiers to guard American embassies. And even that job might be privatized.

World War II ended in 1945. It is time that the Europeans paid for their own defense instead of asking us to do it for them. They have more people than the United States does anyway. Enough is enough. Why are we still defending Japan? And Korea? The Korean War ended in the early 1950s. South Korea has a strong, vibrant economy and can afford to defend itself. Various Korean politicians and thousands of protesters over the years have told us that we are no longer welcome there. So why do we remain? Let's save a couple hundred billion dollars a year and bring the troops home.

My own view is that the government that governs best governs least. I don't think that government should be doing the vast majority of the things it is doing now, at any level of government. It certainly should not tell us what to do on or with our own property. It should not prohibit smoking in restaurants because someone owns those restaurants. It should not dictate what landlords can charge for their apartments because that violates the property and contract rights of landlords.

There is no such thing as an overriding public interest that requires the violation of property and contract rights. Government, if it has any proper functions at all, should be limited to functions that protect things like property and contract rights. It should do things to prevent internal violence and fraud by criminals and external violence by foreign armies. Those are the only functions that benefit the vast majority of the people. Every other thing that government does protects some special interest, usually at the expense of the general public. In other cases, like rent control, it violates the rights of a minority -- landlords -- in the name of untrammeled majoritarianism. Majorities have no right to infringe on the rights of minorities, whether that minority is landlords or some other disfavored group.

GOVERNMENT AS MONOPOLIST

Even if we can identify some functions that benefit the vast majority, it does not follow that they should be performed by government. Arriving at such a conclusion would be another non sequitur. Just because government might be able to protect against violence and fraud does not mean that government should engage in such activities, especially if some private group can do the job better,

Even if we concede that government does have some legitimate functions, it does not follow that the government should be the only entity performing those functions. Most governments have a monopoly on the provision of national defense. In many countries, they also have a monopoly on health and education. Some countries do not have any privately owned schools at all. In other countries, there may be a few private schools that have managed to survive, but the majority of children cannot attend them, either because the cost is prohibitive or because there is no private school in their neighborhood.

There are at least two characteristics of monopoly. A monopoly provides products and services of lower quality than would be the case with competitive markets, and the cost of providing them is higher than would be the case with competitive markets. Monopolies are not the result if markets are allowed to operate freely. They are the result of government protection. The record has shown that a monopoly cannot exist for any extended period of time without government support. Historically, the government has had to keep competitors from competing in order for a monopoly to exist.[33] Some economists have realized this and have called for the total repeal of the antitrust laws, since companies use these laws to protect themselves from competition.[34]

That being the case -- that monopolies result in higher prices and lower quality -- the argument that only government should provide certain services doesn't make a lot of sense. Private sector providers should be able to offer the same services that governments offer. And they already do.

In the case of police protection, for example, the number of private security guards in the shopping malls in some communities outnumber the police on the community's police force. Private gated communities provide for their own protection and safety and use the local police force for supplementary protection. These communities, as well as many others that do not have gates, have their own private roads, which they maintain without the assistance of taxpayers.

The private sector also takes care of dispute resolution. The American Arbitration Association handles thousands of commercial disputes every year. If governments started charging for protection like their private sector counterparts, there would probably be even more private providers of protection, since the government's police force would have to compete in terms of price and quality. Government involvement in police work would likely shrink if their services were not provided free of charge. If the government police force had to charge enough to cover its costs, some consumers would likely choose to hire some private protection agency instead, since the private sector can do just about anything better and cheaper than the government sector.

The point I am trying to make is that much of what government does can be done by the private sector, usually cheaper and better. So if we are trying to figure out how to pay for government services, which is what taxation and public finance are all about, the threshold question to ask is how much needs to be raised in the form of taxes to pay for these things that we want government to provide? It is only then that we should be asking how we are going to raise the funds to pay for the services we decide that government should provide. Yet this first question is seldom asked. The way public finance systems work, politicians and bureaucrats spend their time making promises to add new services and expand existing services, then scramble about trying to find ways to increase taxes to pay for the services.

Another problem with the argument that government should do whatever individuals cannot do for themselves is that perhaps some things should not be done at all, either by governments or by individuals. This argument, too, is based on a non sequitur. To rephrase the argument in clearer terms: Something is not perfect; therefore, somebody has to do something about it. That somebody may be government, but it may also be someone working in the private profit sector or in the nonprofit sector. Or it may be nobody at all. Just because someone perceives that something is not perfect, it does not follow that anything needs to be done to improve the situation. Sometimes inaction is better than taking action. That is definitely the case when any action taken will make things worse rather than better. So the argument that something is wrong, therefore someone must do something about it is structurally defective because it omits one possibility -- do nothing.

Many government regulations fall into this category. Government regulations are sometimes aimed at making some situation better. I say *sometimes* because not all government regulations fall into this category. Some government regulations or laws are clearly aimed at benefiting some special interest at the expense of the general public. Just about any trade regulation you can think of falls into this category. All trade regulations benefit some special interest at the expense of the general public. We will not go into any more detail, however, because doing so would take us too far afield of the main argument. Besides, this topic has been covered thoroughly elsewhere.[35]

CONCLUDING COMMENTS

The bottom line is that the first question to ask is not "How can we raise the money we need to keep the wheels of government running?" The initial question should be "What should government do?" It is only then that we need to ask where the money is going to come from to support the government functions that we think we need. The remainder of this book addresses this second question from a variety of perspectives.

NOTES

[1] Robert W. McGee, A Trade Policy for Free Societies: The Case Against Protectionism, Westport, CT and London: Quorum Books, 1994; Robert W. McGee, The Case to Repeal the Antidumping Laws, Northwestern Journal of International Law & Business 13(3): 491-562 (1993); Robert W. McGee, The Moral Case for Free Trade, Journal of World Trade 29(1): 69-76 (1995).

[2] Marvin Olasky, editor, Loving Your Neighbor: A Principled Guide to Personal Charity. Washington, DC: Capital Research Center, n.d.; Tibor R. Machan, Generosity: Virtue in Civil Society. Washington, DC: Cato Institute, 1998.
[3] [www.privatization.org].
[4] Robert Albon. The Future of Postal Services. London: Institute of Economic Affairs, 1991; Ian Senior. The Postal Service: Competition or Monopoly? London: Institute of Economic Affairs, 1970; Ian Senior, Liberating the Letter: A Proposal to Privatise the Post Office. London: Institute of Economic Affairs, 1983; Douglas K. Adie, Monopoly Mail: Privatizing the U.S. Postal Service. New Brunswick, NJ and Oxford: Transaction Publishers, 1989; Peter J. Ferrara, editor, Free the Mail: Ending the Postal Monopoly. Washington, DC: Cato Institute, 1990; Edward Lee Hudgins, editor, Mail at the Millennium: Will the Postal Service Go Private? Washington, DC: Cato Institute, 2001.
[5] Dean Baim, Private Ownership Incentives in Professional Sports Facilities, in Calvin A. Kent, editor, Entrepreneurship and the Privatization of Government. New York, Westport and London: Quorum Books, 1987, pp. 109-121.
[6] Burton W. Folsom, Jr., Private Industry Puts Michigan Railroads Back on Track, in Lawrence W. Reed, editor, Private Cures for Public Ills: The Promise of Privatization, Irvington-on-Hudson, NY: Foundation for Economic Education, 1996, pp. 65-67; Donald J. Senese, Privatizing Japan's Railroads, in Lawrence W. Reed, editor, Private Cures for Public Ills: The Promise of Privatization, Irvington-on-Hudson, NY: Foundation for Economic Education, 1996, pp. 84-89.
[7] John Semmens, Highways: Public Problems, Private Solutions, in Lawrence W. Reed, editor, Private Cures for Public Ills: The Promise of Privatization, Irvington-on-Hudson, NY: Foundation for Economic Education, 1996, pp. 68-77; Richard Barbarick, Government Highways: Unsafe at any Speed, in Lawrence W. Reed, editor, Private Cures for Public Ills: The Promise of Privatization, Irvington-on-Hudson, NY: Foundation for Economic Education, 1996, pp. 78-83; Geoffrey F. Segal, Adrian T. Moore and Samuel McCarthy, Contracting for Road and Highway Maintenance, How-to Guide No. 21, Reason Public Policy Institute, March 2002 [www.privatization.org].
[8] Clint Bolick, Public Lands and Private Incentives, in Lawrence W. Reed, editor, Private Cures for Public Ills: The Promise of Privatization, Irvington-on-Hudson, NY: Foundation for Economic Education, 1996, pp. 95-101; Lawrence W. Reed, Privatization: Best Hope for a Vanishing Wilderness, in Lawrence W. Reed, editor, Private Cures for Public Ills: The Promise of Privatization, Irvington-on-Hudson, NY: Foundation for Economic Education, 1996, pp. 102-111.
[9] Nancy Seijas and Frank Vorhies, Private Preservation of Wildlife: A Visit to the South African Lowveld, in Lawrence W. Reed, editor, Private Cures for Public Ills: The Promise of Privatization, Irvington-on-Hudson, NY: Foundation for Economic Education, 1996, pp. 112-120; David Haarmeyer and Elizabeth Larson, Zoo, Inc., in Lawrence W. Reed, editor, Private Cures for Public Ills: The Promise of Privatization, Irvington-on-Hudson, NY: Foundation for Economic Education, 1996, pp. 121-125.
[10] Charles H. Logan, Competition in the Prison Business, in Lawrence W. Reed, editor, Private Cures for Public Ills: The Promise of Privatization, Irvington-on-Hudson, NY: Foundation for Economic Education, 1996, pp. 136-145; Charles H. Logan, Private Prisons: Cons & Pros. New York and Oxford: Oxford University Press, 1990; Geoffrey F. Segal and Adrian Moore, Weighing the Watchman: Evaluating the Costs and Benefits of Outsourcing Correctional Services, Part 2: Reviewing the Literature on Cost and Quality Comparisons, Policy Study 290, Reason Public Policy Institute, January 2002 [www.privatization.org]; Geoffrey F. Segal and Adrian Moore, Weighing the Watchman: Evaluating the Costs and Benefits of Outsourcing Correctional Services, Part 1: Employing a Best Value Approach to Procurement, Policy Study 289, Reason Public Policy Institute, January 2002 [www.privatization.org]; Adrian T. Moore, Private Prisons: Quality Corrections at Lower Cost, Policy Study 240, Reason Public Policy Institute, April 1998 [www.privatization.org].

[11] David Honigman and George Leef, It's Time to Privatize Unemployment Insurance, in Lawrence W. Reed, editor, Private Cures for Public Ills: The Promise of Privatization, Irvington-on-Hudson, NY: Foundation for Economic Education, 1996, pp. 146-151.

[12] Anna David, Disestablishing Public Education, in Lawrence W. Reed, editor, Private Cures for Public Ills: The Promise of Privatization, Irvington-on-Hudson, NY: Foundation for Economic Education, 1996, pp. 152-157; Saralee Rhoads, Can Private Schools Survive "Privatization?" in Lawrence W. Reed, editor, Private Cures for Public Ills: The Promise of Privatization, Irvington-on-Hudson, NY: Foundation for Economic Education, 1996, pp. 158-165; Sheldon Richman, Separating School & State: How to Liberate America's Families, Fairfax, VA: The Future of Freedom Foundation, 1995; Myron Lieberman, Privatization and Educational Choice, New York: St. Martin's Press, 1989; Samuel L. Blumenfeld, Is Public Education Necessary? Boise, ID: The Paradigm Company, 1985; David Boaz, editor, Liberating Schools: Education in the Inner City, Washington, DC: Cato Institute, 1991; Marva Collins and Civia Tamarkin, Marva Collins Way, Los Angeles: Jeremy P. Tarcher, Inc., 1982; Jack E. Bowsher, Educating America: Lessons Learned in the Nation's Corporations, New York: John Wiley & Sons, Inc., 1989.

[13] Edwin S. Rubenstein, Medicaid, in E.S. Savas, editor, Privatization for New York: Competing for a Better Future, A Report of the New York State Senate Advisory Commission on Privatization, January, 1992, pp. 44-76.

[14] Robert W. Poole, Jr., Airports, in E.S. Savas, editor, Privatization for New York: Competing for a Better Future, A Report of the New York State Senate Advisory Commission on Privatization, January, 1992, pp. 77-105; Robert W. Poole, Jr., Guidelines for Airport Privatization, How-to Guide No. 13, Reason Public Policy Institute, October 1994 [www.privatization.org].

[15] Wendell Cox and Jean Love, Bus Service, in E.S. Savas, editor, Privatization for New York: Competing for a Better Future, A Report of the New York State Senate Advisory Commission on Privatization, January, 1992, pp. 154-185.

[16] Steve Steckler and Lavinia Payson, Infrastructure, in E.S. Savas, editor, Privatization for New York: Competing for a Better Future, A Report of the New York State Senate Advisory Commission on Privatization, January, 1992, pp. 186-214; Randall Fitzgerald, When Government Goes Private: Successful Alternatives to Public Services. New York: Universe Books, 1988, pp. 149-181; Adrian T. Moore, Geoffrey F. Segal and John McCormally, Infrastructure Outsourcing: Leveraging Concrete, Steel, and Asphalt with Public-Private Partnerships, Policy Study 272, Reason Public Policy Institute, September 2000 [www.privatization.org].

[17] Barbara J. Stevens, Solid Waste Management, in E.S. Savas, editor, Privatization for New York: Competing for a Better Future, A Report of the New York State Senate Advisory Commission on Privatization, January, 1992, pp. 215-243; Lynn Scarlett and J.M. Sloan, Solid Waste Management: A Guide for Competitive Contracting for Collection, How-to Guide No. 16, Reason Public Policy Institute, September 1996 [www.privatization.org]; Geoffrey Segal and Adrian T. Moore, Privatizing Landfills: Market Solutions for Solid-waste Disposal, Policy Study 267, Reason Public Policy Institute, May 2000 [www.privatization.org].

[18] Jack Richman, Housing in New York City, in E.S. Savas, editor, Privatization for New York: Competing for a Better Future, A Report of the New York State Senate Advisory Commission on Privatization, January, 1992, pp. 244-265.

[19] Randall Fitzgerald, When Government Goes Private: Successful Alternatives to Public Services. New York: Universe Books, 1988, pp. 47-48, 163-166, 170-172; Robert W. Poole, Jr., How to Enable Private Toll Road Development, How-to Guide No. 7, Reason Public Policy Institute, May 1993 [www.privatization.org].

[20] Randall Fitzgerald (1998), pp. 166-169.

[21] Randall Fitzgerald (1998), pp. 248-251.

[22] Randall Fitzgerald (1998), pp. 72, 79.

[23] Randall Fitzgerald (1998), pp. 93-119.

[24] Adrian T. Moore, Integrating Municipal Utilities into a Competitive Electricity Market, Policy Study 270, Reason Public Policy Institute, June 2000 [www.privatization.org].
[25] Robert W. Poole, Jr., Privatizing Emergency Medical Services: How Cities Can Cut Costs and Save Lives, How-to Guide No. 14, Reason Public Policy Institute, November 1995 [www.privatization.org].
[26] Robin A. Johnson, John McCormally and Adrian T. Moore, Long-Term Contracting for Water and Wastewater Services, How-to Guide No. 19, Reason Public Policy Institute, May 2002 [www.privatization.org].
[27] E.S. Savas, Privatizing the Public Sector: How to Shrink Government. Chatham, NJ: Chatham House Publishers, 1982; Robert W. Poole, Jr., Cutting Back City Hall. New York: Universe Books, 1980; James T. Bennett and Manuel H. Johnson, Better Government at Half the Price, Ottawa, IL and Ossining, NY: Caroline House Publishers, 1981; John C. Goodman, editor, Privatization. Dallas: National Center for Policy Analysis, 1985; Michael James, editor, Restraining Leviathan: Small Government in Practice. St. Leonard's, Australia: The Centre for Independent Studies, 1987; Madsen Pirie, Privatization: Theory, Practice and Choice. Hants, UK: Wildwood House, 1988; Pauline Rosenau, editor, Public-Private Policy Partnerships, Cambridge, MA: MIT Press, 2000; Bill Bradshaw and Helen Lawton Smith, editors, Privatization and Deregulation of Transport, Palgrave Macmillan, 2000.
[28] F.A. Hayek, Denationalisation of Money -- The Argument Refined, 3rd edition. London: Institute of Economic Affairs, 1990.
[29] Larry V. Ellis, The Privatization of Money: A Survey of the Issues, in Calvin A. Kent, editor, Entrepreneurship and the Privatization of Government. New York, Westport and London: Quorum Books, 1987, pp. 135-144; R.G. King, On the Economics of Private Money. Journal of Monetary Economics 12: 127-158 (1983); R. Vaubel, The Government's Money Monopoly: Externalities or Natural Monopoly? Kyklos 37: 27-57 (1984); Cento Veljanovski, Privatization: Monopoly Money or Competition? In Cento Veljanovski, editor, Privatisation & Competition: A Market Prospectus. London: Institute of Economic Affairs, 1989, pp. 26-51.
[30] Martin L. Gross, The Government Racket: Washington Waste from A to Z, New York: Bantam Books, 1992; J. Peter Grace, Burning Money: The Waste of Your Tax Dollars, New York: Macmillan, 1984; Randall Fitzgerald and Gerald Lipson, Pork Barrel: The Unexpurgated Grace Commission Story of Congressional Profligacy, Washington, DC: Cato Institute, 1984.
[31] United States General Accounting Office, The Navy Overhaul Policy -- A Costly Means of Insuring Readiness for Support Ships, Report by Comptroller General of the United States: LCD-78-434, December 27, 1978, p. 42, reproduced in James T. Bennett and Manuel H. Johnson, Better Government: Private Production of Public Services. Ottawa, IL and Ossining, NY: Caroline House Publishers, 1981, p. 53.
[32] For some statistics on cost savings, see John Hilke, Cost Savings from Privatization: A Compilation of Findings, How-to Guide No. 6, Reason Public Policy Institute, March 1993 [www.privatization.org].
[33] Gabriel Kolko, The Triumph of Conservatism: A Reinterpretation of American History, 1900-1916. Glencoe: The Free Press, 1963; Gabriel Kolko, Railroads and Regulation 1877-1916. Princeton: Princeton University Press, 1965.
[34] Dominick T. Armentano, Antitrust: The Case for Repeal, 2nd revised edition. Auburn: The Ludwig von Mises Institute, 1999; Dominick T. Armentano, Antitrust and Monopoly: Anatomy of a Policy Failure, 2nd edition. New York and London: Holmes & Meier, 1990.
[35] Robert W. McGee, A Trade Policy for Free Societies: The Case Against Protectionism. Westport, CT and London: Quorum Books, 1994; Robert W. McGee, The Case to Repeal the Antidumping Laws, Northwestern Journal of International Law & Business 13(3): 491-562 (1993).

PART TWO

WHEN CAN TAXATION BE JUSTIFIED?

Chapter 2

WHEN CAN TAXATION BE JUSTIFIED?

> But you might say, if government didn't do all that it's doing we wouldn't have a *just* society. What's *just* has been debated for centuries but let me offer my definition of social justice: I keep what I earn and you keep what you earn. Do you disagree? Well then tell me how much of what I earn *belongs* to you --- and why? (Walter Williams)[1]

WHEN IS TAX EVASION UNETHICAL?

This chapter involves several related questions, including -- When can taxation be justified and When is tax evasion unethical? In some ways, these two questions are really the same question. When taxation is justified, it seems to follow that tax evasion constitutes unethical conduct. And when a tax is not justifiable, it seems to follow that evasion is not unethical. It then becomes a question of how we can determine when, and under what circumstances, taxation is justified.

One of the most comprehensive treatises on the topic of the ethics of tax evasion, from a Catholic perspective at least, was done by Martin Crowe in 1944.[2] This 177-page treatise raises most of the major issues concerning the morality of tax evasion. But even here, Crowe distinguishes "just" taxes from other kinds of taxes. One might conclude from the title of Crowe's work that one is morally obligated to pay just taxes and not morally obligated to pay taxes that are unjust. So it then becomes a question of what is a just tax?

Is tax evasion ever justified on moral grounds? If your taxes go to finance Hitler's war machine, it seems clear that there is nothing immoral about tax evasion.[3] Indeed, it might even be argued that one has a moral duty to evade such taxes where possible. But the issue becomes less clear for less extremist cases. Is it ethical to evade taxes when the proceeds are used to feed the hungry, house the homeless or clothe the poor? Or what if the proceeds are used to provide services that you use, such as police protection, health care, education, and so forth? What if your taxes go toward the support of activities that you do not use, such as the welfare system? What about taxes that are used to pay for "porkbarrel" legislation? In other words, does the use to which the proceeds are put have anything to do with the ethics of tax evasion, or is the end use irrelevant?

Crowe[4] and others[5] divide the taxing power into three categories: fees, such as licenses, franchises and permits; special assessments, such as an assessment to pave a road; and taxes proper, such as the income tax, where those paying the tax have no special claim on any of the proceeds. In the case of fees and assessments, those paying are entitled to some right. Those who pay for an automobile license are entitled to drive.[6] Those who pay for a business permit are entitled to operate a business.[7] Those who pay to have their road paved are entitled to have it paved. But in the case of taxes, those who pay do not have any automatic right to any of the proceeds. New York residents who pay a federal income tax may have their money used to construct a bridge in California, even though they derive no direct benefit for their tax dollars. And they have no right to demand that a bridge be built in New York. All the taxes the government collects go into a common pool and are distributed as the government sees fit. Taxpayers have an obligation to pay, but they have no specific right to any of the proceeds.[8]

Crowe refers to these three sources of revenue as noncontractual revenue sources. Then there are contractual revenue sources, such as user fees. This chapter will concentrate on taxes proper, although many of the same arguments can be used for the other two forms of noncontractual revenue.

WHAT IS A TAX?

Crowe defines a tax as follows:

> A tax is a compulsory contribution to the government, imposed in the common interest of all, for the purpose of defraying the expenses incurred in carrying out the public functions, or imposed for the purpose of regulation, without reference to the special benefits conferred on the one making the payment.[9]

This definition is fairly comprehensive. It includes not only charges that are imposed to raise revenue but also charges that are imposed to regulate, such as tariffs, liquor and tobacco taxes. And the definition separates those who pay from those who benefit, since those who pay may not be the same ones who benefit.

But his definition could be improved. He states that taxes are compulsory contributions that are imposed in the public interest. But what about compulsory contributions that are used to benefit special interests? Many present day government expenditures are used to benefit special interests, often at the expense of the general public. Tariffs on foreign clothing, for example, protect domestic textile manufacturers from foreign competition at the expense of the millions of consumers who would otherwise pay less for clothes.[10] Tariffs, import quotas and domestic content laws benefit domestic auto manufacturers at the expense of the millions of people who buy automobiles. Social Security taxes benefit retired people at the expense of those who work for a living. None of these levies can be said to be in the public interest because they benefit special interests at the expense of the general public. Yet they should be considered taxes because that is what they are. But whether they are just taxes is another question.

A more comprehensive, and accurate, definition of taxes might be the compulsory taking[11] of property by government, without regard to whether the proceeds are used to further public or private interests. But even this definition does not cover all the costs imposed by government on private individuals because it excludes the cost of regulation.[12] For example, if government imposed a regulation that required a business to incur a particular cost, property is, in effect, being taken, in the sense that the individual no longer has use of the property. But it is not a tax in the strict sense because the transfer is not from the taxpayer to the government. If the local rent control board forbids a landlord from charging more than $400 a month for an apartment that would rent for $700 in a free market, is it any less of a compulsory taking than if the landlord charged $700 and had to pay $300 as a tax? In either case, the landlord has $400 instead of $700.[13] Taxes, in the broad sense of the term, should include these kinds of compulsory behavior modifications imposed by government.

A less comprehensive but otherwise accurate definition of tax is offered by Podolsky -- "any revenues collected by the government on any basis whatever with the sole exception of fees paid for the consumption of tangible goods or materials."[14] This definition is more accurate and descriptive than Crowe's definition but excludes the cost of government regulation, since it is not the government that is receiving the money.

WHEN IS A TAX JUST?

What makes a tax just? Crowe sets out three criteria.[15] For Crowe, a tax is just only if it is imposed by legitimate legislative authority;[16] for a just cause;[17] and where there is just distribution of the tax burden.[18] Thus, in countries where there is no legitimate legislative authority, no tax can be just. And where the cause is not just, as where a tax is imposed on Mass wine for the purpose of hindering or hampering its use, there seems to be no obligation to pay.[19] But just taxes, for Crowe, would include taxes that are imposed to fund spiritual, cultural and moral welfare, such as concerts, monuments and art museums.[20]

The Just Distribution Argument

And what about the just distribution of the tax burden? Those who have no income pay no income tax. And those who have high incomes often (but not always) pay a large income tax. Those who have lower incomes may pay a higher percentage of their income for sales taxes than those who have higher incomes. But so what? Is there anything unjust about this relationship? If so, what makes it unjust?

What should constitute a just distribution of the tax burden? In 2000, nearly 38 percent of the California state income tax that was collected was paid by one-third of 1 percent of the taxpayers.[21] It seems like the distribution of the tax burden in this case is grossly unfair to the small minority who is at the top of the income scale. They are being exploited by the less wealthy minority, or rather the politicians who created the present tax structure in California are immorally buying the votes of the majority by promising them benefits that will be paid with the tax dollars of this minority.

If poor people receive more government benefits than rich people, should the poor be required to pay a higher percentage of their income for taxes? If not, could it be said that the poor (which are in the majority) are exploiting the rich minority? Should taxes be based on the ability to pay, or on the amount of benefit received? Are these two approaches mutually exclusive, or can they somehow be reconciled? Is one approach just and another unjust? Or could it be that both approaches are unjust? If so, what determines whether a tax is just? We shall address these questions later. Suffice it to say for now, though, that Crowe takes the position that "moralists are unanimous in their teaching that the ultimate basis of apportioning a tax is the ability of the citizen to pay."[22]

It must be pointed out that this statement is not true. While it might reasonably be said that a majority of "moralists" (whoever they are) would choose the ability to pay principle over the benefit principle, it can in no way be said that there is unanimity. And even if there were, that does not make it so. The fact that a majority approaching 100% thinks that something is just does not make it just. The vast majority of people in the pre-Civil War southern United States thought that slavery was just, and even in keeping with God's law. Even many of the slaves did not think that it was unjust. But what they thought had nothing to do with the justice of the matter. Justice does not depend on opinion or on a majority vote.

Some Religious Arguments

Crowe examined the views of a number of religious and secular writers on the topic of the moral obligation to pay taxes. Angelus of Clavisio,[23] for example, when discussing the moral obligation to pay the tax that the sovereign imposed for those who passed through his territory, said:

> ... When those who impose these taxes do not provide for the common good, for example, in caring for roads,

> bridges, the safety of people and other things, according to their ability as they are bound to do, the subjects do not sin if they evade the tax without lying and perjury, nor are they bound to restitution...Nor do I believe that those sin who defraud taxes, even when the aforesaid (i.e., those who impose the tax) do provide for the common good.[24]

Based on this view, it would seem that Angelus would consider it a sin if the taxpayer had to resort to perjury or lying to evade a tax that is not morally owed. It must be assumed that in such cases it is the lie or perjury and not the tax evasion that is the sin. But how can it be a sin to lie to someone who is not entitled to the truth in the first place? It would not be a sin to tell a Gestapo agent that you are not hiding a Jew in your basement when in fact you are. And it is not a sin to tell a thief that you have given him all of your money when in fact you have not. So how can it be a sin to lie to a tax authority when you do not morally owe the tax? Lying is not a sin, per se. It depends on the circumstances.[25]

Berardi, a later thinker on the subject, takes the position that there is probably no moral duty to pay a tax even if lying and deceit are involved.

> What therefore about subjects who have found a way to avoid paying a tax? ... probably there is no obligation of restitution after the tax has been evaded. For the duty of paying taxes probably does not arise from a tacit pact by which the subjects bind themselves to pay the prince whatever is necessary for the public expenses -- each one contracting to pay an allotted percentage of the debt; but this duty arises rather from the law of the prince who determines how that sum of money which is necessary shall be raised.[26]

Basically, Berardi is saying that where there is no contract there is no obligation, and there is no contract between the prince and the taxpayers. This view becomes complicated when one tries to apply it to a modern democracy, since, in theory at least, some sort of contract does exist between the people and the sovereign. This contract theory approach raises some interesting questions, which we shall examine later.

An early twentieth century scholar takes the position that partial evasion is justified on the grounds that the government does not have a right to the full amount, and that it would be unfair to impose heavier taxes on conscientious men while wicked men usually pay less.[27] Crolly takes the position that there is no obligation to pay taxes, but that there is an obligation to pay when evasion would result in violence.[28] Other theologians takes the position that confessors should not make penitents make restitution for unpaid taxes if the penitents themselves do not feel bound to do so.[29]

> ... the confessor should not oblige a penitent to make restitution if the penitent certainly or probably has persuaded himself that in the multitude of taxes which he has paid there were some unjust taxes, or that the number of taxes itself is too great and excessive, or that, having regard for his state in life and his business, the penitent judges that he has sufficiently contributed to the public necessities.[30]

This is in keeping with the view that something is a sin only if you think it is a sin.

Scholars over the centuries have debated the morality of evading taxes from other perspectives as well. Some would argue that one is obligated to pay only those taxes that are not wholly penal in nature,[31] but others have argued that all taxes should be paid regardless of whether the purpose is wholly penal, partially penal or not penal at all. Others would debate the relative merits of paying or evading direct taxes such as per capita taxes, inheritance, land, building, or income taxes, as compared to indirect taxes, such as customs, duties, imposts and sales taxes.[32]

Those who take the position that there is a moral duty to pay only direct taxes are in a curious position. For example, in 1881, the U.S. Supreme Court held that the income tax was an indirect tax.[33] But in 1895, it reversed its position and held that the income tax is a direct tax.[34] Does that mean that anyone who evaded the U.S. income tax before 1895 was not committing a sin, but those who evaded it thereafter were sinners? But in France, certain income taxes are legally classified as indirect taxes, which means that evaders do not commit a sin, which leaves one in the curious position of being a sinner if one evades the U.S. income tax but not the French tax.[35]

Others have argued that the morality of paying a tax has nothing to do with whether the tax is direct or indirect. Some scholars over the last two thousand years have taken the position that it is a sin to evade a tax only if payment is refused after the tax collector has demanded payment. Others have said that payment is required even if no demand for payment has been made. Some scholars have taken the position that it is a sin to break any law.

The logic for this position is as follows. "It is sinful to act unreasonably. But it is unreasonable to break a law. Therefore, it is sinful to break a law."[36] But this line of reasoning begs the question: What if the law is unreasonable or unjust? Few, if any, modern theologians would take this position. But this position was common when it was thought that the king derived his authority from God. This divine right of kings is supported by Romans 13, 1-2, which says:

> "Let every soul be subject unto the higher powers. For there is no power but of God: the powers that be are

> ordained of God. Whosoever therefore resisteth the power, resisteth the ordinance of God: and they that resist shall receive to themselves damnation."

Some theologians take the position that the state is like a servant, and just as a servant is entitled to wages, so is the state entitled to taxes.[37] In an ideal state, this might be true, if, indeed the state is the servant and the people are the masters. But how many modern states really fall into this category? Who is the master and who is the servant if the state can extract whatever it demands and individual citizens who do not comply are arrested, jailed or perhaps killed?

Another question debated over the centuries has been whether tax evasion is a mortal or venial sin.[38]

> Subjects who without the consent of the prince use fraud and other means to evade just taxes due because of a pact or from ancient and legitimate custom, or even those recently imposed ... sin mortally by committing the sin of theft and are bound to restitution.[39]

Assessing mortal sin for tax evasion seems a bit severe, especially in cases where the amount involved is small, and it is unlikely that many theologians would classify all tax evasion as mortal sin.[40] Voit takes the position that it is probable that one commits a grave sin for tax evasion even if payment is not demanded, and that those who fail to pay must make restitution.[41]

There seems to be no clear cutoff point between what constitutes a mortal sin and what is merely a venial sin, at least in the case of theft.[42] Where a theft is of a penny, the sin would likely be venial, but where the theft is a million dollars, it might be mortal. Where the amount stolen is $100, the sin is more grave if the victim is poor than if the victim is rich. And the severity of the sin is affected by the circumstances of the person who is evading the tax. "Those who defraud taxes imposed on the necessities of life (pro usualibus) probably can be excused from mortal sin and from the obligation of making restitution."[43] Bonacina takes the position that it is not a sin to evade taxes if the burden is too large.[44]

What does the bible have to say about taxes?[45] Taxes are mentioned in several places. In the Old Testament, it says that the Pharaoh taxed the people according to their ability to pay.[46] But it does not say whether this practice was considered just. In the New Testament, when Jesus was asked whether it was legal to give tribute to Caesar, he said, "Render therefore unto Caesar the things which are Caesar's; and unto God the things that are God's."[47] But all this means is that individuals should give people what they are entitled to have. It says nothing about whether Caesar (the State) is entitled to anything. This point is reiterated by Paul: "Render therefore to all their dues: tribute to whom tribute is due; custom to whom custom; fear to whom fear; honour to whom honour."[48]

But not all scholars have interpreted the scriptures in this way. Beia, for example, interprets the passage from Romans 13 to mean that justly imposed taxes are due to the prince by divine law because they are the ministers of God.[49] But he does not consider whether taxes are required by divine law to be paid to evil princes, such as Hitler, Stalin, Mao or lesser sandlot dictators. And he does not question whether atheists should be made to pay a tax under divine law.

According to some interpreters of Jewish law, there is an obligation to pay taxes.

> Anyone who cheats on income taxes transgresses the law prohibiting robbery, whether the king (government) be Jewish or non-Jewish; for the *law of the country is the Law*. Some scholars held that this law implied no more than the obligation to pay taxes and to help the country against enemies, but the majority opinion holds that conformity to all laws imposed by a legally constituted government is compulsory.[50]

There are several problems with this view. For one thing, it takes the position that what is legal is moral, and what is illegal is immoral, at least where the government is legally constituted. When one considers that the governments of the Third Reich and fascist Italy were legally constituted, in the sense that Hitler and Mussolini were both came to power through the democratic process, one must question whether there are exceptions to this rule. Another problem with this view is that it cites majority opinion as authority. But majorities have nothing to do with right. Something is either right or wrong regardless of majority opinion.

The Fair Share Argument

Another argument that has been put forward in justification of taxation is that if some people don't pay their "fair share," then others must pay more than their fair share. If this is true, then it would appear that tax evasion is immoral, since you are forcing someone else to pay for your benefits. You are acting as a parasite, since you are receiving benefits that others are being forced to pay for.

Lehmkuhl (1834-1917) takes the position that commutative justice is involved whenever the failure of one person to pay "just taxes" results in others having to pay more than their fair share.[51] But even if this were true, it still does not answer the question of whether it is unethical for someone to evade an unjust tax where the result would be that others must pay more. According to Crowe, "commutative justice directs the relations of one private individual with another."[52] Crowe later says: "Commutative justice directs the actions of one private individual in relation to the strict right of another private individual."[53]

This fair share argument suffers from several weaknesses. For one thing, it is not easy to determine what is one's fair share. The problem is complicated by the fact that governments often squander large sums of money. Should one pay only the fair share of the money that is not squandered, or should one pay a portion of the funds that are squandered as well? A corollary to the fair share argument that theologians over the centuries have made, which supports the practice of partial evasion, is that " ... the state does not seem to have a right to the whole tax, and that it would be unjust to burden conscientious men with heavier taxes while wicked men usually pay less."[54] Davis expresses a similar view.

> It appears unreasonable to expect good citizens, who certainly are in the minority, to be obliged in conscience to pay taxes, whereas so many others openly repudiate the moral obligation, if there is one. It seems unjust that good people should feel an obligation to be mulcted and to pay readily, in order to balance the evasions of many.[55]

Another variation of the fair share argument is that one has a moral duty to pay if benefits are received. But this line of reasoning also suffers from many defects. What if the government provides benefits but you did not ask for them? For example, what if the government provides free abortions but you do not believe that abortion is morally permissible? Or what if the government requires that you contribute to a Social Security system, but a private pension system -- which you cannot invest in because Social Security taxes have taken all of the income that would have been available for this purpose -- would have been a much better investment?[56] Is there any moral duty to pay a Social Security tax if you are being forced to pay for what amounts to a bad investment?[57]

A Cost Benefit Approach

In a broader sense, is there any relationship between what you are asked (forced) to pay and what you receive in return? As a general rule, taxpayers receive less than what they pay for because of the administrative costs of government.[58] Economists call this phenomenon a deadweight loss. And the deadweight loss increases as the distance between the tax collection agency and the taxpayer increases. For example, taxpayers who pay a local tax, on average, only get back 80% or 90% of what they have paid in the form of services.[59] Only perhaps 70% of state government taxes are returned in the form of services. Only perhaps 30% or 40% of the taxes paid to the federal government are returned in services, depending on the service.[60]

The farther away the collecting agency is from the source, the lower the return. In the case of some federal welfare programs, the cost of administering the program far exceeds the amount that is actually spent on the target recipients. And residents of some states get less back from the federal government than others. Some senators and members of Congress are more skilled at getting federal funds for their state than others.

It is as though the federal government took your automobile to satisfy your tax liability and gave you a bicycle in return.[61] True, you are receiving some benefits from the government. But does that mean that you have a moral duty to give them your car? Does the fact that you may have another car in your garage change the answer? Or the fact that the car the government took from you was given to someone who had no car? Or two cars?

Not all wealth transfers go from the rich to the poor. In fact, many go from the poor to the rich, or from the middle class to the middle class. In the case of tax-supported college education, for example, those in the middle and upper middle classes tend to use the service, but those in the middle and lower income classes tend to pay for it. In effect, the poor are subsidizing the rich.

Does the disposition of the property have nothing to do with the moral duty to pay a tax to a government that has been elected, in theory at least, by a majority or plurality of the eligible voters who voted in the last election. In other words, do you have a moral duty to pay all the taxes the government thinks you should pay even though you receive much less in benefits than what you are being forced to pay?

If there is a moral duty to pay the government something in exchange for the benefits received, what amount is justifiable? If you receive a bicycle from the government, are you morally obligated to give the government whatever it demands in return, including your car? Or would you be justified in giving just a tire or two? Where the tax is extracted by force, or the threat of force, as in the case of the income tax, there seems to be no moral duty to give anything whatsoever, since the recipient is a robber.

Is there ever a moral obligation to pay government for the services received if, for some reason you are not forced to contribute? For example, nonprofit organizations receive exemptions from the payment of property taxes. Yet they still receive local police and fire protection, city water and sewage treatment, and so forth. A strong case can be made that there is some duty to pay for the value of the services received (not what the government would charge to a taxpayer, which may be different from the value of the services provided).

This situation is different from that where the government forcibly takes the tax because the government, in this example, is not legally entitled to assess any tax, although it must provide certain services. The author knows of one exempt organization that takes this position. For years, it did not apply for tax exempt status because it felt it had some moral duty to pay for the government services it received. But when property taxes became outrageously high, it decided to apply for a tax exemption, which it received. It then started to make voluntary contributions to the local government each year, based on the value of the services the government provided.

So in cases where there is no force involved, and where services are provided, there may be a duty to pay something for the services, if the services have some value to the recipient. But if the services provided by government have no value, or where the person does not use the service, as in the case of an exempt organization that has the option of contributing for the support of the local school system that it does not use, there is no moral duty to pay for the support of such services. In fact, there may be an ethical duty not to contribute to the support of such services, since the people who contributed to the support of the exempt organization want their money to be used for other purposes. Otherwise, they would have contributed to the local school system themselves.

The Legitimacy Argument

The question of legitimacy also needs to be raised here. How legitimate is the average government? In the United States, for example, perhaps half of the eligible voters tend to vote in national elections. Even fewer vote in purely local elections, and in primaries. And not all individuals over the age of 18 (the legal voting age) register to vote. And many of those who do vote, do not really vote for the candidate of their choice. They vote for the least bad candidate who is on the ballot.[62] And it is a commonly recognized fact in political science texts that all countries, whether democratic or otherwise, are actually run by political elites, not "the people."[63]

So how legitimate are governments? It could be argued that, if a government falls below some degree of legitimacy, there is no longer a duty to pay taxes. Indeed, this position is taken in the U.S. Declaration of Independence, which supports the view that, at some point, the people have the right to withdraw their support from the government. The exact cutoff point, however, is difficult to define, since all governments are illegitimate to some extent, because they do not do just what every citizen wants and nothing else.

The Duty Argument

Another argument that has been used to support the position that there is a duty to pay taxes is based on Kant's categorical imperative.[64] Kant's categorical imperative asks the question, "What would happen if everyone did it?" Kant would conclude that if the universal practice of some act results in something bad, then the act is unethical. If nothing bad results from the universal practice of the act, then it is not unethical.

The weakness of this line of reasoning is highlighted when applied to the question of tax evasion. If taxation is theft -- the taking of property without the owner's consent -- one might ask, "What would happen if everyone refused to allow their property to be taken without their consent?" One result would be a marked decline in the amount of theft and an increase in the amount of justice. Another result would be a vast shrinking in the scope of government, since it would no longer be able to maintain the level of spending it now enjoys.[65] It would no longer be able to force fundamentalist Christians, Moslems and Jews to support abortion clinics. It would no longer be able to force pacifists to pay for national defense. It would no longer be able to subsidize farmers or enforce protectionist legislation, which means that consumers would be able to purchase products at lower prices.

But all these arguments are, at their base, merely utilitarian -- the greatest good for the greatest number. Even if it would benefit the general population if government were to get out of the wealth transfer business, the real question is whether someone's rights are being violated by the government's tax policy. It is not a question of whether the good outweighs the bad; it is a question of whether rights are being violated.

A more difficult question arises in the case of user fees, the charge that the government places only on those who use a particular government service. Examples include entrance fees to government parks and fees for using toll roads. Is it ethical to sneak into a government park without paying or to go through a toll booth without paying?[66]

Morality and Choice

Morality involves choice. Where there is no choice, there is no morality. If one must either use the government's roads or stay at home, there is not much of a choice. One must go to the grocery store, to work, and so forth, and the government has a monopoly on roads, so individuals do not have a choice of whether to use the government's roads or a road that is privately owned.[67] That being the case, there appears to be no moral duty to pay the toll, although there is a legal obligation.

But if the road is privately owned, that may be a different matter, because in the case of a privately owned road, failure to pay the fee for the use of the road violates the owner's right to property. In the case of using a privately owned road, there is an implied contract that if you use the road, you agree to pay the price for using the road. But where the road is owned by some government, no such implied contract exists. For one thing, the government holds a monopoly position. For another, the government obtained the road by confiscating someone's property, either by the process of eminent domain or by taxes, the proceeds of which were then used to purchase the land and hire the construction workers, material, and so forth needed to build it.

The argument for sneaking into a government-owned park without paying is not quite as strong, especially in cases where the park is supported 100% by user fees, because the necessity argument does not apply. Whereas individuals must use roads in order to have a normal life, such is not the case with government parks. Although privately owned parks are generally in better shape than government parks and cost less to maintain,[68] individuals still have a choice of whether to use the facility or not, so there is a moral dimension. And there is a strong argument that all parks should be privately owned rather than government owned. But exploring this question goes rather far afield from the subject of this chapter, which is tax evasion.

NOTES

[1] Walter Williams, All It Takes Is Guts: A Minority View, Washington, DC: Regnery Books, 1987, p. 62.

[2] Rev. Martin T. Crowe. 1944. The Moral Obligation of Paying Just Taxes, The Catholic University of America Studies in Sacred Theology No. 84. For a more recent comprehensive discussion of this topic that does not limit itself to the Catholic perspective, see Robert W. McGee, editor. 1998. The Ethics of Tax Evasion. Dumont, NJ: The Dumont Institute for Public Policy Research.

[3] Some authors have disagreed with this position. Writers writing from the Jewish and Baha'i positions have argued that tax evasion is always unethical. For examples, see Meir Tamari, "Ethical Issues in Tax Evasion: A Jewish Perspective," in Robert W. McGee, editor, The Ethics of Tax Evasion (Dumont Institute, 1998), 168-179; Gordon Cohn, "The Ethics of Tax Evasion: A Jewish Perspective," in Robert W. McGee, editor, The Ethics of Tax Evasion (Dumont Institute, 1998), 180-189; Wig DeMoville, "The Ethics of Tax Evasion: A Baha'i Perspective," in Robert W. McGee, editor, The Ethics of Tax Evasion (Dumont Institute, 1998), 230-241. Other writers have failed to find justification for taxation in the relevant literature. See Walter Block, "The Justification for Taxation in the Economics Literature," in Robert W. McGee, editor, The Ethics of Tax *Evasion* (Dumont Institute, 1998), 36-88.

[4] *Id.*, at 6-12.

[5] E.R. Seligman, Essays in Taxation 406 (1931).

[6] One might argue that one has the right to drive (or to walk, or to speak) without first obtaining a government license. But we will not go into that here.

[7] One might argue that individuals have a right to operate a business with or without the government's permission, and that a government that interferes with the conduct of personal affairs such as operating a business violates the owner's rights, since regulating private conduct is not a legitimate function of government. We will not go into that issue here, either.

[8] Crowe, *supra*, at 11.

[9] *Id.*, at 14-15.

[10] For more on this point, *see* James Bovard, The Fair Trade Fraud (1991), especially 35-64; Robert W. McGee, "The Trade Policy of a Free Society," 19 Capital University Law Review 301-41 (1990); Robert W. McGee, A Trade Policy for Free Societies: The Case Against Protectionism. Westport, CT and London: Quorum Books, 1994; Robert W. McGee, The Case to Repeal the Antidumping Laws. Northwestern Journal of International Law & Business 13(3): 491-562 (1993).

[11] For a comprehensive discussion of the Fifth Amendment takings clause and the concept of governmental takings, see Richard A. Epstein, Takings: Private Property and the Power of Eminent Domain (1985).

[12] The cost of regulation is not insubstantial. Various estimates have placed the annual cost of regulation in the UA at hundreds of billions of dollars. Robert Genetski, The True Cost of Government, Wall Street Journal, February 19, 1992, at A14, col. 3; Thomas D. Hopkins, Cost of Regulation, A Rochester Institute of Technology Public Policy Working Paper, December, 1991; Ronald Utt, The Growing Regulatory Burden: At What Cost To America, The Institute for Policy Innovation, Policy Report No. 114, November, 1991; George F. Will, Purring Along the Potomac, Newsweek, November 30, 1992, at 96; William G. Laffer, III, George Bush's Hidden Tax: The Explosion in Regulation, Backgrounder No. 905, The Heritage Foundation, July 10, 1992. The Cato Institute [www.cato.org], the Heritage Foundation [www.heritage.org] and several other organizations have published a number of studies that estimate the cost of various regulations. The U.S. International Trade Commission publishes studies estimating how much its regulations cost the general public. One such study is The Economic Effects of Significant U.S. Import Restraints, Third Update 2002, USITC Pub. 3519 (June 2002), available at [www.usitc.gov]. Also see James Rolph Edwards, Regulation, the Constitution, and the Economy. Lanham, MD, New York and London: University Press of America, especially pp. 166-191(1998). A good reference on the economic costs of regulation is Alfred E. Kahn, The Economics of Regulation: Principles and Institutions, 2 volumes, Cambridge, MA and London: MIT Press, 1989.Another good question to ask is whether it is sinful or unethical to evade a regulation. But we will save discussion of this point for another time.

[13] It should not be overlooked that the landlord might also have to pay a tax on the $400 received, if the expenses incurred in operating the apartment are less than the revenue received.

[14] Robert E. Podolsky, Titania: The Practical Alternative to Government, Boca Raton, FL: The Titania Group, Inc., 2002, pp. 129-130.

[15] Crowe, *supra*, at 22-26.

[16] Id., at 22-23.

[17] Id., at 23-24.

[18] Id., at 24-26.

[19] Id., at 23.

[20] Id. One wonders whether Crowe, who is a Catholic, would mind being taxed to support a Protestant spiritual or cultural event, or a showing at an art museum that includes artworks of crucifixes or photos of Christ that are soaked in urine, as was done at one art exhibition, with the support of government funds. And one might question whether it is just to impose taxes on Georgia residents to help pay for a monument to General Sherman, who helped to destroy their state during the American Civil War (more properly called the War for Southern Independence).

[21] George F. Will, California, Ugly: Recall war headed downhill, New York Post, September 4, 2003, p. 27.

[22] Crowe, *supra*, at 24.

[23] 1411-1495.

[24] Crowe, *supra*, at 29, is quoting from the 1494 Lyons edition of Angelus' Pedagium section of Summa Angelica.

[25] Of course there is another possibility -- that lying is never a sin because there is no such thing as a sin. To hold this view, one must define sin as an offense against God and the person arguing the point must be an atheist. If sin can include unethical conduct against an individual, then sin can exist, since sin, in this case, is an example of immoral conduct.

[26] Crowe, supra, at 35, quoting Berardi, praxis confessariorum II (1898).

[27] Crowe, supra, at 37, discussing the view of Genicot-Salsmans, as espoused in Institutiones Theologiae Moralis I (1927). The exact pages are not given, but it is likely that his views appear around page 572.

[28] Crowe, *supra*, at 38, referring to Crolly's Disputationes Theologicae de Justitia et Jure III (1877), at 1001 ff.
[29] Crowe, supra, at 39, citing Frassinetti, Compendio della Teologia Morale I (1866), at 304.
[30] Crowe, *supra*, at 53, is quoting Lugo's citation of Molina's De Justitia et Iure, III, disp. 674, n. 9, concl. 5 (1611), which is in Gabriel Vasquez, De Restitutione, cap. 6, para. 3, dub. 2, n. 43 (1631).
[31] Crowe, *supra*, at 6-7 and elsewhere throughout the text. Castro defines a purely penal law as one that does not prescribe or forbid the doing of anything but merely imposes a penalty on someone who does something or omits to do something. A mixed penal law, for Castro, is one that prescribes or forbids doing something and prescribes a penalty for violators. A purely moral law prescribes or forbids something but does not provide a penalty. Castro, De Potestate Legis Poenalis I, c. IX, col. 1613 (1571), as cited in Crowe, *supra*, at 88.
[32] Crowe, *supra*, at 17 and elsewhere in the text.
[33] Springer v. U.S., 102 U.S. 586 (1881).
[34] Pollock v. Farmers Loan & Trust Co., 157 U.S. 429; 158 U.S. 601.
[35] Crowe, *supra*, points this out at 139.
[36] Crowe, *supra*, at 97.
[37] Concina, Theologia Christiana Dogmatico-moralis, VI, 309 (1774), as cited in Crowe, supra, at 55. Patuzzi (1700-1769) also takes this position in his Ethica Christiana sive Theologia Moralis I, 90 (1770), who is cited by Crowe at 57.
[38] For those unfamiliar with the distinction between mortal and venial sin, Catholic doctrine holds that someone who commits a mortal sin must spend eternity in hell, whereas someone who commits a venial sin must spend some time in a place called purgatory, where punishment is imposed for some temporary period, after which the sinner is transferred to heaven.
[39] St. Antoninus, Summa Sacrae Theologiae II (1571), at about page 63, as quoted by Crowe, *supra*, at 42.
[40] Here I am falling prey to the same line of philosophical reasoning I warned against. Whether a majority of theologians say this or that really has nothing to do with the fact of the matter. Something is either a mortal sin or not, regardless of what a majority of theologians say. Molina (1536-1600) makes the following statement in this regard: "When a tax is imposed ... those who do not pay, sin mortally provided the amount is sufficient for a mortal sin of theft, and they are bound in the forum of conscience to make restitution ....The common opinion of the doctors affirms this." *De Iustitia et Iure*, tr. II. disp. 674, n. 3 (1611), III, col. 555 ff., as quoted in Crowe, *supra*, at 43.
[41] E. Voit, Theologia Moralis I, 855 (1833), p. 372, as cited in Crowe, supra, at 57.
[42] Murder, for example, is always a mortal sin, regardless of whether the person murdered is rich or poor, pious or sinful, young or old, Christian or not. But some sins can be mortal or venial, depending on the facts or circumstances, such as the amount of the theft and the nature of the victim.
[43] Bonacina, De Morali Theologia, Tractatus de Restitutione, disp. II, q. IX, n. 5 (1687), II, p. 449, as quoted in Crowe, *supra*, at 48.
[44] Crowe, *supra*, at 48.
[45] This is an important question for people who believe that God wrote the Bible, in spite of overwhelming evidence to the contrary. For discussions by persons who dispute the divine authorship of the Bible, see William Henry Burr, Self-Contradictions of the Bible, New York: A.J. Davis & Company, 1860, reprinted by Prometheus Books, Buffalo, 1987; C. Dennis McKinsey, The Encyclopedia of Biblical Errancy, Amherst, NY: Prometheus Books, 1995; Joseph Wheless, Is It God's Word: An Exposition of the Fables and Mythology of the Bible and the Fallacies of Theology, Montana: Kessinger Publishing Co., 1997; Ruth Hurmence Green, The Born Again Skeptic's Guide to the Bible, Freedom from Religion Foundation, 1999; Michael Martin, The Case against Christianity, Philadelphia: Temple University Press, 1993; Joseph Wheless, Forgery in Christianity: A

Documented Record of the Foundations of the Christian Religion, Montana: Kessinger Publishing Co., 1997; Robert G. Ingersoll, Some Mistakes of Moses, Buffalo: Prometheus Books, 1986; Charles Templeton, Farewell to God: My reasons for rejecting the Christian faith, Toronto: McClelland & Stewart, 1996; Joseph Lewis, The Bible Unmasked, New York: The Freethought Press Association, 1926; Dan Barker, Losing Faith in Faith: From Preacher to Atheist, Madison, WI: Freedom from Religion Foundation, 1992. Additional books of this genre can be .found on the Prometheus Books website [www.prometheusbooks.com] and the Freedom From Religion Foundation website [www.infidels.org/org/ffrf/].. For an author who takes an opposite view, that God really did write the Bible, see John W. Haley, Alleged Discrepancies of the Bible, Grand Rapids, MI: Baker Book House, 1977.

[46] 2 Kings 23:35.

[47] Matthew 22:21.

[48] Romans 13:7.

[49] Crowe, *supra*, at 32, citing Beia's Responsiones Casuum Conscientiae, cas. 13, 53ff. (1591).

[50] Leo Jung, Business Ethics in Jewish Law 112 (1987). Italics in the original.

[51] Lehmkuhl, Theologia Moralis I, n. 981 (1902), as cited in Crowe, *supra*, at 76.

[52] Crowe, *supra*, at 114.

[53] Crowe, *supra*, at 116.

[54] Crowe, *supra*, at 37, citing the views of Genicot-Salsmans as expressed in Institutiones Theologiae Moralis (1927).

[55] H. Davis, Moral and Pastoral Theology 339 (1938), as quoted by Crowe, *supra*, at 40.

[56] The Social Security system is a bad investment for the vast majority of people. Individuals are forced to pay thousands of dollars into the system over their working lives, yet have no right to claim any benefits before age 62 or later. If they die before they collect, their heirs get nothing. And even if they do collect a monthly check, the amount they receive is generally less than what they would receive if they had made equal contributions to a private pension fund. For more on this point, *see* Peter J. Ferrara, Social Security: The Inherent Contradiction (1980); Social Security: Prospects for Real Reform (Peter J. Ferrara ed. 1985). Volume 3, No. 2 (Fall, 1983) of The Cato Journal is also devoted to this topic. The Cato Institute is conducting a major study of Social Security. Many of these papers may be found at the Cato Institute website, http://www.cato.org.

[57] In many cases, individuals do not have a choice. They do not have the option of either paying or evading the Social Security tax because it is taken from their paychecks before they receive them. But self-employed individuals can evade the Social Security (self-employment) tax by not declaring all of their self-employment income.

[58] This point is discussed in most public finance texts, and in the public finance chapters of general economics texts.

[59] Of course, people who pay property taxes to educate other people's children get no return for their payments, and may even be adversely affected, since these recently educated students -- who are computer literate -- will soon compete with them for jobs that may require computer literacy.

[60] These percentages are used only for illustrative purposes. The actual percentages will differ depending on a number of factors. For example, senators and representatives in some states are more skillful in obtaining federal money for their constituents than are others. And some taxpayers derive very little benefit for the taxes they pay, whereas others get a great deal back in the form of services. And those who pay little or no taxes can receive much more in services at all levels of government than what they pay, since they pay so little.

[61] I would like to thank Marshall Fritz for introducing me to this example.

[62] A number of commentators over the years have speculated as to why the best individuals do not run for political office or gravitate to positions of authority in government. For one of the better expositions on this point, see *Why the Worst Get on Top*, which is chapter 10 of Friedrich A. Hayek, The Road To Serfdom 134-52 (1944).

[63] Another point might also be made here. The Public Choice School of Economics, founded by James Buchanan and Gordon Tullock, has been pointing out for several decades that government officials are motivated by the same things that motivate the rest of us -- self-interest. They act in their own interest, not the public interest.

[64] Kant's categorical imperative permeates his works. For some discussions and examples of it, *see* Immanuel Kant, The Metaphysics of Morals (1797); Immanuel Kant, Ethical Philosophy (1983); W.L. Reese, Dictionary of Philosophy and Religion 278-79 (1980); Ernst Cassirer, Kant's Life and Thought 245-54 (1981); 4 The Encyclopedia of Philosophy 317 (1967).

[65] It could still support some activities through voluntary revenue raising means, such as lotteries and user fees.

[66] It may be difficult, as a practical matter, to avoid paying a toll if there is someone at the booth who is ready to take either your money or your license plate number if you do not pay. But some toll booths allow users to pay by throwing in coins or tokens, which provides a greater opportunity for beating the fare. However, the more sophisticated toll booths now have cameras that take photographs of the license plates of cars that pass through the toll booth without paying the toll.

[67] There are a few exceptions. A few roads are privately owned. A number of studies take the position that at least some roads should be privatized -- turned over to private owners -- because privately owned roads are better maintained at a much lower cost. Thus, government ownership of roads results in the squandering of resources, relatively speaking. For more on this point, *see* Steve Steckler and Lavinia Payson, Infrastructure, in Privatization For New York: Competing For A Better Future, A Report of the New York State Senate Advisory Commission on Privatization (1992), at 186-214; Randall Fitzgerald, When Government Goes Private: Successful Alternatives to Public Services 47-8, 163-74 (1988); Robert W. Poole, Jr., Cutting Back City Hall 148-49 (1980).

[68] The Yellowstone Primer (John A. Baden and Donald Leal eds. 1990); Randall Fitzgerald, When Government Goes Private: Successful Alternatives to Public Services 68-71, 193-207(1988); Robert W. Poole, Jr., Cutting Back City Hall 99-107 (1980).

Chapter 3

IS TAXATION THEFT?

THE QUESTION OF CONSENT

Those who take the position that tax evasion is unethical or a sin often do so because they view tax evasion as theft -- the taking of property that does not belong to them or the failure to give up property that belongs to someone else, namely, to some government. If you are supposed to render unto Caesar what is Caesar's and you do not, then you are depriving Caesar of his property. But can that argument be turned around? Could it be argued that taxation is theft, and that tax evasion is merely an attempt to prevent a theft from taking place?

Theft is generally defined as the taking of property without the owner's consent. But when it is some government that does the taking, it is called taxation. However, there is a difference between taxation and robbery because robbery is a one-time thing, whereas taxation is something that occurs at regular intervals, which makes it more akin to exploitation or slavery.[1] Does it make any substantive difference whether some government takes one-third of your income or merely forces you to work for it without pay for four months out of the year? Could it be argued that it is the tax collectors rather than the tax evaders who are the sinners or thieves since it is they who are taking property that does not belong to them?

If a robber wants to raise $1,000 and forces you and your friends to empty your pockets, is it unethical not to tell the thief that you have $20 in your shoe, even if the failure to declare the $20 results in having your friends pay a larger share, because you are paying less? Is the argument any different when the robber is government?

The morality of the failure to pay does not revolve around whether the effect of nonpayment might result in a more severe burden on others, but whether you have a moral duty to pay in the first place. If taxation is theft, then the fact that others might be forced to pay what you do not is of no consequence. Robbery is in no way more justified if the robber takes equal portions from all of the victims. But is taxation really theft, or do taxpayers consent to be taxed?

It might be argued that taxation is not really coercive because voters, somewhere along the line, have consented to be taxed. But there are a number of flaws in this line of reasoning. For one thing, the voters who consented to be taxed did so sometime in the past. In the case of the individual income tax in the United States, for example, they gave their consent in 1913, indirectly, through their elected representatives.[2] Many if not all of the people who gave their consent then are now dead. And many of those who were alive and of voting age back then did not give their consent.

It is a fundamental principle of both common law and basic justice that one person cannot be held for the contract of another, so even if consenting to be taxed is viewed as a contract between citizens and the state, the contract is null and void as far as those who did not consent are concerned. So taxation cannot be said to be noncoercive just because some group of voters agreed to be taxed sometime in the past.

Thomas Jefferson makes the following point:

> We may consider each generation as a distinct nation, with a right, by the will of its majority, to bind themselves, but none to bind the succeeding generation, more than the inhabitants of another country.[3]

Jefferson elaborates on this point as follows:

> The question Whether one generation of men has a right to bind another, seems never to have been started either on this or our side of the water. Yet it is a question of such consequences as not only to merit decision, but place also, among the fundamental principles of every government...no such obligation can be transmitted ... the earth belongs ... to the living...[4]

By reviewing statistics of his time (1789), Jefferson determined that the average life expectancy of those still living at age 21 was 55.[5] He reasoned that, since the majority of those twenty-one year-olds who belonged to a particular generation would be dead nineteen years after entering into a social contract with the state, the contract becomes null and void after nineteen years.[6]

This rule applies to constitutions, public debt and all laws. Every law and constitution expires naturally at the end of that time, and any law or constitution that is enforced beyond that time is done so by force and not because of right.[7] Thus, there is a strong philosophical argument that even laws that are passed by majorities -- or unanimously -- expire after some period of time because one generation cannot bind another. So even if one subscribes to some social contract theory, by which some majority can bind everyone, the contract has a limited life. One generation cannot bind another.

Another problem regarding the obligation of citizens to the state involves the concept of majoritarianism. Under majoritarianism, if 51% vote some item into law, the other 49% must go along with it whether they want to or not. Majoritarianism is a basic weakness of democracy, but it is endured so that democracy can function. It is a pragmatic compromise. If unanimous consent were required for everything, governments would not be able to pass many laws (which some say is not such a bad idea).[8]

But the fact that a law is passed by a majority does not mean that it is not coercive, because a large minority might disapprove of the law. The law is coercive at least for those who did not consent to the tax. It is also coercive for those who did give their consent, since they will feel the full force of government if, at some time in the future, they decide not to pay whatever the government says they owe.

Government is force, regardless of how many individuals might have been in favor of passing a particular law.[9] And in cases where democracy is representational rather than direct, it sometimes happens that the peoples' representatives pass a law of which the majority of citizens do not approve.

The concept of majoritarianism is tied in with the concept of a social contract, the view that some group of people have somehow entered into a contract with the state and that they can bind the entire population. They give up a part of their freedom in exchange for certain benefits that the state can provide. Some social contract theorists (like Hobbes) would argue that individuals give up all of their rights in exchange for protection by the state. Others (like Locke) would argue that individuals give up some of their rights, and that they can reclaim these rights if the state fails to do its job.[10]

Some commentators would go farther than Jefferson and Locke and assert that there is no such thing as a social contract, and that such agreements, even if they did exist, are not binding on anyone who did not agree to their terms. For example, Spooner states that:

> The Constitution has no inherent authority or obligation. It has no authority or obligation at all, unless as a contract between man and man. And it does not so much as even purport to be a contract between persons now existing. It purports, at most, to be only a contract between persons living eighty years ago. And it can be supposed to have been a contract then only between persons who had already come to years of discretion, so as to be competent to make reasonable and obligatory contracts. Furthermore, we know, historically, that only a small portion even of the people then existing were consulted on the subject, or asked, or permitted to express either their consent or dissent in any formal manner. Those persons, if any, who did give their consent formally, are all dead now. Most of them have been dead forty, fifty, sixty, or seventy years. *And the Constitution, so far as it was their contract, died with them.* They had no natural power or right to make it obligatory upon their

> children. It is not only plainly impossible, in the nature of things, that they *could* bind their posterity, but they did not even attempt to bind them. That is to say, the instrument does not purport to be an agreement between any body but "the people" *then* existing; nor does it, either expressly or impliedly, assert any right, power, or disposition, on their part, to bind anybody but themselves.[11]

So it appears that those who would say that taxation is not coercive because "the people" consented to it are standing on shaky ground, philosophically. Taxation is coercive whenever it forces people to part with their property without their explicit consent.

In a society where freedom and private property are valued, voluntary forms of revenue raising are superior to coercive forms. If government is viewed as the servant rather than the master of the people, then coercion is to be minimized and the possibilities for voluntary exchange maximized. Forms of revenue raising (like lotteries and user fees) that do not depend on coercion are to be preferred to forms of revenue raising that rely on coercion.

One argument that has been made against voluntarism in the area of government finance is that the government cannot raise all the funds it needs through voluntarism. Coercion is necessary for the state to function. While it would take a book to explore this issue, a few points can be made here. For one thing, this line of reasoning is pragmatic rather than philosophical or ethical. This pragmatic view basically holds that coercion is necessary to raise the necessary funds, therefore coercion must be used. Fairness, equity and property rights are totally absent from this line of reasoning.

Even if one concedes the point that coercion is needed to raise the "necessary" funds, one must still ask "how much is necessary?" If the goal of a free society is to minimize coercion and allow maximum room for individual choice, then government expenditures must be kept at a minimum, so that the amount of coercion needed to raise funds is minimized. Thus, the role of government must be minimized.[12]

EXPLOITATION AS OFFICIAL STATE POLICY

> There is an obligation in justice for all the subjects to contribute to the expenses of the state according to the ability and means of each.[13]

The ability to pay principle involves exploitation. The government exploits the producers -- the wealth creators -- and redistributes a portion of their income to wealth consumers -- those who use the various government programs. In that sense, it is a parasitical system.

The cost-benefit principle, on the other hand, attempts to match costs with benefits. Those who use government services pay for them, and those who do not use the services are not forced to pay. Thus, the cost-benefit principle appears to be fairer than the ability to pay principle because it is based on principles of equity rather than exploitation. So a tax that is based on the cost-benefit principle is to be preferred to a tax that relies on the ability to pay principle, all other things being equal.

But even a system based on cost-benefit does not eliminate the deadweight loss question or the fact that some of the services provided are services that some taxpayers do not want -- or the fact that the money is being taken without the owner's consent. So if there are degrees of badness, one might say that a tax system based on the cost-benefit principle is less bad than one based on the ability to pay because one is based on exploitation and the other is based on recouping money for services rendered. But both systems are bad, in the sense that they rely on coercion and the taking of property without the owners' consent.

CONCLUSIONS AND IMPLICATIONS

Is tax evasion a sin? Is it unethical? The arguments that have been put forth over the centuries do not support the position that tax evasion is a sin. Taxation is the taking of property without the owner's consent, which makes it the equivalent of theft, with some government as the robber. But unlike normal theft, the perpetrator is the State rather than an individual. And the taking is continuous rather than a one-time thing, which likens taxation to exploitation or slavery rather than robbery.

The fact that a majority of eligible voters who voted in some previous election[14] does not change the substance of the transaction. And the fact that taxpayers receive some benefits from government does not alter the morality of the matter either. The fact that nonevaders may have to pay more as a result of the act of evasion does not alter the morality of the act because taxation is based on theft rather than paying each what one is morally required to pay.

While theologians and others have often argued that there is a duty to pay a just tax, the fact is, there is no such thing as a just tax. Gury has suggested that there is a presumption that a tax is just where it has existed over a long period of time and where it has been paid without protest.[15] But this might also be said of slavery, which existed for thousands of years with nary a protest, even from the slaves, for the most part.

While Gury might offer that there is a presumption that certain taxes can be just, this presumption can always be overcome where rights are being violated, as where property is taken by force or the threat of force without the owner's consent. All taxes are the taking of property without the owner's consent, so there is no justice about it, even if some of the proceeds are used for good causes.

Theft is wrong regardless of whether the thief uses the proceeds of the theft to distribute food to the poor or to gamble, drink or go wenching. It is the act itself that is either good or bad, not what happens afterward. Rather than regarding tax evaders as sinners or cheats, it might be more accurate to say that it is the tax collectors who sin or rob because it is they who facilitate the taking of property without the owners' consent.

NOTES

[1] Nozick would say that income taxation is the theft of the fruits of one's labor. Robert Nozick, Anarchy, State and Utopia (1974).

[2] The Sixteenth Amendment to the U.S. constitution, which made income taxation constitutional, was passed in 1913. Before that, the government raised the money it needed through excise taxes and tariffs.

[3] Letter of Thomas Jefferson to John Wayles Eppes, Monticello, Virginia, June 24, 1813, reprinted in Thomas Jefferson: *Writings* 1280-86 (1984). The quote is from 1280-81.

[4] Letter of Thomas Jefferson to James Madison, Paris, September 6, 1789, reprinted in Thomas Jefferson: *Writings* 959-64 (1984). The quote is from 959.

[5] *Id.*, at 960.

[6] *Id.*, at 1281.

[7] *Id.*, at 962-63.

[8] Some political commentators regard John Tyler as America's greatest president because not a single law was passed during his administration. Actually, a tariff and a treaty (and perhaps some other laws) were passed during his administration, so it cannot strictly be said that "no laws" were passed during his administration. Actually, it might better be said that Harrison was the greatest president, since he died a few weeks after taking the oath of office, thus not having time to do much damage.

[9] One advantage of a democracy over a dictatorship is that, under a dictatorship, one person tyrannizes the other 99.99%, whereas under a democracy, at worst, 51% tyrannize the other 49%. Herbert Spencer expresses a similar view in Social Statics 189 (1970). He expresses the view on page 210 of the 1851 London edition. Others would say that the difference between a democracy and a dictatorship is the number of feet on your throat.

[10] For various views on the theory of the social contract, see Thomas Hobbes, Leviathan (1651); John Locke, Two Treatises on Government (1689); Jean Jacques Rousseau, The Social Contract (1762). The U.S. Declaration of Independence (1776) reflects Locke's view, that a government that fails to protect basic rights can be replaced by the people with one that will protect these rights.

[11] Lysander Spooner, No Treason: The Constitution of No Authority, originally self-published by Spooner in Boston in 1870, reprinted by Rampart College in 1965, 1966, and 1971, and by Ralph Myles Publisher, Inc., Colorado Springs, Colorado, in 1973. The quote is from page 1 of the 1971 edition (p. 11 of the 1973 edition). The constitution Spooner is referring to is the U.S. Constitution, which was adopted about eighty years before he wrote this essay. Emphasis is in the original.

[12] Much of what is now done by government can be done more efficiently and cheaper by the private sector. The growing body of privatization literature points this out clearly. For examples, see Robert W. Poole, Jr., Cutting Back City Hall (1980); Randall Fitzgerald, When Government Goes Private (1988); James T. Bennett and Manuel H. Johnson, Better

Government at Half the Price (1981). One way to minimize the tax bite would be to privatize as much as possible.

[13] S.E. le Card. Gousset, Théologie Morale I, 504 (1869), as quoted in Rev. Martin T. Crowe. 1944. The Moral Obligation of Paying Just Taxes, The Catholic University of America Studies in Sacred Theology No. 84, at p. 59.

[14] Or their representatives, in the case of a representative democracy.

[15] Gury, Compendium Theologiae Moralis (1850), as cited in Crowe, *supra*, at 61.

Chapter 4

SHOULD ACCOUNTANTS AND ATTORNEYS BE PUNISHED FOR AIDING AND ABETTING TAX EVASION?

THE PREMISE

The knee-jerk response to the question, "Should accountants and attorneys be punished for aiding and abetting tax evasion?" is "yes." But that response is self-serving. Few accountants or attorneys would publicly state that their colleagues should not be punished for aiding and abetting an act that is illegal and widely regarded (in some circles at least) as unethical as well.[1] Furthermore, having an accountant state that accountants should not be punished for aiding and abetting tax evasion would lead the accounting profession to be perceived in a bad light by the general public. However, it does not logically follow that an *illegal* act should necessarily be punished by the profession. Likewise, it does not logically follow that an *unethical* act should necessarily be punished. That being the case, it also does not logically follow that an act that is both illegal and unethical must *necessarily* be punished. It depends.

A CLOSER LOOK AT THE ISSUE

Acts that are illegal today may be legal tomorrow, and vice versa. During prohibition, it was illegal to sell alcoholic beverages. Yet before and after prohibition, it was perfectly legal to do so. In some states, it was illegal to drive before age 18 at some times and before age 16 at others. So, depending on a person's age, location and time period, a seventeen year-old might be driving either legally or illegally. Both driving illegally and selling alcoholic beverages are victimless crimes, as are ticket scalping, bigamy and dwarf tossing.[2] If one takes the plausible position that only perpetrators of crimes that have victims should be punished, then the initial question is whether the crime in question has a victim or is victimless. Does tax evasion have a victim? If so, perhaps tax evaders should be punished. If not, then perhaps they should not be punished.

In the realm of ethics, it does not logically follow that someone who acts unethically should automatically be punished. Not every unethical act is a crime, and even if an act is unethical and a crime, the crime may have no victim. In the case of accounting or law, the ethical question is complicated by the fact that what might have been regarded as unethical by the profession in the past might be considered perfectly ethical today. For example, advertising was labeled as unethical conduct by the accounting and legal professions at one point, until several court cases found that punishing accountants and attorneys for advertising violated their rights to free speech and press. Indeed, it might even be argued that preventing accountants or attorneys (or anyone, for that matter) from exercising their rights to free speech and press constitutes unethical conduct.

Yet that is exactly what the accounting and legal professions did until courts told them they couldn't do it any more. Punishing accountants and attorneys for advertising their services was a self-serving, rent seeking activity. It was supposedly done in the public interest, but was actually done because the old established firms did not want to lose clients to new, smaller firms that could compete on price and perhaps on quality as well.

Another problem is that what is ethical or unethical is not always readily apparent. Reasonable people disagree as to what constitutes unethical conduct. Should some majority determine what is ethical, or is ethical conduct a highly individual matter?

Is tax evasion always unethical or only sometimes? Or perhaps never? Certainly if tax evasion is never unethical, it logically follows that someone who is guilty of it should not be punished by the profession. But what if it is illegal? Illegal activities should be punished. Or should they? Is someone who lives in Nazi Germany obligated to follow the laws? People who are unfortunate to live under such regimes might have an ethical obligation to break some laws, at least if the penalty for doing so is small or nonexistent. So it does not follow that individuals act unethically just because they broke some law. It depends on what law they violated. if the law is unjust, then there seems to be no ethical problem with breaking such a law.

Bigamy is illegal in many places, but not in all places. Prostitution is also illegal in many places, but not in all places. It used to be a felony in some states to marry someone of a different race. Some religious sects of fundamentalist Christians still think it is an abomination. Engaging in sodomy, which includes having oral sex with your spouse, is still considered a felony in some places, as is engaging in homosexual activity. In some places, such acts are punishable by death. Does that mean that tax practitioners who engage in these activities should be punished, and perhaps have their licenses to practice revoked?

The point is that it cannot be stated categorically, once and for all that tax professionals should be punished by their profession for aiding and abetting their clients to evade taxes. It depends on whether the tax is just. If the law is unjust, tax practitioners who help them to evade the unjust law should not be punished by their profession. Yet both the accounting and legal professions have rules that sanction members for engaging in acts that are illegal just because they are illegal, without regard to whether they are also unethical or whether they harm someone who does not deserve to be harmed. The better policy, from an ethical standpoint, would be to sanction members only for acts that harm the public. or some individual who does not deserve to be harmed. Such a policy would prevent tax practitioners from being unjustly punished for breaking unjust laws and engaging in activities that may be unethical, like prostitution and dwarf tossing, but that have no victims.

An even bigger question, which we shall not go into here, is whether some profession, or rather some organized subset of a profession, should be able to punish members of the profession for any reason whatsoever. A related question is whether anyone should need government permission to engage in a line of work such as accounting, medicine or law. If there is such a thing as the right to work, and the right to engage in voluntary exchange with consenting adults, it would seem that government has no such right. If so, then government should not be involved in the certification of accountants or the licensing of doctors, lawyers or anyone else. Milton and Rose Friedman have advocated a constitutional amendment that would prohibit occupational licensure because such licensure benefits special interest groups at the expense of the general public.[3] But we will leave discussion of these questions for another day.[4]

If there is nothing ethically wrong with tax evasion, it seems to follow that attorneys, accountants and financial planners should not be penalized for advising their clients to evade taxes, or even for helping them to evade taxes. Yet it is probably safe to assume that the vast majority of professional codes of ethics for attorneys, accountants and financial planners -- perhaps all -- would consider any kind of activity that aids in tax evasion to be unethical and subject to sanction.[5]

This prohibition also has some First Amendment implications, since the freedom of an advisor to advise a client to evade taxes is being impinged. Counselors cannot tell their clients to evade taxes, or show them how to do it, or help them to do it, without opening themselves up to punishment,[6] which has a chilling effect on free speech.

While suggesting that these codes of ethics remove any prohibition on the advocacy of tax evasion is extremely controversial, perhaps it is time that someone at least raised the question. If the advocacy of tax evasion is not unethical, and it appears that it is not, then a code of ethics that punishes individuals for advising their clients to evade taxes may itself be perpetrating an injustice, since it is punishing someone for advocating something that is not unethical.

NOTES

[1] For discussions of the question of whether, and when, tax evasion might be unethical, see Robert W. McGee. 1994. Is Tax Evasion Unethical? University of Kansas Law Review 42(2): 411-435. For discussions of diverse perspectives, see Robert W. McGee, editor. 1998. The Ethics of Tax Evasion. Dumont, NJ: The Dumont Institute for Public Policy Research.

[2] For an exposition of the dwarf tossing case as a victimless crime, see Robert W. McGee. 1993. If Dwarf Tossing Is Outlawed, Only Outlaws Will Toss Dwarfs: Is Dwarf Tossing a Victimless Crime? American Journal of Jurisprudence (38): 335-358.

[3] Milton and Rose Friedman, Free to Choose, New York and London: Harçourt Brace Jovanovich, 1979 and 1980, at p. 293 of the paperback edition and p. 305 of the hardcover edition.

[4] For a classic treatment of these issues, see Milton Friedman, Capitalism and Freedom, Chicago: University of Chicago Press, 1962 at pp. 137-160. For other discussions on the economics and ethics of occupational licensure, see Simon Rottenberg, editor, Occupational Licensure and Regulation, Washington, DC: American Enterprise Institute, 1980; S. David Young, The Rule of Experts: Occupational Licensing in America. Washington, DC: Cato Institute, 1987; Robert Albon and Greg Lindsay, editors, Occupational Regulation and the Public Interest: Competition or Monopoly? St. Leonard's, Australia: The Centre for Independent Studies, 1984; Mary J. Ruwart, Healing Our World, Kalamazoo, MI: Sun Star Press, 1992, pp. 55-70.

[5] E.g., *ABA Model Rules of Professional Conduct* Rule 1.2(d) cmt. (1983) ("[A] lawyer should not participate in ... a transaction to effectuate criminal or fraudulent escape of tax liability.").

[6] See id; Charles W. Wolfram, *Modern Legal Ethics* § 13.3.6, at 700-01 (1986).

Chapter 5

JEWISH VIEWS ON THE ETHICS OF TAX EVASION

INTRODUCTION

This chapter summarizes and comments on the ethics of tax evasion from the Jewish perspective. The Jewish literature on this subject, although scant, is consistent in holding that tax evasion is generally unethical. One hesitates to comment on "the" views of any particular religion, especially when the religion is thousands of years old with vast quantities of literature published in numerous languages. One is especially hesitant when one was not raised in the tradition of that religion. However, one must start somewhere, so I will attempt to summarize and comment on the Jewish view on the ethics of tax evasion as best I can.

After much searching, I was unable to find more than two authors who have published anything on this topic.[1] Thus, my analysis and comments will be based on the scant literature I was able to find on this classic ethical issue.

Unlike the Christian views, which seem to span the full range of possibilities,[2] the Jewish view seems to be quite consistent, based on the two scholars who have written on the subject. Based on these authors, the Jewish view is that tax evasion is almost always or perhaps always unethical. Presumably, this view would hold true even if Hitler were the tax collector.

JEWISH VIEWS

Tamari's Views

Tamari's analysis starts with a look at the conceptual framework of the Jewish system. He states that

> There exists a moral obligation on society to fund the social costs of that society and this gives it the right to tax its members for that purpose. These social costs are recognised by halakhah (lit. to walk but referring to the corpus of Jewish Law) as going beyond defense and infrastructure to include the needs of the poor, the sick

> and the old as well as religious study and the religious needs of the community.[3]

There are at least three problems with this statement. For one, only living, breathing human beings can have any kind of moral obligation. "Society" does not exist. Society is just a collective term to refer to a group of living, breathing individuals who may have some things in common, like geographical proximity and economic and social interaction. Thus, society has no moral obligation because society does not exist except as a dictionary term for a collection of individuals. Individuals may have some moral obligations, but society does not and cannot.

The second problem with Tamari's statement is that it includes a non sequitur. Assuming for the sake of argument that "society" *does* exist, it does not logically follow that society has the moral right to tax its members. The so-called "right" to tax involves force or the threat of force.

If some individual or group of individuals has a moral obligation to do something, it does not follow that they have the right to force anyone to do anything. Indeed, morality by definition involves choice. If one is not free to choose, there is no morality. If one has a moral obligation, it is the individual who must do or refrain from doing something. There is no such thing as having a moral obligation to force others to pay for some agenda that you may personally think is right and just.

The third problem is Tamari's view of government. He would include as legitimate government expenditures items that could only be construed as payments to special interests,[4] such as the poor, the sick and the old. He also finds nothing morally repugnant about supporting religious study.

In a society that is 100 percent Jewish, the argument in favor of supporting religious study with taxes may be somewhat stronger than in a pluralistic society, where many religions (and no religion) reign with equal freedom. But even in totally Jewish communities there may be problems with forcing some Jews to pay for the religious instruction of other Jews. Should orthodox Jews be forced to pay for the religious education of reform, conservative or reconstructionist Jews? Should orthodox Jews from one synagogue be forced to support religious training that takes place at another orthodox synagogue? Should Jews who do not have children be forced to pay for the religious education of other people's children, even if the other children attend the same synagogue? There are a number of problems inherent in forcing anyone to do anything, even if some individual or group might benefit.

Tamari later states that "taxes may not be confiscatory nor arbitrary nor discriminatory."[5] He goes on to point out that the Jewish literature permits Jews to disregard laws, including tax laws, that are capricious or discriminating.[6] However, he later contradicts this view that would seemingly condone tax evasion in certain circumstances. For example, he states that "Jewish legal literature is clear that non-payment of taxes is theft and is therefore forbidden."[7] He thus turns the definition of theft on its head. While theft is usually defined as the taking of property without the owner's consent, Tamari would define it as not allowing someone (the state's tax collectors) to take your property without your consent.

One might argue that "the people" have consented to be taxed, but this line of reasoning is faulty on several grounds. First of all, "the people" does not exist, just as "society" does not exist. Secondly, at best, only a majority of people voted to delegate to some legislative or executive the authority (not the right) to tax all the people. It could also be pointed out that elected representatives often do not represent the will of the majority. A whole body of literature has developed that shows case after case where elected representatives are in the pockets of special interests and act against the interests of the people who elected them. And even if elected representatives *did* follow the will of the majority, there is still a problem with majority rule because majorities can, and often do, disparage the rights of the minority.[8] It should be remembered that both Hitler and Mussolini came to power through the democratic process.

Jewish religious thought regards tax funds that are raised to fund "social" obligations as *holy* money rather than *stolen* money.[9] Again he points out that Jewish religious teachings require one to contribute to communal costs. Since the money is holy, it must not be wasted or spent on frivolous things. But what if it is wasted or spent on frivolous things? While Tamari rightly points out that tax collectors and public officials have a moral obligation not to squander tax funds, he fails to mention whether tax evasion might be justified in cases where squandering is widespread.

One of Tamari's strongest arguments is that, in order to evade taxes, it is necessary to falsify records and lie.[10] The assumption here is that falsifying records and telling lies is morally indefensible, which is usually the case. Falsifying records and telling lies do tend to corrupt an individual's moral fiber. But telling lies is not always an unethical act, as Plato[11] and Aristotle[12] both pointed out more than 2,000 years ago. It is not immoral to tell a spouse who is contemplating suicide that you do not know where the pistol is kept even if you do know where it is kept. It is not immoral to tell an armed robber that you have given him all your money when in fact you have money hidden in your shoe.

If one defines theft as the taking of property without the owner's consent, then it could reasonably be argued that taxation is theft, since individuals representing some government are taking property without the owner's consent. If the owner consented, there would be no need to use force or the threat of force to obtain the property. But Tamari instead states that tax evasion is theft, since, for him, some mythical community has a superior claim on an individual's assets than the individual himself.

Even where tax evasion seems morally justified because of high tax rates or wasteful spending, Tamari suggests the ballot box, political pressure or a tax revolt, perhaps involving jail sentences, rather than bend to the personal corruption that would take place if individuals evaded taxes.[13]

There are several problems with this solution. For one, there is the problem of majoritarianism. What if the majority approves of high tax rates (or perhaps graduated tax rates for the rich)? Since Jews comprise a small minority of voters in practically every country, the ballot box does not seem like a probable solution. Political pressure would also likely be ineffective. Going to prison as a protest seems like a rather high price to pay.

One issue Tamari avoids completely is whether tax evasion might be justified if tax proceeds are used to fund downright evil activities. One of the best examples of evil activity would be where a Hitler or Stalin uses tax funds to kill or persecute Jews. If tax evasion can be justified at all, it would seemingly be justified in such a case. Tamari does not cover this point or cite any Jewish literature that might be quoted to support tax evasion in such a case.

Cohen's Views

In the first sentence of Cohn's chapter[14] he states that his paper presents the orthodox Jewish view regarding the obligation to pay taxes, which begs the question – are the reform, conservative or reconstructionist Jewish views different from the orthodox view? Perhaps it is an unfair criticism, since Cohn is an orthodox rabbi and has stated up front which view he is representing. But if the orthodox view differs from other Jewish views, it would have been nice for him to point out the differences. If there are differences, it would make a good topic for an article since, to my knowledge, no such articles presently exist in the literature.

Cohn's chapter overlaps somewhat with Tamari's, but there is not a complete overlap. Cohn makes some points that Tamari does not, and vice versa. But they are in basic agreement that tax evasion is unethical.

> The *Halachic* (Jewish legal) perspective on paying taxes has four components. First, there are laws related to a citizen's duty to follow his country's statutes. This is called *dina damalchusa dina*. Second, laws prohibit lying. Third, a Jewish person may not do anything which could discredit the religion. This is known as *Chillul Hashem*. Finally, since it is essential for a Jewish person to perform the maximum number of mitzvos (commandments and good deeds), he is required to refrain from any activity

> which could result in confinement in a place where Judaism cannot be properly practiced, e.g., jail.[15]

The next four parts of his paper go into some explanation of these four points. Several questions immediately come to mind when reading this passage. For one, must one always follow the laws of the country where one lives, even if the laws are unjust? Again, one might cite the Hitler/Stalin example.[16] Is lying always unjustifiable or only most of the time? The third point – not doing anything that would discredit the religion – is more complex than first appearance would suggest because this view involves the issue of self-ownership versus ownership by some mystical collective. The fourth point, paying taxes in order to stay out of jail, would seemingly contradict what Tamari suggested – tax protest, including jail, as a means of changing what is perceived to be an unjust law. One might also point out that it might be possible to perform even more mitzvos in jail than in society at large, since there might be more of a need for good deeds in a prison situation.

Cohn cites several Talmudic passages to support the view that one must obey the laws of the king.

> There are three principal reasons for *dina damalchusa dina*. First, the king owns the country and therefore everyone is required to give him a portion of their income as rent. Second, a country can be considered a partnership. The king or president is the organizational leader. Third, according to the Torah the descendants of Noah were assigned seven laws to follow. One of these laws requires each nation to establish a government which provides for the welfare of its citizens.

The first reason, that the king is entitled to rent from his subjects, holds true at best only in the few countries that still have kings. Modern political theory begins with the premise that the government is the servant and the people are the masters. At least that is the case for democratic regimes. Even in some nondemocratic regimes, lip service is paid to the idea that the government is there to serve the people instead of the other way around. In countries that recognize private property, individuals own the country, not the government.

The second point, that a country can be considered a partnership, seems plausible on the surface. But here we run into the problem of untrammeled majoritarianism crushing the rights of the minority. Furthermore, partnerships are voluntary associations whereas governments are not. Government involves force whereas partnerships exist only through voluntary cooperation.

The third point, that God told us to establish governments, even if true involves a non sequitur. If governments must provide for the welfare of its citizens, it does not follow that it must do so through taxes.

Governments can and have raised funds to operate through voluntary contributions such as lotteries and user fees. Under Islam, Judaism and some branches of Christianity, there is a moral obligation to tithe or give some portion of one's income or assets to the church or to the poor. Before 1913 the United States raised the necessary funds through tariffs without any income tax. Even if government does have some moral right to extract taxes from the populace, it does not follow that individuals have a moral duty to pay whatever the tax collector demands.

Cohn goes on to elaborate on the three points he made. For example, some Jewish literature holds that the king's subjects only owe the king the income that is derived from the land, since the king owns only the land and not the people. Other Jewish scholars take the position that the king owns his subjects as well, and is thus entitled to a portion of their labor.

As evidence of this ownership Cohn points out that the king may force his subjects to work or draft them into the army. However, this ownership exists only where the ruler is legitimate. Where he forces himself into a country, there is no such ownership or moral authority. Cuba and Eastern Europe are pointed out as examples of where "*dina damalchusa dina* could not suffice to forbid tax evasion."[17]

Cohn next describes a case in the Jewish literature where "people agree that a person is their ruler and they see themselves as servants to him."[18] He states that *dina damalchusa dina* would apply in such places, which would include modern democratic states. Again, the problem is one of majoritarianism since, in a democracy, only some of the people voted for the people who were elected. Also, very few people in a democracy view themselves as servants to their elected officials. It is more likely that elected officials are viewed as servants who are derelict in their duties to the people.

Cohn expands on the partnership theory by stating that when individuals join partnerships, they are expected to abide by the partnership rules, and if they don't like the rules, they should leave the partnership. All this is true of partnerships. The problem is that governments are not partnerships. Governments rely on force whereas partnerships rely on voluntary cooperation.

Furthermore, no one "joins" a government. One is born into some political jurisdiction and perhaps has the option of voting with his feet and moving to another political jurisdiction if he is allowed out of the country of birth and into the country of choice. Cohn's statement that "continuing to live in a country is an implicit agreement to abide by its rules"[19] is not true. For one thing, not everyone is allowed to leave the country of his birth. The Soviet Union did not allow its people (with the exception of Jews, who were considered undesirable) to leave the country until shortly before its collapse. Even in countries where individuals are able to leave, they must be able to find a country that is willing to take them. The United States, Switzerland and many other countries limit immigration.

But the consent argument is weak even in cases where people are free to leave and can find refuge in another country. Again, we face a non sequitur. The non sequitur might go something like this: You live in country X, therefore you agree to abide by the rules of country X. The second statement does not logically follow from the first.

Cohn's elaboration on the third reason for *dina damalchusa dina* is interesting and involves several arguments that have been repeated through the ages. One of the more interesting points he makes is that, according to the Jewish literature, the laws given to Noah and his descendants are laws that non-Jews are bound to follow. Supposedly, these laws include a tax system.

According to the *Schulchan Aruch*, one need not follow the government's tax statutes unless "the tax system is fair."[20] But the government is permitted to practice discrimination and charge one group more than others. In such cases the *dina damalchusa dina* is to be followed.

It seems like any tax system that charges one group more than others is inherently unfair. The groups Cohn uses as examples are Jews, Italians or people from Alabama. However, a case can be made that where one group benefits more by taxes, it should also be required to pay more.

For example, if the government uses extra tax money to provide grammar and diction lessons for the people who live in Alabama, it seems reasonable that they should be charged more, since they receive more benefit.[21] However, an even larger question is whether the government should provide such lessons for anyone, since these lessons can be provided by the private sector. It does not seem fair to charge the people of Boston (who might also need lessons on when to pronounce the 18th letter of the alphabet) for lessons received by people who live in Alabama.

The Jewish literature says that people should not lie and should not say things that come close to lying. Writing a falsehood is also a violation of Jewish law. From this Cohn concludes that someone who signs a falsified tax form violates the prohibition against falsehoods.[22]

However, Cohn correctly points out that lying is permitted in certain well-specified circumstances. Lying is only a relative inequity according to Jewish law. Lying may be permitted to prevent an even greater injustice. Cohn states that one may lie in order to prevent an illegal government from unlawfully collecting a tax.[23]

However, even where lying is permitted to circumvent an injustice, one may never swear falsely or give false testimony in court.[24] Because it is not always easy to determine when lying is acceptable and when it is not, some rabbis have suggested that only those who are learned in the Jewish law (like rabbis) should be permitted to lie, since otherwise people might wrongly conclude that lying is permitted in certain cases where it is forbidden.

Speaking of lying, what about politicians who lie? During his re-election campaign, George Bush the elder promised "no new taxes," yet he imposed them anyway. Is there any ethical duty to pay such increased taxes? How about politicians who come close to lying. Bob Dole said he would not raise tax "rates," but what he did not say is that he had no qualms about eliminating deductions, which amounts to the same exact thing as a rise in tax rates, since more taxes are extracted. Perhaps in the future some Jewish scholar can address what the Jewish law and tradition have to say about these cases.

So far, it seems like the Jewish tradition would permit tax evasion in certain limited circumstances, like where the ruler is illegitimate or where the tax is unfair. However, tax evasion even under these circumstances might be considered unethical if the person who evades the tax causes the Jewish religion to be seen in a bad light (*Chillul Hashem*).

> ...even if there is a type of tax evasion which did not require lying and was not a violation of *dina damalchusa dina*, if it could come to *Chillul Hashem* it would not be allowed.[25]

Thus, one is ethically obligated to pay an unjust tax or to pay a tax to an illegitimate ruler if doing so would prevent the Jewish religion from being shown in a bad light. The underlying philosophy here is that individuals lose the right to their property if keeping their property somehow causes some people to think negatively on other people. The main problem with this position is that it results in rights violations. Any policy that results in the violations of a person's rights is an inherently bad policy.

> ...it is important for a Jewish person to pay taxes in order to avoid jail. For example, someone living in a society where there is an illegitimate dictatorship should still pay taxes in order to avoid prison. Being in jail has two major drawbacks for a Jewish person. First, there are many mitzvos which cannot be performed there. There may not be kosher food, a synagogue, Torah study, etc. Second, the fellow prisoners will not be the types of individuals who will encourage one to have a proper Jewish attitude.[26]

Cohn makes a good point, of course. A non-Jewish person might also decide to pay taxes to stay out of jail. That is just common sense and a practical decision. However, it says nothing about the ethics of the matter.

> In order to stay out of jail, a Jewish person should even pay taxes to an illegitimate government.[27]

This view is rather severe. However, if one holds the ability to live a religious life more dear than parting with one's assets by giving them to an illegitimate government, then there is a certain logic to it. It is a value judgment, one that comes down in favor of religious freedom over property rights. But what if the proceeds of the taxes surrendered are used for evil purposes, such as munitions factories the products of which are used to kill Jews? How much religious freedom can a Jew have if he is dead? Does it make any difference if the products of the munitions factory are used to kill gentiles? Perhaps at some point it might be ethical to evade taxes and risk jail rather than allow a portion of your assets to be used to commit unethical or immoral acts. Apparently, the Jewish law and tradition do not allow for this possibility, at least according to Cohen.

CLOSING THOUGHTS

So what is the bottom line? If Tamari's and Cohn's interpretations of the Jewish literature on tax evasion are accurate, one must conclude that tax evasion is always, or at least almost always, unethical. There are several problems with such an absolutist view. I have tried to point out the weaknesses in their arguments and line of reasoning on a point by point basis.

If one expands the argumentation to include non-Jewish sources, several other arguments could be used to ethically justify tax evasion in certain situations. For example, one does not necessarily owe the state whatever the state demands. There are limits. This brings to mind a statement by a famous Jewish rabbi who also doubled as a carpenter: "Give to Caesar what is Caesar's, and to God, what is God's."[28] Neither author mentions this famous quote.

Also, the state is supposed to be the servant and the people the masters. If and when it gets to the point when the state starts acting like the master and starts treating the people like servants, perhaps tax evasion is not unethical.

NOTES

[1] Gordon Cohn, The Jewish View on Paying Taxes, Journal of Accounting, Ethics & Public Policy, 1(2): 109-120 (Spring 1998), reprinted in slightly different form under the title The Ethics of Tax Evasion: A Jewish Perspective, in Robert W. McGee, editor, The Ethics of Tax Evasion, Dumont, NJ: The Dumont Institute for Public Policy Research, 1998, 180-189. All citations are to the book. The second paper on the topic is by Meir Tamari, Ethical Issues in Tax Evasion: A Jewish Perspective, Journal of Accounting, Ethics & Public Policy, 1(2): 121-132 (Spring 1998), reprinted under the same title in

Robert W. McGee, editor, The Ethics of Tax Evasion, Dumont, NJ: The Dumont Institute for Public Policy Research, 1998, 168-178. All citations are to the book.
[2] Robert W. McGee, Christian Views on the Ethics of Tax Evasion, Journal of Accounting, Ethics & Public Policy, 1(2): 210-225 (Spring 1998).
[3] Tamari at 169.
[4] For definitional purposes, special interests may be defined as any group that constitutes less than a majority of some relevant population. Forcing the general public (taxpayers) to pay for some benefit that is received by some minority is inherently immoral. Forcing the general public to pay for a benefit that is received by a majority of less than 100 percent may also be considered immoral but, if one can distinguish degrees of immorality, it seems that forcing 100 percent of the population to pay for a benefit that 99 percent receive is somehow less immoral than forcing 100 percent to pay for a benefit received by less than a majority. We will leave a detailed discussion of this point for another day.
[5] Tamari, at 169.
[6] Mishnah Torah Hilkhot Gezeilah Chap. 5 halakhah 11, cited by Tamari at p. 169, n. 2.
[7] Tamari, at 170.
[8] Space does not permit a more detailed discussion of the consent aspect of taxation. However, this discussion has been had elsewhere. For example, see Robert W. McGee, When Is Tax Evasion Unethical? in Robert W. McGee, editor, The Ethics of Tax Evasion (Dumont, NJ: The Dumont Institute for Public Policy Research, 1998), 5-35; Robert W. McGee, Is Tax Evasion Unethical? University of Kansas Law Review 42(2): 411-435 (Winter 1994).
[9] Tamari, at 174.
[10] Tamari, at 176.
[11] Plato, The Republic.
[12] Aristotle, The Politics.
[13] Tamari, at 177.
[14] Cohen, at 180.
[15] Cohen, at 182.
[16] I have mixed feelings about continuing to pick on these two tyrants to the exclusion of others who might have been even worse. Hitler only killed a few million nonsoldiers; Stalin killed more Russians than Hitler did. China's Mao killed perhaps 30 or 40 million of his own people, mostly because of stupid economic policies that led to starvation. Cambodia's Pol Pot, while being responsible for the deaths of only a few million people, killed a higher percentage of the population of his small country than Hitler, Stalin or Mao. Whew! Now I feel better.
[17] Cohen, at 183.
[18] Cohen, at 183.
[19] Cohen, at 183.
[20] Cohen, at 184.
[21] This is the present author's example, not Cohn's.
[22] Cohen, at 184.
[23] Cohen, at 185.
[24] Cohen, at 185.
[25] Cohen, at 186.
[26] Cohen, at 186.
[27] Cohen, at 187.
[28] Matthew 22:17, 21, cited in D. Eric Schansberg, The Ethics of Tax Evasion Within Biblical Christianity: Are There Limits to "Rendering Unto Caesar"? in Robert W. McGee, editor, The Ethics of Tax Evasion (Dumont, NJ: The Dumont Institute for Public Policy Research, 1998), 144-157, at 148.

Chapter 6

CHRISTIAN VIEWS ON TAX EVASION

INTRODUCTION

One hesitates to make general statements about "Christian" views on anything, given the fact that Christians of various sects have persecuted and even killed each other (not to mention Jews and Muslims) over the centuries because of doctrinal disputes.[1] Nevertheless, I will attempt to make some general statements regarding Christian doctrine on the ethics of tax evasion. The literature on this topic is scant, or at least was scant until the late 1990s.[2] Therefore, I will necessarily be limited in my discussion to some Biblical passages, a few articles,[3] the views of some Popes and a doctoral dissertation that was written in the 1940s.[4]

THE POPE'S VIEWS

Pope John Paul II's view, as expressed in the most recent edition of the Baltimore Catechism, is that tax evasion is a sin.[5] Unfortunately, it does not go into any detail, nor does it explain how that conclusion was arrived at. One wonders whether the view, as expressed in the most recent edition – the first since 1566 – would consider tax evasion to be a sin if Hitler were the tax collector, or if the tax were so high as to deprive a poor family of basic needs. I think not, based on my understanding of Catholic doctrine. In fact, Christian scholars have taken the position that it is probably not a sin to evade a tax that is imposed on the necessities of life or to evade a tax if the burden is too large.[6]

Thus, even though a publication approved by the Pope states that tax evasion is a sin, serious Catholic scholars cannot take seriously the possibility that tax evasion is always a sin. Furthermore, the Pope is not speaking *ex cathedra*, meaning that his statement cannot be taken as the word of God,[7] but is merely his opinion, at best. I say at best because the Pope did not write the new edition of the Baltimore Catechism but only approved it after numerous scholars spent many years revising it.

Other Popes have addressed taxation from time to time. Leo XIII recognized the right to property and thought that the advantages of private property could be attained only if private wealth was not drained away by crushing tax burdens. He also rejected the concept of egalitarian and redistributive taxation. An American Bishops' letter issued in 1933 agreed with this position.[8]

Another interesting point, which was not mentioned either in the Baltimore Catechism or by any Popes (to my knowledge) in any of their statements, is how tax evasion can be an offense against God, which is necessary in order for something to be a sin, at least according to some dictionaries.[9] If tax evasion is an offense at all, it is an offense against the state.[10] If one stretches a bit, one might argue that evading a tax makes it necessary for others to pay more, since the tax evader is paying less. But that argument leaves a lot to be desired, especially if the tax is an unfair one, or one where the proceeds are used to do evil things. Thus, the recent Roman Catholic Church view, as expressed in the Baltimore Catechism, must be deeply discounted, since it leaves out so much detail and contradicts hundreds of years of Catholic scholarship.

OTHER CHRISTIAN VIEWS

If one wants more detail than is provided by the Baltimore Catechism – which represents only one branch of Christianity in any event – it is possible to find some detail in the ethical and religious literature. Perhaps the most comprehensive treatise on the ethics of tax evasion from a Christian – mostly Catholic[11] – perspective was that done by Martin Crowe in 1944. Crowe's review of the Christian literature quickly reveals that tax evasion is not always unethical. Christian scholars over the centuries have often conceded that, at times at least, tax evasion is not unethical. However, they do not always agree on the fine points.

If one were to summarize Crowe's thesis in a single sentence, it would be that there is a moral obligation to pay just taxes, but there is no moral obligation to pay unjust taxes. That conclusion begs the question, of course, since one must first determine what is a just tax and what is not. But before we examine that question, let's try to define exactly what a tax is. Crowe's definition of a tax is as follows:

> A tax is a compulsory contribution to the government, imposed in the common interest of all, for the purpose of defraying the expenses incurred in carrying out the public functions, or imposed for the purpose of regulation, without reference to the special benefits conferred on the one making the payment.[12]

This definition seems fairly comprehensive on its face. However, it leaves out a number of things that could be considered taxes. For example, any so-called tax that benefits some private interest at the expense of the general public would seemingly not fit this definition. Exactions by government that do not fit this definition could therefore logically be considered to be exactions that could ethically be evaded. What are some of these so-called taxes that benefit special interests at the expense of the general public? Tariffs, for one, because, in most modern societies at least, tariffs are less a means of raising revenue than a means of reducing foreign competition.[13] Tariffs raise the prices of products that the general public buys while special interests benefit due to the decreased competition.

Another, perhaps less obvious special interest exaction is Social Security. The only people who benefit from Social Security taxes are people who receive benefits, which is a distinct minority. Those who must pay the tax, on the other hand, constitute the majority. Thus, Social Security taxes benefit special interests (those who receive benefits) at the expense of the general public. One might push the point farther by pointing out that Social Security is a bad investment, since a much higher rate of return – and pool of cash at the time of retirement – could be had by investing in the average mutual fund. Forcing people to make a bad investment cannot be deemed in the public interest even if they get some or all of their money back eventually.

Another special interest tax is the property tax, to the extent that it is used to finance public schools. Anyone who owns a house has to pay property taxes. Tenants also pay indirectly, since landlords try to pass along the tax as part of the rent. Yet many people do not have children, and many people who do have children do not send them to public schools. Thus, the portion of the property tax that goes to finance public education constitutes special interest subsidization at the expense of the general taxpaying public. Thus, according to Crowe's definition, it appears that there is no ethical duty to pay these taxes, since they benefit special interests rather than the general public. A letter issued by the American Bishops in 1933 seems to justify this position.

> ...state taxation could never be justified for special interests. The placing of the interest of one group of people over another, in terms of taxation, was unjust. The state should not be permitted to tax particular groups within society to benefit other specific groups. Thus, taxation should serve the citizenry in common and not a particular group as the redistributive tax system of socialism is constructed to do.[14]

For Crowe,[15] a tax is just only if it meets three criteria. It must (1) be imposed by legitimate legislative authority, (2) for a just cause, and (3) where there is just distribution of the tax burden. Presumably, there is no ethical duty to pay any tax that meets less than all three of these criteria. Thus, failing to pay taxes to Hitler would not be unethical because the taxes were not used for a just cause, although it could not be said that his authority was illegitimate because he, as well as the Nazi legislature, was elected. This conclusion lends evidence to the argument that tax evasion is not always a sin, even though the revised Baltimore Catechism states that tax evasion is a sin.

While Crowe's doctoral thesis provides an excellent review of the Christian literature on the topic of tax evasion, his logic and line of reasoning sometimes leave a lot to be desired. For example, he states that "moralists are unanimous in their teaching that the ultimate basis of apportioning a tax is the ability of the citizen to pay."[16] There are several problems with this statement. For one, moralists are not unanimous in this view. Secondly, even if they were unanimous, it does not follow that a tax should be based on ability to pay. Morality and ethics are not majoritarian. If the world consisted of 100 moralists and they all agreed that the world was flat, it would not mean that the world is flat, but only that the moralists are unanimously wrong in their opinion.

The most important flaw in Crowe's reasoning is his premise: that some individuals should be exploited for the sake of others. There are basically only two kinds of taxes, those based on the premise that individuals are the masters and the state is the servant, and those based on the premise that the state is the master and the people are the servants. The ability to pay viewpoint is based on the premise that the state is the master and the people are the servants.

Karl Marx said it best when he stated: "From each according to his ability, to each according to his needs."[17] The Marxian view treats people as ends rather than means. It exploits the most productive citizens by forcing them to pay for benefits that others receive just because they have the funds to do so. It begins with the premise that individuals exist to serve the state rather than the other way around. The ability to pay principle is parasitical because it forces the producers in society to transfer wealth to wealth consumers, those who consume government benefits.[18]

Modern democracies are based on the premise that the only reason for the state to exist is to benefit the people, to perform functions that benefit the vast majority, such as providing police protection from internal thugs and military protection from external threats.[19] The Marxian premise, on the other hand, is that the people exist to serve the state. How else could Marx have made such an utterance? Thus, Crowe's view, that taxes should be based on the ability to pay, is morally bankrupt, even if a majority of "moralists" agree with him.

The other view of taxation, that the state provides services for the people, is more tied in to the cost-benefit principle. The cost of government services should be borne by those who benefit. The purest form of "tax" in this regard is actually a user fee. An example would be a gasoline tax, since the only people who pay gasoline taxes are those who use the roads. If the gasoline tax is used solely to build and maintain roads, then those who pay gasoline taxes are not being exploited to pay for services that others use. Another example of a user fee would be charging admission to a public park or a museum. The only people who have to pay for such things are the people who use the facility. This is the fairest kind of tax, since it does not require one group of people to pay for the benefits that other people receive.

In the strictest sense, however, such user fee taxes are not really taxes at all, since they do not involve the force of government. A real tax involves coercion. People must be forced to pay because they will not pay voluntarily. A user fee is different because no one is forced to pay park admission fees. If they don't want to pay, they don't have to pay. But if they don't pay, they are not entitled to the service. That seems fair. No one is forced to pay anything and no one is being used to pay for someone else's benefit. Neither Crowe nor most of the moralists he refers to, however, mention this point. The Christian literature neglects this very important distinction between coercion and volunteerism.

Some Christian scholars take the position that one is morally bound to pay direct taxes but not indirect taxes. Other Christian scholars have held that whether a tax is direct or indirect has nothing to do with the morality of paying or not paying.[20] The matter is further complicated by the fact that people (and governments) cannot agree on what is a direct tax and what is an indirect tax. For example, in the United States, income taxes are considered to be direct taxes but in France they are classified as indirect taxes,[21] which puts one in the curious position of committing a sin if one evades the U.S. income tax but not if one evades the French income tax. I wonder what God would have to say about this?

Some Christian scholars have taken the position that it is a sin to break any law. This position was common during the period when it was thought that the King derived his power from God. This view is supported in the Bible. In Romans 13, 1-2, for example, it states:

> "Let every soul be subject unto the higher powers. For there is no power but of God: the powers that be are ordained of God. Whosoever therefore resisteth the power, resisteth the ordinance of God: and they that resist shall receive to themselves damnation."

Almost no one believes this gibberish these days. To believe such a statement would be to support the regimes of Hitler, Mao, Stalin, Pol Pot and all the other dictators who have killed millions of people. Such a belief would give credence to the Marxist view that religion is the opiate of the people.

Several other passages in the Bible have something to say about taxes. In the Old Testament, it says that the King taxed people according to their ability to pay (2 Kings 23:35) but it does not say whether such a practice is moral. In the New Testament, when Jesus was asked whether it was legal to give tribute to Caesar, he said: "Render therefore unto Caesar the things which are Caesar's; and unto God the things that are God's." (Matthew 22:21). But all this statement really says is that we are supposed to give individuals and institutions (the state) what they are entitled to. It does not address the main issue, which is what the state might be entitled to. One might infer from this passage that Jesus said it is all right to evade the tax if the state is not entitled to the tax. In fact, such would be the logical conclusion to draw from this statement.

St. Paul made a similar statement in Romans 13:7: "Render therefore to all their dues: tribute to whom tribute is due; custom to whom custom; fear to whom fear; honour to whom honour."

The "paying one's fair share" argument also leaves a lot to be desired. Must one pay one's fair share of whatever taxes the state sees fit to impose, or only the fair share of the taxes that are not squandered or given to special interests? This is a very real question at present, since every western democracy squanders large sums of taxes and spends vast quantities of taxpayer dollars (or Euros, Pesos, Yen or Rubles) on questionable projects. Does it make sense for one person to pay more so that others will be exploited by the state less?

What about the "everybody does it" argument, which states that it is all right to evade taxes since everybody does it? One Christian scholar makes the following point:

> It appears unreasonable to expect good citizens, who certainly are in the minority, to be obliged in conscience to pay taxes, whereas so many others openly repudiate the moral obligation, if there is one. It seems unjust that good people should feel an obligation to be mulcted and to pay readily, in order to balance the evasions of many.[22] (Davis 339)

While a case might be made that there is no moral duty to pay a tax where no benefits are received – such as a tariff where the benefits go to some special interest like the textile industry, or Social Security payments, which are transferred directly to people who do not work – what about the case where some benefits are received? Does it depend on how much benefit is received compared to the amount of tax paid, or are taxes morally due in cases where any benefit whatsoever is received?

Most of the time, individuals receive less in benefits from government than they pay in taxes. There are several reasons for this. For one, there is an administrative fee associated with the collection of taxes. Taxpayers in Oregon who send their money to Washington, for example, do not necessarily get it all back. The bureaucracy eats up a substantial portion of their tax payments. If their Senator or Congressman is more skilled than his colleagues, he might be able to push through legislation that results in a higher than average return of tax dollars to Oregon. But half the members of Congress are less skilled than average at this sort of thing. For some federal programs, only about 10 percent of their budget goes to the people intended to be helped. The other 90 percent goes for administration costs.

Another problem with the view that individuals owe some duty to pay taxes if they receive benefits is that the benefits they receive are often benefits they would not pay for if they had to get them from the market rather than the government. Also, the benefits the government bestows on the populace might be of inferior quality compared to what the market would provide, or more costly than what could be had if the market were permitted to provide the same or a similar service. What then? Is one morally obligated to pay the full cost, including the waste that is inherent in the government provision of services? Or is one only obligated to pay the price that would exist if the market provided the service instead of the government? To my knowledge, the Christian literature on tax evasion does not address these points.

What about barter? We all engage in it at some point, even if it is only to take turns carpooling our children to school – You do it today and I will do it tomorrow. Barter transactions are taxable (but probably not the present example). If I pay someone to take my child to school, the person who receives the money is subject to the income tax, or at least that is the case in some countries. What if, instead of paying someone, we agree to take turns instead? Isn't it basically the same as if I got paid for my services and the other person got paid for hers? Is it ethically any different whether we decided to barter to evade the tax rather than because barter would be more convenient? As Schansberg points out, I Corinthians 4:5 states that God will judge men by their motives.[23] So if tax evasion is a sin (a big IF), and if I barter to evade taxes, then I will be guilty of a sin. Of course, I could always estimate the value of the service I receive and declare that on my tax return.

The pacifist wing of Christianity, represented by Quakers among others, does not place much emphasis on whether a tax is just. Their emphasis is on what the tax is used for. If it is used to finance war, the moral thing to do is resist and evade.[24] Some pacifists refuse to pay only that portion of the tax that represents military expenditure. For example, if military expenditures represent 40 percent of the budget, some objectors will refuse to pay 40 percent of their income taxes.

Resisters generally respect and obey the law, but recognize that there is a higher law that must be obeyed. The moral law is higher than the law of the state, so when the two conflict, the state loses. They take the position that it is not only not immoral to break an immoral law, but also that one has a moral duty to break it.

The pacifist argument against paying taxes leaves something to be desired. It begins with the premise that some taxes are legitimate; it is merely the use to which some taxes are put that makes them immoral. Consistent pacifists would resist paying taxes to repel an invading army. Many pacifists think that taxes should be used on social programs like Social Security or welfare, which are merely transfer payments. Many pacifists also think that there is nothing morally wrong with the graduated income tax or other taxes that are based on the ability to pay. They often see nothing wrong with using the force of government to pay for their social agenda. They only see the force of government as evil when it involves killing people. They see nothing wrong with a government that fleeces its people or threatens to imprison them if they resist the fleecing.

Some pacifists are selective in their resistance to war taxes. They would resist payments of taxes to support some wars but not others. They are not consistent in their pacifism. Perhaps they should not be called pacifists in such cases, since war tax resister seems more descriptive.

> If much of what government does is sinful or promotes sin, a case could be made for a subsequent level of tax evasion ... If taxation is so stringent that it prevents a believer from giving to God, tax evasion would be a conceivable alternative.[25]

Thus, if government supports sinful activity, there may not be any ethical duty to pay to support such activities. There may even be an ethical duty not to pay, as in cases where the government supports or subsidizes abortion, systematically disparages property rights, etc. Likewise, if the tax burden makes it difficult or impossible to give to the church, tax evasion might not be considered unethical. Schansberg sums up his view on tax evasion as follows:

> ...the Bible does not endorse tax evasion except in cases where obedience to God supersedes obedience to the state. Moreover, a spirit of the law interpretation recognizes that tax evasion of some sorts is a necessary aspect of life. The bottom line from the perspective of a Biblical Christian ethic is to "render unto Caesar" --- most of the time.[26]

Some Catholic scholars point out that the Catholic view is not completely internally consistent. For example, traditional Catholic sources like Encyclicals and bishops' letters take a more or less classical liberal view of taxation, whereas the recent views of American bishops are more statist and collectivist.[27]

Another interesting view is that presented by the Church of Jesus Christ of Latter-day Saints, also known as the Mormons. While the authors of the only article I could find on this viewpoint (Smith and Kimball) are quick to point out that the views in their article are their own and do not represent the views of their church, they also state that they "derived their conclusions from a historical background unique to the Church."[28] Their conclusion is basically that tax evasion and both legally and ethically wrong. Section 134, Verse 5 of the Mormon Doctrine and Covenants states that individuals should support their governments.[29]

> We believe that all men are bound to sustain and uphold the respective governments in which they reside, while protected in their inherent and inalienable rights by the

> laws of such governments; and that sedition and rebellion are unbecoming every citizen thus protected, and should be punished accordingly; and that all governments have a right to enact such laws as in their own judgments are best calculated to secure the public interest; at the same time, however, holding sacred the freedom of conscience.[30]

This view that governments should be supported is also contained in the Articles of Faith, *The Pearl of Great Price*: "We believe in being subject to kings, presidents, rulers, and magistrates, in obeying, honoring, and sustaining the law."[31] To further bolster their position, Smith and Kimball also quote the *General Handbook of Instructions* of the Church of Jesus Christ of Latter-day Saints, which is reprinted in the *Encyclopedia of Mormonism*, Volume 3:

> Church members in any nation are to obey applicable tax laws. "If a member disapproves of tax laws, he may attempt to have them changed by legislation or constitutional amendment, or, if he has a well-founded legal objection, he may attempt to challenge them in the courts. A member who refuses to file a tax return, or to pay required income taxes, or to comply with a final judgment in a tax case is in direct conflict with the law and with the teachings of the Church.[32]

Based on this quote, it seems that there is little room for disputing the Mormon position that tax evasion is considered unethical. One of the Mormon twelve apostles, who later became the president of the Mormon Church, likened tax evasion to theft.[33] He likened tax evaders to meter robbers and purse snatchers.[34]

One might ask whether the Mormon doctrine would view tax evasion as unethical even if the tax collector were Hitler (one of my rules of thumb for judging the absolutism of someone's position on tax evasion). But in the Mormon case, the Mormon Church was persecuted and some church members were killed, not by Hitler but by fellow nineteenth century Christians who were equally tolerant of different lifestyles as was Hitler. So it could reasonably be concluded that the Mormon doctrine would support the payment of taxes to the Hitlers of the world. According to the Mormon authors of this article (Smith and Kimball), "tax evasion is not consistent with gospel principles."[35]

CONCLUSION

What conclusions can be drawn from this review of Christian literature? The main conclusion is that Christian writers cannot agree on whether, and under what circumstances, tax evasion might be unethical.

Some Christians believe that tax evasion is always unethical. Others believe that it is not unethical at least sometimes. Jesus's oft-quoted view that we should render unto Caesar what is Caesar's is also subject to differing interpretations.

The Catholic Popes apparently do not agree on whether tax evasion is unethical. Neither do the American Catholic Bishops. Christian scholars cannot even agree on whether the ability to pay principle is morally bankrupt or the ethical way to tax. Some scholars believe that there is nothing ethically wrong with evading indirect taxes and others think that it is ethically improper to evade any tax, even if the state does evil things with the proceeds. In short, the only thing that can be said about the Christian position on tax evasion is that there is no coherent, unified, noncontradictory position.

NOTES

[1] As someone who has gone through the Catholic school system to grade 16 (university) I even hesitate to claim to know what Roman Catholic doctrine is, since I learned several, contradictory versions of it during the course of my studies.

[2] See Robert W. McGee, editor. 1998. The Ethics of Tax Evasion. Dumont, NJ: The Dumont Institute for Public Policy Research.

[3] Robert T. Pennock, Death and Taxes: On the Justice of Conscientious War Tax Resistance. Journal of Accounting, Ethics & Public Policy (1998) 1: 58-76, reprinted in Robert W. McGee, editor, The Ethics of Tax Evasion. Dumont, NJ: The Dumont Institute for Public Policy Research, 1998: 124-142; D. Eric Schansberg, The Ethics of Tax Evasion Within Biblical Christianity: Are There Limits to "Rendering Unto Caesar"? Journal of Accounting, Ethics & Public Policy (1998) 1: 77-90, reprinted in Robert W. McGee, editor, The Ethics of Tax Evasion. Dumont, NJ: The Dumont Institute for Public Policy Research, 1998: 144-157; Sheldon R. Smith and Kevin C. Kimball. Tax Evasion and Ethics: A Perspective from Members of The Church of Jesus Christ of Latter-day Saints. Journal of Accounting, Ethics & Public Policy (1998) 1: 337-348, reprinted in Robert W. McGee, editor, The Ethics of Tax Evasion. Dumont, NJ: The Dumont Institute for Public Policy Research, 1998: 220-229; Gregory M.A. Gronbacher, Taxation: Catholic Social Thought and Classical Liberalism. Journal of Accounting, Ethics & Public Policy (1998) 1: 91-100, reprinted in Robert W. McGee, editor, The Ethics of Tax Evasion. Dumont, NJ: The Dumont Institute for Public Policy Research, 1998: 158-167; Robert W. McGee, Is Tax Evasion Unethical? University of Kansas Law Review (1994) 42: 411-435. Future references to Pennock, Schansberg, Smith & Kimball and Gronbacher are to the book, not the journal article.

[4] Martin T. Crowe, The Moral Obligation of Paying Just Taxes. Catholic University of America Studies in Sacred Theology No. 84 (1944). Doctoral Dissertation.

[5] New Rules for an Old Faith, Newsweek, November 30, 1992, p. 71; Sins, Ancient and Modern. The Economist, November 21, 1992, p. 50.

[6] Bonacina. 1687. De Morali Theologia, Tractatus de Restitutione, disp. II, q. IX, n. 5 (1687), II, p. 449, as quoted in Crowe at 48.

[7] Roman Catholic doctrine has considered the Pope to be infallible, meaning incapable of stating error on Catholic doctrine or morals, only since 1870, when the doctrine was approved by majority vote of some council. Even then, infallibility applies only to certain statements. Of course, just because some council says so doesn't make it so. But we will leave discussion of this issue for another day.

[8] Gronbacher, 163-4.

[9] The Catholic position, or at least the one that was beat into my head by the nuns, was that a sin is an offense against God. However, not all dictionaries agree with this view. Some dictionaries say that a sin is something that is in violation of some community standard. These dictionaries leave God out of the picture entirely.

[10] Crimes such as murder are considered crimes against the state for some reason. In fact, they are crimes against some individual. Yet the state is the one that prosecutes and punishes rather than the individual, or more accurately the surviving family of the murdered individual. Whether, and under what circumstances, something can be a crime against the state is an interesting question that is, unfortunately beyond the scope of the present paper.

[11] I say mostly Catholic because some of Crowe's references were to Christian scholars who wrote before the Reformation. Prior to the Reformation, there was no distinction between Christian and Catholic.

[12] Crowe, 14-15.

[13] Robert W. McGee, A Trade Policy for Free Societies: The Case Against Protectionism. Westport, CT: Quorum Books, 1994; Robert W. McGee, The Trade Policy of a Free Society. Capital University Law Review (1990) 19: 301-341.

[14] Quoted in Gronbacher, 165.

[15] Crowe, 22-26.

[16] Crowe, 24. He cites several Christian scholars to buttress his position. For example, "There is an obligation in justice for all the subjects to contribute to the expenses of the state according to the ability and means of each." S.E. LeCard, 1869. Gousset, Theologie Morale I, p. 504, as quoted in Crowe at 59.

[17] Marx, Karl. 1875. Critique of the Gotha Program.

[18] President John F. Kennedy espoused the same view when he said: "Ask not what your country can do for you; ask what you can do for your country." This view is incompatible with the view that the government is the servant and the people are the masters.

[19] Even these functions are not necessarily monopolies that only the state can provide. The majority of police protection in the United States, for example, is provided by private security guards, who are retained by shopping malls, warehouses and businesses to protect their customers and property. There are thousands of private roads, private schools, private parks, etc. as well. Many of these things are provided by the private sector better and cheaper than by the state, which leads one to wonder what we need a state for anyway.

[20] Crowe, p. 17 and elsewhere.

[21] Crowe, 139.

[22] H. Davis, 1938. Moral and Pastoral Theology, p. 339, as quoted in Crowe at 40.

[23] Schansberg, p. 151.

[24] Pennock.

[25] Schansberg, 155.

[26] Schansberg, 157.

[27] Gronbacher, 159.

[28] Smith and Kimball, 220.

[29] Smith and Kimball, 221.

[30] Quoted in Smith and Kimball, 222.

[31] Quoted in Smith and Kimball, 222.

[32] Quoted in Smith and Kimball, 224.

[33] Smith and Kimball, 224.

[34] Smith and Kimball, 225.

[35] Smith and Kimball, 228.

Chapter 7

TAX EVASION IN ISLAM

Scholars have not written too much about the ethics of tax evasion specifically,[1] although a few scholars have mentioned it in a book about something else, like business ethics. According to Islam, Muslims have a moral obligation to pay zakat for the support of the poor and for the legitimate functions of government. Thus, evading one's duty to pay zakat is classified as an immoral act. The Islamic system of taxation is a voluntary one, at least partially, although Islamic literature makes it clear that a government is justified in forcing people to pay taxes if the amount raised by zakat is insufficient to cover all the legitimate costs of government. However, "This right of interference with the individual's personal property will be limited to the extent required by the general welfare of the society ..."[2]

Also, it does not follow that Muslims have a moral obligation to pay whatever taxes the government demands,[3] and it does not follow that any and all forms of taxation are legitimate. Thus, a case can be made that some forms of tax evasion, under certain conditions, may not be immoral. For example, if the government engages in activities that are beyond its legitimate functions, it might not be immoral to withhold taxes.[4] It might also not be immoral to evade certain kinds of taxes.

Ahmad[5] cites Yusuf's *Economic Justice in Islam*, which provides a list of practices that would be immoral for an Islamic state to engage in:

(a) It is immoral on the part of the state to use its power and privilege to make monopolistic gains or to tax the common people indirectly for replenishing the exchequer thereby.[6]

(b) There is no room in Islam for custom barriers, restrictive tariffs or exchange control. The Islamic state, therefore, must not resort to them.[7]

(c) It is illegitimate and unlawful for the state to tax directly or indirectly the general body of consumers and to give "protection" to the interests of a class of producers in the name of industrialization.[8]

(d) Since it is the duty of the state to dispense justice free of charge, therefore, there must not be any court-fees, revenue stamps or fees of any kind for the transaction of any official business.[9]

(e) There must not be any "income" tax as such. Besides curbing the initiative it assumes illegitimacy of the income of the rich. The state should levy, if need be, a proportional tax on the pattern of zakat on the accumulated wealth of the capable taxpayers.[10]

(f) The state should not resort to indirect taxation. If the state has to tax, then, it should do so directly so that the taxes represent a conscious contribution of the people to the cause of public interest.[11]

(g) That there is no justification for imposing death duty. Islamic laws of inheritance take care of the wealth left by the deceased.[12]

If these are the parameters, then it would seemingly not be immoral for a Muslim not to pay indirect taxes, which include excise taxes, customs duties and perhaps corporate income taxes.[13] Muslims could also morally evade paying tariffs and could engage in smuggling, as long as the good smuggled is not against Islam, such as alcohol or cocaine. Evading income taxes would also not be immoral although evading a property tax might be. The evasion of inheritance, estate and gift taxes would not be immoral.

Ahmad elaborates on some of the points made by Yusuf. Protectionism is condemned because it amounts to a direct or indirect tax placed upon consumers by the state. The general public must pay higher prices because the favored few (domestic producers) are being enriched. Traders and consumers are not morally bound to pay the increased price, whether the price increase is the result of protectionism or price fixing.[14]

According to Ahmad, "the adoption of any methods that create an artificial rise in the prices is strictly forbidden."[15] Price fixing and protectionism are only two actions that cause prices to artificially rise. Other causes mentioned by Ahmad include the sales tax and excise taxes.

> "The term *maks* is used for sales-tax. The Prophet (peace be on him) had reportedly said: 'He who levies *maks* shall not enter Paradise'. Since the imposition of sales-tax (or, for that matter, of octroi and excise duties) results in raising the prices unjustly, therefore, Islam does not approve of it. The Caliph 'Umar ibn 'Abd al-'Aziz had abolished *maks*, interpreting it as *bakhs* (diminution in what is due to others) which is expressly prohibited by the Qur'an."[16] (Ahmad: 123)

This prohibition on sales taxes places Muslims in a bit of a quandary, since nearly every state in the USA levies a sales tax. Many European and other countries levy value-added taxes, which are basically the same thing as a sales tax. While it might be expedient for a Muslim consumer to pay a sales tax, and for a Muslim merchant to charge a sales tax, because they are required to do so by law, there is apparently nothing immoral about not collecting or paying them according to Islam.

Excise taxes are more difficult to avoid paying, since they are incorporated into the price of certain products. Of course, the excise tax on alcohol is easy to avoid. Just refrain from purchasing alcoholic beverages. But the excise tax on gasoline is more difficult (but not impossible) to avoid. In fact, the only way I can think of offhand to avoid paying the excise tax on gasoline is to buy gas from certain gas stations on Long Island, where the local mafia has made the evasion of the excise tax on gasoline into a profitable business. However, doing business with the mafia might run afoul of other Islamic tenets.

Another, less obvious form of tax evasion that is not immoral is the evasion of compliance with certain government regulations. A number of studies have pointed out that regulations can be equivalent to a tax,[17] and many examples can be given. One of the more obvious examples is rent control. If a landlord who owns a rent controlled building is prohibited from charging more than $500 a month for an apartment that would fetch $1,500 in a free market, he is, in effect, being forced to subsidize his tenant to the tune of $1,000 a month. The effect of this regulation is exactly the same as if the landlord were allowed to charge the $1,500 market rate, then pay a tax of 66 2/3 percent. Rent control laws force the transfer of wealth from property owners to a favored group (tenants), which is immoral according to the tenets of Islam.

The strongest argument for complying with government regulations is when the regulation benefits the general public. However, many regulations are not of this genre. At least two other categories of regulations exist, those that benefit some special interest at the expense of the general public and those that are actually harmful to the general public. A number of trade regulations fall into one or both of these categories. The United States Trade Representative publishes a book each year that summarizes some of these protectionist regulations.[18]

Numerous studies in recent years have attempted to measure the cost of various regulations. Some of these studies have concluded that certain regulations cost more than they are worth, or actually do more damage than good.[19]

Since there is no moral obligation for a Muslim to comply with a law that causes prices to rise unnecessarily or that enhances the wealth of some protected group at the expense of the general public -- such as price fixing and protectionist trade legislation -- and since some regulations cause prices to rise unnecessarily or protect some favored group at the expense of the general public, it is logical to conclude that Muslims have no moral duty to comply with regulations that either cause prices to rise unnecessarily or that protect some special interest at the expense of the general public. It would also be logical to conclude that there is no moral duty for a Muslim (or anyone, for that matter) to comply with a regulation that is actually harmful to the general public.

Whether, and under what circumstances, a Muslim has a duty to evade certain taxes or regulations is a question we will leave for another day.

NOTES

[1] Two scholars who have written specifically about the ethics of tax evasion in Islam are Athar Murtuza and S.M. Ghazanfar. 1998. Tax as a Form of Worship: Exploring the Nature of Zakat. Journal of Accounting, Ethics & Public Policy 1(2): 134-161.

[2] Mushtaq Ahmad. 1995. Business Ethics in Islam. Islamabad, Pakistan: The International Institute of Islamic Thought and the International Institute of Islamic Economics, p. 134.

[3] S.M. Yusuf. 1971. Economic Justice in Islam. Lahore: Sh. Muhammad Ashraf, p. 96.

[4] For more on the legitimate role of the government under Islam, see M. Nejatullah Siddiqi. 1996. Role of the State in the Economy: An Islamic Perspective. Leicester, UK: The Islamic Foundation.

[5] pp. 135-136.

[6] Yusuf, 96.

[7] Yusuf, 68, 101.

[8] Yusuf, 9-10.

[9] Yusuf, 67.

[10] Yusuf, 67. Since there must not be any income tax, there definitely must not be any graduated income tax, which necessarily treats the rich less favorably than the poor. According to Yusuf (p. 67): "There is no tax on income, which curbs initiative and enterprise. The progressive taxation assumes illegitimacy of the income of the rich. The rising slabs represent taxation with vendetta. Only a proportional tax at a fixed rate (on the pattern of Zakat) is to be levied on the accumulated wealth of the capable taxpayers without any distinction." S.M. Yusuf. 1971. Economic Justice in Islam. Lahore: Sh. Muhammad Ashraf.

[11] Yusuf, 67.

[12] Yusuf, 67.

[13] A simplified definition of a direct tax is a tax that individuals or corporations pay directly. Joseph E. Stiglitz. 1988. Economics of the Public Sector, second edition. New York: W.W. Norton & Company, p. 387. Indirect taxes are taxes on commodities. However, the burden of a corporate income tax is ultimately borne by individuals, either shareholders, consumers or the corporation's employees. So a case can be made that a corporate income tax is actually an indirect tax. For more on the distinction between direct and indirect taxes, as well as the ethics of tax evasion in general, see Robert W. McGee. 1994. Is Tax Evasion Unethical? The University of Kansas Law Review 42:2 (Winter): 411-435.

[14] Ahmad, 122.

[15] Ahmad, 123.

[16] Ahmad, 123.

[17] For examples, see Ronald Utt.. 1991. The Growing Regulatory Burden: At What Cost To America? IPI Policy Report No. 114, Lewisville, TX: Institute for Policy Innovation. November; James L. Payne. 1992. Unhappy Returns: The $600-Billion Tax Ripoff. Policy Review (Winter): 18-24; Murray L. Weidenbaum and Robert DeFina. 1978. The Cost of Federal Regulation of Economic Activity. Washington, DC: American Enterprise Institute. May; Lawrence J. MacDonnell. 1989. Government Mandated Costs: The regulatory burden of environmental, health and safety standards. Resources Policy 15(1): 75-100. March 1; U.S. General Accounting Office. 1993. Regulatory Burden: Recent Studies, Industry Issues, and Agency Initiatives. GAO/GGD-94-28. December; Wayne B. Gray. 1987. The Cost of Regulation: OSHA, EPA and the Productivity Slowdown. American Economic Review 77: 998-1006; Thomas D. Hopkins. 1991. Cost of Regulation. An RIT Public Policy Working Paper, Rochester Institute of Technology; Jonathan H. Adler.1996. Property Rights, Regulatory Takings, and Environmental Protection. Washington, DC: Competitive Enterprise Institute; Bruce Yandle. 1994. Regulatory Takings, Farmers, Ranchers and the Fifth Amendment. Center for Policy Studies, Clemson University.

[18] For example, see United States Trade Representative, 2003 National Trade Estimate Report on FOREIGN TRADE BARRIERS (Washington, DC: Superintendent of Documents).

[19] For a study that discusses some regulations that actually make things worse rather than better see Richard L. Stroup and John C. Goodman. 1989. Making the World Less Safe: The Unhealthy Trend in Health, Safety, and Environmental Regulation. NCPA Policy Report #137, Dallas: National Center for Policy Analysis.

Chapter 8

THE BAHA'I PERSPECTIVE ON TAX EVASION

The Baha'i religion incorporates viewpoints from numerous other religions. Thus, one would think that the Baha'i religion would have the most diverse views on the ethics of tax evasion. But such is not the case. At least, that is what one may conclude from reading the one article I could find that has been written about the ethics of tax evasion from the Baha'i perspective.[1]

The Baha'i position is remarkably similar to the Mormon position, although the literature cited is different. Basically, tax evasion is never justified, presumably even in cases where tax proceeds are used to kill members of the Baha'i faith. DeMoville's article focuses on the ethics of tax evasion as a form of civil disobedience and on the relationship of the individual to the State. Basically, individuals must obey the laws of the State in which they live.

> In every country where any of this people reside, they must behave towards the government of that country with loyalty, honesty and truthfulness. This is that which hath been revealed at the behest of Him Who is the Ordainer, the Ancient of Days.[2]

> ...the Baha'is are the well-wishers of the government, obedient to its laws and bearing love towards all peoples. Such obedience and submission is made incumbent and obligatory upon all by the clear Text of the Abhá Beauty. Therefore the believers, in obedience to the command of the True One, show the utmost sincerity and goodwill towards all nations; and should any soul act contrary to the laws of the government he would consider himself responsible to God, deserving divine wrath and chastisement for his sin and wrongdoing.[3]

Perhaps the most interesting and revealing quote DeMoville makes is a letter written by a Baha'i religious leader to the Baha'i community in Germany in 1934, shortly after Hitler's rise to power.

> At the outset it should be made indubitably clear that the Baha'i Cause being essentially a religious movement of a spiritual character stands above every political party or

group, and thus cannot and should not act in contravention to the principles, laws, and doctrines of any government. Obedience to the regulations and orders of the state is indeed, the sacred obligation of every true and loyal Baha'i. Both Baha'u'llah and Abdu'l-Bahá have urged us all to be submissive and loyal to the political authorities of our respective countries. It follows, therefore, that our German friends are under the sacred obligation to whole-heartedly obey the existing political regime, whatever be their personal views and criticisms of its actual working. There is nothing more contrary to the spirit of the Cause than open rebellion against the governmental authorities of a country, specially if they do not interfere in and do not oppose the inner and sacred beliefs and religious convictions of the individual. And there is every reason to believe that the present regime in Germany which has thus far refused to trample upon the domain of individual conscience in all matters pertaining to religion will never encroach upon it in the near future, unless some unforeseen and unexpected changes take place. And this seems to be doubtful at present.[4]

Although the religious literature cited by DeMoville is different than that cited in the Mormon article, the content is remarkably similar. Individuals must submit to the laws of the State in which they live. Thus, the criticisms I made of the Mormon view could be made of the Baha'i view as well. There is no need to repeat my criticisms here.

NOTES

[1] Wig DeMoville, The Ethics of Tax Evasion: A Baha'i Perspective, 1 Journal of Accounting, Ethics & Public Policy (Summer 1998), also published in The Ethics of Tax Evasion 230-240 (Robert W. McGee, ed. 1998). All references are to the book.

[2] Baha'u'llah, Tablets of Baha'u'llah 22-23 (1978), cited in DeMoville, supra, at 233.

[3] Abdu'l-Baha, Selections from the Writings of Abdu'l-Baha 293 (1978), as cited in DeMoville, supra, at 234.

[4] Shoghi Effendi, The Light of Divine Guidance, Vol. 1 54-55 (1982), cited in DeMoville, supra, at 234-235. The letter was written by Abdu'l-Baha's grandson.

Chapter 9

TAX EVASION IN EMERGING ECONOMIES

INTRODUCTION

Although all countries have somewhat of a problem collecting all the taxes they think are due to them, this problem is especially acute in emerging economies. There are a number of reasons for this problem. Although the specific situation is different in each country, each country that may be labeled as an emerging economy or a transition economy has certain common characteristics that make tax evasion easier to do and easier to get away with. The focus of this chapter is on Armenia because I happened to live there for more than a year and I was able to observe what went on around me and how the economy worked. However, similar stories could probably be told of any country where the people view their government negatively and where the mechanism for collecting taxes is not in place.

Practically no one in Armenia pays the correct amount of taxes. Many people pay no taxes at all. One wonders how a government can function and provide needed services in such a situation.

While working as a consultant in Armenia, I concluded that there were two principal reasons for the massive underpayment of taxes: there is no mechanism in place to collect taxes and the people feel no moral obligation to pay taxes to a corrupt government that does not provide services.

NO COLLECTION MECHANISM IN PLACE

With the exception of a few multinational companies that have offices in Armenia, there is basically no mechanism set up to collect and pay taxes. Many local businesses do not "hire" employees. They hire independent contractors and let them take care of their own taxes. Almost none of the independent contractors I met paid all of the taxes that were legally due and many of them paid nothing. There were a few exceptions, such as in the case of the independent contractors who worked for U.S. companies that had U.S. government contracts. The U.S. government agency with which they did business insisted that the names of these independent contractors should be turned over to the Tax Inspectorate and since the Tax Inspectorate knew that these independent contractors were earning money, they felt that they had to pay.

The United States Agency for International Development (USAID) had a project in Armenia to help "reform" the Armenian tax system. Part of the reform was to set up a mechanism for the collection of taxes. Another USAID project was to reform the accounting system, which includes providing training in accounting for Tax Inspectorate employees.

From my interviews with people who have visited the Tax Inspectorate, it appears that many tax inspectors do not have much of an accounting background and do not need much of an accounting background to collect taxes. They merely go into various businesses and engage in shakedowns. Those who pay a bribe see their tax liability reduced dramatically. The Tax Inspectorate is notorious for its corruption and bribetaking. Although officially a branch of the Ministry of Finance and Economy, the Tax Inspectorate seemingly reports to no one. The people I spoke to in the Finance Ministry seemed somewhat afraid to confront the people who worked for the Tax Inspectorate, even though the Tax Inspectorate is supposed to be subordinate to the Finance Ministry.

NO MORAL DUTY TO PAY TAXES

The interviews I conducted as part of this study all had the same underlying theme: People do not pay taxes because of the widespread feeling that the government does not deserve the fruits of people's labor. There are a variety of reasons why this feeling is so widespread but the basic reasons revolve around corruption and the lack of services. I found this reason to be the main reason why the people I chatted with in several Latin American, Caribbean and East European countries do not feel any moral obligation to pay taxes as well. The existing literature supports this view.[1]

The main moral justification for not paying taxes is because the government is thoroughly corrupt.[2] I was told about the Minister of Internal Affairs[3] who left the country with millions of dollars from the Armenian Social Security fund. I was also told that people don't trust banks because the government confiscated bank funds a few years ago and because the value of the currency was destroyed by high inflation rates.[4]

The second moral reason for justifying tax evasion was that the government does not provide much in the way of services. Under the old Soviet system, the people expected to get everything for free. Now that there is a move toward a market economy, they find that they have to pay if they want something. The government no longer provides everything for free. Now, the government does not provide much of anything, whether for free or for a fee.

Pensions are extremely low, less than $10 a month in many cases and although it is possible to buy about 50 loaves of bread for $10, that is not really enough to live on. Some people pay rent and some still live in government owned buildings where rent is not collected and maintenance is nonexistent. Back in the early 1990s, the winters in Armenia were extremely cold and there was no heat, so people cut down trees for fuel and even removed and burned the wooden doors at the entrance of state-owned apartment buildings. Those doors have still not been replaced.

One person I interviewed told me that the government authorities told her that her house was too big for just one family, so they were going to make her give up half of the rooms to another family. So she tried to purchase the house from the government and was successful only after paying a bribe to close the deal.

Corruption in the army was also a frequently cited reason why people feel no moral obligation to pay taxes. Much of the tax money that is collected goes to support the army. All men are required to serve for some period of time but it is almost always possible to escape service by paying a bribe, often to some general.

One person I interviewed told me he was paying some general $300 a month. There were a few months when he had difficulty coming up with the money (a family can live on $100 a month in Armenia) and he was afraid that they would come and get him. He eventually worked out a deal whereby he would pay $5,000 and be exempt from service forever. One wonders how this contract would be enforced in the Armenian courts. Apparently, there is some honor among thieves.

One woman complained that she did not feel morally compelled to pay taxes because the sons that are in the army still have to be supported by their families. The army does not provide adequate food for the soldiers, so family members have to pay frequent visits to their sons to give them food and money for food (and for bribes).

The army does not provide adequate medical care. There is much dysentery and disease among the army troops. Parents have to pay for medicine for their sons. One mother told me that her son almost died because of an appendicitis attack that went untreated for too long.

One person told me that the military police took one of his friends, who was in the army, and beat him several times over a period of months, for what reason no one knows. He could have avoided the beatings by paying a bribe, but his parents were not wealthy enough to pay.

Another interviewee told me that, as the sole support of his mother, he was legally exempt from service in the army, but the army came after him anyway. One morning at 7am a few weeks before Christmas, soldiers appeared at his mother's house, broke in and demanded to take her son into the army. Apparently, they needed a little money for the holidays and saw this as a good way to get it. When they discovered that the son was not there, they took his mother hostage. He told me that it is common practice to take a family member hostage until the son appears for duty (or, more likely, to pay the bribe). The soldiers in this case wanted $1,000.

One businessman who could be classified as a member of the "white" mafia[5] makes regular "gratuity" payments to the Defense Ministry so that he can keep the Tax Inspectorate off his back. He is proud of the fact that his businesses support more than 700 families and he feels a responsibility to them. He said that he will start paying taxes when the government starts doing something for the people. Until then, he needs to use the money he earns so that the people he employs can take care of their own families, since the government does nothing for them.

Police corruption is another reason people give for justifying the nonpayment of taxes. I experienced police corruption within minutes after arriving at the airport in Yerevan, the capital of Armenia. Customs officials were hassling people at the airport for no apparent reason other than to solicit bribes in exchange for allowing them to keep some of the property that was in their baggage. As I left the airport, my driver was pulled over and had to pay a bribe to continue the journey. He was pulled over for no apparent reason other than to help increase the policeman's income. He was not speeding or driving recklessly. I later learned that this shakedown is common practice.

Whenever one drives around the capital city one sees police everywhere, with their little black and white striped (or sometimes orange) sticks, waiving people over to the side of the road. I was waived over once myself. I was in the passenger seat and the police had a nice little chat with the ex-pat who was driving who could speak a little Armenian. The policeman changed his attitude 180 degrees as soon as the ex-pat asked for the policeman's name and picked up his cellular phone and started pressing a few buttons. The policeman let us go without having to pay anything.

The police in Russia operate in a similar, but somewhat different manner. My experience in Siberia was that the police only pull you over if you have broken the law. Then they solicit a bribe. My driver actually had been speeding and was pulled over. The police accused her of speeding, which she was. She paid the bribe and we left. However, the bribe in Siberia was somewhat higher than the bribe in Armenia.

One of the people who worked for me in Armenia was pulled over twice by the police while in my employ. Both times the police followed him to the office because he had to borrow money from me to pay the bribe and they did not want to let him out of their sight.

This situation brings to mind an interesting ethical question. Is it unethical for a CPA to lend money to an employee so that the employee can pay a bribe? This is a case where the CPA is clearly facilitating the bribe transaction. However, penalizing the CPA would seem unfair in this case, since he was merely trying to come to the aid of an employee who was being victimized.

CONCLUDING COMMENTS

In a country where there is no mechanism in place to collect taxes and where there is widespread agreement that there is no moral duty to pay taxes, it is no wonder that tax evasion is rampant. The U.S. government (U.S. taxpayers) are helping the Armenian government to establish an efficient mechanism for collecting taxes, which beings to mind another question: Is it moral to help set up a mechanism for collecting taxes in a country where the widespread opinion is that there is no moral duty to pay taxes?[6]

As Armenia establishes a rule of law it is likely that the degree of corruption will decrease, perhaps dramatically. In countries where there is a strong rule of law there is generally not much corruption.[7] But until the rule of law can be established, it appears that Armenians are likely to continue to find moral justification for evading the payment of taxes.[8]

Another, larger question, might also be asked. What services should government provide for its citizens? Just about any service the government provides can be provided better and cheaper by the private sector without the use of coercion.[9] Perhaps it is better that the people of Armenia and other countries in the CIS and Eastern Europe continue to evade taxes and start depending on themselves rather than government to provide for them. Dependence on government is unhealthy, both psychologically and economically. The mental and economic health of the people could improve if they removed the need for their governments to provide any services. Self-sufficiency would take away the excuse that governments use to collect taxes, since they would not have to provide much in the way of services.

NOTES

[1] Alfonso Morales, Income Tax Compliance and Alternative Views of Ethics and Human Nature, in Robert W. McGee, editor, The Ethics of Tax Evasion, Dumont, NJ: The Dumont Institute for Public Policy Research, 1998, at pp. 242-258 (regarding Latin America); Apostolos A. Ballas and Haridimos Tsoukas, Consequences of Distrust: The Vicious Cycle of Tax Evasion in Greece, in Robert W. McGee, editor, The Ethics of Tax Evasion, Dumont, NJ: The Dumont Institute for Public Policy Research, 1998, at pp.284-304; Vladimir V. Vaguine, The "Shadow Economy" and Tax Evasion in Russia, in Robert W. McGee, editor, The Ethics of Tax Evasion, Dumont, NJ: The Dumont Institute for Public Policy Research, 1998, at pp.306-314; Gueorgui Smatrakalev, Walking on the Edge: Bulgaria and the Transition to a Market Economy, in Robert W. McGee, editor, The Ethics of Tax Evasion, Dumont, NJ: The Dumont Institute for Public Policy Research, 1998, at pp.316-329.

[2] I was told that some World Bank study listed Armenia as the eighth most corrupt nation on earth. I do not have the cite for this study but when I relayed this information to various Armenians, they were really quite proud that they made the top ten and invariably asked me who was number one. A recent study lists corruption as one reason why economic growth and investment have been retarded in Armenia. *See* Bryan T. Johnson, Kim R. Holmes and Melanie Kirkpatrick, 1999 Index of Economic Freedom (The Heritage Foundation and the Wall Street Journal, 1999), 79.

[3] It should be pointed out that he was never convicted due to lack of evidence. However, there is a widespread perception that he did it.

[4] Since gaining independence in 1991, the annual inflation rate has been well over 500 percent [Johnson, Holmes and Kirkpatrick, *supra*, at 79], although in 1998 it was less than 20 percent, if measured by the amount of local currency needed to buy dollars. Since 1998, the inflation rate has declined even more.

[5] Perhaps a few words need to be said about the difference between the white mafia and the black mafia. The term white mafia is used in Eastern Europe and the CIS to describe people who engage in voluntary exchange in activities that just happen to be illegal in some way or other. They do not use force, they just happen to be operating outside the law. The black mafia uses force or the threat of force as part of its normal operating procedures.

[6] Another question that could be asked is where the authority to help the Armenian government -- or any government, for that matter -- comes from. My reading of the U.S. Constitution failed to find a single sentence or phrase that gives the federal government the authority to spend money for this purpose. It cannot be justified under the "Necessary and Proper" clause, since it is neither necessary nor proper to help a corrupt government collect taxes. It does nothing to ensure domestic tranquility in the United States and may actually reduce the amount of domestic tranquility in Armenia and the other countries where U.S. taxpayers are being called on to establish mechanisms for collecting taxes. For more on systems of public finance in emerging economies, see Robert W. McGee, Principles of Taxation for Emerging Economies: Some Lessons from the U.S. Experience, Dickinson Journal of International Law 12(1): 29-93 (Fall 1993); Robert W. McGee, Tax Advice for Latvia and Other Similarly Situated Emerging Economies, International Tax & Business Lawyer 13(2): 223-308 (1996). For a more philosophical approach to public finance, see Robert W. McGee, Taxation and Public Finance: A Philosophical and Ethical Approach, Commentaries on the Law of Accounting & Finance 1: 157-240 (1997).

[7] For some discussions on the factors that influence economic development, see Robert W. McGee, editor, The Market Solution to Economic Development in Eastern Europe (The Edwin Mellen Press, 1992).

[8] For a treatise on the justification of taxation from an economic perspective, see Walter Block, The Justification for Taxation in the Economics Literature, Canadian Public Administration/Administration Publique du Canada 36(2): 225-262 (Summer/Été, 1993), reprinted in Robert W. McGee, editor, The Ethics of Tax Evasion (Dumont, NJ: The Dumont Institute for Public Policy Research, 1998), 36-88.

[9] Government must resort to coercion (the collection of taxes) in order to provide services. Before it can use assets to provide services, it must first take assets from the rightful owners. Thus, the government provision of services must necessarily include coercion -- force or the threat of force -- since otherwise the people would not part with their money to fund government activities.

PART THREE

PHILOSOPHICAL ISSUES

Chapter 10

TAXATION AND SOCIAL ENGINEERING

INTRODUCTION

Excise taxes, or any taxes for that matter, violate property rights, since they take property without the owner's consent. The argument that voters consent to be taxed is a phony argument when subjected to analysis, but we will not get into that issue here, since it has been discussed elsewhere.[1] The point of this chapter is to discuss another abuse of the tax system, the use of taxes to alter or punish behavior rather than to raise revenue. Although this chapter emphasizes how the excise tax is used as a tool of social engineering, any tax could be used to alter taxpayer behavior, so much of what is said about excise taxes could also be said about other taxes.

One hesitates to subdivide a discussion on this topic into legal, economic and ethical aspects, since the three aspects of the discussion are interrelated. The legal aspect also involves ethical and economic issues, the ethics of using the excise tax as a tool of social engineering also involves a discussion of legal and economic issues, and so forth. This topic cannot be neatly subdivided into separate little boxes. However, I have decided to discuss these three aspects separately to give the chapter some structure.

LEGAL ISSUES

Assuming for the sake of argument that some taxes are legitimate at least some of the time,[2] it does not follow that all taxes are always legitimate. Some taxes are better than others. Some taxes better serve the legitimate role of raising revenue than do other taxes. Some taxes result in less distortion to the economy and do less damage to the structure of government than others.

Perhaps the central legal issue involving the use of excise taxes as a tool of social engineering revolves around the legitimate scope of government and the relationship of the government to the governed. There are basically just two philosophies of government, and most legal systems have elements of both.

One view of government begins with the premise that governments are formed to provide services to the people. Governments are formed to protect property and liberty and (perhaps) to provide other functions.[3] If government fails to provide some minimum level of safety and services, the people have the right to abolish it and form a new government that is more to their liking.[4] That is the principle upon which the government of the United States was founded. It was a radical concept back in the 1770s, although this concept had been floating around since at least 1690 when John Locke wrote a book that discussed this viewpoint.[5] One might say that this view sees government as the servant and the people as the masters.

The other view of government is just the opposite. The government is the master and the people are the servants. This view of government is older than the Lockean view,[6] but it is a view that is still with us. The Lockean view has by no means replaced it.

The governments of any communist or socialist country subscribe to this philosophy, as did the Fascist (really socialist)[7] governments of Nazi Germany and Mussolini's Italy. Individuals are means, not ends in themselves. As Karl Marx said, "From each according to his abilities; to each according to his needs."[8] Those who are productive and who have more wealth than others must have some of their wealth confiscated and distributed to others. "Society" has a claim on the assets of individuals. That is the rationale behind the graduated income tax, a tax that most modern industrial nations have adopted. There is no economic rationale for the graduated income tax. The evidence is clear on that point.[9] The graduated income tax was adopted for purely social engineering purposes, to equalize income. Karl Marx advocated a heavy, graduated income tax as a way to destroy capitalism.[10]

This second view of government, that the state is the master, sometimes includes the concept of the state being a benevolent father figure, who looks after the needs of his children. The western welfare states and the now defunct socialist states in Eastern Europe and the CIS would like their subjects to believe that the state should be viewed in such a manner. The state provides cradle to grave security and the people are forced to pay for it. A corollary of this "state as father figure" viewpoint is that the father knows what is best for his children. Thus, the state makes policies to regulate personal behavior because the father has better judgment about the needs of his children than the children do themselves.

Having identified the two philosophies of government, we must now look at the excise tax to see which philosophy of government is the underlying rationale for using the excise tax to regulate personal behavior. Clearly, the philosophy that government is the servant is not at work here, since servants do not use force to regulate the behavior of their masters. The only other possibility is the view that government is the master. That being the case, the excise tax, at least when used for social engineering purposes, is illegitimate, since the philosophical foundation for the tax is based on a faulty premise -- that government is the master and the people are the servants.

Another political issue is that of social harmony. Legal intrusions into the lives of individuals reduce social harmony. In the case of taxing alcohol and tobacco products merely because some government officials view such consumption as undesirable, the effect is to separate citizens into two groups, those whose behavior is deemed acceptable and those whose behavior is deemed unacceptable. Using the excise tax as a tool of social engineering divides individuals into classes for no legitimate reason. The concept of equal protection under the law becomes tarnished when government arbitrarily divides its citizens into separate groups and treats one group better than another group. It chips away at respect for government and reduces the legitimacy of government, since dividing citizens into classes is not a legitimate function of government.

ECONOMIC ISSUES

The main economic issue is efficiency. Is the excise tax efficient?[11] More precisely, is raising excise tax rates to regulate personal behavior an efficient way to regulate personal behavior?

The evidence is clear that excise taxes on alcohol and tobacco are not an efficient way to reduce consumption of these products. That is because the demand curves for these products are highly inelastic, meaning that a large increase in price will have little effect on demand, and therefore on consumption.[12]

Changing the excise tax rate can have an effect of the relative demand for various related products, however. For example, increasing the excise tax on alcoholic beverages can entice consumers to purchase more potent alcoholic beverages.[13] Increasing the excise tax on cigarettes can entice consumers to purchase more potent cigarettes.[14] Thus, if the goal of increasing the excise tax is to reduce consumption of harmful substances, the excise tax is not only inefficient but also counterproductive.

ETHICAL ISSUES

There are basically two ethical approaches that may be taken to determine whether using excise taxes as a tool of social engineering is ethical. The first approach is utilitarian. The second is based on rights.[15] We have already applied the utilitarian approach, which is basically the economic approach. Using that approach, we found that using the excise tax as a tool of social engineering is unethical because it is inefficient.[16] Now we shall apply the rights approach to determine whether the excise tax can be justified as a tool of social engineering using rights as the basis for analysis.

The nonaggression axiom holds that "no man or group of men may aggress against the person or property of anyone else."[17] In other words, the initiation of force is never allowed. The initiation of force is always unethical. The excise tax is based on force. People must pay or face penalties, including fines, possible confiscation of property and possibly incarceration. Thus, according to the rights approach to ethics, the excise tax is unethical because people's property rights and the right to liberty are violated.

Can there be an exception if force is used for the individual's own good? No, the nonaggression axiom does not allow an exception for cases when force is used to protect an individual from himself. Also, it is not a legitimate function of government to protect individuals from themselves. The only legitimate activities of government, if there are any, are to protect liberty and property from aggression by others.

CONCLUDING COMMENTS

There are a number of ethical, economic and legal problems with using the excise tax as a tool of social engineering. Perhaps the basic problem is the use of government force to alter personal, non-rights-violating behavior. It is not a legitimate function of government to punish people for engaging in activities that do not violate rights. Yet that is what the excise tax does.

The excise tax is economically inefficient. From a purely economic point of view, it should be abolished, at least as far as the excise tax on alcohol and tobacco are concerned.

Using the excise tax as a tool to alter behavior is ethically bankrupt. That is because using force to alter non-rights-violating behavior is ethically bankrupt.

There are numerous legal, economic and ethical problems with using the excise tax as a tool of social engineering. This chapter has merely summarized some of the main problems. Yet even this summary makes it clear that there is no legitimate reason for using excise taxes as a tool of social engineering. Since that is the main goal of the excise tax on alcohol and tobacco, these taxes should be abolished, the sooner the better. Social harmony and respect for government will be enhanced by abolition.

NOTES

[1] Lysander Spooner, No Treason: The Constitution of No Authority, originally self-published by Spooner in Boston (1870), reprinted by Rampart College (1965, 1966 & 1971), and by Ralph Myles, Publisher, Inc., Colorado Springs (1973); Robert W. McGee, Some Tax Advice for Latvia and Other Similarly Situated Emerging Economies, International Tax & Business Lawyer 13: 223-308 (1996), at 229-233; Robert W. McGee, Taxation and Public Finance: A Philosophical and Ethical Approach, Commentaries on the Law of Accounting & Finance 1:157-240 (1997), at 160-165.

[2] This premise is subject to dispute. Reviews of the economics and public finance literature failed to find a single justification for taxation that would hold up to close analysis. See Walter Block, The Justification for Taxation in the Economics Literature, in The Ethics of Tax Evasion 36-88 (Robert W. McGee, ed. 1998); Walter Block, William Kordsmeier and Joseph Horton, The Failure of Public Finance, 2 Journal of Accounting, Ethics & Public Policy (Winter 1999); Walter Block, William Kordsmeier and Joseph

Horton, Public Finance, Perfect Competition and Externalities, Commentaries on the Law of Accounting & Finance (1998).

[3] Whether providing functions other than the protection of liberty and property is a legitimate function of government is highly questionable. When government goes beyond these basic functions, the result is the disparagement of property rights and liberty rather than their protection. We will leave discussion of this point for another day. See Walter E. Williams, More Liberty Means Less Government, Stanford: Hoover Institute Press, 1999; James Bovard, Freedom in Chains: The Rise of the State and the Demise of the Citizen, Palgrave Macmillan, 1999; James Bovard, Lost Rights: The Destruction of American Liberty, New York: St. Martin's Press, 1995; James Bovard, Shakedown: How the Government Screws You from A to Z, New York: Penguin, 1995; Robert Higgs, editor, Hazardous to Our Health? FDA Regulation of Health Care Products, Independent Institute, 1995; James T. Bennett and Thomas J. DiLorenzo, The Food and Drink Police: America's Nannies, Busybodies & Petty Tyrants, New Brunswick, NJ: Transaction Publishers, 1999; Walter K. Olson, The Excuse Factory: How Employment Law is Paralyzing the American Workplace, Free Press, 1997; Richard K. Vedder and Lowell E. Gallaway, Out of Work: Unemployment and Government in Twentieth-Century America, New York: New York University Press, 1997; Richard A. Epstein, Mortal Peril: Our Inalienable Right to Health Care? Perseus Publishing, 1997.

[4] For more on the theory of secession, see David Gordon, editor, Secession, State & Liberty, New Brunswick, NJ; Transaction Publishers, 1998; Robert W. McGee, The Third Liberal Theory of Secession, Liverpool Law Review 14: 45-66 (1992); Robert W. McGee, The Theory of Secession and Emerging Democracies: A Constitutional Solution, Stanford Journal of International Law 28: 451-476 (1992); Robert W. McGee and Danny Lam, Hong Kong's Option to Secede, Harvard International Law Journal 33: 427-440 (1992); Robert W. McGee, Secession and Emerging Democracies: The Kendall and Louw Solution, Journal of International Law & Practice 2: 321-335 (1993); Robert W. McGee, Secession Reconsidered, Journal of Libertarian Studies 11: 11-33 (1994).

[5] John Locke, Two Treatises on Government (1690). Locke's ideas are discussed in many places, including Richard A. Epstein, Principles for a Free Society: Reconciling Individual Liberty with the Common Good, Perseus Books Group, 1998, pp. 25-28, 251-264; Richard A. Epstein, Simple Rules for a Complex World, Cambridge, MA: Harvard University Press, 1995; Robert Nozick, Anarchy, State and Utopia, New York: Basic Books, 1974; Murray N. Rothbard, For a New Liberty, revised edition, New York: Libertarian Review Association, 1978, pp. 31-36; Murray N. Rothbard, The Ethics of Liberty, New York and London: New York University Press, 1998; Tom Bethell, The Noblest Triumph: Property and Prosperity Through the Ages, New York: St. Martin's Press, 1998.

[6] When France's Louis XIV heard that the people were complaining about excessive taxes, he remarked that "since everything belonged to him, he was only taking what was his." Charles Adams, For Good and Evil: The Impact of Taxes on the Course of Civilization, Madison Books, 1993, p. 217.

[7] Hitler's party was the National Socialist Party, yet people labeled him a Fascist. In reality, there is not much difference between the two. Under socialism, the means of production are owned by the state. Under fascism, the means of production are privately owned but so heavily regulated that owners have practically no property rights left. For a summary of the attributes of the four classifications of political systems, see The World's Smallest Political Quiz at www.theadvocates.org/quiz.html.

[8] Karl Marx, Critique of the Gotha Program (1875). The original wording was "Jeder nach seinen Fähigkeiten, jedem nach seinen Bedürfnissen." Louis Blanc, the French socialist, said basically the same thing in 1848. George Seldes, The Great Thoughts, New York: Ballantine Books, 1985, p. 274.

[9] A number of studies have shown that the graduated income tax cannot be supported on economic grounds. See Walter J. Blum and Harry Kalven, Jr., The Uneasy Case for Progressive Taxation, Chicago: University of Chicago Press, 1953; F.A. Hayek, The Case Against Progressive Income Taxes, The Freeman 229-232 (1953).

[10] Karl Marx, The Communist Manifesto (1848).
[11] For discussions of taxation and efficiency, see Richard A. Posner, Economic Analysis of Law 523-525 (5th ed. 1998); Harvey S. Rosen, Public Finance 284-334 (5th ed. 1999); John Cullis and Philip Jones, Public Finance and Public Choice 159-166 (2nd ed. 1998); Michael L. Marlow, Public Finance: Theory and Practice 139-141, 449-458 (1995); David N. Hyman, Public Finance: A Contemporary Application of Theory to Policy 53-57, 68-73, 96-97, 410-413 (6th ed. 1999).
[12] The Ramsey Rule suggests that high excise taxes be imposed on products that have a highly inelastic demand curve because high tax rates will not discourage consumption. For more on the Ramsey Rule, see Taxing Choice: The Predatory Politics of Fiscal Discrimination 4, 13-18, 81, 97 (William F. Shughart, II, ed. 1997); Richard A. Posner, Economic Analysis of Law 389-391 (5th ed. 1998); John Cullis and Philip Jones, Public Finance and Public Choice 376, 380-381 (2nd ed. 1998); Harvey S. Rosen, Public Finance 310-312, 318 (5th ed. 1999); Michael L. Marlow, Public Finance: Theory and Practice 455 (1995); David N. Hyman, Public Finance: A Contemporary Application of Theory to Policy 426n (6th ed. 1999).
[13] Paula A. Gant and Robert B. Ekelund, Jr., Excise Taxes, Social Costs, and the Consumption of Wine, in William F. Shughart, editor, Taxing Choice: The Predatory Politics of Fiscal Discrimination, New Brunswick, NJ and London: Transaction Publishers, 1997, pp. 247-269; Adam Gifford, Jr., Whiskey, Margarine, and Newspapers: A Tale of Three Taxes, William F. Shughart, editor, Taxing Choice: The Predatory Politics of Fiscal Discrimination, New Brunswick, NJ and London: Transaction Publishers, 1997, pp. 57-77 at 67.
[14] William F. Shughart, II, The Economics of the Nanny State, William F. Shughart, editor, Taxing Choice: The Predatory Politics of Fiscal Discrimination, New Brunswick, NJ and London: Transaction Publishers, 1997, pp. 13-29 at 15.
[15] Some philosophers would have more than two classifications for ethical systems. However, upon closer analysis, these other categories break down into some subcategory of utilitarianism. For a discussion of the various subcategories of the utilitarian philosophy, see William H. Shaw, Contemporary Ethics: Taking Account of Utilitarianism, Oxford: Blackwell Publishers, 1999.
[16] According to utilitarian ethical theory, an act that produces the greatest good for the greatest number is ethical and all other acts are unethical. Since excise taxes are inefficient, thus not producing the greatest good for the greatest number, they are unethical according to utilitarian ethical theory. Richard A. Posner, Economic Analysis of Law 284-285 (5th ed. 1998); William H. Shaw, Contemporary Ethics: Taking Account of Utilitarianism 10 (1999). A variation on the utilitarian theme is the wealth maximization view, which holds that "...the criterion for judging whether acts and institutions are just or good is whether they maximize the wealth of society." Richard A. Posner, The Economics of Justice, Cambridge, MA: Harvard University Press, 1983, p. 115.
[17] Murray N. Rothbard, For a New Liberty 23 (rev. ed. 1978).

Chapter 11

THE VOID FOR VAGUENESS DOCTRINE

WHAT IS THE VOID FOR VAGUENESS DOCTRINE?

The void for vagueness doctrine basically states that a law is void if it is vague. The problem is that all statutes are vague to some extent. The void for vagueness doctrine itself is not entirely clear and easy to understand once one digs beneath the surface a bit.[1]

> That the terms of a penal statute creating a new offense must be sufficiently explicit to inform those who are subject to it what conduct on their part will render them liable to its penalties, is a well-recognized requirement, consonant alike with ordinary notions of fair play and the settled rules of law. And a statute which either forbids or requires the doing of an act in terms so vague that men of common intelligence must necessarily guess at its meaning and differ as to its application violates the first essential of due process of law.[2]

> There must be ascertainable standards of guilt. Men of common intelligence cannot be required to guess at the meaning of the enactment.[3]

> Vague laws offend several important values. First, because we assume that man is free to steer between lawful and unlawful conduct, we insist that laws give the person of ordinary intelligence a reasonable opportunity to know what is prohibited, so that he may act accordingly. Vague laws may trap the innocent by not providing fair warnings. Second, if arbitrary and discriminatory enforcement is to be prevented, laws must provide explicit standards for those who apply them. A vague law impermissibly delegates basic policy matters to policemen, judges, and juries for resolution on an *ad hoc* and subjective basis, with the attendant dangers of arbitrary and discriminatory applications.[4]

The void for vagueness doctrine originally applied to criminal statutes.[5] However, in recent decades it has expanded its scope to apply to civil liberties as well.[6] The void for vagueness doctrine may also be applied in at least two different ways. A statute may be void on its face –

for all cases.[7] Or it may be void as applied to a particular person, case or set of circumstances.[8]

IS THE INTERNAL REVENUE CODE VOID FOR VAGUENESS?

The Internal Revenue Code forms the basis of the tax law in the United States. But it is only the basis. There are also regulations that explain what the Code means. These regulations are much longer than the Code itself. But that is still not the end of it. There are three federal court systems[9] that interpret what the Code and regulations really mean.

To make matters more interesting, these three federal court systems are not always in agreement. Sometimes one federal court will find a person not liable for a tax whereas another federal court will find a person liable, even when the fact situations are identical or nearly so. Over the years the various federal courts have heard and decided literally thousands of tax cases, many of which still have precedential value. If one were to place the Code, regulations and all the tax cases into a single average sized room, the room would probably be filled. There is no way that anyone can find the time to read all the official materials that exist on tax law, let alone understand and remember them.

But that is still not the end of it. There are also unofficial materials. The Internal Revenue Service publishes various kinds of guidance, including, but not limited to, Revenue Rulings and Revenue Procedures. It also publishes booklets on various tax topics to help individuals understand and apply the tax code. Some of these publications contain mistakes and even those that do not have mistakes sometimes present a less than complete picture of the various tax topics because IRS publications tend to be biased in favor of the tax collector.

But even this pile of publications does not complete the list of available tax materials. Various commercial publishers publish loose-leaf tax services[10] as well as paperback and hardcover books that discuss various aspects of the tax Code. These publications have to be revised frequently in order to keep up with changes in the tax Code. Then there are the thousands of articles that have been written about various tax laws. Each annual volume of the Accounting & Tax Index lists several hundred pages of them.

Another issue also comes to mind. Rather than asking whether the Internal Revenue Code is void for vagueness, we might ask whether the "tax law" is void for vagueness, since the Internal Revenue Code and the tax law are not quite the same. The Internal Revenue Code is statutory. Various Congresses over the years have passed portions of the Internal Revenue Code we have today. But the tax law consists of much more than the Internal Revenue Code. As previously mentioned, there are three federal court systems that interpret (and some would say also make) tax law. The number of pages these cases comprise easily surpasses the number of pages in the Internal Revenue Code. The tax regulations also comprise part of the tax law. Regulations have the practical effect of law even though Congress never passed them. Congress delegated the authority to the Treasury Department to issue regulations, and while this delegation might violate the Separation of Powers clause of the Constitution, such delegation has never been successfully challenged. Then there are the various IRS publications such as Revenue Rulings and Revenue Procedures, which are not quite law but which should not be ignored lest one wants to risk the wrath of the IRS.

To make matters worse, sometimes the Treasury Department issues a tax regulation retroactively, which makes it impossible to know what the law is by the date the tax return must be filed, because the law may change. While it seems that issuing a regulation retroactively would constitute an ex post facto law, and therefore automatically be null and void, the courts have not so held. So the retroactivity problem remains.[11]

There is no doubt that the Internal Revenue Code is complex. But is it vague? There is a difference between being complex and being vague. A law can be complex but not vague. Another law can be vague but not complex.

> When we reach the level where most taxpayers with relatively uncomplicated economic circumstances are unable to function without professional help, something is badly wrong.[12]

Interestingly enough, not only have we reached the point where the average taxpayer needs professional help; we have reached the point where the professionals are unable to give that help without making mistakes on a regular basis. Even the people who work for the IRS do not know what the rules are. A General Accounting Office report found that 44 percent of the penalties that IRS agents assessed under the payroll tax rules were wrong. The payroll tax rules are so complex that one-third of all U.S. employers are assessed penalties each year.[13] But complexity is not limited to the payroll tax rules. Many other areas of the tax code are also overly complex. The IRS assessed 29 million penalties in 1990, many of which were later abated.[14]

In November, 1997, for the eighth time since 1987, MONEY magazine conducted a test of practitioners to see how accurately they were able to prepare the tax return for a middle class family.[15] They sent a hypothetical fact situation to sixty tax professionals who agreed to prepare the family's tax return. Forty-six tax practitioners completed the return. All of them were seasoned pros – 31 certified public accountants, 12 enrolled agents and three other professional tax return preparers.

For the seventh time since MONEY started conducting this test, no two tax experts came up with the same tax liability figure. It was also the third time that no one turned in an error-free return.[16] Thirty experts calculated a tax liability that was excessive, by an average of $7,207. Sixteen underestimated the tax liability, by an average of $1,080. No one calculated the correct tax liability, which was $37,105. The tax law has become even more complicated since those surveys were done.

If men of common intelligence cannot be expected to guess at the meaning of the law, how about tax experts? If none of the forty-six tax experts could apply the tax law correctly, can we conclude that the tax law is void for vagueness? If so, is it void in all cases or only in certain cases? If it is void for vagueness in so many cases that the courts would be clogged with void for vagueness cases, would it be administratively expedient just to declare that the whole tax code is void for vagueness even though there might be some provisions that are not vague enough to be void?

WHAT CONSTITUTES VAGUENESS?

Another set of questions also arises. What if the average tax expert is able to correctly handle 17 or 18 of the 20 tax issues that might be included in an average tax return, even though almost no tax practitioner can make the correct decision for all 20 tax issues? For example, if we were to list the tax issues present in an average tax return numerically, from one to twenty, and tax expert #1 made mistakes only on tax issues 2, 5 and 7, tax expert #2 made mistakes only on issues 3, 6 and 11, and so forth, could we conclude that the whole tax code is void for vagueness?

Another issue, one that is perhaps more relevant, is what we should do with the tax code if we gave the same test to the "person of average intelligence," who probably never even took an accounting course, much less a tax course? What if the average person who does not have a tax background misapplied the law in 15 or 18 of the 20 cases in this theoretical tax return? Could we then conclude that the tax code is void for vagueness? Or would we have to look at each particular provision in the code to determine which provisions could be understood and correctly applied by someone who does not have a tax background? If 40 percent of the people of common intelligence made a mistake involving a particular tax issue, would that percentage be sufficiently high to warrant voiding that provision of the tax Code? Or would more than 50 percent be required?

Perhaps it is time we looked more closely at the Void for Vagueness Doctrine to see whether it should be applied to the Internal Revenue Code, and under what circumstances it should be applied. Certainly, if a law is so complex that even professionals who specialize in that area of the law cannot apply the law correctly, there should be a presumption that, at the very least, the Code sections that they cannot apply correctly should be classified as void.

The Void for Vagueness Doctrine is based on the equitable concepts of fair play and settled rules of law. It seems like the equitable thing to do would be to declare those sections of the Internal Revenue Code that cannot be understood by the person of common intelligence to be void.[17]

THE MOST LIKELY CANDIDATES

What are the most likely parts of the Internal Revenue Code to be held void for vagueness? If one uses the person of common intelligence standard to measure vagueness, perhaps so many Code sections would be held void that it would be easier to scrap the entire Internal Revenue Code and start over.[18]

There are far too many Code provisions to possibly examine them all in depth in the limited space we have here. So let's take a look at the Code provisions that are too complicated for even the professionals to understand and apply properly. If professional tax preparers are unable to properly apply a Code provision, a strong case can be made that the person of common intelligence who does not have a tax background also cannot know what the law is.

How can we determine which Code provisions are too complex for even a tax professional to understand and apply properly? Luckily, MONEY magazine as already done the job for us. MONEY magazine has been conducting surveys of tax preparers almost annually since 1987 to see whether they can prepare the tax return of a hypothetical family without making a mistake. In November, 1997, for the eighth time since 1987, MONEY sent a hypothetical tax situation to a group of tax preparers and asked them to prepare the family's tax return.[19] Forty-six tax professionals prepared the return in that survey – 31 CPAs, 12 enrolled agents and 3 other professional tax preparers. For the seventh time since MONEY has been conducting these surveys, no two tax preparers came up with the same tax liability. For the third time since the surveys started, no one calculated the correct tax. They all made at least one mistake. Some of the tax rules have changed since the 1997 survey, but the concepts are the same. Also, the tax rules have, in general, become more complex since the 1997 survey, which makes the void for vagueness argument even stronger now than it would have been in 1997.

Retirement Payouts

In the 1997 survey, MONEY magazine listed the six most common mistakes in terms of costliness. The most costly mistake occurred in miscalculating the tax due on a retirement payout.[20] Ken, the hypothetical taxpayer, was entitled to five-year averaging when he took his early retirement payout because he was 59 1/2. Four of the preparers didn't realize that he was eligible, even though the fact situation they were given clearly listed his birthdate on the first page of the hypothetical example. As a result of this oversight, he had to pay an extra $26, 558 in tax.[21] Fourteen other tax professionals carelessly used the wrong tax rate, which resulted in overstating the amount of tax due by $420. Two other professionals made a mistake in his favor by incorrectly applying the ten-year average rules, which save him an extra $1,010 in taxes. Ten-year averaging is available only for taxpayers who were born before 1936, so he did not qualify, but the tax preparers who used ten-year averaging did not know about this requirement, even though it is spelled out (somewhere) in the Code. If 20 out of 46 tax professionals (43 percent) cannot apply this Code provision properly, what percentage of people from the community in general would be able to do it? This provision looks like a strong candidate for voidness.

The Home Sales Rules

The second most costly mistake was in the home sale rules.[22] In the fact situation given to the tax professionals, the family bought and moved into a new home in May, 1995 but were unable to sell their old home, so they rented it out for two years. Under the tax law passed in 1997, they could avoid paying a tax on the sale if they had lived in the house for two of the last five years before the sale, a requirement they clearly met. Eight preparers did not know of that rule (17%), which resulted in an additional tax of $8,718.

Double-counting the Tax on Stock Options

The third most costly mistake involved double-counting income from the exercise of nonqualified stock options. The difference between the stock's market value and the option price was properly reported as income on Ken's W-2. But seven of the tax professionals didn't realize that it was already included in his taxable income, so it got taxed twice, once as ordinary income and once as short-term capital gains.[23] That error cost him $2,408 in taxes on his $8,000 gain.

401(k) Loan

The next most costly error involved overlooking a loophole on a 401(k) loan. When Ken's wife switched jobs she still owed more than $15,000 on a loan she took out on her IRA. Before her employer rolled it over into an IRA the employer deducted the outstanding loan balance from her account. She had 60 days to put in an amount equal to the loan balance but she didn't do it, which would normally trigger a 10 percent penalty for a premature withdrawal. But there was a loophole that 43 of the 46 practitioners (93%) didn't know about. The penalty could have been reduced because she had a medical expense deduction in the same year. Only 3 of the practitioners took that fact into account when they prepared her taxes.[24]

Overstating Capital Gains on Mutual Fund Redemptions

There are four ways to compute the gain on the sale of mutual fund shares: first-in, first-out, single-category averaging, double-category averaging and the specific identification method. Twenty-eight of the professionals (61%) chose a method that would not have minimized the tax liability.[25]

Claiming Dependents

Claiming dependents is one of the most frequently occurring decisions in tax return preparation. In this hypothetical example, 30 tax professionals (65%) claimed the wrong number of dependents.[26]

For three of these six mistakes, more than half of the tax professionals got the wrong answer. On another item, 43 percent got it wrong. So even if one were to use the "professional of average intelligence" standard, at least three, and perhaps four of the Code provisions in this theoretical tax return would be good candidates for voidness. If the person of common intelligence standard were applied, perhaps all six Code areas would be found void. At the very least, penalties should be waived for taxpayers (or their representatives) who incorrectly apply the law in these areas.

WHEN ARE PREPARERS NEGLIGENT?

There are a number of areas where tax advisors and tax return preparers face liability. For tax claims brought between 1979 and 1989, the breakdown by category is as follows: failure to advise, 39%; filing errors, 19%; election errors, 14%; estate tax errors, 8%; liquidation errors, 7%; Subchapter S errors, 7%; other tax errors, 6%.[27]

For smaller accounting firms, making tax mistakes is the number one cause of losses, even more than audit failures.[28] It is a problem for larger firms as well. Numerous cases have held accountants or other tax preparers liable for giving bad advice or making mistakes in the preparation of tax returns.

Traditional Reasons for Finding Liability

The general rule is that practitioners may be found liable if their standard of care falls below that of the average or usual standard of care.[29] That means that practitioners are not necessarily liable for making a mistake. They are liable only if they exercised less than the usual or average standard of care. According to the community standard of care, a practitioner who gives the same advice as other practitioners in the same geographic location will not be guilty of negligence for giving bad advice.[30] A frequently used method courts use to determine the community standard of care is to have several local practitioners testify as to what they think the standard of care is in their community.[31] IRS Circular 230[32] has a due diligence requirement.

An alternative standard of care is that of a tax specialist. According to this standard, a higher standard of care may be applied if (1) a general practitioner takes on an engagement that calls for the skills of a specialist, or (2) a practitioner advertises or holds himself out to be capable of performing special services.[33] In at least one case, the standard of care applicable to an accounting firm was for tax generalists to identify tax problems and refer them to individuals who were specialists in the area.[34] An attorney who is a generalist may have a duty to refer his client to a tax specialist if a reasonably careful practitioner would do so.[35] Where practitioners hold themselves out to be specialists, some courts have called on expert witnesses to determine what the standard of care is for the specialty.[36] However, expert testimony is not conclusive of the standard to be followed.[37] A jury can make its own standard, based on the facts and circumstances of the case.[38]

A preparer may be liable for failure to use the loss carryforward rules or for changing an accounting method without IRS consent.[39] Liability may also accrue for failure to make tax return elections.[40] Failure to file or revoke an S corporation election because of incorrect advice has also been a cause of liability.[41]

Other causes of liability for accountants or other tax advisors have included failure to advise a client that savings could be had by disclaiming all or part of an estate interest;[42] failure to file an estate tax return on time, which led to loss of the use of the alternative valuation date;[43] giving defective advice on Sec. 351 asset transfers;[44] giving incorrect advice on recapture of inventory profits upon sale of a business;[45] failure to investigate the effect that financing by industrial development bonds would have on a corporate reorganization;[46] giving incorrect advice on the redemption of stock involving a controlled corporation;[47] giving bad advice on tax free exchanges;[48] preparation of a defective trust instrument;[49] negligent preparation of a tax return that resulted in an IRS assessment;[50] incorrectly advising a client that she could sell stock at a loss and offset the gain on the sale of other stock;[51]

erroneous preparation of a tax return that results in penalties;[52] failure to advise a client about tax return elections or to file elections on a timely basis;[53] concealing the failure to prepare a corporate tax return;[54] failure to prepare documents;[55] failure to file liquidation papers on a timely basis.[56] These examples are not meant to be comprehensive but merely to show some areas where liability has been found in the past.

An Overlooked Defense Argument

The rule of thumb for determining whether a tax return preparer has been negligent in the preparation of a tax return seems to be related to what other practitioners would do. Generally speaking, if all or most practitioners would have done or not done the same thing, the defendant tax return preparer will be found not guilty of negligence or malpractice.

This standard does not have clearly defined borders. As was previously mentioned, there really seems to be several standards. The IRS has a due diligence standard. Then there are community or geographic standards and standards for specialists. In jury trials, the ultimate decider of whether the standard of care has been met is the jury.

What I propose in this chapter is not a new standard but merely a refinement of an existing standard. What exactly are the standards for tax return preparation? I propose that the answer to that question should be viewed both from a macro and micro perspective. But before we discuss the macro and micro perspectives, let's take another look at those very interesting MONEY surveys.

Survey Data on Tax Prep Accuracy

In November, 1997, for the eighth time since 1987, MONEY magazine asked professional tax preparers to prepare a hypothetical tax return based on information it provided.[57] For the seventh time, no two tax preparers computed the same tax liability.[58] For the third time, every practitioner who participated made at least one mistake.[59]

Forty-six professional tax preparers participated in the 1997 survey – 31 CPAs, 12 enrolled agents and 3 other tax prep professionals. The tax liabilities they computed ranged from $34,240 to $68,912, a difference of slightly more than 100 percent.[60] MONEY listed the six most frequent mistakes. They were as follows:

• 93% overlooked a tax-saving loophole on a 401(k) loan.[61] When Barbara changed jobs she still owed more than $15,000 on a loan she took out on her 401(k). Her former employer deducted the amount she owed from the sum that was eventually rolled over into an Individual Retirement Account. That would ordinarily expose her to tax plus a 10% penalty since she did not put the amount of the loan into the IRA and roll it over within the 60-day deadline. But there is a provision in the Code that would reduce the penalty for taxpayers who also claimed a medical expense deduction in the same year, which she did. Forty-three tax preparers overlooked that Code provision.

• 65% misjudged who could be claimed as a dependent.[62] Thirty preparers mistakenly classified the couple's daughter, who was a full-time student, as a dependent, even though they did not provide more than half of her support (she banked the money they gave her rather than using it for support.)

• 61% overstated the capital gain on a mutual fund redemption.[63] There were four acceptable methods for computing the gain on the sale of mutual funds. Twenty-eight preparers chose a method that did not result in the lowest tax liability.

• 43% miscalculated the tax due on a retirement payout.[64] Ken, the hypothetical husband, was entitled to use five-year averaging. Four preparers didn't know he could use five-year averaging and another 14 preparers used the wrong rate to calculate the tax liability. Two preparers wrongly applied the ten-year averaging rules, for which Ken does not quality.

• 17% failed to use the new tax rules on home sales.[65] When the hypothetical family bought and moved into their new home, they were not able to sell their old home, so they rented it for two years. The eventual sale of their home was tax free, yet 8 preparers classified the sale as a taxable event.

• 15% double counted the tax due on the exercise of nonqualified stock options.[66] The $8,000 gain was correctly reported on Ken's W-2, but 7 tax preparers didn't realize that the gain was already included in his taxable wages, so they caused the same gain to be taxed twice, once as ordinary income and once as short-term capital gain.

The Macro View

Since none of the tax preparers in several of the MONEY magazine surveys could complete the hypothetical tax return without making at least one mistake, a case can be made that every tax preparer is presumptively entitled to make one mistake per tax return without being found guilty of negligence or malpractice. Preparers who make just one mistake on a tax return are definitely operating at the same level of competence as their colleagues.

We might expand on that concept a bit. If one mistake is within the standard, how about two mistakes? The MONEY surveys did not disclose much information about how many mistakes each practitioner made, but it is highly probable that many of them made at least two mistakes, and perhaps as many as four. In the survey for the 1997 tax year, 93% of them missed the 401(k) loan loophole and more than half of them missed the capital gain item and the claiming a dependent item. More than 40% miscalculated the retirement payout. So the argument could be made that a practitioner could still be within the nonnegligent category if he made four mistakes on a single tax return. Making more than four mistakes may or may not constitute negligence, depending on the facts and circumstances.

Although the MONEY magazine article for the 1997 tax year survey did not give a breakdown of the number of mistakes each practitioner made, we can use probability theory to make our own estimate. If 93% of the preparers made at least one mistake (actually, they all made at least one mistake), then it is probable that more than 60% of them made at least two mistakes [.93 x .65]. It is also probable that 37% of them made at least 3 mistakes [.93 x.65 x.61] and about 16% of them made at least 4 mistakes [.93 x .65 x .61 x .43].

Actually, these figures are conservative, for several reasons. First, 100% of the tax preparers in the survey made at least one mistake. Second, the probability calculation just given makes the assumption that mistakes are randomly distributed, which is not the case. A practitioner who makes 4 mistakes, for example, is more likely to make a fifth mistake than one who makes only 3 mistakes.

The MONEY surveys did discuss the number of mistakes per practitioner in a few places. For example, in the survey for the 1992 tax year, 95% of the participants made more than one mistake.[67] The person who came closest to the correct answer in the 1991 tax year survey made three mistakes.[68] So a defense attorney could make the case that making two mistakes does not constitute negligence, since 95% of the participants in one of the MONEY surveys made at least that many mistakes. A case could also be made that making three mistakes on one tax return does not constitute negligence, since the person who came closest to the correct answer on a MONEY survey made three mistakes.

If negligence is defined as being more than 3 standard deviations from the mean in a random distribution, then someone who makes 4 mistakes on a tax return is not negligent, since he is less than 3 standard deviations from the mean (100% - 16% = 84%).[69]

The Micro View

The micro view would look at individual tax items to attempt to determine whether a tax preparer is about as competent as his colleagues. Looking at the survey for the 1997 tax year, a strong case can be made that a tax preparer who overlooked the tax-saving loophole on the 401(k) loan would not be guilty of negligence, since 93% of his colleagues would also have made the wrong calculation. The defense attorney of any client who made the same mistake could point to this MONEY magazine survey as strong evidence that his client is as competent as his peers.

Presumptively, any item that was missed by more than half of the participants in any of the MONEY surveys would also constitute strong evidence that negligence was not the cause of the error. Thus, there is strong evidence that tax preparers who calculate the wrong amount of a capital gain on a mutual fund redemption or those who incorrectly determine the correct number of dependents would not be found guilty of negligence because more than half of their colleagues would make the same mistake. Miscalculating the tax due on a retirement payout also seems to fall into the nonnegligent category, since such a high percentage of tax preparers (43%) would make the same mistake.

CONCLUDING COMMENTS

The complexity of the Internal Revenue Code makes it difficult, if not impossible, even for tax professionals to prepare an error free tax return. The person of ordinary intelligence has even less of a chance of not making a mistake. That being the case, it seems like the IRC would be thrown out for being vague if the judge hearing the case could be disinterested enough to merely look at the facts of the case, without thinking of the consequences of what ruling the IRC void might lead to. If a law is so bad, so unclear as to be vague even to experience tax professionals, asking question like "What would happen if..." are not appropriate. If the law is so vague as to be void, it should be thrown out, regardless of the short-term consequences. Throwing it out would force Congress to do its job and pass a tax law that can be understood and applied with a reasonable amount of certainty.

Then there is the question of what to do with tax practitioners who make mistakes advising clients or preparing tax returns. What is the proper standard for measuring negligence if the IRC is basically void for vagueness? It seems unfair to punish them for making certain mistakes, if the mistakes they make are due to excessively vague wording in the tax law. Fairness would demand that tax practitioners not be found guilty of negligence if they exercised as much diligence and skill as the average practitioner. If it is not the practitioner's fault that mistakes were made, the practitioner should not be punished.

NOTES

[1] Comment, Reconciliation of Conflicting Void-for-Vagueness Theories by the Supreme Court, Houston Law Review 9: 82 (1971); Note, Void for Vagueness: An Escape from Statutory Interpretation, Indiana Law Review 23: 272, at 283 (1948).

[2] Connally v. General Construction Co., 269 U.S. 385, 391 (1926), cited by Evans, infra at note 12.

[3] Winters v. New York, 333 U.S. 507, 515 (1948). Also see Colten v. Kentucky, 407 U.S. 104, 110 (1972).

[4] Grayned v. City of Rockford, 408 U.S. 104, 108-09 (1972), quoted in Village of Hoffman Estates v. The Flipside, 455 U.S. 489, 498 (1982).

[5] Criminal laws "must be defined with appropriate definiteness" lest they run afoul of the Due Process clause. Cantwell v. Connecticut, 310 U.S. 296, 308 (1940).

[6] Jeffrey Merle Evans, Void-for-Vagueness – Judicial Response to Allegedly Vague Statutes – State v. Zuanich, 92 Ut. 2d 61, 593 P.2d 1314 (1979), Washington Law Review 56: 131 (1980), n. 86.
[7] Papachristou v. City of Jacksonville, 405 U.S. 156, 92 S. Ct. 839 (1972) [An ordinance that prohibited "loafing," "strolling" or "wandering around from place to place" was struck down as being void for vagueness because it did not adequately warn people what kinds of conduct would be subject to prosecution.]; Smith v. Goguen, 415 U.S. 566 (1974). Vague laws that involve the First Amendment will generally be considered void for vagueness in all cases. Winters v. New York, 333 U.S. 507, 509 (1948).
[8] Palmer v. City of Euclid, 402 U.S. 544 (1971); Village of Hoffman Estates v. The Flipside, 455 U.S. 489 (1982).
[9] Tax cases can originate in the federal district court, the Claims Court or the Tax Court. Appeals can then be made to a federal appellate court and finally to the United States Supreme Court.
[10] Looseleaf tax services have become a necessity for any practitioner who wants to keep current on recent changes in the tax law. That is because the tax law changes on a weekly basis. Dozens of tax cases are decided each week by the three federal court systems. The IRS continues to issue Revenue Rulings and Revenue Procedures. Congress continues to make changes in the tax code every year. In years when Congress passes a so-called tax reform bill, the changes could number more than one thousand. Some loose leaf tax services have weekly updates. The Bureau of National Affairs publishes a daily tax update that sometimes runs to more than 50 pages.
[11] D.W. Ball, Retroactive Application of Treasury Rules and Regulations, New Mexico Law Review 17: 139 (1987); J.S. Bryant, Retroactive Taxation: A Constitutional Analysis of the Minimum Tax on IDCs, Oklahoma Law Review 36: 107 (1983); Brian T. Camp, The Retroactivity of Treasury Regulations: Paths to Find Abuse of Discretion, Virginia Taxation Review 7:509 (1988); T. Robinson, Retroactivity: The Case for Better Regulation of Federal Tax Regulators, Ohio State Law Journal 48: 773 (1987); To What Extent Can Taxpayers Rely on IRS Regulations and Rulings to Predict Future IRS Conduct? Gonzaga Law Review 25:281 (1989/90).
[12] James S. Eustice, Tax Complexity and the Tax Practitioner, Tax Law Review 45: 7-24, at 9 (Fall 1989).
[13] James L. Payne, Unhappy Returns: The $600 Billion Tax Ripoff, Policy Review 21 (1992)
[14] Id., at 21-22.
[15] Joan Caplin, 6 Mistakes Even the Tax Pros Make, MONEY 104-106 (March 1998).
[16] Caplin, supra, at 104.
[17] If one concedes that equity and fair play are involved here, a logical application of fair play would be to consider the vagueness of a law when a practitioner is accused of malpractice or negligence for failing to apply the vague law.
[18] Harry Browne, the Libertarian Party candidate for President in 1996, said we should scrap the Internal Revenue Code and replace it with nothing. He made the case that, if federal spending were limited to the few areas where the federal government is constitutionally authorized to operate, it could raise the funds it needs without an income tax. So scrapping the Internal Revenue Code and starting over is only one option.
[19] Joan Caplin, 6 Mistakes Even the Tax Pros Make, MONEY 104-106 (March 1998).
[20] Caplin (1998), supra at 104-105.
[21] Id., at 105.
[22] Id.
[23] Id.
[24] Id.
[25] Id., at 105-106.
[26] Id., at 106.
[27] George Spellmire, Wayne Baliga and Debra Winiarski, Accountants' Legal Liability Guide 5.02 (1990).

[28] Denzil Y. Causey, Jr. and Sandra A. Causey, Duties and Liabilities of Public Accountants, 5th ed. 324 (1995).
[29] Id.
[30] Smith v. St. Paul Fire & Marine Insurance Co., 366 F.Supp. 1283 (M.D. La. 1973), aff'd per curiam, 500 F.2d 1131 (5th Cir. 1974).
[31] Richard v. Staehle, 434 N.E.2d 1379 (Ohio App. 1980), cited in Causey, supra at 324.
[32] 31C.F.R. §10.
[33] Causey, supra at 326.
[34] Billings Clinic v. Peat Marwick Main & Co., 797 P.2d 899 (Mont. 1990), cited in Causey, supra at 326, n. 6.
[35] Horne v. Peckham, 158 Cal.Rptr. 714 (Cal. App. 1979), cited by Causey, supra at 326, n. 7.
[36] Wright v. Williams, 121 Cal.Rptr. 194 (Cal. App. 1975), cited in Causey, supra at 326, n. 8.
[37] United States v. Simon, 425 F.2d 796 (2d Cir. 1969), cert. denied, 397 U.S. 1006 (1970).
[38] SEC v. Seaboard Corp., 677 F.2d 1301 (9th Cir. 1982).
[39] Causey, supra at 327-328; Sladky v. Lomax, 538 N.E.2d 1089 (Ohio App. 1988), cited in Causey at 328, n. 19.
[40] Causey, supra at 327; Atkins v. Crosland, 417 S.W.2d 150 (Tex. 1967); Isaacson, Stolper & Co. v. Artisan's Savings Bank, 320 A.2d 130 (Del. 1974); Leonhart v. Atkinson, 289 A.2d 1 (Md. App. 1972); cited in Causey at 328, n. 20.
[41] Feldman v. Granger, 257 A.2d 421 (Md. 1969), cited in Causey at 328, n. 21.
[42] Linck v. Barokas & Martin, 667 P.2d 171 (Alaska 1983), cited in Causey at 328, n. 22.
[43] Cameron v. Montgomery, 225 N.W.2d 154 (Iowa 1975), cited in Causey at 328, n. 23.
[44] Snydergeneral Corporation v. KPMG Peat Marwick, No. 90-14145-K (District Court of Dallas County 1992), cited in Causey at 329, n. 24.
[45] Deloitte Haskins & Sells v. Green, 403 S.E.2d 818 (Ga. App. 1991), cited in Causey at 329, n. 26.
[46] Billings Clinic v. Peat Marwick Main & Co., 797 P.2d 899 (Mont. 1990).
[47] Lien v. McGladrey & Pullen, 509 N.W.2d 421 (S.D. 1993); Bancroft v. Indemnity Insurance Co. of North America, 203 F.Supp. 49 (W.D. La. 1962), aff'd mem., 309 F.2d 959 (5th Cir. 1963), cited in Causey at 329, n. 28 & 29.
[48] Mills v. Garlow, 768 P.2d 554 (Wyo. 1989), cited in Causey at 330, n. 30.
[49] Horne v. Peckham, 158 Cal.Rptr. 714 (Cal. App. 1979), cited in Causey at 330, n. 31.
[50] H & R Block v. Testerman, 338 A.2d 48 (Md. App. 1975); Jerry Clark Equipment, Inc. v. Hibbits, d/b/a AAA Bookkeeping Service, 612 N.E.2d 858 Ill. App. 1993); Slaughter v. Roddie, 249 So.2d (La. App. 1971); Dial v. Adamson, 570 N.E.2d 1167 (Ill. App. 1991); cited in Causey at 330, n. 35 & 36.
[51] Rassieur v. Charles, 188 S.W.2d 817 (Mo. 1945), cited by Causey at 331, n. 39.
[52] L.B. Laboratories v. Mitchell, 244 P.2d 385 (Cal. 1952); Sorenson v. Fio Rito, 413 N.E.2d 47 (Ill. App. 1980); Dail v. Adamson, 570 N.E.2d 1167 (Ill. App. 1991); Jerry Clark Equipment, Inc. v. Hibbits, d/b/a AAA Bookkeeping Service, 612 N.E.2d 858 (Ill. App. 1993); Bick v. Peat Marwick and Main, 799 P.2d 94 (Kan. App. 1990). Cited in Causey at 331, n. 41 & 42.
[53] Sladky v. Lomax, 538 N.E.2d 1089 (Ohio App. 1988), cited in Causey at 335, n. 61.
[54] Jerry Clark Equipment, Inc. v. Hibbits, d/b/a AAA Bookkeeping Service, 612 N.E.2d 858 (Ill. App. 1993), cited by Causey at 353.
[55] Consolidated Management Services, Inc. v. Halligan, 368 S.E.2d 148 (Ga. App. 1988), affirmed, Halligan v. Consolidated Management Services, Inc., 369 S.E.2d 745 (Ga. 1988), cited by Causey at 353.
[56] Warmbrodt v. Blanchard, 692 P.2d 1282 (Nev. 1984), cited by Causey at 354.
[57] Joan Caplin, 6 Mistakes Even the Tax Pros Make, MONEY 104-106 (March, 1998).
[58] Id., at 104.
[59] Id.
[60] Id.

[61] Id., at 105.
[62] Id., at 106.
[63] Id., at 105-106.
[64] Id., at 104.
[65] Id., at 105.
[66] Id.
[67] Teresa Tritch, Keep an Eye on Your Tax Pro, MONEY (March, 1993), at 100.
[68] Teresa Tritch and Deborah Lohse, Tax Payers, Start Worrying! MONEY (March, 1992), at 90.
[69] The 16% figure was taken from the 1997 survey calculation given above.

Chapter 12

IS TAX COMPETITION HARMFUL?

INTRODUCTION

One of the benefits of globalization is that it is bringing economies closer together. As trade and investment barriers fall, investors are able to take advantage of an ever increasing number of investment opportunities. That sounds like good news, doesn't it? The problem with this scenario, if you are one of the bloated, high-tax Western European welfare states, is that you are witnessing an exodus of investment capital to jurisdictions that are more tax friendly. Corporations that are headquartered in one of these high tax countries are increasingly exercising their options to invest elsewhere. The result is a loss of jobs and tax revenue to the high tax jurisdictions and an influx of capital, jobs and economic growth to the countries that offer lower corporate tax rates.

Bureaucrats and politicians from these tax gouging states are yelling and screaming for something to be done about this "unfair" tax competition. The health of their welfare states is in jeopardy if investors are allowed to invest their funds as they see fit. The bureaucrats are even banding together to stem the flow of investment capital to more friendly tax climates.

The Organisation for Economic Cooperation and Development (OECD) is spearheading an effort to end tax competition, although it doesn't come right out and say it. The OECD and the public servants in the high tax jurisdictions prefer to call it tax harmonisation. They just want to harmonize tax rates so that all countries charge about the same rate for doing business within their jurisdiction. That rate is high, of course, but they prefer not to dwell on that point. The European Union wants potential new members to agree to charge some minimum value added tax (VAT) rate as a condition of joining their club. They don't want some transition economy to be able to undercut them by charging 5% when everyone else is charging 15 or 20 percent. That would undercut the whole idea of "cooperation."

If private parties engage in rate fixing, they are subject to fines and jail, but when government officials do basically the same thing, it is perfectly legal. Why is that? Their excuse is that they are doing it in the public interest. But how is it in the public interest to raise tax rates? If private business people get together to keep prices high, it is bad for the public, but when our elected (and unelected) government officials do it, it is supposed to be good for the general population. I fail to see the logic.

WHAT'S WRONG WITH COMPETITION?

It is curious that the same politicians and bureaucrats who are so concerned about maintaining competition when it comes to acquisition and merger activity within their borders take a completely opposite view when their cushy little fiefdoms start to feel the pressure of tax competition. Why is it that competition is good when private firms engage in it, but bad when governments have to engage in it? Economists who recognize the superiority of the market over central planning and the closed economy agree that competition leads to innovation, lower prices and higher quality products and services whenever private firms engage in it. But these public servants, whether elected or unelected, refuse to see that holding governments' feet to the fires of competition will also lead to lower prices (taxes) and higher quality services. There is no evidence to suggest that governments are not subject to the same laws of supply and demand as every other provider of goods and services.

Part of the problem is that our public servants have forgotten that they are our servants. They think and act as though they were our masters, which might indeed be true, since they can throw us in jail if we refuse to pay them whatever they demand. Luckily, investors are free to choose where they invest their money, which allows them to escape oppressive and abusive jurisdictions whose only concern is how to take an ever increasing share of people's income to spend or squander on their pet projects.

There is an inverse relationship between the rates a government charges and the rate of economic growth. Countries that have the lowest tax rates tend to have the highest economic growth. One reason for that is because investment capital tends to flow into low tax countries and out of high tax countries. But that is not the only reason, Another reason has to do with economic efficiency. The private sector can do just about anything more efficiently than the government sector, so the more funds that remain in private hands, the more efficient the economy works. Taking money out of the more efficient private sector and spending it on government projects distorts the economy and causes it work operate less efficiently.

Ireland is an excellent example of what can happen if a country decides to shrink the size of its welfare state, cut tax rates and become friendly to business. In 2000 this little country of less than 4 million people was able to attract more foreign direct investment than either Japan or Italy.[1] It slashed its corporate tax rate to 10 percent and now has one of the highest standards of living in the world.[2] The EU, of which Ireland is a member, is very upset because it sees investment capital that could flow to the continent flowing into Ireland instead. But that doesn't bother the Irish government all that much. For decades, if not centuries, people who were born in Ireland have been emigrating to other countries where the economic opportunities are better. All that has changed since Ireland got smart and dropped its tax rates. Many of the Irish who left Ireland are going back. The flow of immigration into the country now exceeds the emigration out of the country.

In 1998 the OECD issued a nasty little report in which it tried to show that tax competition is harmful.[3] Curiously, on page 2 it repeats its Article 1 goals, which are to promote policies designed:

- to achieve the highest sustainable economic growth and employment and a rising standard of living in Member countries, while maintaining financial stability, and thus to contribute to the development of the world economy;
- to contribute to sound economic expansion in Member as well as non-member countries in the process of economic development; and
- to contribute to the expansion of world trade on a multilateral, non-discriminatory basis in accordance with international obligations.

If the OECD were really interested in achieving such goals, it is hard to understand why it is pressuring low tax jurisdictions to raise their tax rates, since the evidence is quite clear that countries that have low taxes tend to have higher economic growth rates than do countries with high taxes. Ireland is an excellent example, although not the only one. Ireland has maintained a high economic growth rate and also expanded employment opportunities precisely because its tax rates are relatively low. The avowed OECD policy of pressuring low tax countries to increase their tax rates would, if successful, have just the opposite effect, and would also violate the terms of Article 1 of its Convention. Its recommendations for dealing with what it calls "harmful" tax competition would actually reduce trade, retard economic development and destroy jobs.

In 2000 it issued another report, further explaining that the goal of its tax competition project was to ensure that "the burden of taxation is fairly shared and that tax should not be the dominant factor in making capital allocation decisions."[4] The report goes on to say that the OECD is concerned that both OECD and non-OECD countries may suffer revenue losses as a result of harmful tax competition, and mentions that erosion of the tax base can be especially harmful to developing countries.

However, it is often the developing countries that are attracting FDI precisely because of their relatively low tax rates. It is touching that the OECD is concerned for the welfare of these countries, especially the countries that are not even OECD members. However, its concern is misplaced. What they should be concerned about is the high taxes that citizens of member and nonmember countries will have to pay if their efforts to raise taxes throughout the world are successful, and the economic stagnation and job losses that would result.

CONCLUDING COMMENTS

The OECD continues to issue progress reports. Apparently, the bureaucrats and economists who issue these reports still do not see the relationship between low tax rates and high rates of economic growth. But some other people see the relationship. A number of scholars and policy makers have written about the harmful effects the OECD initiative would have if successful. Writing from the U.S. perspective, Daniel Mitchell sees the OECD's tax harmonization and information exchange proposals as something that would undermine the competitive advantage that the United States now has in the global economy.[5] Other commentators point out potential dangers to national sovereignty,[6] the likelihood of higher taxes and less privacy,[7] and the likelihood that carrying out the sanctions OECD proposes would get OECD member nations into trouble with the World Trade Organization, which has rules against imposing economic sanctions.[8]

If the OECD were truly concerned with harmonizing tax rates so that all nations would have similar rates, why is it threatening to sanction the nations that have relatively low rates? Why not target the nations that have relatively high rates? Since low rates foster economic growth and the expansion of employment, and since these are among the OECD's stated goals, it seems inappropriate that it should be targeting low tax countries instead of high tax countries. Targeting low tax countries makes the OECD's claim that it is not trying to raise tax rates very difficult to believe.

The OECD's repeated use of the level playing field argument is especially curious, given the fact that it employs so many economists (who should know better). Basically, the level playing field argument has no place in economic analysis. It is a sports concept, nothing more. In a horserace, a horse that has a jockey who is lighter than the other jockeys will have a few pounds of sand placed in a bag so that the horses will all be carrying equal weight into the race. In a 100 meter dash, all participants start at the same place. That's because it's the fair thing to do.

Sporting events are a win-lose proposition. They are a zero-sum game. Business is not like that. Business is a win-win game. Both participants -- buyer and seller -- benefit by any voluntary, mutually agreed upon exchange. Trade is a positive-sum game, so the level playing field argument is inappropriate. David Ricardo knew that as far back as 1817 when he wrote his classic book, Principles of Political Economy and Taxation.[9]

Not only is a level playing field inappropriate in business; it is also undesirable. If Florida and Maine both could grow oranges at the same cost, Florida would not be able to export any oranges to Maine, since there would be no competitive advantage. Likewise, if it were possible to grow potatoes in Florida at the same cost as it costs Maine farmers, Maine would not be able to export potatoes to Florida because Florida would be growing its own potatoes.

The fact that the level playing field does not exist in business makes trade possible. If there were no competitive advantage, there would be no trade and little economic growth, since being able to trade with other nations makes it possible to have a high degree of division of labor, which increases efficiency, and therefore the standard of living.

Nations that have chosen not to have bloated welfare states have a competitive advantage over nations that have chosen to have welfare states because the cost of maintaining a small state is less than the cost of maintaining a bloated welfare state. If the bloated welfare states of Western Europe want to be competitive with the lean non-welfare states, they can be competitive. All they have to do is relinquish their welfare states and let taxpayers keep more of the money they have earned. They should not use the force of government to impose sanctions that only do harm to nations that have done nothing wrong.

NOTES

[1] United Nations, World Investment Report 2001, New York: United Nations Conference on Trade and Development (UNCTAD), 2001, p. 291, as cited in Chris Edwards and Veronique de Rugy, International Tax Competition: A 21st-Century Restraint on Government, Policy Analysis No. 431, Washington, DC: Cato Institute, April 12, 2002, at p. 3. [www.cato.org].

[2] Edwards and de Rugy, p. 3.

[3] OECD, Harmful Tax Competition: An Emerging Global Issue, Paris: OECD, 1998. www.oecd.org.

[4] OECD, Towards Global Tax Co-operation: Report to the 2000 Ministerial Council Meeting and Recommendations by the Committee on Fiscal Affairs; Progress on Identifying and Eliminating Harmful Tax Practices, Paris: OECD, 2000, p. 5. www.oecd.org.

[5] Daniel J. Mitchell, A Tax Competition Primer: Why Tax Harmonization and Information Exchange Undermine America's Competitive Advantage in the Global Economy, Backgrounder No. 1460, Washington, DC: Heritage Foundation, July 20, 2001 [www.heritage.org].

[6] Bruce Zagaris, Application of the OECD Harmful Tax Practices Criteria to the OECD Countries Shows Potential Dangers to the U.S. Sovereignty, April 25, 2001, posted at www.freedomandprosperity.org.

[7] Daniel J. Mitchell, An OECD Proposal to Eliminate Tax Competition Would Mean Higher Taxes and Less Privacy, Backgrounder No. 1395, Washington, DC: Heritage Foundation, September 18, 2000 [www.heritage.org].

[8] Cordia Scott, OECD 'Harmful' Tax Competition May Violate WTO Obligations, Expert Says, Tax Notes International, April 24, 2001, reproduced at www.freedomandprosperity.org.

[9] David Ricardo, Principles of Political Economy and Taxation, 1817.

Chapter 13

IS THE ABILITY TO PAY PRINCIPLE ETHICALLY BANKRUPT?

INTRODUCTION

The cost-benefit approach takes as its premise the view that people should pay taxes based on the benefits they receive from government. If you receive benefits, you should pay for them. This approach seems fair, since any other alternative would be to charge people for the costs of government on some basis other than benefit. Some people would pay more than what they get in services while others would pay less. Those who pay more are exploited, while those who pay less are parasites.

One problem with the cost-benefit approach is that it is impossible to measure benefits. Different people place different values on things. It is the principle upon which subjective value theory and marginal utility are based.[1]

The ability to pay principle "maintains that taxes should be distributed according to the capacity of taxpayers to pay them."[2] This principle has been justified on several grounds over the years.[3] A dollar taken from a rich man reduces total utility less than does a dollar taken from a poor man, or so the saying goes. The problem with this philosophical approach is that a closer analysis reveals that "progressive taxation cannot be justified by reference to the principle of diminishing marginal utility of income."[4] Individuals have different interpersonal marginal utilities and it is impossible to measure them, although some scholars have taken the position that it is better to make a rough estimate than none at all.[5]

Several philosophical approaches may be taken to determine whether the ability to pay principle is ethically sound. Utilitarianism is one. Rights is another. We shall examine both.

THE UTILITARIAN APPROACH

Utilitarianism is a kind of ethical philosophy, an approach to making moral judgments. There are several ways to look at utilitarianism. Some utilitarians would say that a policy is good, just and ethical if it results in the greatest good for the greatest number.[6] Other utilitarians would say that a policy is good if its implementation would result in increasing total utility. Economists would say that a policy is good if it results in a positive-sum game, where the winners exceed the losers.

Jeremy Bentham would say that human suffering and enjoyment are the only sources of right and wrong.[7] Where the amount of pleasure exceeds the amount of pain, the action is ethical. If total pain exceeds total pleasure, the action or policy is unethical.

The utilitarian ethic has been applied to the philosophy of public finance in an attempt to determine the optimal tax policy. For example,

> The real income ... after any taxes should be equal, except (a) for supplements to meet special needs, (b) supplements recompensing services to the extent needed to provide desirable incentive and allocate resources efficiently, and (c) variations to achieve other socially desirable ends such as population control.[8]

Economists almost universally subscribe to utilitarian ethics. Economists are wealth maximizers. A policy is good if it increases wealth and best if it maximizes wealth. They would argue that there is no inconsistency between morality and efficiency.[9]

If we accept the premise that what is efficient is also moral,[10] we run into ethical problems with the ability to pay principle because it is inefficient. Economists have given a number of utilitarian reasons against the graduated income tax.[11] For one thing, it destroys the incentive of the most productive people. And since it is primarily the most productive people who save, invest and create jobs, a graduated tax will retard economic growth by reducing the amount of capital available for investment.

A progressive tax system, which is the kind of tax system one has if one begins with the premise that the tax system should be based on the ability to pay, causes the inefficient substitution of leisure for work because it increases the price of work relative to that of leisure.[12] A progressive tax also decreases the amount of risk taking relative to that that would take place where the tax system is not progressive.[13] As risk taking is reduced, so is income mobility. Aversion to risk taking can have an adverse effect on economic growth, capital accumulation and expansion of employment.

There are also social costs of having a progressive tax system. People who are in a high tax bracket will find it profitable to pay accountants and attorneys huge sums to reduce their tax liability.[14] Someone who owes $100,000 in taxes should logically be willing to pay an accountant or an attorney up to $99,999 to find ways to avoid the tax. This money could better be spent on investment in some project that generates income and creates employment rather than being diverted in defense of retaining property that the tax collector would otherwise take. A large chunk of the U.S. Internal Revenue Code exists solely to prevent people from finding ways around the progressivity of the income tax.[15]

Countries that have adopted a progressive tax system tend to have highly complex tax systems with multiple rates, numerous exemptions, etc. These complications greatly decrease the efficiency of tax collection.[16] Complex tax systems also cost billions of dollars in administration costs. According to one estimate, the cost of administering the federal tax system in the United States is $600 billion.[17]

Another inefficiency with a graduated tax system is that it increases animosity between the rich and the poor. It is divisive in the sense that it forces high income earners to pay what might be perceived to be more than their "fair share" of the tax burden. And it exacerbates the envy that the lower income earners already have toward high-income earners.[18] Thus, it decreases social harmony and stability.

One might argue that it is only fair that the rich pay more in total than the poor do, because the rich have more property to protect than the poor do. Since protecting property is a function of government, it seems only fair that those who have more property will pay more, in total, for government services than those who own less property. This line of reasoning seems reasonable on the surface. But if one digs beneath the surface, problems start to appear with this line of reasoning.

For one thing, there may be little or no relationship between the cost of protecting property and the amount of property to be protected. It may cost more to protect 100 acres of land worth $10,000 than to protect a bank vault that contains $100 million.[19] One might logically argue that if it costs 10% more to protect the property of someone who earns $1 million a year than someone who earns $10,000 a year, then one might conclude that the person with the $1 million income should pay 10% more in taxes than the person who earns $10,000. Critics of this approach would be quick to claim that such a tax system is "regressive," as though there is something somehow wrong with regressivity.

The ability to pay principle does not stand up to utilitarian ethical analysis because it is inefficient and thus unethical. However, the utilitarian approach to ethics suffers from at least two major weaknesses: (1) There is no accurate or precise way to measure gains and losses and (2) utilitarian ethics totally ignores rights.[20]

Even though a utilitarian approach makes it easy to see that the ability to pay principle leads to inefficiency, and is thus unethical from a utilitarian perspective, it is not possible to measure the degree of inefficiency. Also, as was mentioned, the utilitarian approach to ethics is defective because it ignores rights.[21]

Immanuel Kant would reject the graduated income tax because it treats individuals as means rather than ends in themselves.[22] The graduated income tax is based on the exploitation of the wealthy by the less wealthy for no other reason than the fact that they have more money than other people.

Ayn Rand, the Russian-American philosopher and novelist would also reject the graduated income tax, for the same reason. Individuals must be treated as ends in themselves, not as mere means to an end.[23] She also rejects utilitarianism and its related concept -- redistribution of income.

> "The greatest good for the greatest number" is one of the most vicious slogans ever foisted on humanity.
>
> This slogan has no concrete, specific meaning. There is no way to interpret it benevolently, but a great many ways in which it can be used to justify the most vicious actions.
>
> ...Because "the good" is not determined by counting numbers and it is not achieved by the sacrifice of anyone to anyone.[24]

> Whoever claims the "right" to "redistribute" the wealth produced by others is claiming the "right" to treat human beings as chattels.[25]

THE RIGHTS APPROACH

The rights approach avoids the two flaws inherent in utilitarianism. If one begins with the premise that an action is unethical if one person's rights are violated, there is no need to measure gains and losses but only to determine whether one person's rights have been violated. A utilitarian would conclude that an action is ethical even though someone's rights might be violated as long as there are more winners than losers or as long as the good exceeds the bad and that is the inherent flaw in the utilitarian approach.

In a progressive tax system, those who have more are exploited by those who have less. There is an inherent injustice in such a system because some people are living at the expense of others. Individuals are being treated as means rather than as ends in themselves. One might say that the family is based on this system -- where some (children) live at the expense of others (parents) -- but this analogy is inapplicable if for no other reason than the fact that the family is a voluntary association whereas the tax system is based on coercion.[26]

AN OVERLOOKED PHILOSOPHICAL POINT

There are two basic and diametrically opposed views of taxation. Those who favor the ability to pay approach view the state as a master, who extracts tribute from its subjects on the basis of how much they are able to pay. Those who take this first approach often also view the state as a benevolent father figure, who distributes tax benefits on the basis of need. In Karl Marx's words, "From each according to his abilities; to each according to his needs."[27]

Those who take the service provider approach view the state as the servant of the people. Government provides services and taxpayers pay for the services. Those who benefit the most from the services should pay the most. And those who do not use a particular government service[28] should not be forced to pay for it at all.[29] Thomas Cooley makes the following point:

> Taxation is the equivalent for the protection which the government affords to the person and property of its citizens; and as all alike are protected, so all alike should bear the burden, in proportion to the interests secured.[30]

A corollary to the service provider approach is that there should be some maximum tax,[31] an amount above which no one should have to pay. Leona Helmsley, for example, who went to prison for tax evasion,[32] would not have been punished if the U.S. tax system were set up under a service provider principle because the amount of taxes she paid -- more than $100 million -- exceeded the benefit she received. Under the service provider principle she would have been entitled to a refund. But because she paid a few million dollars less than she "owed" under the graduated, ability to pay system, and because she resorted to illegal means to prevent the government from assessing the "proper" amount, she was sentenced to prison. It is difficult to believe that she received more than $100 million in services from the federal government over the years. It seems like a clear case of the government exploiting one of its more productive citizens.[33]

CONCLUDING COMMENTS

The ability to pay principle involves exploitation. The government exploits the producers -- the wealth creators -- and redistributes a portion of their income to wealth consumers -- those who use the various government programs. In that sense, it is a parasitical system. The service provider principle, on the other hand, attempts to match costs with benefits. Those who use government services pay for them, and those who do not use the services are not forced to pay. Thus, the service provider principle is fairer than the ability to pay principle because it is based on principles of equity rather than exploitation. So a tax that is based on the service provider principle is to be preferred to a tax that relies on the ability to pay principle, all other things being equal.

However, it should be pointed out that both taxes raised under the ability to pay principle and under the service provider approach are generally raised by the use of force or the threat of force, except in the case where the method used is a user fee or lottery. So both methods suffers from defects, although the service provider approach at least attempts to match costs and benefits equitably, whereas the ability to pay concept makes no such attempts.

NOTES

[1] The benefit principle is discussed in many places in the public finance literature. See Liam Murphy and Thomas Nagel, The Myth of Ownership: Taxes and Justice. Oxford: Oxford University Press, 2002, pp. 16-19; Richard A. Musgrave, The Theory of Public Finance. New York: McGraw-Hill, 1959, pp. 61-89; Richard A. Musgrave and Peggy B. Musgrave, Public Finance in Theory and Practice, second edition, New York: McGraw-Hill, 1976, pp. 211-215; James M. Buchanan and Marilyn R. Flowers, The Public Finances. Homewood, IL: Richard D. Irwin, 4th edition, 1975, pp. 183-187; Michael L. Marlow, Public Finance: Theory and Practice. Orlando: The Dryden Press, 1995, pp. 416-422.

2 David N. Hyman, Public Finance: A Contemporary Application of Theory to Policy, 6th edition. Orlando: Dryden Press, 1999, p. 663.Adam Smith's first Canon of taxation was that individuals should contribute "as nearly as possible in proportion to their respective abilities." Adam Smith, The Wealth of Nations 310 (1776; 1937), as quoted in John Cullis and Philip Jones, Public Finance and Public Choice, second edition, Oxford: Oxford University Press, 1998, p. 244. Rosen defines ability to pay as the "Capacity to pay a tax, which may be measured by income, consumption, or wealth." Harvey S. Rosen, Public Finance, 5th edition. Irwin/McGraw-Hill, 1999, p. 529.

[3] For discussions of the ability to pay principle, see Liam Murphy and Thomas Nagel, The Myth of Ownership: Taxes and Justice. Oxford: Oxford University Press, 2002, pp. 20-30; Richard A. Musgrave, The Theory of Public Finance. New York: McGraw-Hill, 1959, pp. 90-115; Richard A. Musgrave and Peggy B. Musgrave, Public Finance in Theory and Practice, second edition, New York: McGraw-Hill, 1976, pp. 215-222; James M. Buchanan, Public Finance in Democratic Process: Fiscal Institutions and Individual Choice. Chapel Hill: University of North Carolina Press, 1967, pp. 157-158; James M. Buchanan and Marilyn R. Flowers, The Public Finances. Homewood, IL: Richard D. Irwin, 4th edition, 1975, pp. 97-100, 233-234; Michael L. Marlow, Public Finance: Theory and Practice. Orlando: The Dryden Press, 1995, pp. 422-425.

4 Richard A. Posner, Economic Analysis of Law, 5th edition, New York: Aspen Law & Business, 1998, p. 547. Posner's Chapter 16: Income Inequalities, Distributive Justice, and Poverty 497-521 completely destroys the notion that the ability to pay concept can be justified on marginal utility grounds. For an exposition of the now discarded theory that total utility can be increased if the rich nations would give money to poor nations, see Ruben P. Mendez, International Public Finance: A New Perspective on Global Relations. Oxford: Oxford University Press, 1992, pp. 104-5.

[5] Liam Murphy and Thomas Nagel, The Myth of Ownership: Taxes and Justice. Oxford: Oxford University Press, 2002, p. 24.

[6] Mill, Bentham and the other classical utilitarians take this position, although it is not the only position they take. There are many variations of utilitarianism, almost as many variations are there are utilitarian philosophers. For various approaches to utilitarianism, see John Stuart Mill, Utilitarianism, On Liberty, Essay on Bentham. New York: New American Library, 1962; Douglas G. Long, Bentham on Liberty: Jeremy Bentham's Idea of Liberty in Relation to His Utilitarianism. Toronto: University of Toronto, 1976; Christopher Biffle and Julius J. Jackson, A Guided Tour of John Stuart Mill's Utilitarianism. New York: McGraw-Hill, 1992; J.J.C. Smart and Bernard Williams, Utilitarianism - For and Against. Cambridge: Cambridge University Press, 1973; Amartya Sen, Utilitarianism and Beyond. Cambridge: Cambridge University Press, 1982; Geoffrey Scarre, Utilitarianism. London and New York: Routledge, 1996; Jeremy Bentham, The

Principles of Morals and Legislation. Amherst, NY: Prometheus Books, 1988; Richard B. Brandt, Morality, Utilitarianism, and Rights. Cambridge and New York: Cambridge University Press, 1992. James A. Yunker, In Defense of Utilitarianism: An Economist's Viewpoint, Review of Social Economy 44(1): 57-79 (April 1986). Robert E. Goodin, Utilitarianism as a Public Philosophy. Cambridge: Cambridge University Press, 1995. For an explanation of Mill's utilitarianism, see Roger Crisp, Mill on Utilitarianism. London and New York: Routledge, 1997.

7 William H. Shaw, Contemporary Ethics: Taking Account of Utilitarianism. Oxford: Blackwell, 1999, p. 69, citing Bentham's *The rationale of judicial evidence, specially applied to English practice*, in The Works of Jeremy Bentham, vol. 6, ed. J. Bowring (1962), at 238. For a defense of utilitarianism, see Shaw at 68-101. For objections to utilitarianism, see Shaw, 102-132. For refutations of the utilitarian ethic, see Murray N. Rothbard, Man, Economy, and State. Los Angeles: Nash Publishing, 1970, pp. 260-268; Robert W. McGee, The Fatal Flaw in the Methodology of Law & Economics, Commentaries on Law & Economics 1: 209-223 (1997); Robert W. McGee, The Fatal Flaw in NAFTA, GATT and All Other Trade Agreements, Northwestern Journal of International Law & Business 14: 549-565 (1994).

8 Richard B. Brandt, A Theory of the Good and the Right. Buffalo: Prometheus Books, 1979, p. 310, as cited by Shaw, *supra*, at 235.

9 Richard A. Posner, Economic Analysis of Law , 5th edition, New York: Aspen Law & Business, 1998, p. 546.

10 There are a number of problems with the premise that what is efficient is moral but we will leave discussion of this issue for another day.

11 For examples, see Walter J. Blum and Harry Kalven, Jr., The Uneasy Case for Progressive Taxation. Chicago: University of Chicago Press, 1953; F.A. Hayek, The Case Against Progressive Income Taxes, The Freeman 229-32 (December 28, 1953).

12 Posner, *supra*, at 544.

13 Posner, *supra*, at 545.

14 Posner, *supra*, at 545-546.

15 Richard A. . Epstein,, Simple Rules for a Complex World Cambridge, MA. Harvard University Press, 1995, p. 147.

16 Robert W. McGee, Taxation and Public Finance: A Philosophical and Ethical Approach, Commentaries on the Law of Accounting & Finance 1: 157-240 (1997); Robert W. McGee, Tax Advice for Latvia and Other Similarly Situated Emerging Economies, International Tax & Business Lawyer 13: 223-308 (1996); Robert W. McGee, Principles of Taxation for Emerging Economies: Some Lessons from the U.S. Experience, Dickinson Journal of International Law 12: 29-93 (1993).

17 James L. Payne, Unhappy Returns: The $600-Billion Tax Ripoff, Policy Review 21 (Winter 1992).

18 Helmut Schoeck, Envy: A Theory of Social Behavior. New York: Harcourt Brace & World, 1966, pp. 194, 217, 221; Robert Sheaffer, Resentment Against Achievement: Understanding the Assault Upon Ability. Buffalo: Prometheus Books, 1988, pp. 177, 186.

19 Murray N. Rothbard makes this point at 115 in Power and Market: Government and the Economy, Menlo Park, CA: Institute for Humane Studies, 1970.

20 I could have said that utilitarian ethics totally ignores "individual" rights but there is no need to include the word "individual" when speaking about rights since individual rights are the only kind of rights that exist. There is no such thing as group rights.

[21] For discussions of this point, see R.G. Frey, editor, Utility and Rights. Minneapolis: University of Minnesota Press, 1984; Parta Dasgupta, Utilitarianism, information and Rights, in Amartya Sen and Bernard Williams, editors, Utilitarianism and Beyond. Cambridge: Cambridge University Press, 1999, pp. 199-218.

[22] This view permeates Kant's work. For examples, see Immanuel Kant, The Critique of Pure Reason. Great Books of the Western World, Vol. 42. Chicago: Encyclopedia Britannica, 1952, pp. 1-250; Immanuel Kant, Fundamental Principles of the Metaphysics

of Morals, Great Books of the Western World, Vol. 42. Chicago: Encyclopedia Britannica, 1952, pp. 251-287; Immanuel Kant, The Critique of Practical Reason. Great Books of the Western World, Vol. 42. Chicago: Encyclopedia Britannica, 1952, pp. 289-361; Immanuel Kant, Preface and Introduction to the Metaphysical Elements of Ethics, Great Books of the Western World, Vol. 42. Chicago: Encyclopedia Britannica, 1952, pp. 363-379; Immanuel Kant, General Introduction to the Metaphysics of Morals, Great Books of the Western World, Vol. 42. Chicago: Encyclopedia Britannica, 1952, pp. 381-394; Immanuel Kant, The Critique of Judgment, Great Books of the Western World, Vol. 42. Chicago: Encyclopedia Britannica, 1952, pp.459-613. If you don't want to go through all this reading, which is uniformly heavy, a good abbreviated introduction to Kant's thought may be found in Immanuel Kant, Ethical Philosophy, James W. Ellington, translator, Indianapolis and Cambridge: Hackett Publishing Company, 1983. For a good intellectual biography that is more pleasant reading than the original, see Ernst Cassirer, Kant's Life and Thought. New Haven and London: Yale University Press, 1981.

[23] She expresses her views on this subject in novel form in Atlas Shrugged. New York: New American Library, 1957.

[24] Ayn Rand, Textbook on Americanism, pamphlet, p. 10, as cited by Harry Binswanger, editor, The Ayn Rand Lexicon: Objectivism from A to Z. New York: New American Library, 1986, p. 519.

[25] Ayn Rand, The Virtue of Selfishness. New York: New American Library, 1964, p. 91.

26 We will leave for another day a discussion of whether any tax can be just, since all taxes seemingly violate the right to property. However, this topic has already been discussed elsewhere. For examples, see Robert W. McGee, Is Tax Evasion Unethical? University of Kansas Law Review 42: 411-435 (Winter 1994); Robert W. McGee, Should Accountants be Punished for Aiding and Abetting Tax Evasion? Journal of Accounting, Ethics & Public Policy 1: 16-44 (Winter 1998); Walter Block, The Justification for Taxation in the Economics Literature, Canadian Public Administration/Administration Publique du Canada 36: 225-262 (Summer/Été 1993), 225-262, revised and reprinted in The Ethics of Tax Evasion (Robert W. McGee, ed. 1998), at 36-88.

[27] Karl Marx, Critique of the Gotha Program (1875). The original wording was "Jeder nach seinen Fähigkeiten, jedem nach seinen Bedürfnissen." Louis Blanc, the French socialist, said basically the same thing in 1848. George Seldes, The Great Thoughts. New York: Ballantine Books, 1985, p. 274.

28 The excise tax on gasoline is an example of the application of the benefit principle. Those who use roads pay a gasoline tax, which is supposed to cover the cost of maintaining the roads. However, not all excise taxes are tied in to benefits received. For example, if the amount of excise tax charged for gasoline is five or ten times the cost of maintaining the roads, it ceases to be a tax that is tied in to benefits. Some excise taxes, like those on alcohol and tobacco, are punitive in nature. Such punitive taxes have no place in a society where government is supposed to be the servant rather than the master. For a discussion of the abuse of excise taxes, see William F. Shughart, II, editor, Taxing Choice: The Predatory Politics of Fiscal Discrimination. New Brunswick, NJ and London: Transaction Books, 1997.

[29] There are problems with both of these approaches. There is no way to objectively determine what someone's ability to pay is, so it must be decided arbitrarily. And there is no way to determine how much benefit someone receives from government services that are made available even if few people want them, since the price of such services is determined by bureaucratic fiat rather than through voluntary exchange.

30 Thomas Cooley, Constitutional Limitations 613 (5th ed. 1883), as quoted in Richard A. Epstein, Principles for a Free Society: Reconciling Individual Liberty with the Common Good. Perseus Books, 1998, p. 129.

31 For more on the concept of a maximum tax, see Robert W. McGee, The Case for a Maximum Tax: A Look at Some Legal, Economic and Ethical Issues, Journal of Accounting, Ethics & Public Policy 1: 294-299 (Spring 1998).

[32] U.S. v. Helmsley, 733 F.Supp. 600, 941 F.2d 71 (2nd Cir. 1991).

---

33 Ross Perot, during one of the televised U.S. presidential debates in October, 1992, announced that he has paid $1 billion in taxes over the years. One must wonder how the federal government could possibly provide him with $1 billion in services. It seems unlikely that he could get his moneysworth even if the government provided him with a large home, free clothing and ten meals a day. But he makes too much money to even qualify for welfare, so he is not able to get food or housing from the government.

Chapter 14

THE CASE FOR A MAXIMUM TAX

INTRODUCTION

Several Congresses have passed various forms of minimum tax, both at the individual and corporate level. They have even passed alternative minimum tax bills to squeeze out additional tax revenue that would not otherwise be forthcoming. The problem was caused by the philosophy of taxation they have adopted over the years.

Rather than have the tax law function solely as a way to raise the revenue needed to keep the government running, various special interest groups and social do-gooders have persuaded Congress to incorporate much social engineering into the tax code. There are special provisions for oil companies, farmers, manufacturing companies, small business, homeowners, heads of household, families, sick people, blind people, people with children, and on and on.

Special incentives are given to encourage individuals to alter their behavior in certain supposedly desirable ways. The problem is that if they respond to too many tax incentives, they will not pay "their fair share" of taxes. Thus the need for a minimum tax, to ensure that (almost) everybody who has income pays at least some income tax.

This article will examine the other side of the coin. Whereas numerous commentators have been yapping about some kind of minimum tax in order to increase their perceived view of equity, no one is talking about establishing a maximum tax to ensure that no one pays too much more than their fair share (whatever that is). Thus, the need for this chapter.

THE TWO PHILOSOPHIES OF TAXATION

There are only two philosophical bases upon which tax policy can be based. Curiously enough, elements of both of these contradictory philosophies are incorporated to some extent in most tax systems. One view is based on the ability to pay. To quote one of the biggest proponents of this view, "From each according to his abilities; to each according to his needs."[1] Those who advance this position advocate policies like a graduated income tax, since they presume that the more money you make, the better able you are to pay. The question of whether anyone should pay based on ability to pay is never raised. When people go into the grocery store to buy a loaf of bread, the person behind the counter never asks how much they earn before quoting a price. A Rockefeller does not have to pay $50,000 for a loaf that would sell to a poor person for $0.10.[2] The very thought is ridiculous. Yet that is the theory upon which the graduated income tax is based.

There are many utilitarian arguments against the graduated income tax.[3] For example, it destroys incentives of the most productive people, the ones who can create jobs and increase capital, which is the only way to achieve economic growth. It causes distortion in the economy, since it alters economic behavior. It leads to a misallocation of resources and economic inefficiency.

There is also a moral argument against the graduated tax.[4] It is exploitative. Thus, an appropriate name for the first theory of taxation is the Exploitative Theory. It is based on the premise that the government has some inherent right to exploit its most productive citizens. This premise, in turn, is based on what political scientists might call the Master-Servant theory of the state, where the state is the master and the taxpayers are the servants. According to this theory, the state can extract whatever it wants from its subjects, since they owe fealty to the state.

The second theory of taxation might be called the Nonexploitative Theory, since it is not based on exploitation. This theory begins with the premise that the government is the servant and the people are the masters. The purpose of taxation is to pay for services that the people want, and the people should pay in proportion to the benefit they receive.

In its pure form, such taxation would include only user fees, which is not really taxation at all, if one defines a tax as the extraction of money by force. With user fees, the people who use the service are the ones who pay for it. Those who do not use the service are not forced to pay for it.

Charging a fee for gaining access to a public park is an example of a user fee. So would charging a fee to enter a public museum or a public library. Gasoline taxes would also be included under this heading.

User fees and lotteries are the only truly "fair" ways to finance government, since they are the only ways to raise revenue that do not include the use of force. User fees and lotteries are completely voluntary forms of public finance.

The problem with voluntary forms of public finance is that they do not raise sufficient revenue to pay for the bloated welfare states that presently exist. Thus, there is a need to resort to coercive forms of public finance.

THE CASE FOR A MAXIMUM TAX

As long as politicians promise to give people something for nothing there will be a need to tax based on the Exploitation Theory of taxation. The problem inherent in such a system is that some people are forced to pay more than what they receive back in the form of government services. As a general rule, it might be said that poor people receive more in benefits from the tax system than what they pay into it and rich people receive less in services than what they pay in.

Leona Helmsley comes to mind as one example of a victim of the present Exploitation Theory of taxation. She paid about $100 million in taxes, yet went to jail because some court determined that she "owed" a few million dollars more than that.[5] Another example of a tax victim is Ross Perot. During one of the televised presidential debates, he said that he estimated that he paid about $1 billion in taxes over the years.

It is hard to imagine that Ross Perot or Leona Helmsley received services from the federal government that was even remotely equal to the amount of individual income taxes they were forced to pay. They were clearly exploited.

What I advocate is as follows. Let's establish some maximum tax beyond which nobody is forced to pay. If it can be determined that individuals do not receive more than, say, $20,000 in benefits from the federal government, let's establish a maximum tax that is some multiple of that amount. Ideally, the multiple should be one, since having a multiple of more than one would establish the legitimacy of exploitation.

However, since some people receive more than what they pay for and others receive less, as long as the tax system is not based exclusively on user fees and lottery revenue, some people will continue to be exploited by government. That being the case, let's limit the amount of exploitation to perhaps twice the benefits received. Thus, if no one (or almost no one) receives more than $20,000 in federal benefits, let's establish a maximum tax of $40,000 per year. If we can't raise enough revenue to cover the cost of government services with a multiple of two, let's cut costs and eliminate government programs until we can raise the revenue that is needed to finance the bloated welfare state with a multiple of two.

Establishing a maximum tax would result in more than just a decrease in exploitation and an increase in equity. It would also eliminate the need for many people and businesses to keep tax records. If they know their tax is going to be no more than $40,000, for example, people who have been paying substantially more than $40,000 would just send a check to the government and be done with it. They would not have to retain the services of high priced accountants and tax attorneys to minimize their tax bill. These tax professionals would then be free to use their talent and energy doing something to increase economic growth rather than squandering their time trying to reduce government exploitation of their clients.

A maximum tax would increase economic efficiency and equity. No one would be exploited by more than 100%, which is a reduction from the present levels of exploitation. It is not a perfect solution to exploitation but it is a step in the right direction.

NOTES

[1] Karl Marx, Critique of the Gotha Program (1875). The original wording was "Jeder nach seinen Fähigkeiten, jedem nach seinen Bedürfnissen." Louis Blanc, the French socialist, said basically the same thing in 1848. George Seldes, The Great Thoughts 274 (1985).

[2] I owe this example to Murray N. Rothbard but I can't remember quite where I read it.

[3] Walter J. Blum and Harry Kalven, Jr., The Uneasy Case for Progressive Taxation (1953); F.A. Hayek, The Case Against Progressive Income Taxes, Freeman 229-232 (1953).

[4] Some would say that utilitarianism is a kind of moral philosophy. If it is, it is defective, for at least two reasons. Its premise is based on the greatest good for the greatest number. It incorporates positive-game theory. One problem with the utilitarian approach is that it is not possible to measure gains and losses accurately enough to determine whether the gains exceed the losses. Another problem -- one might call it a fatal flaw -- is that utilitarianism completely ignores property rights. For more on this point, see Robert W. McGee, The Fatal Flaw in the Methodology of Law & Economics, Commentaries on Law & Economics 1: 209-223 (1997); Robert W. McGee, The Fatal Flaw in NAFTA, GATT and All Other Trade Agreements, Northwestern Journal of International Law & Business 14: 549-565 (1994).

[5] United States v. Helmsley, 941 F.2d 71 (2d Cir. 1991). Interestingly enough, she actually received a refund because she paid too much tax. The reason she went to jail was because she submitted a fraudulent tax return.

Chapter 15

SECESSION AS A TOOL OF PUBLIC FINANCE

INTRODUCTION

Politicians have always found it easier to spend money than to raise it. That accounts for the fact that the federal government of the United States has not been able to balance its budget more than a few times in the last two or three generations. But the problem of overspending is not confined to the federal level. Governments at all levels have problems restraining their spending habits and being responsive to the needs of the people.

Americans are paying a higher percentage of their incomes in taxes now than ever before, and many of them feel that they are not getting their moneysworth.[1] Some measures, such as balanced budget amendments,[2] line-item veto authority,[3] term limitations[4] and sunset laws,[5] act as brakes on government spending and unresponsiveness, and many articles and books have been written about these tools as means that can be used to curb government spending and make it more responsive.[6]

The right to secede can also be used to restrain government spending and make politicians more responsive to the needs of their constituency, but this option has all but been ignored in the literature. The purpose of this chapter is to help fill that gap, or at least to start a discussion on the possibilities. We begin with a philosophical discussion of the theory of secession and conclude that secession is always justified at any level, at least theoretically, on philosophical grounds. We then apply the Kendall and Louw model of secession to states and municipalities in the United States. Finally, we conclude that secession should be considered a viable option and should be added to the toolbox of constitutional provisions that can be used to restrain government spending and make political leaders more responsive.

THE THEORY OF SECESSION

Philosophical Foundations

Secession involves the right of individuals to divorce themselves from their present political affiliation and either form a new affiliation or merge with another existing political entity. The right to secede has been a part of our political philosophy for hundreds of years.[7] Once the idea of the divine right of kings was scrapped, people began to realize that government exists for the benefit of people, not the other way around. If and when the government no longer has the support of the people, they have the right to change it. Democratically elected officials can be changed in countries where voters have the power to vote. But being able to choose elected officials does not mean that the right to secede no longer exists. It is still a viable option,[8] especially when the politicians who get elected represent special interests rather than the interests of the people who elected them, as is quite often the case in the present day United States.

The Declaration of Independence is the American political document that outlines this right most clearly.

> We hold these truths to be self evident, that all men are created equal; that they are endowed by their Creator with certain unalienable rights; and that among these, are life, liberty, and the pursuit of happiness. That to secure these rights, governments are instituted among men, deriving their just powers from the consent of the governed; that whenever any form of government becomes destructive of these ends, it is the right of the people to alter or to abolish it, and to institute a new government, laying its foundation on such principles, and organizing its powers in such form, to effect their safety and happiness ... when a long train of abuses and usurpations, pursuing invariably the same object, evinces a design to reduce them under absolute despotism, it is their right, it is their duty, to throw off such government, and to provide new guards for their future security.

In other words, whenever the government does not have the support of the people, it is no longer legitimate and the people have the right to replace it with something that is more to their liking. In a sense, then, no government is totally legitimate because the percentage of citizens who support their government is never 100% but always something less. But just because a government is not totally legitimate is not necessarily sufficient reason to replace it because the new government formed may be no better than the one that was abolished. Also, there is the transaction cost aspect of it, to use an economic term. The amount of effort expended to replace the existing government may not be worth the benefit received. So, as a practical matter, people choose not to replace their government with every whim. But if the government becomes abhorrent to a large enough percentage of the population, secession is one possible remedy.

While the most clear-cut support for the right of secession appears in the Declaration of Independence, some commentators have also read the Tenth Amendment to include the right to secede.[9]

> The right of secession is not something ... outside of and antagonistic to the Constitution ... So far from being against

> the Constitution or incompatible with it, we contend that, if the right to secede is not prohibited to the States, and no power to prevent it expressly delegated to the United States, it remains as reserved to the States or the people, from whom all the powers of the General Government were derived.[10]

Abraham Lincoln also believed in the right to secede at one time, although he later changed his mind.

> Any people anywhere being inclined and having the power have the right to rise up and shake off the existing government, and form a new one which suits them better. This is a most valuable, a most sacred right -- a right which we hope and believe is to liberate the world. Nor is this right confined to cases in which the whole people of an existing government may choose to exercise it. Any portion of such people than can may revolutionize and make their own so much of the territory as they inhabit.[11]

This view differs markedly from the one he took years later. In his first inaugural speech, Lincoln said:

> I hold that, in contemplation of universal law and of the Constitution, the Union of these States is perpetual. Perpetuity is implied, if not expressed, in the fundamental law of all national governments. It is safe to assert that no government proper ever had a provision in its organic law for its own termination. Continue to execute all the express provisions of our National Constitution, and the Union will endure forever -- it being impossible to destroy it except by some action not provided for in the instrument itself.[12]

The right to self-determination is also recognized in international law. For example, the United Nations Charter supports the right of self-determination and secession in several places,[13] as do other United Nations documents.

> [1] By virtue of the principle of equal rights and self-determination of peoples enshrined in the Charter of the United Nations, all peoples have the right freely to determine, without external interference, their political status and to pursue their economic, social and cultural development, and every State has the duty to respect this right ...
>
> [2] Every State has the duty to promote, through joint and separate action, realization of the principle of equal rights and self-determination of peoples...

> [4] The establishment of a sovereign and independent State, the free association or integration with an independent State or the emergence into any other political status freely determined by a people constitute modes of implementing the right of self-determination by that people ...
>
> [5] Every State has the duty to refrain from any forcible actions which deprives peoples ... of their right to self-determination and freedom and independence...[14]

There are many forms of secession. Theoretically, any political unit of any size can secede from another political unit to which it is attached. But the kind most Americans are familiar with is the case where a state, or a group of states, tries to secede from a larger group of states, as was the case during the American Civil War (1861-65).[15] This very costly war could have been prevented if the right to secede had been an explicit part of the Constitution.[16] Some scholars believe that the right to secede was not an explicit part of the Constitution because the right was assumed, just like the right to free speech and press.[17]

While the kind of secession we are most familiar with involves the case of a section of one nation wanting to split and form a new nation, such as India and Pakistan or Quebec and Canada, a number of other possibilities also exist.[18] A section of one country may want to secede and become part of another country.

For example, some Canadian provinces that border the United States, such as British Columbia, Alberta, Saskatchewan, Manitoba, Ontario or New Brunswick, may want to become part of the United States because of the perception that the Canadian central government is giving them a raw deal. Or some Muslim republics in the former Soviet Union may want to join a neighboring Muslim country such as Turkey or Iran. Or perhaps the Kurds living in Iran, Iraq, Syria, Turkey and the former Soviet Union might want to form their own sovereign state.[19] Latvia,[20] Lithuania,[21] or any of the former Soviet Republics[22] should be able to secede and form their own sovereign nations if they want to.

If we begin with the premise that all groups have a right to the government of their choice, there should be no philosophical problem preventing these groups from forming a government that is more responsive to their needs. However, all parties to the *new* regime must agree. If Manitoba wants to become part of the United States, both the citizens of Manitoba and the United States must agree. But if Quebec wants to leave Canada and form its own sovereign nation, the government of Canada need not be consulted because it has no right to keep the province of Quebec if it wants to leave.

Seceding to either form a new country or joining with a contiguous country is the usual path secession takes. But there is nothing wrong with seceding and joining with another political entity that is not adjacent. For example, East and West Pakistan could be a single country, although separated by hundreds of miles of India.

The cases of Alaska and Hawaii present interesting examples. Alaska is actually much closer to Russia than it is to the continental United States, and is separated from the other states by hundreds of miles of Canada. Yet it is one of the 50 states. Hawaii is separated from the mainland by thousands of miles of ocean, yet it is fully integrated into the American political system. Would it make any difference if Hawaii were separated from California by land rather than water? There is no reason why France and Quebec could not merge to form a single country if they wanted to. Or Belgium and Scotland. Geographic location does not seem to be an insurmountable obstacle, as long as people and goods can move freely.

Secession of Political Sub-Units

Most treatises on secession address questions of secession at the national level. But secession at lower levels may also be justified on philosophical grounds. Whenever a group of individuals does not support the present government, they have several options. They can attempt to vote in a new group of leaders. They can resign themselves to living under the present government. They can move. Or they can secede. Once the right of secession is recognized, there is no logical stopping point. Theoretically, secession can take place at the individual level -- the anarchist position.[23] Murray Rothbard's view is as follows:

> ... would a laissez-fairist recognize the right of a region of a country to *secede* from that country? Is it legitimate for West Ruritania to secede from Ruritania? If not, why not? And if so, then how can there be a logical stopping-point to the secession? May not a small district secede, and then a city, and then a borough of that city, and then a block, and then finally a particular individual? Once admit *any* right of secession whatever, and there is no logical stopping-point short of the right of *individual* secession, which logically entails anarchism, since then individuals may secede and patronize their own defense agencies, and the State has crumbled.[24]

Ludwig von Mises would not go quite as far as Rothbard, for technical reasons.

> The right of self-determination in regard to the question of membership in a state thus means: whenever the inhabitants of a particular territory, whether it be a single village, a whole district, or a series of adjacent districts, make it known, by a freely conducted plebiscite, that they no longer wish to remain united to the state to which they belong at the time, but wish either to form an independent state or to attach themselves to some other state, their wishes are to be respected and complied with. This is the only feasible and effective way of preventing revolutions and civil and international wars.
>
> ... It is not the right of self-determination of a delimited national unit, but the right of the inhabitants of every territory to decide on the state to which they wish to belong.
>
> ... However, the right of self-determination of which we speak is not the right of self-determination of nations, but rather the right of self-determination of the inhabitants of every territory large enough to form an independent administrative unit. If it were in any way possible to grant this right of self-determination to every individual person, it would have to be done. This is impracticable only because of compelling technical considerations, which make it necessary that a region be governed as a single administrative unit and that the right of self-determination be restricted to the will of the majority of the inhabitants of areas large enough to count as territorial units in the administration of the country.[25]

Philosophically, if we believe that government receives its legitimacy from the consent of the governed, then secession can be justified at the individual level. If an individual does not want the services of government, then why should he or she have to pay for it?

> Singly, or in coalitions of any size, persons would be allowed to withdraw simultaneously from both the tax and benefits sides of the fiscal account, which would require that they provide *all* public services, including legal order, on their own. Such an internal exit option is a meaningful addition to the set of liberties normally considered, and a society in which this equal liberty of secession exists clearly is superior ... to a society where this liberty does not exist.[26]

Unfortunately, most people don't see things that way, so individuals who do not support their government will just have to make the best of an imperfect situation. But just because secession at the individual level is not viable for the moment does not mean that we should not consider the possibility of secession at the sub-national level, since secession can be used to make government more responsive to the needs of the governed.

If part of a state wants to secede and form a new state, why should it not be able to do so? Some western counties of Virginia seceded from Virginia during the War Between the States and formed a new state -- West Virginia. If residents of northern California want to break away from California or if southern New Jersey wants to break away from New Jersey, there is no good reason why they should not be allowed to do so.

Staten Island, et al.

If part of a county or city wants to secede and either form a new political unit or merge with an existing political unit, there is no justification for not allowing the residents of that political unit to secede. The case of Staten Island, one of the five boroughs of New York City, is an example.[27] Staten Island residents felt they are being shortchanged by being part of New York City and many of them wanted to secede and form an independent City of Staten Island.[28]

A study showed that an independent City of Staten Island could be fiscally independent.[29] The study projected a 3% budget surplus in the first year,[30] which would be sufficient to eliminate the corporate and bank taxes that New York City presently levies on local businesses, or reduce the local sales tax by one cent or lower property taxes by 10%.[31] Or it could hire about 500 extra police, firemen or teachers.[32]

One method proposed to effectuate the secession was the constitutional amendment route.[33]

> The New York State Constitution can be amended so as to free Staten Island from New York City by the passage in both houses of the Legislature, at two separately elected legislative sessions, of a proposed constitutional amendment. The New York State Constitution provides that upon such passage, the proposed amendment must be submitted to the people (of the entire state) for approval. (Article XIX §1 New York State Constitution) If approved, such amendment shall become a part of the Constitution on the first day of January next after such approval. This procedure does not require the Governor's approval, nor does it require an act of the City Council or Mayor.[34]

New York State Senator Marchi introduced legislation[35] that would allow Staten Island to become an independent city and the Senate actually passed the bill, but it never became law.[36] New York City's mayor opposed the secession move because:

> New York City has been a five-county federation since 1898. Each borough makes a unique contribution to the development and continued success of the City of New York.[37]

Such a statement gives no good reason at all why a dissatisfied segment of a political unit should not be able to leave and form a new political unit that is more to its liking. It is like a plantation owner telling his slaves that they cannot leave because their ancestors have worked his plantation for three generations and they make a unique contribution to the development and continued success of his plantation. If Staten Island wants to secede, it should be able to, and New York City should not be able to prevent or delay the change, just as a plantation owner should not be able to prevent or delay the retreat of his slaves if they no longer want to be a part of the plantation. Secession is a matter of right, not something that people have to ask permission for.[38]

Staten Island is only one of any number of examples that could be cited where one political entity wants to secede and either form a new entity or merge with an existing entity. Some residents of Greenburgh in Westchester County, New York threatened to secede because they did not want a housing project that was scheduled to be built for the homeless.[39] Residents of Mount Olive Township, New Jersey wanted to secede from Warren County to protest a landfill scheduled for their town.[40]

In another New Jersey case, some residents of Essex County wanted to break away and become part of the neighboring Morris County. The desire to secede arose because the welfare system in the city of Newark (located in Essex County) did not have sufficient funds to pay for all the promises that had been made by the Newark politicians. A tax increase was needed, so a property tax increase was assessed on the citizens of Essex County, which included many affluent homeowners in the suburbs who could not vote in the Newark city elections. In many cases, their annual property taxes increased by more than $1,000, which caused a storm of controversy.[41] At least one Essex County politician who advocated the increase was voted out of office at the next election, but the tax increase was not repealed. Had these disgruntled taxpayers been able to join Morris County, they could have avoided being exploited by the Newark politicians who did not represent their interests.

Los Angeles

Los Angeles is spread over 470 square miles.[42] It occupies a geographic mass that is ten times as large as San Francisco.[43] It has nearly five times as many people.[44] In the last hundred years, it has expanded enough to swallow Cleveland, St. Louis, Milwaukee, Minneapolis, Boston, San Francisco, Pittsburgh and Manhattan.[45] Some LA residents think that LA has become too big and unmanageable.[46]

Several sections of Los Angeles would like to secede and become separate cities. Support for secession of the San Fernando Valley has been building since 1915, when LA officials forced it to become part of LA in exchange for cheap water.[47] Secession moves during the 1960s and 1970s were quashed by California state laws,[48] but the secession movement is now more alive and aggressive than ever.

During the November 2002 election, the issue was actually placed on the ballot and defeated narrowly. The vote on secession for the San Fernando Valley would have succeeded if California would have adopted my secession proposals. If the secession vote would have succeeded, the San Fernando Valley, one of the seceding entities, would have become the sixth largest city in the United States, with a population of 1.3 million,[49] about the same size as Phoenix.[50] The secession would have caused Los Angeles to become the third largest city, behind New York and Chicago.[51] It now has the second largest population in the United States.[52]

The San Fernando Valley[53] and Hollywood,[54] both of which are neighborhoods of Los Angeles, wanted to secede because of the perception that they were not getting their fair share of services.[55] They were paying in a great deal in taxes but their money was being spent in the inner city or in other parts of the city. Business owners are complaining about the level of city business fees and gross receipts taxes[56] they have to pay. They also want more police presence, especially in shopping malls.[57]

There is some evidence to support this claim. In the two years leading up to the secession vote, Valley taxpayers subsidized the rest of the city by $124 million.[58] They paid out 6.3 percent more than what they got back in services.[59] At least one study has estimated that the San Fernando Valley could provide superior services for about 25 percent less than what residents now pay in taxes.[60]

Per capita police coverage in Los Angeles is nearly twice what it is in the Valley.[61] Only $4 million of the $28 million that Los Angeles spends repairing streets is spent in the Valley.[62] That is 14 percent, compared to the Valley's one-third plus percentage of the total population. Only one of the city's 34 museums is in the Valley.[63] The Valley has nine libraries per hundred square miles, compared to 18 for the rest of the city.[64] The Valley also does not have as many bus and mass transit lines or parks as other parts of the city.[65]

There is also a question of quality. The buses in nearby Santa Monica cost 50 cents, are clean and run every 15 or 20 minutes. The MTA in Los Angeles charges three times as much and provides much poorer service.[66]

It seems like the disgruntled sections of Los Angeles might be better off as part of a different political entity. They would have more control over how government services are provided and they could have it done at lower cost. Secession would allow them to improve their lives and would also send a message to the politicians in Los Angeles that if they did not do a better job of providing services, other parts of the city could also secede.

SECESSION AS A TOOL TO RESTRAIN GOVERNMENT EXCESSES

Balanced budget amendments, line-item vetoes and term limitations can be used as tools to restrain government excesses.[67] So can the threat of secession. If politicians know that a portion of their constituency can leave, they will be less likely to try to exploit them or to neglect their needs. But more importantly, citizens will have a choice. They will no longer have to pick up and move if they do not like their local, county or state government. They will be able to change their political affiliation by seceding, just like West Virginia did during the War Between the States.

One method of entrenching this right is by constitutional amendment. The amendment should be clearly worded, so that the procedures for secession are clear. And it should be unilateral -- the segment seceding should not have to ask anyone's permission. An amendment to the United States Constitution should give a segment of one state the opportunity to secede and join with another state,[68] and the various state constitutions should have a provision that allows one political sub-unit to secede and either form a new sub-unit or merge with an existing sub-unit. Kendall and Louw,[69] two South African political theorists, have proposed such a solution for post-apartheid South Africa. Article XVII of their Model Bill of Rights states:

> Every canton and every part of a canton may, by referendum, as provided in the Constitution, break away from or amalgamate with any other canton.[70]

The relevant part of Article IV, which deals with referendums, states:

> No canton boundary may be changed, including splitting from or amalgamating with another canton, unless approved by a majority of all the registered voters directly affected thereby. If a part of a canton wishes to split from an existing canton, the citizens in the remainder shall not have a vote in the referendum. But if that part is to amalgamate with or be incorporated into another canton, all the citizens of the latter shall be entitled to vote in a separate referendum.[71]

Thus, if a political sub-unit wants to break away and form its own state (canton), it may do so without the permission of the state it plans to leave. But if the political sub-unit of one state wants to become part of another state, both groups must approve, just like in a marriage.

How would this work in practice? Let's take the case of New York. New York State residents pay higher taxes than the residents of any other state.[72] It is bordered by Vermont, Massachusetts, Connecticut, New Jersey and Pennsylvania, as well as Canada. New Hampshire, which has no state income tax, is only a few miles away, separated from New York by a few miles of Vermont.

If the U.S. Constitution had a provision allowing New York State's political sub-units to secede and join neighboring states, it is conceivable that some counties, cities and townships in New York would decide to become part of another state. This is especially true of upstate New York residents,[73] who feel that all their tax money is going to support the transportation, education and welfare systems of New York City. And there is no reason why some New York counties would not be able to become part of New Hampshire, since the two states are separated by only a few miles of Vermont. Rensselaer County New York (and the city of Troy) is much closer to New Hampshire than they are to Chautauqua County, New York, which is on the extreme western end of the state. The fact that Rensselaer County New York and New Hampshire are not contiguous should be prevent them from merging if both sides want to merge. After all, Hawaii and California are part of the same political unit, although they are separated by thousands of miles of ocean.

The effect that such a constitutional provision would have on the politicians of New York State would be tremendous. If New York did not offer its residents a better deal than the neighboring states, New York could shrink rapidly -- and its (former) citizens would be better off. Counties bordering Vermont could merge with Vermont, and the same thing could happen with counties bordering New Jersey, Pennsylvania, Connecticut and Massachusetts. Citizens would have a choice. They would no longer have to either move or put up with the politicians in Albany, who may not represent their interests. They could keep their homes and jobs and vote to become part of a neighboring (or distant) political entity that better meets their needs. In economic terms, one would say that the situation has changed from one of monopoly[74] to one of oligopoly.[75]

Where is the cut-off point? What is the smallest political unit that can secede? All government derives its legitimacy from the consent of the governed; if they do not consent, the government is not legitimate. "No people and no part of a people shall be held against its will in a political association that it does not want."[76] Theoretically, the smallest unit that can secede is an individual. Any other answer results in injustice to anyone who is forced to be part of a political affiliation he or she does not want to be a part of. But, unfortunately, the chances of passing a constitutional amendment allowing an individual to secede are slim, at least for the near future. However, Kendall and Louw have found a partial solution to this dilemma that would minimize the amount of injustice that results by not allowing individuals to secede. Their Model Bill of Rights. Article VI (iv) states that:

> Any landowner or group of landowners whose land is on a boundary between cantons may opt at any time for the boundary to be adjusted so as to place such land under the jurisdiction of a neighboring canton subject to the agreement of that canton.[77]

Thus, it is possible for a political unit as small as an individual to secede, as long as the individual lives on the border between cantons -- or states, cities, townships, etc. -- and obtains the other political entity's permission to join. However, the individual still is not free to secede and form his or her own country or join a contiguous country. So the Kendall and Louw solution goes farther than that advocated by Mises,[78] but not quite as far as that of Rothbard.[79] The Kendall and Louw approach provides more choice than that advocated by Mises, since Mises would stop short of advocating secession at the individual level.[80]

Allowing individuals to secede and join another city, county or state could lead to some interesting results. For example, if some businesses on the New York City side of the Hudson River felt they were being overtaxed, they could decide to secede and become part of New Jersey, where taxes are lower. Thus, their property would become within the borders of New Jersey. Once they became part of New Jersey, their neighbors' property would be on the New Jersey border, and they would have the same option -- to become part of New Jersey. It is not inconceivable that all the Broadway theaters in New York City could become part of New Jersey in a very short time, since they are all on the west side of New York, just a few blocks from the Hudson River. Theater owners would benefit by the move because their property and income tax bills would be cut. But New York residents would also benefit because the theaters would be able to charge (lower) New Jersey sales taxes on the tickets they sell.

Secession might be able to do what balanced budget amendments and other tax limitation strategies have not been able to do. Secession could be another arrow in the taxpayer's quiver to restrain government excesses and offer protection against excessive taxes.

CONCLUSION

Secession is a right that should be incorporated into the federal and state constitutions. It is an additional tool that can be used to place restraints on government excesses at all levels. If a group of individuals would rather be a part of a different political entity than the one to which they are currently a part, they have an inalienable right to form a political entity that is more to their liking, or to join with an already existing political entity. It is not a matter of permission. It is a matter of right. And there is no theoretical reason why the size of the seceding group cannot be as small as a single individual, although there may be some technical difficulties involved when the entity seceding is this small.

NOTES

1 The Tax Foundation conducts studies every year to calculate Tax Freedom Day, the day when U.S. taxpayers can start working for themselves. The premise is that people work for the government first, and start working for themselves only after they have satisfied their annual tax liability. If the annual tax liability is one-third of income, then Tax Freedom Day comes around the first of May. Most recent estimates have placed Tax Freedom Day sometime in May for people in most states and perhaps in early June for people who live in high tax states. Tax Freedom Day comes even later in some European countries.

2 See Article III Problems in Enforcing the Balanced Budget Amendment, Columbia Law Review 83: 1065-1107 (1983); David Dreier and William Craig Stubblebine, The Balanced Budget/Tax Limitation Amendment, Hastings Constitutional Law Quarterly 10: 809-819 (1983); E. Donald Elliott, Constitutional Conventions and the Deficit, Duke Law Journal 1077-1110 (1985); Gale Ann Norton, The Limitless Federal Taxing Power, Harvard Journal of Law & Public Policy 8: 591-625 (1985); Note, The Balanced Budget Amendment: An Inquiry Into Appropriateness, Harvard Law Review 96: 1600-1620 (1983); Note, "The Monster Approaching the Capital:" The Effort To Write Economic Policy Into the United States Constitution, Akron Law Review 15: 733-751 (1982); Note, The Proposed Federal Balanced Budget Amendment: The Lesson from State Experience, Cincinnati Law Review 55: 563-583 (1986); Peter W. Rodino, Jr., The Proposed Balanced Budget/Tax Limitation Constitutional Amendment: No Balance, No Limits, Hastings Constitutional Law Quarterly 10: 785-807 (1983).

3 See Constitutional Law -- The Governor's Item Veto Power, Missouri Law Review 39: 105-110 (1974); The Constitutionality of a Line-Item Veto: A Comparison With Other Exercises of Executive Discretion Not To Spend, Golden Gate University Law Review 19: 305-345 (1989); Louis Fisher and Neal Devins, How Successfully Can the States' Item Veto be Transferred to the President? Georgia Law Journal 75: 159-197 (1986); Eugene Gressman, Is the Item Veto Constitutional? North Carolina Law Review 64: 819-23 (1986); Arthur J. Harrington, The Propriety of the Negative -- The Governor's Partial Veto Authority, Marquette Law Review 60: 865-89 (1977); The Item Veto Power in Washington, Washington Law Review 64: 891-912 (1989); David Schoenbrod, Presidential Lawmaking Powers: Vetoes, Line Item Vetoes, Signing Statements, Executive Orders, and Delegations of Rulemaking Authority, Washington University Law Quarterly 68:533-60 (1990); Glen O. Robinson, Public Choice Speculations on the Item Veto, Virginia Law Review 74: 403-22 (1988); J. Gregory Sidak and Thomas A. Smith, Four Faces of the Item Veto: A Reply To Tribe and Kurland, Northwestern University Law Review 84: 437-79 (1990); Washington's Partial Veto Power: Judicial Construction of Article III, Section 12, University of Puget Sound Law Review 10: 699-720 (1987); The Wisconsin Partial Veto: Past, Present and Future, Wisconsin Law Review 1395-1432 (1989).

4 Ronald D. Elving, Congress Braces for Fallout From State Measures, Congressional Quarterly 3144-6 (September 29, 1990); John H. Fund, Term Limitation: An Idea Whose Time Has Come, 141 Policy Analysis (Cato, Oct. 30, 1990); Janet Hook, New Drive to Limit Tenure Revives an Old Proposal, Congressional Quarterly 567-9 (February 24, 1990); Albert R. Hunt, Congress's Terms: Just Fine As They Are, The Wall Street Journal, Apr. 24, 1990, at

A-18, col. 3; Charles R. Kesler, Bad Housekeeping: The Case Against Congressional Term Limitations, Policy. Review 20-25 (Summer 1990); John R. Lott, Jr. and W. Robert Reed, Shirking and Sorting in a Political Market With Finite-Lived Politicians, Public Choice 61: 75-96 (1989); Cleta Deatherage Mitchell, Insider Tales of an Honorable Ex-Legislator, The Wall Street Journal, Oct. 11, 1990, at A-14; Neal R. Peirce, Zeroing in on 'Permanent Incumbency,' National Journal, Oct. 6, 1990; Mark P. Petracca, The Poison of Professional Politics, 151 Policy Analysis (Cato, May 10, 1991); Robert Reinhold, Voters Propose to Put a Lid on Their Representatives, The New York Times, Apr. 29, 1990, at 4E, col. 1; David Shribman, Drive to Restrict Tenure in Congress to 12 Years Is Pressed in Capital and One-Third of the States, The Wall Street Journal, March 12, 1990, at A-12, col. 1; The Term Limit Train, The Wall Street Journal, Oct. 11, 1990, at A-14; Terms of Limitation, The Wall Street Journal, Dec. 11, 1989, at A-14.

[5] Robert D. Behn, The False Dawn of the Sunset Laws, Public Interest, 103-18 (Fall 1977); Sunset Act of 1980: Report of the Committee on Governmental Affairs, United States Senate, to accompany S. 2, To Require Authorizations of New Budget Authority for Government Programs at Least Every Ten Years, To Provide for Review of Government Programs Every Ten Years, and for Other Purposes, July 24, 1980 (Report No. 96-865); A Compilation of State Sunset Statutes with Background Information on State Sunset Laws, A Staff Report prepared for the Committee on Rules, U.S. House of Representatives, by the Subcommittee on the Legislative Process, October, 1983.

[6] Much has also been written about the dangers inherent in holding a constitutional convention and about the various ways that amendments may be made to a constitution. However, those issues will not be discussed in this chapter. See Article III Problems in Enforcing the Balanced Budget Amendment, Columbia Law Review 83:1065-1107 (1983); Arthur J. Goldberg, The Proposed Constitutional Convention, Hastings Constitutional Law Quarterly 11: 1-4 (Fall 1983); James L. Gattuso, Amending the Constitution by the Convention Method, State Backgrounder (Heritage Foundation April 19, 1988); Francis H. Heller, Limiting a Constitutional Convention: The State Precedents, Cardozo Law Review 3: 563-79 (1982); Thomas H. Kean, A Constitutional Convention Would Threaten the Rights We Have Cherished for 200 Years, Detroit College of Law Review 4: 1087-91 (1986); Cal Ledbetter, Jr., The Constitutional Convention of 1975 And Some Remaining Constitutional Problems, Arkansas Law Review 29: 199-214 (1975); Robert M. Rhodes, A Limited Federal Constitutional Convention, University of Florida Law Review 26: 1-18 (1973).

[7] For background, see Lee C. Buchheit, Secession: The Legitimacy of Self-Determination, New Haven and London: Yale University Press, 1978. For discussions of secession movements in various developing and developed countries, see Viva Ona Bartkus, The Dynamic of Secession, Cambridge University Press, 1999; Leopold Kohr, The Breakdown of Nations, London and New York: Routledge & Kegan Paul, 1957 & 1986; Allen Buchanan, Secession: The Morality of Political Divorce from Fort Sumter to Lithuania and Quebec, Boulder, CO and Oxford: Westview Press, 1991; David Gordon, editor, Secession, State & Liberty, New Brunswick, NJ and London: Transaction Publishers, 1998.

[8] Problems can arise when a substantial segment of the population wants things to remain as they are, as is the case in Northern Ireland. Many people there want to remain a part of Great Britain, but many others want to unite with Southern Ireland, and both sides are willing to fight and die for their cause. Many people in Southern Ireland would also like to see the North become part of Ireland. For a discussion of the Irish question, see Richard J. Harvey, The Right of the People of the Whole of Ireland to Self-Determination, Unity, Sovereignty and Independence, New York Law School Journal of International and Comparative Law 11: 167-206 (1990). The Palestinian question presents another problem, since the Palestinian and Jewish populations are mixed and the government in the State of Israel (or is it occupied Palestine?) is making a major effort to populate Gaza and the West Bank. For more on the Palestinian question, see "Measuring Up": Do the Palestinian Homelands Constitute a Valid State Under International Law? Dickinson Journal of International Law 8: 339-48 (Winter

1990); J. Quigley, Palestine's Declaration of Independence: Self-Determination and the Right of the Palestinians to Statehood, Boston University International Law Journal 7: 1-33 (Spring 1989); Self-Determination: the Case of Palestine, Am. Soc'y. Int'l. L. Proc.: 334-51 (1988).

[9] The Tenth Amendment states: "The powers not delegated to the United States by the Constitution, nor prohibited by it to the States, are reserved to the States respectively, or to the people."

[10] Jefferson Davis, The Rise and Fall of the Confederate Government 168 (1958), cited in H. Newcomb Morse, The Foundations and Meaning of Secession, Stetson Law Review 15: 419-433 (1986) at 424.

[11] This passage is taken from Abraham Lincoln's "If you can secede you may" (Mexico) speech. The Speeches of Abraham Lincoln (1908) cited in Rupert Emerson, From Empire to Nation 450 (1967).

[12] 1 Abraham Lincoln, The War Years 128 (Carl Sandburg ed. 1939). What would North America be like today if Lincoln had not changed his mind on the idea of secession?

[13] U. N. Charter, art. 1, para. 2 and art. 55.

[14] Declaration on Principles of International Law concerning Friendly Relations and Co-operation among States in accordance with the Charter of the United Nations, G.A. Res. 2625, Annex, 25 U. N. GAOR, Supp. 28, at 121, U.N. Doc. A/5217 (1970). Cited in Buchheit, supra, at 247-8.

[15] I hesitate to use the term "Civil War" because "the War Between the States" is more appropriate. By using the term "civil war," one might assume that the war took place between different states that were part of the same nation. But in the case of the American conflict that took place between 1861 and 1865, the Confederate States were a separate nation, if we believe that all government derives its legitimacy from the consent of the governed. Since the government of the United States was deemed by the majority of the population in the Confederate States to be illegitimate based on this standard, we must logically conclude that the Confederacy was legally a separate country.

[16] More than a half million American lives were lost in the war between the states, which was more than either World War II (400,000) or World War I (117,000). The 1987 Information Please Almanac 308 (1986).

[17] See Forrest McDonald, Novus Ordo Seclorum: The Intellectual Origins of the Constitution, Lawrence, KS: University Press of Kansas,1985, p. 281; Gottfried Dietze, The Federalist: A Classic of Federalism and Free Government, Baltimore: Johns Hopkins University Press, 1960, p. 283.

[18] See John R. Wood, Secession: A Comparative Analytical Framework, Canadian Journal of Political Science 14: 107-34 (1981).

[19] Buchheit, supra, discusses the Kurd situation at 153-62.

[20] Latvia Is an Independent, Democratic Republic, The Wall Street Journal, May 5, 1990, at A-14, col. 3.

[21] Lithuania on brink of leaving U.S.S.R.: It's only a question of how and when, The (Bergen County, New Jersey) Record, Feb. 25, 1990, at A-20, col. 1; Bill Keller, Can Gorbachev Stay On if Lithuania Chooses to Leave? The New York Times, Jan. 14, 1990, at E-3, col. 1; Top-level plea for Soviet unity, The (Bergen County, New Jersey) Record, Jan. 13, 1990, at A-5, col. 4.

[22] Soviet Decolonization, The Wall Street Journal, Jan. 3, 1990, at A-6, col. 1; Gorbachev's turbulent south, The Economist, Jan. 13, 1990, at 45; Gorbachev's bolshie republics, The Economist, Jan. 13, 1990, at 13-4.

[23] I am not rejecting the idea of anarchism, since no other logical conclusion is possible once the right of secession is recognized. If groups have the right to secede, then so do individuals, since groups cannot possess any rights that individuals do not possess. But this is one instance where pure theory may have to be sacrificed for practical considerations, at least for the present, until more individuals accept the idea of anarchism as a possibility. Part of the problem most people have with accepting anarchism is their (incorrect) perception that the

absence of government means chaos. But such is not necessarily the case. Government is one thing; society is another. Society can exist without government and society can provide order. See Terry L. Anderson and P.J. Hill, An American Experiment in Anarcho-Capitalism: The Not So Wild, Wild West, Journal of Libertarian Studies 3: 9-29 (1979); Bruce L. Benson, The Enterprise of Law: Justice Without the State, San Francisco: Pacific Research Institute, 1990; Bruce L. Benson, Enforcement of Private Property Rights in Primitive Societies: Law without Government, Journal of Libertarian Studies 9: 1-26 (Winter 1989).

[24] Murray N. Rothbard, The Ethics of Liberty, New York and London: New York University Press, 1998, p. 181.

[25] Ludwig von Mises, Liberalism, Irvington-on-Hudson, NY: Foundation for Economic Education and San Francisco: Cobden Press, 109-110 (3rd ed. 1985). Also published as The Free and Prosperous Commonwealth, Princeton, NJ: Van Nostrand, 1962. First published in German as Liberalismus (1927).

[26] James M. Buchanan, Liberty, Market and State: Political Economy in the 1980s, New York: New York University Press, 1986, p. 170. Chapter 15 of this book, from which this quote was taken, first appeared in the Scandinavian Journal of Economics 86: 102-14 (1984).

[27] Elizabeth Kolbert, Staten Island Is Voting, but It's Only a Sitcom Secession, The New York Times, March 11, 1990, at 22E, col. 1.

[28] According to one poll, 96% of Staten Islanders want to secede from New York City. See Remedies of a Proud Outcast: The Legal Probability and Implications of Restructuring the Government and Boundaries of the City of New York, A New York State Senate Finance Committee Staff Report, July, 1983, at 3, citing The New York Post, July 21, 1983 and S.I. Advance, July 8, 1983, at 1. Hereinafter referred to as Remedies of a Proud Outcast.

[29] Remedies of a Proud Outcast, supra at Appendix A, 20.

[30] Id.

[31] Id.

[32] Id.

[33] Other methods were State legislative action, see Remedies of a Proud Outcast, supra, at 19-20, or a New York City Charter revision, id., at 21-2.

[34] Remedies of a Proud Outcast, supra, at 23.

[35] S. 2341, 1989-90 N.Y. Reg. Sess. (February 15, 1989).

[36] Kolbert, supra

[37] Memorandum in Opposition, issued by James Brenner, Legislative Representative, City of New York, Office of the Mayor, March 29, 1989.

[38] Admittedly, the analogy of slaves and a plantation owner is somewhat different than that of Staten Island residents and New York City. The plantation owner owns the land, so the slaves would have to vacate the premises, whereas Staten Island residents would not have to pick up stakes and move because they already own or rent the land they are on.

[39] Kolbert, supra.

[40] Id.

[41] This statistic is based on television news reports.

[42] Geoffrey F. Segal and Samuel R. Staley, City of Angels, Valley of Rebels, Cato Policy Report, Vol. XXXIV, No. 5, September/October, 2002, pp. 1, 12-14, at 12.

[43] Paul Wilborn, Los Angeles Has Become Too Big, Say Those Who Want to Break It Up, Associated Press, November 2, 2002, available at www.sfgate.com.

[44] Ibid.

[45] Geoffrey F. Segal and Samuel R. Staley, City of Angels, Valley of Rebels, Cato Policy Report, Vol. XXXIV, No. 5, September/October, 2002, pp. 1, 12-14, at 12.

[46] Paul Wilborn, Los Angeles Has Become Too Big, Say Those Who Want to Break It Up, Associated Press, November 2, 2002, available at www.sfgate.com.

[47] Geoffrey F. Segal and Samuel R. Staley, City of Angels, Valley of Rebels, Cato Policy Report, Vol. XXXIV, No. 5, September/October, 2002, pp. 1, 12-14, at 12.

[48] Paul Wilborn, Los Angeles Secession Efforts Getting Closer to Winning Spots on the Ballot, Associated Press, May 19, 2002. www.sfgate.com.
[49] Most news reports cite 1.3 million as the population of the San Fernando Valley. However, other estimates have been given. For example, Christopher Hawthorne cites 1.4 million. See Christopher Hawthorne, Breaking Up Is Hard To Do, Architecture, Vol. 90, No. 3, March, 2001, pp. 64-66.
[50] Paul Wilborn, Los Angeles Has Become Too Big, Say Those Who Want to Break It Up, Associated Press, November 2, 2002, available at www.sfgate.com.
[51] Paul Wilborn, Los Angeles Secession Efforts Getting Closer to Winning Spots on the Ballot, Associated Press, May 19, 2002. www.sfgate.com.
[52] Los Angeles Police Protective League, White Paper On Secession, July, 2002, available at www.lapd.com.
[53] The people in the San Fernando Valley voted 51-49 to secede but the citywide vote was 67-33 percent against secession. Lisa Mascaro, Beth Barrett and James Nash, Breakup Leaders Weigh Methods to Sustain Clout, Los Angeles Daily News, November 6, 2002. Gregory J. Wilcox, Commerce Back to Business as Usual? Los Angeles Daily News, November 6, 2002 report that the Valley vote was 50.77% in favor in the Valley but 66.53% opposed citywide.
[54] The secession initiative failed in Hollywood. A majority of Hollywood residents and LA as a whole both voted against it. Paul Wilborn, Failed Secession Forces Pressure LA Mayor for Better Services, Associated Press, November 6, 2002. www.sfgate.com.
[55] The San Fernando Valley and Hollywood are not the only parts of Los Angeles that have secession on their mind. In 1998, some communities on the West side of Los Angeles were talking about breaking away from Los Angeles and forming a new city that would have a population of 643,000. Chris Warren, Some Westsiders Want to Follow the Valley to Independence from L.A., Los Angeles Magazine, September, 1998.
[56] Harrison Sheppard, VICA Backs Cityhood, Los Angeles Daily News, September 24, 2002.
[57] Gregory J. Wilcox, Commerce Back to Business as Usual? Los Angeles Daily News, November 6, 2002.
[58] Geoffrey F. Segal and Samuel R. Staley, City of Angels, Valley of Rebels, Cato Policy Report, Vol. XXXIV, No. 5, September/October, 2002, pp. 1, 12-14, at 1.
[59] Ibid.
[60] Joseph Kahn, Valley Girls (and Guys) Push to Secede from Los Angeles, The New York Times, April 20, 2002.
[61] The Los Angeles police union's White Paper states that per capita police protection is 2.0 for the city but only 1.2 for the Valley. If this statistic were accurate, it would mean that there are 2 police officers for every Los Angeles resident. Something is obviously wrong with this statistic, but if the ratio is correct, then Valley residents get substantially less police protection, per capita, than residents of Los Angeles as a whole. See Los Angeles Police Protective League, White Paper On Secession, July, 2002, available at www.lapd.com.
[62] Los Angeles Police Protective League, White Paper On Secession, July, 2002, available at www.lapd.com.
[63] Ibid.
[64] Ibid.
[65] Paul Wilborn, Los Angeles Secession Efforts Getting Closer to Winning Spots on the Ballot, Associated Press, May 19, 2002. www.sfgate.com.
[66] Chris Warren, Some Westsiders Want to Follow the Valley to Independence from L.A., Los Angeles Magazine, September, 1998.
[67] Anyone who needs documentation of government excesses need only read the daily newspaper. This paper will not attempt to prove that government excesses exist. For one study on the subject of government waste at the federal level, see J. Peter Grace, Burning Money: The Waste of Your Tax Dollars (1984).
[68] Citizens of any state should also have the right to secede and form another sovereign national entity, too, as was attempted by the Confederate States during the War Between the

States, but it is unlikely that such an amendment could be adopted in the near future in the United States. However, such an amendment might defuse much political tension in some of the emerging democracies in Eastern Europe, Asia and Africa, especially those having diverse languages, cultures and religions.

[69] Leon Louw and Frances Kendall, South Africa: The Solution, Ciskei: Agami Publishers,1986. A slightly different American edition was published by Frances Kendall and Leon Louw under the title After Apartheid: The Solution for South Africa, San Francisco: ICS Press, 1987) All references will be to the 1987 American edition unless otherwise stated. The book advocates a Swiss cantonal system for South Africa that will guarantee the rights of all groups.

[70] After Apartheid 218 (1987); The Solution 161 (1986).

[71] After Apartheid 215 (1987); The Solution 159 (1986).

[72] Based on a study by the Tax Foundation. Tax Freedom Day 1991 Is May 8 -- Latest Date Ever: State Tax Freedom Days Range from April 24 to May 26, 35 Tax Features (April 1991) 1ff.

[73] "Upstate New Yorkers" is a loosely defined term. It might be defined to include any New York State resident who lives more than about 20 or 30 miles from New York City, with the exception of those living on Long Island.

[74] A single provider of goods or services.

[75] A small number of providers of goods or services.

[76] Ludwig von Mises, Nation, State, and Economy, New York: New York University Press, 1983, p. 34. This book first appeared in German as Nation, Staat, und Wirtschaft (1919).

[77] After Apartheid 216 (1987); The Solution 159 (1986).

[78] Mises, supra.

[79] Rothbard, supra.

[80] It is interesting to speculate what Mises would have thought of the Kendall and Louw proposal (Mises died in 1973). Although Mises was against allowing secession at the individual level, his refusal was based on technical considerations. Kendall and Louw seem to have found a partial solution to these problems.

Chapter 16

FINANCING EDUCATION

INTRODUCTION

One of the largest expenditures of state and local governments in the USA,[1] and of various governments at all levels in other countries, is for the provision of education. In the USA, states provide a free government (public school) education to students for the first twelve years, and subsidize tuition at state universities thereafter. As a result, government education has become a near monopoly,[2] especially at the primary and secondary level because privately provided education finds it difficult to compete on price. Where private education exists, it can compete only because of nonprice advantages.

This near monopoly position with regard to education exhibits many of the attributes of monopolies in general -- the price (total cost) is higher than would be the case in a market system and the quality is lower.[3] This phenomenon has been recognized, and some economists and others have advocated breaking up this monopoly by the use of a voucher system whereby parents can purchase education for their children by presenting these vouchers to the appropriate authority.[4] Vouchers inject choice and competition into the public education system, which, it is thought, will overcome the disadvantages of the present near-monopoly situation. The funds for these vouchers would be provided by taxation, just as the government school system is presently funded by taxation, except that parents would have some power to decide where the tax proceeds flow.

While the use of vouchers would trigger markets, and would cause the price of education to decrease while improving quality of service,[5] vouchers are only a half-way measure because they ignore some fundamental issues, such as whether government should be in the business of providing education in the first place.

This chapter explores the possibility of privatizing education and attempts to answer questions such as:

• How would education be funded if government didn't do it?

• How would a privately funded education system provide for those who couldn't pay?

THE PROBLEM WITH GOVERNMENT EDUCATION

There are many problems with government-provided education. It can be a means to indoctrinate rather than teach. Indeed, one of the main reasons why John Dewey and others pushed for a free system of government schools in the USA was so that the children of immigrants could be indoctrinated with American values. Plato, Hitler, Mussolini, King Frederick William I of Prussia and others favored education as a means of instilling loyalty to the state. John Calvin, Martin Luther and others have urged that the school be used to indoctrinate children with certain religious values.[6] Modern attempts at indoctrination take different forms, such as culturally diverse curriculums and the adoption of textbooks that are politically correct.

Some parents would like to indoctrinate their children with certain values, so it cannot be said that all indoctrination is bad per se. Such judgments are subjective. Different consumers have different values and preferences. Problems arise when the schools indoctrinate children with values that their parents do not approve of. But in a government monopoly school situation, parents have little choice but to accept whatever programs the local school offers because there are no other options.

Because government schools are free, they maintain a near-monopoly position, making it difficult or impossible for private educational institutions to compete. Education monopolies are not any different than other monopolies. They have the same attributes that most monopolies have -- high cost and low quality. In Newark, New Jersey, for example, it costs about $10,000 to educate one high school student in the inner-city for a year, whereas private schools in Newark can do a better job for about half as much. Many graduates of Newark's high schools are barely literate. Yet the government school system allows them to graduate anyway. And Newark is not a special case. The same could be said for many inner-city government schools.[7]

If educational consumers have no options regarding where to send their children, what incentive is there for schools to provide high quality education? What incentive is there to cut costs if taxpayers are picking up the tab anyway and they cannot take their business elsewhere?

Government educational systems have a tendency to become bloated in the absence of market forces. The New York City school system, for example, has more administrators than it has teachers. Private schools, on the other hand, run a much leaner program. Many Catholic grade schools, for example, may have just a principal and one or two administrators.

Government education can be, and often is, a one-size-fits-all system, which must necessarily lead to suboptimal results. Programs are more or less standardized. Decisions regarding what to offer and what policies to adopt are made politically, by bureaucrats and politicians, rather than by consumers and entrepreneurs. There are not many options. Parents generally must send their children to the school that is geographically closest to their home. They are not free to shop around for the school that offers the best mix of offerings and policies according to their own subjective preferences. Indeed, most government schools offer similar or identical programs, although the quality of those programs tends to be better in the suburbs than in the inner city.

Below is a partial list of the choices educational consumers would have under a private system:

- Length of school day: 5 hours; 6 hours; 8 hours; 9 hours
- Length of school year: 183 days; 200 days; 240 days
- Saturday classes or not
- Sports programs: strong programs; weak programs; no programs
- Emphasis on academics; emphasis on socialization
- Course offerings: many electives; few electives
- Should schools be co-ed or should boys and girls go to separate schools?
- Should the schools provide condoms?
- Should children from outside the neighborhood be bused in or out to achieve some sort of racial balance?
- Should admission criteria be different for different ethnic and racial groups?
- Should school employees be hired or promoted partially on the basis of race or ethnic background (affirmative action)?
- What should graduation requirements be?
- Should school officials be able to expel disruptive students?
- Who determines which textbooks are used? Teachers? School board members? Should parents have any input? Should only politically correct texts be adopted? Should only religious textbooks be adopted?
- What should be taught?
  - Creationism v. evolution
  - Religion; no religion; which religion? How much time should be spent on religion? Should prayer be permitted? What kind of prayer?
  - Sex education; no sex education; what kind of sex education? starting in which grade?
  - Diversity: Should diverse cultures and lifestyles be taught?
    - Minority cultures? Which ones? How much time should be spent on each?
    - Gay and lesbian lifestyles?
  - Foreign language courses: strong program; weak program; omit completely
  - Vocational courses: many offerings; few offerings; no offerings
- Faculty
  - Should they be able to get tenure?
  - What qualifications should they have?

Arguably, children could learn more if they spent more time in school. Perhaps they could learn more if they went to school 8 hours a day than if they went only 5, or if they went on Saturdays rather than just Monday through Friday. Of course, if the school day or school year is increased in length, the cost of providing the education would also likely increase. Criticisms have been made of the school system in the USA because children in government schools have classes about 183 days a year, whereas children in other countries go to school 200 days a year or more. Parents don't have any options about the length time their children spend in school. That choice is taken from them by the local bureaucrats or government officials. Under a private system, parents would likely have more options.

Some parents have strong preferences about the kind of education they want their children to receive. The problem is, they don't all have the same preferences. Some parents would prefer to send their children to a school that has a strong academic program, one that emphasizes math, science or languages and prepares their children for college. Others would rather send their children to a school that places more emphasis on socialization or that teaches a trade.

Some parents prefer a school that hammers western civilization into their children's heads. Others prefer a curriculum that includes exposure to diverse cultures. Some parents would like to have their children exposed to gay and lesbian lifestyles, and have condoms distributed free to students, while other parents abhor the very idea. Some parents want their children to be exposed to religion in school and others think that religion be best taught at home (or not at all).

Because of various accreditation standards, laws and regulations, it is often not possible to hire the best teachers. For example, if someone wants to learn a language, it may be best to have a teacher who is a native speaker of that language. But schools are pressured to hire people who have taken the requisite number of courses even if they barely know how to speak the language. And because the supply of qualified teachers is artificially pinched as a result of these rules, the cost of the teacher you can get is higher than would be the case in a free market. A recent college graduate who took a few Spanish courses would cost more, and would know less Spanish, than an immigrant from a Spanish-speaking country. Yet accreditors would prefer that a school hire the college graduate even though he or she is less qualified than the native speaker. Thomas Edison would not be able to get a job teaching high school science under present accreditation rules because he never graduated from grade school.

A totally privatized system would find ways to deal with these blockages to market entry. Schools would be free to hire the best people they could afford without regard to arbitrary regulatory restraints.[8] A privatized system would also offer more options than a government school system. From the above list of more than two dozen options and preferences, it is obvious that it is highly improbable that most parents would be able to find a government school that offers all of their preferred options. Government schools tend to offer standardized curricula and uniform standards. Private schools, on the other hand, could cater to a particular segment of the market that has specific preferences.

The problem with any democracy, even where elected officials and unelected bureaucrats actually serve the needs of the majority --which is not always the case -- is that some minority -- perhaps as high as 49 percent -- must settle for something less than what they prefer because the majority rules. In a privatized, competitive system, what the majority wants becomes less relevant because consumers have more choices. In a privatized system, if 51 percent of all parents in some local community want to send their children to a school that emphasizes socialization, political correctness and free condoms over strong academics, western civilization and prayer, the other 49 percent are still free to send their children to a school that offers different preferences. In a one-size-fits-all government system, the 49 percent must either be content to send their children to a suboptimal government school, or pay to send their children to a private school while continuing to pay taxes to support the government school system that they do not want to use.

THE VOUCHER SYSTEM

The Benefits of Vouchers

The main benefit of vouchers is that they serve to break-up, or at least water down, the government school monopoly.[9] Even where vouchers may only be used to pay for government schools, vouchers allow market forces to operate, thus injecting a degree of competition where none previously existed. Voucher systems that allow their use for private schools do an even better job of breaking up the government school monopoly because it gives educational consumers the opportunity to send their children to private schools, an option they could not always afford without vouchers.

Thus, some voucher systems are better than others. A voucher system that permits parents to use vouchers only for government schools is an improvement over the present system because any kind of voucher system injects some choice and competition into the education industry. Having some options is better than not having any options. But a system that allows vouchers to be used only for government schools is inferior to one that allows parents to use vouchers for any school of their choice because the government-school-only approach limits both choice and competition.

Numerous papers and several books have been written about various voucher systems. The purpose of this chapter is not to summarize previous work, or to suggest a new and improved version of the voucher system. The remainder of this chapter will summarize the deficiencies inherent in any voucher system, and will explore options for providing education without any government involvement.

The Problems with Vouchers

The main problem with vouchers is that they are paid for out of tax funds. Taxpayers are forced to pay for the education of other people's children. Tax supported education is really just a form of special interest legislation, since the general public (taxpayers) are forced to pay for benefits received by a minority of the population (those who have children in government schools). At any particular time, there are more people paying taxes to support government schools than there are users of government schools. Thus, there is an inherent degree of unfairness in any tax-supported educational system because people who do not utilize the service are forced to pay for it.

Another problem with vouchers is that it does not cut off government involvement. Where government pays the bill, it also regulates.[10] There is nothing to prevent legislators or government bureaucrats from setting standards that schools must meet in order to qualify for vouchers. If the standards are good ones, standard setting would not be a problem. But the history of regulation, in the USA at least, is full of examples where regulators have made things worse rather than better.[11]

Not only is there no guarantee that government involvement would improve things, there is a high probability that government involvement would make things worse. While the market does not always operate perfectly, there is much evidence to show that government does not do a good job of serving taxpayers in the field of education. One need only look at the history of the last few decades to see increasing costs of government schools and declining test scores.[12] Literacy rates in the USA were actually higher in the mid-1800s, before the advent of public schools, than they are today in many communities.[13]

FINANCING A TOTALLY PRIVATE SYSTEM

Financing Education without Government

The main question to be answered is how a totally private educational system can be financed if there is no government involvement. The obvious answer is user fees. Those who use the service should be the ones who pay for it. The user fee approach is the only moral solution, because it is the only one that does not rely on force. Under any other system, education is paid for by taxes, which involves the forcible transfer of property from those who own it to those who don't. [14]

Unfortunately, most economists and other policymakers do not hold moral solutions in high regard when it comes to financing special interest programs such as education. They quickly give up the high moral ground by debating the merits of various second-best solutions, such as whether education could best be financed by property taxes, income taxes or sales taxes, or which mix of the various coercive forms of financing is optimal in a given situation. They start from the premise that some form of taxation is needed to finance education.

User fees would probably be the main source of financing a totally private educational system. But it need not be the only one. Private businesses might also pay for part of the cost through voluntary contributions.[15] Schools could solicit funds from corporations, and corporations could set aside part of their earnings to support schools. Many corporations already have a policy of giving a portion of their profits to good causes. All they would have to do is add education to their list of potential recipients. Many corporations already give to educational institutions, although much corporate giving is presently restricted to colleges and universities. Corporate charity could be expanded or shifted to provide for primary and secondary schools in the neighborhoods where its employees live.

Corporations could include education as a fringe benefit in one way or another. Large corporations could sponsor their own school, which would be available to the children of employees. It would probably cost a medium-sized or large corporation less money to fund its own school than to pay local property taxes. Corporations could also offer their own tuition vouchers as a fringe benefit to employees. Corporations that have a sufficient number of employees could have their own school on corporate premises. They could provide a free education for the children of employees and could admit the children of nonemployees if their parents could pay the requisite fee. Smaller businesses that cannot afford to have their own school for employees' children could pool their resources, just like small businesses now do for health care coverage.

Philanthropists and private foundations could also contribute to the support of private schools. Bill Gates, the multibillionaire founder of Microsoft, gave $51 million to the New York City public school system to establish 61 new, small high schools.[16] The Bill and Melinda Gates Foundation has a $24 billion endowment, which is more than the GDP of many countries. And Bill Gates is only one of several hundred billionaires living in the United States.

The schools themselves could generate some of the revenue they need by providing services. Some private schools rent out their classrooms at night to various community groups. The Learning Annex in New York City, for example, rents space several evenings a week from a local Catholic high school so that it can run its adult education programs. Private schools can also run their own adult education programs to help defray the cost of their daytime program. Students can hold bake sales or walkathons to raise money for books or school trips. The number of money-generating activities is limited only by the creativity of the school's employees and students.

The USA has a history of strong private religious education in spite of the near monopoly position of government schools. Although their importance has dwindled over time, many Catholic primary schools still provide a free or low-cost education to children in the community. In some cases, parents are asked to pay some nominal monthly fees. In other cases, the education is completely paid for by the individual church, which holds summer festivals and weekly bingo to defray the cost. Discounts are offered to large families. Scholarships are given to needy students. In many cases, schools are able to provide religious education whether students are able to pay or not. Other religious groups also have their own schools.

Religious high schools also exist. These schools usually charge some tuition. Part of the cost of obtaining a religious high school education is often defrayed by the local religious group. In the case of some Catholic high schools, for instance, each parish is assessed a certain fee for each of its students who attend a Catholic high school. The diocese also pays part of the cost of the school system. The total cost of providing a religious school education, at whatever level, if often far less than the cost of a government school education. In many cases, the cost is about half.[17]

An often overlooked option is home schooling. More than 300,000 students in the USA are educated at home by their parents.[18] An extensive network of home schoolers has evolved through the market process to provide information about home schooling and educational materials for a wide range of subjects. One of the more prominent products of home schooling is Sandra Day O'Connor, a justice on the U.S. Supreme Court.

Home schooling can take many forms. The simplest form involves one parent (usually the mother) teaching one or more of her own children in her home. But, in the absence of government intervention and regulation, there would be nothing to prevent one of the neighborhood moms from taking in a few of her friend's children and educating them as well. Home schooling is an attractive option from a public finance perspective because there is no "public" finance involved.

While some home schools are better than others, the same can be said for any other school. Many products of home schooling receive a better education than their government school counterparts, partly because of the flexibility and choice their parents have in determining their curriculum and partly because home schooling includes much closer parental involvement and participation than is possible to receive in a government school.

What About the Poor?

Another important question is how would students from poor families be able to obtain an education if their parents could not afford to pay for a private school and there were no government funding available? At the philosophical level, this question is a non sequitur. In effect, it could be reworded to say: *Poor people can't afford a private education, therefore, someone must be forced to pay for one for them.* Of course, it does not follow that one person or group should be forced to pay for the education of someone who cannot afford it. Yet this presumption is usually implicit in any argument in favor of government schools in spite of its moral bankruptcy.

Those who have no qualms about taking morally bankrupt positions such as this insist on utilitarian-based answers. Fortunately, the history of private school financing offers some solutions. As was previously mentioned, religious schools have traditionally admitted students whether they could pay or not. Many religious schools offer their programs at little or no cost to the student, and provide scholarships for those who cannot pay.

One criticism that can be raised at this point is "What about nonreligious students? While religious schools may be able to provide for their own, what about students who do not have a religious preference? Who will provide for them?" For one thing, many religious schools will admit students regardless of religious preference. But even if they don't, it does not follow that someone else must be forced to pay for the education of these students. Nonreligious students can still go to nonreligious private schools. Their parents can pay tuition. They can obtain scholarships or receive charity.

Furthermore, if all education were private -- if the government school monopoly were broken -- the cost of education would be much less and the quality would be higher. Poor students who attend private schools would be getting a better education than they could have received in many government schools, and the cost of providing that education would be much less. If the cost of a private education could be cut in half, which seems likely,[19] and taxes could be reduced, most parents even of modest means would be able to send their children to a private school.

If, for some reason, some school-age children did not attend school, they may not be any worse off than if they attended a government school in the inner city. Many high school graduates of inner-city schools cannot read well enough to fill out an employment application form.[20] How much worse off would they be if they dropped out of formal education and got an entry-level job that would give them the opportunity to learn some job skills? A good on-the-job training program may be more beneficial for them than a government school that has drug and violence problems yet cannot teach its students to read.

If taxpayers did not have to pay thousands of dollars in property, income and sales taxes each year to pay for government schools, most of them could afford to send their children to a private school. They would also have more money available to contribute to educational charities. Thus, the pool of funds available for scholarships would increase. The schools themselves could also provide scholarships. Private schools currently provide scholarships based on either need or merit. There is no reason to expect that this situation would change under a totally privatized system. The provision of scholarships might even increase as a larger number of private schools have to compete for a small pool of good students.

The argument has been made that living off charity is demeaning. Students who have their education financed through charity are thought to be psychologically burdened because of the perception that they are freeloaders. Regardless of whether such students are actually freeloaders or not, isn't it better if their education were financed by voluntary means -- charity -- rather than by the force of government, which extracts taxes from the general public by force or the threat of force? Isn't it better to have your education paid for by voluntary contributions than with money that is confiscated from taxpayers? Noncoercive solutions are better than coercive ones, and charity is noncoercive, whereas taxation is coercive. Thus, charity is always morally superior to taxation as a means to finance any worthwhile program.

SUMMARY AND CONCLUSIONS

- Private education costs about half as much as government education.
- Taxpayers would save thousands of dollars a year in property, income and sales taxes if the government school system were abolished. They could then spend the thousands of dollars they save on private education or other goods and services and charities of their choice.
- The quality of private education is higher than that of government school education.
- Educational consumers would have more choices under a totally private system. There would be more diversity.
- Poor students would not be any worse off under a totally private system, and many would be better off.
- The amount of coercion in society would be reduced under a totally private system, as taxpayers would no longer be forced to pay for the education of other people's children.

The above arguments are all utilitarian-based. Private education is to be preferred to government education because it is better and cheaper. But the real issue is not utilitarian but moral.[21] If there were a total separation of education and state, the general public (taxpayers) would not be forced to pay for the education of a special interest group (students). Those who receive the benefits would also pay for the benefits or, in the case of charity, would have the benefits provided to them in a noncoercive manner. Property would no longer be confiscated for the purpose of providing a government education.

Not only is it possible to totally remove government from the provision of education, it is also the only moral solution, since it is the only solution that does not involve coercion.

NOTES

[1] More than one-third of state and local government expenditures are for education. Roger LeRoy Miller, (1994). Economics Today: The Micro View, eighth edition. New York: Harper Collins College Publishers, 1994, p. 116.

[2] Everhart, Robert B., editor (1982). The Public School Monopoly. San Francisco: Pacific Institute for Public Policy Research.

[3] Randall Fitzgerald, When Government Goes Private: Successful Alternatives to Public Services. New York: Universe Books, 1988; James T. Bennett and Manuel H. Johnson, Better Government at Half the Price: Private Production of Public Services. Ottawa, IL & Ossining, NY: Caroline House Publishers, Inc., 1981; Robert W. Poole, Jr., Cutting Back City Hall. New York: Universe Books, 1980; E.S. Savas, Privatizing the Public Sector: How To Shrink Government. Chatham, NJ: Chatham House, 1982.

[4] Milton Friedman, Capitalism and Freedom. Chicago: University of Chicago Press, 1962; David W. Kirkpatrick, Choice in Schooling: A Case for Tuition Vouchers. Chicago: Loyola University Press, 1990.

[5] David F. Salisbury, What Does a Voucher Buy? A Closer Look at the Cost of Private Schools. Policy Analysis No. 486, Washington, DC: Cato Institute, August 28, 2003.

[6] Plato, The Republic; Sheldon Richman, Separating School & State. Fairfax, VA: Future of Freedom Foundation, 1994; Joel Spring, The Public School Movement vs. the Libertarian Tradition, Journal of Libertarian Studies 7(1): 61-79 (1983); E.G. West, Education and the State, second edition. London: Institute of Economic Affairs, 1970.

[7] David Boaz, editor, Liberating Schools: Education in the Inner City. Washington, DC: Cato Institute, 1991.

[8] For treatises on the negative effects that occupational licensure laws have on various trades and professions, see Milton Friedman, Capitalism and Freedom, Chicago: University of Chicago Press, 1962; Robert Albon and Greg Lindsay, editors, Occupational Regulation and the Public Interest. St. Leonard's, New South Wales: The Centre for Independent Studies, 1984; Simon Rottenberg, editor, Occupational Licensure and Regulation. Washington, DC: American Enterprise Institute, 1980; S. David Young, The Rule of Experts: Occupational Licensing in America. Washington, DC: The Cato Institute, 1987.

[9] John E. Coons and Stephen D. Sugarman, Education by Choice: The Case for Family Control. Berkeley: University of California Press, 1978.

[10] Dwight Lee, The Political Economy of Educational Vouchers, The Freeman, July, 1986, 244-248; Myron Lieberman, Privatization and Educational Choice. New York: St. Martin's Press, 1989; Sheldon Richman, Separating School & State. Fairfax, VA: Future of Freedom Foundation, 1994.

[11] Philip K. Howard, The Death of Common Sense: How Law Is Suffocating America. New York: Random House, 1994.
[12] James T. Bennett and Manuel H. Johnson, Better Government at Half the Price: Private Production of Public Services., Ottawa, IL & Ossining, NY: Caroline House Publishers, Inc., 1981; John Taylor Gatto, Dumbing Us Down: The Hidden Curriculum of Compulsory Schooling. Philadelphia: New Society Publishers, 1992; Sheldon Richman, Separating School & State. Fairfax, VA: Future of Freedom Foundation, 1994.
[13] Gatto; Richman.
[14] The argument has been made that taxes are not really coercive because "the people" gave their consent to be taxed. Space does not permit a discussion of this argument, but it has been discussed -- and refuted -- elsewhere. See Robert W. McGee, Is Tax Evasion Unethical? University of Kansas Law Review, 42: 411-435 (1994); Robert W. McGee, Principles of Taxation for Emerging Economies: Lessons from the U.S. Experience, Dickinson Journal of International Law, 14:29-93 (1993).
[15] Publicly traded corporations could be in breach of their fiduciary duty to their shareholders if they donated money for things that do not benefit the corporation but we will not go into that issue here. One of the classic articles on this point was written by Milton Friedman. See Milton Friedman, The Social Responsibility of Business, The New York Times Magazine, September 13, 1970, pp. 33, 122-126, reprinted in many places, including Kurt R. Leube, editor, The Essence of Friedman, Stanford: Hoover Institution Press, 1987, pp. 36-42. Also see Henry G. Manne and Henry C. Wallich, The Modern Corporation and Social Responsibility, Washington, DC: American Enterprise Institute, 1972.
[16] Campanile, Carl. 2003. Billionaire Gives $51M to City Schools. New York Post, September 18, p. 2.
[17] Randall Fitzgerald, When Government Goes Private: Successful Alternatives to Public Services. New York: Universe Books, 1988.
[18] Richman.
[19] Fitzgerald.
[20] Samuel L. Blumenfeld, The New Illiterates. Boise, ID: The Paradigm Company, 1988.
[21] Some people think that utilitarian solutions are moral solutions. This issue is discussed elsewhere in this book, so we will not discuss it again here.

Chapter 17

SOCIAL SECURITY: REFORM, PRIVATIZE OR ABOLISH?

INTRODUCTION

The fact that social security is a rip-off is becoming more generally known as the system approaches bankruptcy.[1] Like any Ponzi scheme, those who got in early stood to gain. But the system has insurmountable problems. People are living longer due to advances in medicine,[2] so they take money out of the system longer. The birth rate has declined, so there are not as many people paying into the system. As the baby boomers near retirement age, more people will be drawing from the system and fewer people will be paying into it.[3] Proposed solutions put forth to avoid or postpone bankruptcy have included reducing benefits, increasing taxes,[4] postponing the retirement age and means testing -- allowing only those who need it to be able to receive benefits.

In theory there is a trust fund. As taxes are withheld from workers' paychecks and as employers are taxed, the money flows into a pool for a few months before it is distributed to current recipients. And a portion of the present surplus is borrowed against to finance the federal budget deficit, which weakens the system and makes it less solvent.[5]

Those who have paid into the fund have no inherent claim on any of the funds.[6] Taxpayers who die before retirement are not entitled to any of the money they have poured into the system and neither are their heirs. If a similar investment scheme were made by a private insurance company, the corporate officers would be arrested for fraud. Yet the social security system has been a sacred cow since it was founded in the 1930s. It is time to slaughter this sacred cow.

REFORM

Some people have been advocating reform of the present system. Suggestions have been made to disallow benefits to individuals who continue working after retirement age, partly because of the belief that people who are still working don't need the money they receive each month from Social Security and partly to stem the outflow of funds, to postpone or avoid eventual bankruptcy. Those who disagree with this proposal argue that they paid money into the system for perhaps 40 years or more, so they are entitled to receive benefits and the fact that they continue to work is irrelevant.

Another proposal is to tax 100% of Social Security proceeds, so that people put more money back into the system, again in the belief that taxing Social Security will prevent or postpone its eventual bankruptcy. Postponing the age at which people are eligible for Social Security benefits would also help to delay the eventual bankruptcy of the system. Back when President Roosevelt instituted the program, the average life expectancy was about 65, so making people eligible to receive benefits when they reached age 65 did not place much of a drain on the system, especially when there were dozens of people putting money into the system for every individual who was drawing money out of the system.

The problem with the various reform proposals is that they do not solve some of the basic problems that are inherent in the system.[7] Continuing to force people to pay into the system while denying them benefits does not seem like an equitable reform. Also, forcing the younger generation to pay retirement benefits for the older generation is not fair to the people who are forced to pay. Such a scheme exacerbates generational conflict.

One way to prevent eventual bankruptcy would be to increase the tax rate. As this chapter is being written, the combined tax rate (worker plus employer) is slightly over 15 percent in the United States. That sounds low by European standards, since some European countries have a combined tax rate of more than 60 percent. They had to keep raising the tax rate to prevent bankruptcy because some of the countries in Eastern (and also Western) Europe have declining birth rates.[8]

When I visited Hungary in the early 1990s I was told that men can retire at 60 and women at age 55 and that the charge made for social security payments was approaching 60 percent. This amount was mostly paid by the employer, which dampened the incentive to hire anyone on the books. As a result of such perverse incentives, many companies in Hungary and elsewhere are pressured to hire people off the books and not pay them benefits, since paying an additional 60 percent or so on top of their salaries would drive them into bankruptcy.

Another problem with the system that cannot be solved by any of the reform proposals is the inconvenient fact that Social Security is a bad investment.[9] Over the last 70 years, the price of the average stock has increased by about 11 percent a year. Admittedly, the market has crashed a few times in the last 70 years, and some companies have gone out of business, but stock prices have also skyrocketed a few times and thousands of new companies have been born and some of them have become profitable giants. But even in a down market, investing in personal account provides a better return than the forced investment into the social security fund.[10]

If individuals could invest the money they (and their employers) now put into Social Security into some good mutual fund instead, they could spread the risk and just about everybody who gets into the system by age 25 will have more than $1 million at retirement. The Cato Institute has a calculator that estimates the amount of funds someone would have at retirement.[11] Also, since the funds would belong to them, they would be able to pass it on to their children, grandchildren or mistresses if they want. Another problem with the present Social Security system is that the people who are forced to pay into the system do not have any property right in the funds they deposit. When they die, that's it. Heirs and mistresses don't get anything.

None of the present reform proposals would alleviate these structural problems. Therefore, reform of the present system is not the solution. At best, reform would only postpone the inevitable bankruptcy of the system, while continuing the injustices.

PRIVATIZATION

Some economists have advocated privatization as the way to save the system.[12] The Cato Institute has many studies that offer many recommendations for privatization.[13] Rather than paying into the government's phony trust fund, workers would pay into a private investment trust that they would actually be able to claim as property when they retire. Since it is their property, their heirs would be able to inherit.

The massive pool of funds that would accumulate would be available for investment, thus leading to a business and stock market boom. Interest rates would drop, making it easier to finance a home. Those who placed money into the system for a number of years would be able to retire millionaires.[14] According to Martin Feldstein of Harvard University, "the combination of the improved labor market incentives and the higher real return on savings has a net present value gain of more than $15 trillion, an amount equivalent to 3 percent of each future year's GDP forever."[15]Any number of good things would happen.

Rather than being mere transfer payments, as they are today, a privatized system would result in a ready pool of wealth that people can tap into when they retire. Monthly retirement checks under such a system could be two or three times larger than what retirees presently receive. Such a reform would be of special benefit to the poor, since poor people receive a higher percentage of their total income from Social Security than do middle class and rich people.[16]

Women would stand to benefit disproportionately from Social Security privatization. Under present rules, benefits are cut by as much as half when the spouse (usually the husband) dies. One study has found that this partial cut-off throws one out of every five widows into poverty.[17] This would change under a privatized system, since the widow would retain the assets that were placed into the fund.

Some countries have started to privatize their Social Security systems, with some success. As the pool of capital builds, it is invested in projects, leading to economic growth. Poor countries that previously could not attract sufficient foreign capital are now exporting capital to other countries. The prospects for continued capital growth and the expansion of employment and a higher standard of living are very real prospects.

Chile was the first country to privatize its Social Security system, in 1981. Ninety-five percent of all workers are now covered under the private system.[18] The compound annual rate of return has been more than 11 percent.[19] Pension benefits in the private system are now 50 to 100 percent higher, adjusted for inflation, than they were in the state-run system. Chile's growth rate jumped from its historic 3 percent annual rate to a rate that has averaged 7 percent over the last 12 years. The savings rate jumped to 25 percent of GDP and the unemployment rate dropped to around 5 percent.[20] Argentina, Peru, Colombia, Bolivia, Mexico and El Salvador have also privatized their Social Security systems.[21]

The big question is how do we get from here (the present system) to there (a private system)? What would happen to those now (or soon to be) on the system if the system went private. Various proposals have been put forth. For example, young people could elect to set aside a portion of their present social security payments in a private fund, and the remainder of their social security taxes could continue to be used by those presently (or soon to be) drawing benefits. That way, those presently (or soon to be) drawing benefits would continue to do so.

One rather scary solution that has been proposed would be for the federal government to invest the funds in the capital markets. If this were done, the federal government would become the largest shareholder in most American businesses, and would be able to influence corporate policy. In all likelihood, corporate decisions would start to be made for political rather than economic reasons.[22] Perhaps there would be restrictions on the types of company that the funds could be invested in. Such a possibility is not far-fetched, judging from what has taken place in the state public employee pension funds.[23]

One problem with partial privatization is that young workers would still be forced to pay for other peoples' benefits. Thus, it is unfair to young workers who have to pay into a system that they cannot draw from. Another solution that has been proposed is to sell federal land and use the proceeds to fully fund the present system. The federal government owns more than fifty percent of some western states, and owns substantial assets in every state. If these assets were sold, some estimates conclude that there would be enough money to fully fund the system for those who are presently on the system and for those who will retire within a few years.

THE MORAL CASE FOR ABOLITION

These proposed solutions all have flaws. For one thing, they all rely on coercion. Under the present system, those who work are forced to pay the pensions of those who don't work. If the system were partially privatized, those who work would be forced to set aside some amount determined by government to provide for their own retirement and would also have to pay to fund the retirement of people they never met. Thus, one fatal flaw in any government regulated pension scheme is that it is based on coercion rather than voluntary exchange.[24]

The popular rebuttal to this line of reasoning goes something like this: If the government didn't force people to pay into some social security system, some of them wouldn't do it, and they would become wards of the state. But just because some people decide to spend their money currently rather than provide for their retirement, it does not follow that the rest of us must be forced to support them. The whole argument is based on a non sequitur. If some people do not exercise individual responsibility, it does not follow that those who are responsible should be forced to help them out. There may be some moral duty to help such people, but that choice should be left to individuals and charities. Morality exists only where there is choice, so it cannot be said that government has a moral duty to help these people, because in order to do so, government must resort to force (taxation), which negates morality.

The present social security system is based on the immoral principle of forced redistribution. Those who work are forced to transfer a portion of their earnings to those who do not work. The only way to end this immoral practice is to abolish social security. Those who advocate gradualism would argue: "What would happen to those presently on the system if we abolished social security today"? But this is not a legitimate question, just as the gradualists of the 1840s and 1850s argued that slavery must be abolished gradually so that the slaves would not be unemployed and so that the plantation owners would not go bankrupt. Such gradualist arguments are themselves bankrupt. If something is unjust, the only solution is to end the practice immediately, regardless of consequences. An injustice cannot continue to be perpetrated just because there may be some short-term losers. Looking at gains and losses is not a legitimate avenue of inquiry when rights are being violated. The only moral solution is to end the injustice.

In order to continue the present system, it would be necessary for present workers to continue to pay a portion of their wages to people who are not working, which is inherently unfair to those who are forced to pay. The argument has been made that those now on social security are entitled to receive benefits because they paid into the system for many years. But this line of reasoning involves another non sequitur. In effect, they are saying: "I was forced to contribute to other peoples' retirement, therefore the younger generation should be forced to contribute to my retirement."

The money the older generation paid into the system has long since been spent. It has been stolen, in effect (since theft is defined as the taking of property without the owner's consent, and many people would not pay social security taxes if they had a choice). But it does not follow that a portion of the younger generation's income should be stolen to pay for someone else's benefits. "They stole from me, therefore I have a right to steal from you" is a morally bankrupt statement (as well as a non sequitur).

The only way to stop this injustice of social security is to abolish the system immediately, regardless of consequences. The sale of government assets plus private charity might or might not provide sufficient funds to take care of those who are presently (or soon to be) on social security, but that is beside the point. The only moral solution is immediate abolition, regardless of consequences.

NOTES

[1] The exact date when Social Security will go bankrupt is not known, of course. However, one recent estimate is 2029. The projected bankruptcy date gets closer each time an estimate is made. Outflows are expected to exceed inflows as early as 2012. See Michael Tanner, The Other Trust Fund Report. www.socialsecurity.org.

[2] Carrie Lips, Bad News for Social Security: There May Be a Cure for Cancer, http://www.socialsecurity.org/articles/art-21.html.

[3] In 1950 there were 16 workers for every Social Security recipient. Now there are only 3.3 and by 2030 there will be less than two. See Michael Tanner, The Other Trust Fund Report. www.socialsecurity.org.

[4] Timothy J. Penny, Please, Not Another Payroll Tax Hike, www.socialsecurity.org.

[5] About 86.5% of the money collected is paid out in benefits. The remaining 13.5% is lent to the federal government to meet operating expenses. So there really is no trust fund. Michael Tanner, Social Security Privatization and Economic Growth, www.socialsecurity.org.

[6] Charles E. Rounds, Jr., Property Rights: The Hidden Issue of Social Security reform, SSP No. 19, Cato Institute, April 19, 2000, www.socialsecurity.org.

[7] Michael Tanner, No Second Best: The Unappetizing Alternatives to Social Security Privatization, SSP No. 24, The Cato Institute, January 29, 2002. [www.socialsecurity.org].

[8] William G. Shipman, Retirement Finance Reform Issues Facing the European Union, SSP. No. 28, January 2, 2003, The Cato Institute [www.socialsecurity.org].

[9] Peter J. Ferrara, Social Security Is Still a Hopelessly Bad Deal for Today's Workers, SSP No. 18, The Cato Institute, November 29, 1999. www.socialsecurity.org.

[10] Andrew Biggs, Personal Accounts in a Down Market: How Recent Stock Market Declines Affect the Social Security Reform Debate, Briefing Paper No. 74, Cato Institute, September 20, 2002. [www.socialsecurity.org].

[11] www.socialsecurity.org.

[12] Michael Tanner, Social Security Privatization and Economic Growth,]www.socialsecurity.org.] Edward H. Crane, The Case for Privatizing America's Social Security System, address to S.O.S. Retraite Sante, Paris, France, December 10, 1997, www.socialsecurity.org.

[13] [www.socialsecurity.org]. For some books on the topic, see Peter J. Ferrara and Michael D. Tanner, Common Cents, Common Dreams: A Layman's Guide to Social Security Privatization, Washington, DC: Cato Institute, 1998; Peter J. Ferrara and Michael D. Tanner, A New Deal for Social Security, Washington, DC: Cato Institute, 1998; Peter J. Ferrara, editor, Social Security: Prospects for Real Reform, Washington, DC: Cato Institute, 1985; Peter J. Ferrara, Social Security: The Inherent Contradiction, Washington, DC: Cato Institute, 1980; World Bank, Averting the Old Age Crisis,: Policies to Protect the Old and Promote Growth, New York: Oxford University Press, 1994; Henry J. Aaron, Barry P. Bosworth and Gary Burtless, Can America Afford to Grow Old? Paying for Social Security, Washington, DC: The Brookings Institution, 1989; Charles P. Blahous, III,

Reforming Social Security, Westport, CT: Praeger, 2000; Dorcas R. Hardy and C. Colburn Hardy, Social Insecurity: The Crisis in America's Social Security System and How to Plan Now for Your Own Financial Survival, New York: Villard Books (Random House), 1991; Martha Derthick, Agency under Stress: The Social Security Administration in American Government, Washington, DC: Brookings Institution, 1990. For some early articles on Social Security that have stood the test of time, see the Cato Journal 3(2) (1983), especially the articles by Buchanan; Weaver; Roberts; Robertson; Pellechio and Goodfellow; DiLorenzo; McKenzie; Ranson; Garrison; Ture; Butler and Germanis; Goodman; Wagner; Ferrara.

[14] According to one estimate, a worker who is 25 stands to get between three and six times greater benefits under a private system than under Social Security. Michael Tanner, The Other Trust Fund Report, http://www.socialsecurity.org/articles/art-tanner4.html.

[15] Michael Tanner, Social Security Privatization and Economic Growth, http://www.socialsecurity.org/articles/art-tanner1.html.

[16] Jagadeesh Gokhale, The Impact of Social Security Reform on Low-Income Workers, SSP No. 23, Cato Institute, December 6, 2001. [www.socialsecurity.org]; Michael Tanner, Privatizing Social Security: A Big Boost for the Poor, SSP No. 4, The Cato Institute, July 26, 1996. www.socialsecurity.org.

[17] Ekaterina Shirley and Peter Spiegler, The Benefits of Social Security Privatization for Women, SSP No. 12, The Cato Institute, July 20, 1998. www.socialsecurity.org.

[18] José Piñera, Empowering Workers: The Privatization of Social Security in Chile, International Center for Pension Reform [www.prnsionreform.org].

[19] L. Jacobo Rodriguez, Chile's Private Pension System at 18: Its Current State and Future Challenges, SSP No. 17, The Cato Institute, July 30, 1999. www.socialsecurity.org.

[20] See José Piñera, In Chile, They Went Private 16 Years Ago, http://www.socialsecurity.org/articles/art-19.html.

[21] Peter Ferrara, Destiny of Freedom for Social Security? http://www.socialsecurity.org/articles/art-11.html.

[22] Krzysztof M. Ostaszewski, Privatizing the Social Security Trust Fund? Don't Let the Government Invest, SSP No. 6, The Cato Institute, January 14, 1997.www.socialsecurity.org.

[23] See Michael Tanner, Tom Daschle's Very Bad Idea, http://www.socialsecurity.org/articles/art-tanner3.html.

[24] Daniel Shapiro, The Moral Case for Social Security Privatization, SSP No. 14, The Cato Institute, October 29, 1998. www.socialsecurity.org.

Chapter 18

EARMARKING TAXES

INTRODUCTION

Taxes can either go into the general fund or be earmarked -- set aside -- for particular purposes. Income taxes are generally deposited into the general fund, to be used for a variety of purposes. Gasoline taxes are often earmarked to maintain highways. They are set aside for a particular purpose. Some people have advocated that a portion of the tax on cigarettes be earmarked for cancer research.

Whether revenues from a particular tax are placed into the general fund or earmarked for special purposes depends on a number of factors. Oftentimes, a tax increase will be more acceptable to the general population if it is earmarked for a particular purpose that is widely accepted.[1] Lottery proceeds that are used for education is an example. Social Security taxes that are set aside for taxpayers' retirement is another.[2] Segregating tax revenue for specific purposes reduces the possibility that the money will be squandered on pork barrel projects. That is one of the advantages of earmarking tax collections, and it is one of the disadvantages of dumping tax revenues into one big pot.

Knut Wicksell, the Scandinavian economist, advocated earmarking taxes for all expenditures.[3] Earmarking tax dollars is a good control device that enhances the chances that the money will actually be spent for its intended purpose. But it is not a device that can be used for every kind of government expenditure. Dumping everything into a common pot gives the government more flexibility to shift spending to where it is needed. So there is a trade-off.

Although there are advantages of earmarking taxes for special purposes, there are also some disadvantages as well as some ethical problems that have been overlooked in the economics and public finance literature. The intent of this chapter is to explore these overlooked ethical issues in the hope that a dialogue can be started to address these overlooked issues.

EARMARKING IN THEORY AND PRACTICE

In theory, earmarking taxes is efficient because the taxes raised are set aside for a specific purpose rather than disappearing into the general fund, where they can be used for anything and everything. Also, if voters perceive that a particular program has costs that exceed benefits, they can vote against it and thus abolish both the program and the taxes that go to support it.[4] The problem is that the benefits of earmarking fade away in a public finance system that has many sources of funds and many programs that use those funds. The result may be suboptimal allocation of total resources.

For example, let's say that lottery proceeds or a portion of sales tax proceeds are earmarked for education and that the amount to be earmarked was formerly paid for out of the general fund. It is highly unlikely that tax rates will be reduced to compensate for the reduced need to finance education out of the general fund. What is more likely is that the money in the general fund will be shifted to pay for some other program that taxpayers may or may not want. Politicians will find a way to spend the money, probably in a way that will benefit them at re-election time.

Most empirical studies confirm that this phenomenon does indeed happen.[5] One study found that there is nearly a dollar for dollar substitution between general revenue appropriations and earmarked lottery revenue for public education.[6] There is also a tendency for state legislatures to reduce general appropriations for higher education whenever schools obtain funding from private sources.[7] The Arkansas soft drink tax was used to fund the state's Medicaid program, which freed up funds for use in other areas.[8]

Practice also diverges from theory where the activities ultimately being funded are far removed from the item being taxed. Funding health care by increasing alcohol and tobacco taxes is one example. Smokers and drinkers benefit from Medicare and Medicaid, but so do nonsmokers and nondrinkers. To force smokers and drinkers to pay higher taxes for consuming alcohol and tobacco products seems grossly unfair if the proceeds raised are used to fund services that are used by millions of nonsmokers and nondrinkers. To make matters worse, many smokers and drinkers do not use Medicare and Medicaid, so they are being forced to pay for services they do not use themselves. When such redistribution occurs, the funds raised by the excise tax can no longer be called user fees.[9]

Although the user fee concept looks good in theory, a closer investigation reveals that the user fee concept cannot be used to justify selective taxes in practice.[10] In practice, people from the lower economic classes are being forced to subsidize middle class programs, since smokers and drinkers tend to be young and/or poor and Medicare and Medicaid are used mostly by people in the middle class.[11]

The Airport and Airway Trust Fund is another example of government failure. The taxes raised from selling airline tickets were supposed to be used to improve air traffic facilities. On the surface, the tax looks like a user fee, since the people who stand to benefit from the expenditures are also the ones who pay for airline tickets.

The problem is that the fund has been in a surplus position for many years. Much more money is collected than spent. The fund surplus reduces the federal budget deficit so Congress finds it advantageous to let the surplus accumulate rather than spend it or reduce the tax. In effect, a small minority, those who buy airline tickets, are helping to reduce the federal budget deficit, which benefits the vast majority.[12] Resources continue to be misallocated because of political expedience.

An often overlooked evil of earmarking involves asset forfeiture laws, which disparage property rights and undermine constitutional government. Various law enforcement agencies confiscate the assets of suspected lawbreakers and use the proceeds from the sale of the assets to fund their law enforcement activities. On the surface it looks like a user fee, since criminals are the ones who are forced to pay for law enforcement. The problem is that many of the people whose property is confiscated are not criminals. Indeed, many of them are never formally charged with a crime, let alone convicted. In many cases, state officials enforce federal laws so that state constitutional prohibitions on forfeiture laws can be circumvented, which undermines constitutional government.[13]

SOME OVERLOOKED ETHICAL PROBLEMS

When one thinks of earmarking taxes, one does not usually think of ethics. Earmarking taxes is almost always seen as merely a tool of public finance that has no connection to ethics. But such is not the case.

There are several ways of looking at ethics. Some ethical systems are better than others. Let's look at utilitarian ethics first, since that is the ethical system that practically all economists subscribe to.[14]

Utilitarian ethics has as its goal the greatest good for the greatest number. There are some problems with utilitarian ethics, such as how to measure utility,[15] which population is the relevant population,[16] and the fact that utilitarianism totally ignores rights,[17] but we will not go into those problems because that would take us too far afield of the main topic, which is to apply utilitarian ethics to earmarking taxes.[18]

Jeremy Bentham coined the term utilitarian and is perhaps the first systematic exponent of the utilitarian philosophy.[19] Bentham's view was as follows:

> ...it is the greatest happiness of the greatest number that is the measure of right and wrong.[20]

For Bentham, one must take into account the effect an action has on everyone affected by the action when determining the rightness or wrongness of the action.[21] John Stuart Mill, another early exponent of utilitarianism, said:

> The creed which accepts as the foundation of morals "utility" or the "greatest happiness principle" holds that actions are right in proportion as they tend to promote

> happiness; wrong as they tend to produce the reverse of happiness.[22]

Henry Sidgwick, another English utilitarian, gives a more precise definition:

> By Utilitarianism is here meant the ethical theory, that the conduct which, under any given circumstances, is objectively right, is that which will produce the greatest amount of happiness on the whole; that is, taking into account all whose happiness is affected by the conduct.[23]

In other words, "an action is right if and only if it brings about at least as much net happiness as any other action the agent could have performed; otherwise it is wrong."[24]

Richard A. Posner, an American jurist and prolific author on law and economics, takes the position that morality and efficiency are consistent.[25] In another work, he states that "the criterion for judging whether acts and institutions are just or good is whether they maximize the wealth of society."[26]

If these views are to be reconciled, one might say that an act or policy or institution is ethical if it is more efficient than any other alternative. Otherwise, it is unethical. Thus, if the act or policy results in the misallocation of resources, it is unethical because it reduces efficiency.

If earmarking taxes increases efficiency, one might conclude that earmarking is ethical,[27] at least in cases where no other method produces more efficiency than earmarking. Likewise, where earmarking reduces efficiency, one may conclude that the practice is unethical.

Where Social Security taxes are earmarked for retirement, one might think that the policy is ethical, since the alternative would be to deposit Social Security tax proceeds into the general fund, which is definitely inefficient, and too tempting for politicians to resist. However, earmarking Social Security taxes is ethical only if it is the most efficient alternative, which it is not. Therefore, earmarking Social Security taxes is unethical.

The problem with Social Security is that it is neither social nor secure. The funds that are taken from workers' paychecks are not deposited into any fund in the true sense of the term. The proceeds are transferred to people who are on Social Security. There is no real trust fund in the economic sense of the term because the funds are not held in trust for the people who deposited them. If a private insurance or investment company tried to establish such a "fund" the owners would be convicted of fraud.

No one in his right mind would voluntarily contribute to Social Security if he knew that the average mutual fund would provide a much better investment vehicle. Privatizing Social Security is the most efficient solution.[28] Thus, it is the only ethical solution.

With a privatized pension system, those who put money into the fund would have a property right in the fund. They would be able to take their money out of the fund or leave it to their heirs. Under the present Social Security system, individuals are not automatically entitled to any of the money that is taxed away as Social Security. They cannot get any of it before reaching a certain age. If they continue to work after retirement age, they stand to lose all or part of their "entitlement" to Social Security. When they die, their heirs receive nothing.

A privatized Social Security system is also more efficient as far as capital accumulation is concerned. With a privatized system, capital would accumulate, thus reducing interest rates, housing costs, etc., and creating jobs. If the greatest good for the greatest number is the measuring device for determining the ethics of a policy, it would seem that a policy that creates wealth and prosperity is to be preferred to a policy that merely redistributes presently existing wealth. Thus, earmarking Social Security funds is unethical because it is inefficient and does not result in the greatest good for the greatest number.[29]

Another use of earmarking is for education. Some states earmark lottery proceeds for education. Other states earmark a portion of sales tax proceeds for education.

One might think that there is nothing unethical with earmarking lottery proceeds for education, since lotteries, along with user fees, are the only forms of public finance that raise funds without violating property rights.[30] But such is not the case. Using the reasoning outlined above, whereby maximizing happiness or maximizing efficiency is the measure of ethical policies, earmarking lottery funds for education fails the test. That is because funding government schools is itself inefficient. Private schools provide a better education at a much lower cost.[31] Thus, any funding of government schools is inefficient and unethical, whether the funding is done by earmarking or otherwise.

CONCLUDING COMMENTS

As can be seen, there are some ethical issues involved in the earmarking of taxes. From a utilitarian perspective, earmarking is ethical only if it is the most efficient way, and provided that the tax is ethical in the first place. Even if we assume that the tax is ethical, it does not always follow that earmarking is ethical because there may be a more efficient method available.

Where the funding takes the form of a user fee, one must look beneath the surface to see whether it is a true user fee. Excise taxes that are called user fees may not always be user fees. It depends on whether the people who pay are also the ones who benefit. In the case of the excise tax on alcohol, tobacco and airline tickets, those who benefit are often not the ones who pay, so earmarking in these cases results in redistribution, which is an unethical practice.[32] Social Security taxes are also not user fees and are not earmarked funds, since the people who receive the funds are not the same people who must pay.

In the case of earmarking, practice often diverges from theory. Where there is divergence, earmarking is an unethical practice from a utilitarian perspective because it is inefficient and is unethical from a rights perspective because it violates rights.

NOTES

[1] James M. Buchanan, The Economics of Earmarked Taxes, Journal of Political Economy. 457-69 (October, 1963), at 457. Buchanan also discusses earmarking in Public Finance in Democratic Process, Chapel Hill: University of North Carolina Press, 1967, at 72-87.

[2] The Social Security taxes that are collected in the USA are not really set aside for the taxpayers' retirement. Those who work pay into the system and those who are retired draw from it, so the Social Security Trust Fund is not a true trust fund.

[3] Knut Wicksell, Finanztheoretische Untersuchungen (1896), reprinted as A New Principle of Just Taxation in Classics in the Theory of Public Finance 72-118 (Richard A. Musgrave and Alan T. Peacock, eds. 1958). Also see James M. Buchanan, Public Finance in Democratic Process 72-87 (1967).

[4] William F. Shughart, II, The Economics of the Nanny State, in Taxing Choice: The Predatory Politics of Fiscal Discrimination 13-29 (William F. Shughart, II., ed. 1997), at 19.

[5] William F. Shughart, II, The Economics of the Nanny State, in Taxing Choice: The Predatory Politics of Fiscal Discrimination 13-29 (William F. Shughart, II., ed. 1997), at 20.

[6] Mary O. Borg and Paul M. Mason, The Budgetary Incidence of a Lottery to Support Education, National Tax Journal 41: 75-85 (1988), cited in William F. Shughart, II, The Economics of the Nanny State, in Taxing Choice: The Predatory Politics of Fiscal Discrimination 13-29 (William F. Shughart, II., ed. 1997), at 26.

[7] Elizabeth Becker and Cotton M. Lindsey, Does the Government Free Ride? Journal of Law and Economics 37: 277-296 (April 1994), cited in William F. Shughart, II, The Economics of the Nanny State, in Taxing Choice: The Predatory Politics of Fiscal Discrimination 13-29 (William F. Shughart, II., ed. 1997), at 26.

[8] Dwight R. Lee, Overcoming Taxpayer Resistance by Taxing Choice and Earmarking Revenues, in Taxing Choice: The Predatory Politics of Fiscal Discrimination 105-116 (William F. Shughart, II., ed. 1997), at 107.

[9] A similar argument is given in William F. Shughart, II, The Economics of the Nanny State, in Taxing Choice: The Predatory Politics of Fiscal Discrimination 13-29 (William F. Shughart, II., ed. 1997), at 20.

[10] Dwight R. Lee, Environmental Economics and the Social Cost of Smoking, Contemporary Policy Issues 9: 83-92 (January 1991), cited in William F. Shughart, II, The Economics of the Nanny State, in Taxing Choice: The Predatory Politics of Fiscal Discrimination 13-29 (William F. Shughart, II., ed. 1997), at 20.

[11] William F. Shughart, II, The Economics of the Nanny State, in Taxing Choice: The Predatory Politics of Fiscal Discrimination 13-29 (William F. Shughart, II., ed. 1997), at 20.

[12] Randall G. Holcombe, Selective Excise Taxation from an Interest-Group Perspective, in Taxing Choice: The Predatory Politics of Fiscal Discrimination 81-103 (William F. Shughart, II., ed. 1997), at 87-89.

[13] Bruce L. Benson and David W. Rasmussen, Predatory Public Finance and the Origins of the War on Drugs: 1984-1989, in Taxing Choice: The Predatory Politics of Fiscal Discrimination 197-225 (William F. Shughart, II., ed. 1997), at 210-215. For a discussion

of asset forfeitures, see James Bovard, Lost Rights: The Destruction of American Liberty 10-17 (1995). "Since 1985, federal, state, and local governments have seized the property of over 200,000 Americans under asset forfeiture laws, often with no more evidence of wrongdoing than an unsubstantiated assertion made by an anonymous government informant." Id., at 1-2. For examples, see James Bovard, Freedom in Chains: The Rise of the State and the Demise of the Citizen 26-27, 98, 114, 167-168, 181-182 (1999).

[14] A few exceptions come to mind -- Walter Block, Hans-Hermann Hoppe and Murray Rothbard, for example.

[15] Murray N. Rothbard, Man, Economy, and State, Los Angeles: Nash Publishing, 1970, pp. 260-268.

[16] William H. Shaw, Contemporary Ethics: Taking Account of Utilitarianism 31-35 (1999); Richard A. Posner, The Economics of Justice 51-54 (1983).

[17] Robert W. McGee, The Fatal Flaw in the Methodology of Law & Economics, Commentaries on Law & Economics 1: 209-223 (1997); Robert W. McGee, The Fatal Flaw in NAFTA, GATT and All Other Trade Agreements, Northwestern Journal of International Law & Business 14: 549-565 (1994); Shaw, supra, at 184-190.

[18] A number of other criticisms could also be made of utilitarianism but we will not make them here. See Shaw, supra, at 15-17, 102-132, 138, 171-172, 190-196, 245-246, 275-276, 280-281 and 286; Richard A. Epstein, Simple Rules for a Complex World 141-142 (1995); Richard A. Posner, The Economics of Justice 51-60 (1983).

[19] William H. Shaw, Contemporary Ethics: Taking Account of Utilitarianism 7 (1999).

[20] Jeremy Bentham, A Fragment on Government, in The Works of Jeremy Bentham, vol. 1 (J. Bowring, ed. 1962), at 227, cited in Shaw, supra, at 8.

[21] Shaw, supra, at 8.

[22] John Stuart Mill, Utilitarianism 7 (G. Sher, ed. 1979), as cited in Shaw, supra, at 9.

[23] Henry Sidgwick, The Methods of Ethics 411 (1966), as cited in Shaw, supra, at 9-10.

[24] Shaw, supra, at 10.

[25] Richard A. Posner, Economic Analysis of Law 284-285 (5th ed. 1998).

[26] Richard A. Posner, The Economics of Justice 115 (rev. ed. 1983).

[27] The underlying premise here is that the tax itself is ethical, which is an entirely different issue. Many (perhaps all) taxes are unethical, since they deprive owners of their property by force or the threat of force. Also, from a utilitarian perspective, they reduce efficiency, since they force people to pay for services that are second best. If it were otherwise, there would be no need for taxes, since people would pay for the services voluntarily. However, discussion of this point would take us too far afield of the main topic of this article. Several studies have found that the economics and public finance literature has failed to find a single justification for taxation that will hold up under analysis. For more on this point, see Walter Block, The Justification for Taxation in the Economics Literature, in The Ethics of Tax Evasion 36-88 (Robert W. McGee, ed., 1998); Walter Block, William Kordsmeier, and Joseph Horton, The Failure of Public Finance, 2 Journal of Accounting, Ethics & Public Policy (Winter 1999).

[28] For alternatives to the present Social Security system, see the Cato Institute's web site, http://www.cato.org; Peter J. Ferrara and Michael Tanner, A New Deal for Social Security, Washington, DC: Cato Institute, 1998.

[29] Since the present Social Security system is unethical, it raises another question. Is evasion of Social Security taxes unethical?

[30] For more on this point, see Robert W. McGee, Some Tax Advice for Latvia and Other Similarly Situated Emerging Economies, International Tax & Business Lawyer 13: 223-308 (1996), at 283-285; Robert W. McGee, Taxation and Public Finance: A Philosophical and Ethical Approach, Commentaries on the Law of Accounting & Finance 1: 157-240 (1997).

[31] Sheldon Richman, Separating School and State, Fairfax, VA: Future of Freedom Foundation, 1995; Robert W. McGee, Brown v. Board of Education: Forty Years of

Asking the Wrong Question & the Case for Privatization of Education, St. Louis University Public Law Review 17(1): 141-155 (1997).

[32] Redistribution is unethical because some people are forced to pay for other people's benefits. For more on this point, see Bertrand DeJouvenel, The Ethics of Redistribution. Forced redistribution violates property rights. It also reduces efficiency, thus violating utilitarian ethics, because it reduces incentives to create wealth. If the size of the pie is smaller with redistribution than without, it cannot be said that redistribution results in the greatest good for the greatest number. The good would be greater if the pie were larger.

Chapter 19

THE SUPERMAJORITY REQUIREMENT

INTRODUCTION

The evidence is clear that the private sector can do just about anything more efficiently than the government. Municipal solid waste disposal costs 61% to 71% more when done by government.[1] Another study found that contracting out waste collection to the private sector saved between 22% and 30%.[2] It takes 68% more federal government employees to remove 21% as much railroad track as private sector employees over the same period of time and under similar conditions.[3]

A study of 121 cities in the Los Angeles county area found that contracting out street cleaning to the private sector saves an average of 43%. The savings in other areas are also substantial: 73% for janitorial services, 42% for refuse collection, 56% for traffic signal maintenance, 96% for asphalt overlay construction, 40% for grass maintenance and 37% for street maintenance.[4]

In spite of the fact that the private sector can provide practically any service at a far lower price than the government, and often at a higher level of quality, the size of government keeps expanding, both in total size and as a percentage of gross domestic product (GDP).[5] There are a number of reasons for this continued growth in spite of the clear conclusion that economies that have the smallest governments are the most efficient and prosperous.[6] The Public Choice School of Economics and the Law & Economics literature over the last few decades has proven this to be true in hundreds, if not thousands of studies.

Basically, government continues to expand in spite of the evidence that expansion reduces total welfare because the representatives that voters elect tend to represent special interests rather than the public interest and because the special interests are concentrated whereas the individuals who have to pay for the programs the special interests want are dispersed unorganized and powerless.

The theory of rational ignorance holds that it is sometimes better, from an economic perspective, to be ignorant of certain things, even if being ignorant costs you money, because the cost of overcoming ignorance is more than the cost of remaining ignorant. For example, it might take a Florida taxpayer days or weeks to learn that a portion of his tax money is going to build a bridge in Oregon. His share of the bridge's cost is perhaps $0.20 but the time and other resources he would have to expend to discover this information might be several hundred dollars. Thus, it just is not worthwhile trying to uncover this kind of information. The elected politicians and the unelected bureaucrats, who are supposed to guard against this kind of abuse are, instead, the reason why such abuses continue and proliferate.

It also is not worth trying to do anything about this injustice. It is irrational from an economic perspective to spend the time and money needed to go to Washington and lobby Congress not to fund a bridge that is only costing you $0.20 but it does make sense for the construction company that would build the bridge to do some lobbying, especially if the same company also wants to build bridges in 15 or 20 other states. From a lobbying perspective,[7] the odds are stacked against those who must pay because it does not make economic sense to do anything about the situation.[8] Furthermore, the members of Congress from each state where a bridge is to be built will be lobbying their colleagues to vote in favor of constructing the bridge. Thus, the representatives, who are supposed to represent the interests of taxpayers, often act in ways that support the interests of some special interest at the expense of the taxpayers.

SUPERMAJORITY REQUIREMENT

A supermajority requirement would require more than a 50.001% majority vote for passage of a bill into law.[9] Various supermajority vote proposals have been suggested in the USA at the federal level, but none have passed,[10] perhaps because Congress does not want to give up some of its power. Establishing a supermajority requirement, for spending bills at least, might be feasible in an emerging democracy, where political power might be more in a state of flux. Such a requirement could be added to the country's constitution. But it is more difficult to establish in a mature democracy, since the status quo is firmly in place.

The higher the percentage requirement, the more difficult it would be to raise taxes and spending. There are several options to choose from. For example, a constitution might require a two-thirds vote for passage of a spending bill and the three-fourths vote for raising taxes. Perhaps a simple majority would be required to reduce taxes or repeal a law.

There is any number of possibilities.[11] A former New Jersey governor proposed a 2/3 supermajority for state tax increases.[12] Members of the New Jersey legislature recommended a less strict 3/5 supermajority.[13] Thirteen other states have some form of supermajority requirement. In nine states, the requirement is stiffer than 3/5. Seven states have a 2/3 requirement and two states[14] have a 3/4 requirement.[15] Five states require voters to approve tax increases and in Florida, a supermajority of voters is required.[16]

A supermajority requirement would not preclude the possibility of future tax increases but it would make tax hikes more difficult.[17] The legislature would have to reach more of a consensus than is now required, which would reduce the influence and power of special interests. But a supermajority requirement would not make it impossible to raise taxes.

For example, since California adopted a two-thirds requirement in 1978, its budget increased from $14 billion to more than $61 billion (as of early 1998). A supermajority requirement would merely slow down the increase in the tax burden and would limit increases to cases where there is a strong consensus.[18]

The evidence is clear that a supermajority decreases the rate of government growth. Between 1980 and 1996, the state tax burden as a percentage of personal income rose five times as fast in states that did not have a supermajority requirement than in states that did have such a requirement.[19] Between 1990 and early 1998, the top tax rate increased in ten states. In all ten states where the top rate was raised, there was no supermajority requirement. During this same time period, the top tax rate was reduced in three of the 13 states that do have a supermajority requirement.[20]

In Arizona, taxes had been raised eight times in the nine years before its supermajority requirement was enacted into law in 1992. Between then and early 1998, Arizona reduced taxes five years in a row.[21]

The rate of government growth at the federal level would also likely be reduced if a supermajority requirement were in place. Four out of five tax federal tax increases would not have passed if a two-thirds vote were needed for passage.[22] The four largest tax increases between 1980 and 1998 [1982, 1983, 1990 and 1993] would not have passed if the two-thirds supermajority requirement would have been in place.[23]

The argument has been made that occasional tax increases are necessary to reduce the deficit. But a closer analysis shows that such is not the case. The history of the last few decades is that when Congress increases taxes, it increases spending by even more. In recent years, Congress has increased spending by $1.59 for each $1 increase in taxes.[24] The evidence is clear that the way to balance the budget or reduce the deficit is to reduce spending, not increase taxes.

ETHICAL ISSUES

The ethical aspect of this issue can be approached from several perspectives. According to utilitarian ethics, an act or policy is ethical if it is efficient. Some ethicists would go farther and say that only the most efficient possibility is ethical. All less efficient possibilities are unethical.

Utilitarian ethics has as its goal the greatest good for the greatest number. Richard A. Posner, an American jurist and prolific author on law and economics, takes the position that morality and efficiency are consistent.[25] In another work, he states that "the criterion for judging whether acts and institutions are just or good is whether they maximize the wealth of society."[26]

If these views are to be reconciled, one might say that an act or policy or institution is ethical if it is more efficient than any other alternative. Otherwise, it is unethical. Thus, if the act or policy results in the misallocation of resources, it is unethical because it reduces efficiency.

Another aspect to consider is the effect that a policy has on stability. All other things being equal, stability is a better condition than instability.[27] So a policy that enhances stability is to be preferred to one that increases instability.

> Benjamin Disraeli in the United Kingdom believed that the use of a simple majority for altering the character of the nation was an immoral exercise of power. He theorized that simple majorities that lead to slender margins of passage suggest only a temporary majority in favor of a policy. Making decisions on such temporary majorities leads to decisions which are likely to be reversed. This leads to instability and is damaging to democratic politics. Echoing the views of Hamilton, Madison and Jay is Disraeli's view that the clearer the majority, the more likely that the proposed policy is correct.[28]

Another ethical perspective is based in rights theory. All taxation is based on the taking of property without the owners' consent. When property is taken without the owner's consent in the private sector, it is labeled theft. But when the government does the taking, it is called taxation. Thus, all taxation involves immoral conduct, since theft is immoral.

No one but the most naïve individuals would seriously state that taxation is voluntary. If one honestly believes such gibberish, all one needs to do to prove the thesis is refuse to pay and see what happens.[29]

A third way to approach the issue is based on fairness. Is it fair to force all the people to pay for the benefits that only some people receive? At the federal level, all taxpayers are forced to pay to construct a bridge in Oregon. All taxpayers are forced to pay for a play that portrays Christ as a homosexual who has sex with his Apostles,[30] for art exhibits that show a crucifix soaked in urine[31] and paintings of the Virgin Mary that have elephant dung thrown on them.[32] Such government expenditures are not only unfair to the vast majority of taxpayers who never get to see the art exhibition they are being forced to subsidize. Such subsidies are also highly offensive to millions of taxpayers.

CONCLUDING COMMENTS

If the goal were to reduce the immorality of government, one way to do that is to reduce the tax burden below current levels. That conclusion can be reached regardless of which of the three ethical approaches mentioned above is applied to the question. From the efficiency perspective, utilitarian ethics would require reduced taxes because the private sector can provide just about any service at a lower cost than the government. Increased efficiency results whenever a function shifts from the public sector to the private sector.[33]

If one takes the rights approach to ethics, the same conclusion can be drawn. Since all taxation involves the violation of property rights,[34] the only way to reduce the violation of such rights is to reduce the tax bite that government takes. The same is true from the fairness perspective. Redistribution is an unethical goal because it forces some people to pay for the benefits that other people receive.[35] There is no convincing argument that can be put forth that justifies forcing taxpayers in Florida and the other states to pay for the construction of a bridge in Oregon.

None but the most naïve individuals could seriously advance the argument that the representatives we elect actually represent our best interests. The literature from the Public Choice School of Economics over the last few decades has conclusively proven that politicians and bureaucrats are just like the rest of us. They act so as to benefit themselves, not the public they represent.

That being the case, it becomes necessary to make structural changes to minimize the damage that is done whenever taxes are collected. The way to minimize inefficiency, property rights violations and unfairness is to limit the amount of taxes that the government is able to collect. One way to do that is to increase the number of votes that are required to pass a tax increase. The more difficult it is to raise taxes, the more likely that the system will not be able to increase the inefficiency that already exists, the less likely that even more property will be taken without the owners' consent, the more likely it will be that Florida taxpayers will not be forced to pay for a bridge constructed in Oregon. Thus, adoption of a supermajority requirement to raise taxes would help to achieve this result.

The question then becomes "What percentage is appropriate?" The best percentage, if one were to maximize efficiency, security of property and fairness, would be to have a 100% requirement -- unanimity. The problem with having a 100% requirement is that the government would not be able to raise any taxes, since it is almost 100% certain that at least one representative or Senator would vote "no" on any given tax bill. Thus, if one believes that government performs some functions that deserve funding, the 100% requirement is unacceptable.[36] If 100% is either not feasible or not acceptable, then some lesser percentage could be chosen as a workable alternative. There is substantial precedent for choosing two-thirds, since that ratio appears in the Constitution ten times. A ratio of three-fourths would be even better.

NOTES

[1] E.E. Savas, Privatizing the Public Sector: How to Shrink Government, Chatham, NJ: Chatham House, 1982, p. 93.

[2] Barbara J. Stevens, Solid Waste Management 215-243, in Privatization for New York: Competing for a Better Future, A Report of the New York State Senate Advisory Commission on Privatization, January 1992.

[3] Randall Fitzgerald, When Government Goes Private: Successful Alternatives to Public Services, New York: Universe Books, 1988, p. 17.

[4] John C. Goodman, editor, Privatization, Dallas: National Center for Policy Analysis, 1985, p. 119. For numerous case studies on privatization, see the Reason Public Policy Institute's website on this topic [www.privatization.org].

[5] One study points out that government spending relative to Gross National Product (GNP) has risen from 10 percent during World War I to nearly 40 percent during the 1990s. At the federal level, the government went from taking $1 out of $12 earned in 1890 to $1 out of $3 earned in 1990. James H. Perry and Peter Cleary, Growth, Prosperity and Honest Government: The Case for Constitutional Tax Limitation, Americans for Tax Reform, [www.atr.org/pressreleases/Issues/i0039.htm].

[6] Hundreds of studies have looked at the relationship between the level of taxation and economic growth. For a few examples, see Daniel J. Mitchell, The Historical Lessons of Lower Tax Rates, Backgrounder No. 1086, Heritage Foundation, July 19, 1996; Daniel J. Mitchell, Taxes, Deficits, and Economic Growth, Heritage Lecture No. 565, Heritage Foundation, May 14, 1996; Scott Hodge, William Beach, John Barry, Mark Wilson and Joe Cobb, Is There a "Clinton Crunch"? How the 1993 Budget Plan Affected the Economy, Backgrounder No. 1078, Heritage Foundation, May 1, 1996. These documents may be found at [www.heritage.org]. Also see Richard M. Bird, Tax Policy & Economic Development, Baltimore and London: The Johns Hopkins University Press, 1992; Taxes and Growth: The London Conference, Critical Issues No. 10, Australian Institute for Public Policy, 14 October 1986.

[7] One study found that 96 percent of the witnesses who testified at 14 congressional hearings that discussed increased spending programs were in favor of more spending. Thus, the voices of those who oppose increased spending are not being heard by those who have the power to change spending levels. Joel Fox (Howard Jarvis Taxpayers Association), Making Taxes Harder, Wall Street Journal, April 15, 1997, cited by National Center for Policy Analysis, Require Two-Thirds Vote to Tax [www.ncpa.org/pi/taxes/april97j.html].

[8] This point has been made many times by Public Choice theorists but the idea has been around at least since the 1840s when Frederic Bastiat, the French economist and philosopher, made the same point in several of his writings. James Buchanan and Gordon Tullock are the founders of the Public Choice School of Economics and they cover this point in many of their writings. Other proponents of Public Choice also discuss this point, since it is one of the central points in the Public Choice worldview.

[9] This chapter does not attempt to present a full and comprehensive economic analysis of the supermajority requirement. The recent literature on this topic is extensive and should be referred to by those who want more detailed information. At least 35 documents exist on this topic at the Americans for Tax Reform website alone. See [www.atr.org]. Numerous other web sites also have documents on this topic. See [www.cato.org] (Cato Institute), [www.heritage.org] (Heritage Foundation), [www.ntu.org] (National Taxpayers Union).

[10] The National Center for Policy Analysis points out that the concept of a supermajority has always been a part of our government.

- The requirement for a two-thirds vote appears 10 times in the Constitution.
- It is necessary in order to ratify a treaty, to override a presidential veto and to convict an impeached official.
- Thirteen states now have some form of super-majority tax limitations.
- Taxes and spending have grown more slowly and economies have expanded faster in those states, according to statistics compiled by Americans for Tax Reform.

See Joel Fox (Howard Jarvis Taxpayers Association), Making Taxes Harder, Wall Street Journal, April 15, 1997, cited by National Center for Policy Analysis, Require Two-Thirds Vote to Tax [www.ncpa.org/pi/taxes/april97j.html].

[11] The constitutional amendment that has been proposed would require a two-thirds majority. This percentage is advocated because it is the percentage found elsewhere in the Constitution. It is mentioned in Art. I, sec. 3, cl. 6 (conviction in impeachment trials), Art. I, sec. 5, cl. 2 (expulsion of a member of Congress), Art. I, sec. 7, cl. 2 (override a presidential veto), Art. II, sec. 1, cl. 3 (quorum of two-thirds of the states to elect the President), Art. II, sec. 2, cl. 2 (consent to a treaty), Art. V (proposing constitutional amendments), Art. VII (state ratification of the original Constitution), Amendment XII (quorum of two-thirds of the states to elect the President and Vice President), Amendment XIV (to remove disability of those who have engaged in insurrection) and Amendment XXV, sec. 4 (presidential disability). For more on this and other points relating to the supermajority requirement, see James H. Perry and Peter Cleary, Growth, Prosperity and Honest Government: The Case for Constitutional Tax Limitation, Americans for Tax Reform [www.atr.org].

[12] Dean Stansel, Supermajority: A Super Idea, Cato Institute, April 15, 1998 [www.cato.org].

[13] Stansel, supra.

[14] The two states are Arkansas and Oklahoma. Editorial, Shackle Congress, Free Taxpayers, Investor's Business Daily, April 21, 1998, cited in National Center for Policy Analysis, Tax Limitation Amendment [www.ncpa.org/congress/apr98b.html].

[15] Stansel, supra.

[16] Stansel, supra. A more recent study reveals that 14 states now have some form of supermajority requirement. See Supermajority at the State Level, Americans for Tax Reform. The number varies from year to yet. See [www.atr.org] for the latest statistics.

[17] It is mostly special interests that stand to lose if a supermajority requirement were passed. They argue that such a requirement would "gut" the budget. Such a possibility is remote. Actually, if such a requirement would gut the budget, that would be a good thing, since the private sector can do just about anything better and cheaper than government. The best thing that could happen would be if a supermajority requirement would gut the budget, since the result would be increased efficiency and a higher standard of living for the vast majority.

Other benefits would also accrue if a supermajority requirement were enacted. The New Jersey Education Association argued before a state Senate committee that adopting a supermajority requirement would threaten the future of public education (Stansel, supra). If that did occur, the general public would benefit, since public education is not only highly inefficient at delivering education but is also unfair, since those who do not have children in public schools are forced to pay for those who do. For more on this point, see Robert W. McGee, Brown v. Board of Education: Forty Years of Asking the Wrong Question and the Case for Privatization of Education, St. Louis University Public Law Review 17(1): 141-155 (1997).

[18] Joel Fox (Howard Jarvis Taxpayers Association), Making Taxes Harder, Wall Street Journal, April 15, 1997, cited by National Center for Policy Analysis, Require Two-Thirds Vote to Tax [www.ncpa.org/pi/taxes/april97j.html].

[19] Stansel, supra.

[20] Stansel, supra.

[21] Stansel, supra.

[22] Editorial, Shackle Congress, Free Taxpayers, Investor's Business Daily, April 21, 1998, cited in National Center for Policy Analysis, Tax Limitation Amendment, http://www.ncpa.org/pi/congress/apr98b.html. This point is also made in James H. Perry and Peter Cleary, Growth, Prosperity and Honest Government: The Case for Constitutional Tax Limitation, Americans for Tax Reform [www.atr.org].

[23] Cato Handbook for Congress: Policy Recommendations for the 106th Congress 65 (1999).

[24] James H. Perry and Peter Cleary, Growth, Prosperity and Honest Government: The Case for Constitutional Tax Limitation, Americans for Tax Reform [www.atr.org].
[25] Richard A. Posner, Economic Analysis of Law, 5th edition, New York: Aspen Law & Business, 1998, pp. 284-285.
[26] Richard A. Posner, The Economics of Justice, revised edition, Cambridge, MA: Harvard University Press, 1983, p. 115.
[27] Stability is not always to be preferred to instability. A dynamic market economy that produces annual growth rates in double digits is to be preferred to an economy that produces no growth, even if a stagnant economy is more stable. Living under a dictator like Stalin is more stable than living in a democracy, especially one that changes governments more than once a year like Italy has been doing since World War II, but most people would prefer to live in Italy rather than Stalinist Russia.
[28] James H. Perry and Peter Cleary, Growth, Prosperity and Honest Government: The Case for Constitutional Tax Limitation, Americans for Tax Reform [www.atr.org].
[29] The Internal Revenue Service of the United States has a reputation for being nasty and disregarding legal procedure to confiscate assets, often without any kind of reasonable due process. For horror stories detailing such abuses, see George Hansen, To Harass Our People: The IRS and Government Abuse of Power, Washington, DC: Positive Publications, 1984; David Burnham, A Law Unto Itself: Power, Politics and the IRS, New York: Random House, 1989.
[30] Edwin Feulner, Welfare for Artists, Views, The Heritage Foundation, June 16, 1998 [www.heritage.org].
[31] This artwork was criticized as being offensive to Christians. It was subsidized by the federal government. As a result of this exhibit there were calls for cutting off federal funding for the arts. For more on this and related points, see David Boaz, The Separation of Art and State, Cato Institute, August 14, 1997; Bill Kauffman, Subsidies to the Arts: Cultivating Mediocrity, Policy Analysis No. 137, Cato Institute, August 8, 1990. These documents may be found at [www.cato.org]. Also see Laurence Jarvik, Ten Good Reasons to Eliminate Funding for the National Endowment for the Arts, Roe Backgrounder No. 1110, The Heritage Foundation, April 29, 1997; William Craig Rice, I Hear America Singing: The Arts Will Flower Without the NEA, 82 Policy Review, March-April 1997; available at [www.heritage.org].
[32] The mayor of New York City threatened to cut off millions of dollars in funding to the Brooklyn Museum of Art if it held an exhibit that included this painting, which was highly offensive to Catholics. Mayor's Press Office Statement Regarding Brooklyn Museum of Art's Board of Director's Vote, Release #381-99, September 28, 1999, http://www.ci.nyc.ny.us/html/om/html/99b/pr381-99.html.
[33] It has been estimated that for every dollar of tax reduction at the federal level, the private sector would expand by $1.38 in the same year. Over seven years, output would expand by $2.45 for each dollar of federal spending restraint. If federal spending had not risen above the 15-25 percent level of GNP after World War II, the average American family's income would be twice what it is in 1999. James H. Perry and Peter Cleary, Growth, Prosperity and Honest Government: The Case for Constitutional Tax Limitation, Americans for Tax Reform [www.atr.org].
[34] User fees and lotteries are exceptions, but these forms of public finance are not taxes in the true sense of the term, since they are voluntary.
[35] For a major treatise on this point, see Bertrand DeJouvenel, The Ethics of Redistribution, Cambridge: Cambridge University Press, 1952.
[36] Some economists, political scientists and philosophers argue that there is nothing that government can do better than the private sector, including the provision of defense. If that is true, then there is no need to fund any governmental function. We will leave discussion of this point for another day.

Chapter 20

SHOULD TAXES BE VISIBLE OR HIDDEN?

INTRODUCTION

A tax can be either visible or hidden. The two possibilities seem to be diametrically opposed to each other. Which possibility is better? That depends on the goals of the individual making the determination. If the goal is to raise as much revenue as possible with a minimum of protest, then a hidden tax is to be preferred to a visible tax. If the goal is to restrain the amount of tax the government takes, or to let taxpayers know exactly what they have to pay for government services, then a visible tax is more likely to help achieve that goal. The real question is whether hiding taxes from those who pay them is ethical.

AN ETHICAL APPROACH TO THE QUESTION

There are basically just two ethical approaches to this question. One can take either a utilitarian approach or a rights approach.

There are several variations of utilitarianism, the philosophy that nearly all economists espouse. But basically, utilitarianism holds that an act is ethical if the result is the greatest good for the greatest number. Acts that do not result in the greatest good for the greatest number are unethical.

Bentham, one of the founders of utilitarianism, stated that "...it is the greatest happiness of the greatest number that is the measure of right and wrong."[1] Sidgwick, a later utilitarian, said that "...an action is right if and only if it brings about at least as much net happiness as any other action the agent could have performed; otherwise it is wrong."[2] According to this view, if an act results in increasing happiness by 10 percent, the act is unethical if another act could have increased happiness by more than 10 percent.[3]

Another variant of utilitarianism, one that economists generally espouse, is that an action is moral if it is efficient. Efficiency and morality are not inconsistent.[4] The problem with this view is that it totally ignores rights. An action can increase efficiency and still be unethical if it violates rights but utilitarianism ignores this possibility.[5]

Ignoring the flaws of the utilitarian approach, let's apply utilitarian theory to the question of whether taxes should be visible or hidden. Hidden taxes reduce administration costs. It costs more to administer a tax if taxpayers know about it. Hiding taxes increases efficiency in tax collection because taxpayers do not protest what they do not know exists. Thus, it would appear that hidden taxes are ethical, since the result is increased efficiency.

However, that is not the end of the analysis. If more taxes are collected, which is likely if the tax is hidden from taxpayers, less money remains in the private sector. Since money is always spent more efficiently in the private sector than by government, one may logically conclude that a transfer of money from the private sector to the government reduces efficiency. Resources are transferred from more highly valued uses to less highly valued uses. Thus, one may conclude that hiding taxes from taxpayers is unethical on utilitarian grounds because it reduces efficiency.

From a rights perspective, a visible tax is to be preferred to a hidden tax. That is because taxpayers have a right to know what they are paying for. Disclosure should be as full and complete as possible. Disclosure is required on corporate financial statements so investors will know something about the stock they are buying. Product labeling laws force manufacturers to disclose the contents of the package.[6] Bankers are required by law to reveal the full interest charges on the loans they make. And people should know the full cost of what they have to pay for government. If they don't, they will not be able to make intelligent decisions at election time, when they are called upon to decide who their political leaders will be.

SOME EXAMPLES

An example of a hidden tax would be the value-added tax.[7] The value-added tax is hidden because the people who ultimately pay it -- consumers -- do not know what portion of their purchase is for the product and what portion is for the tax. As a result, they may tend to blame the company that makes or sells the product for the high price, when in fact a significant portion of the price represents a tax.

Excise taxes on alcohol, tobacco and gasoline could be used for examples of hidden taxes. Although the tax may be stated on the package or gas pump, consumers seldom read these things. The tax they pay is part of the stated price.

An example of a visible tax would be a user fee. If people have to pay $4 to enter a national park, they are made aware immediately of the cost of that particular government service. It is not hidden. But if admission is free, the real cost is hidden. Someone has to pay to maintain the park, to pay the salaries of the employees who work there, and so forth. If the cost of maintaining the park is funded through general tax revenues, those who use the park for free are being subsidized at the expense of everyone else. The result is overuse of the park. If individuals had to pay the full cost of using the facility, fewer of them would use it, which would have beneficial effects on the environment, which is being harmed by overuse of government-owned recreational facilities.

Some taxes are partly visible and partly hidden. For example, the personal income tax in the USA is collected by having the employer take the tax directly from employee paychecks before they even receive their pay. The amount of the tax taken is disclosed on their pay stub, but they do not feel the full "bite" of the tax because they never actually saw the money. The tax would be more visible if the employer did not take it out of their checks, since they would then have to write out a check to the government for the amount they owe. Such a requirement would place more pressure on politicians to keep taxes low, since taxpayers would have a better feel for what they are actually paying for government services. But it would also increase collection problems, since not everyone would pay the tax when it is supposed to be paid.

But where there is a tradeoff between disclosure and efficiency, the only ethical choice would be disclosure. If the government is the servant of the people, then the people should know exactly how much their servant costs. The full cost should not be hidden, even if the tax collection process would run more smoothly without disclosure. In the long-run, a full disclosure system would probably result in lower taxes, since taxpayers who are aware of the full cost of government will have a tendency to put pressure on their representatives to keep taxes low.

CONCLUDING COMMENTS

The question of whether a hidden tax is ethical can be viewed from the perspectives of utilitarianism or rights theory. Utilitarianism yields mixed results because, on the one hand, hidden taxes are more efficient to collect than visible taxes because they entail fewer administrative problems and cause the tax collection process to be more efficient. But on the other hand, hiding taxes makes it easier to collect more taxes, which reduces happiness, since all taxes are forced takings, which require taxpayers to forcibly part with a portion of their property.

Applying rights theory to the question produces more clear-cut results. Hiding taxes from those who must pay them is unethical because taxpayers have a right to know what they pay for the cost of government. Thus, hiding taxes from taxpayers is always unethical, even if hiding them makes tax collection more efficient.

NOTES

[1] Jeremy Bentham, A Fragment on Government, in The Works of Jeremy Bentham, vol. 1, 227 (J. Bowring, ed. 1962), as cited in William H. Shaw, Contemporary Ethics: Taking Account of Utilitarianism 8 (1999).

[2] Quoted in Shaw, supra, at 10.

[3] One problem with any utilitarian approach is that it is impossible to measure increases in happiness. It is also not possible to measure interpersonal utility. Measurement problems also result if a few individuals stand to gain a lot from an act while many

people stand to lose just a little. Such is the case with tariffs, quotas and other trade restraints.

[4] Richard A. Posner, Economic Analysis of Law 284-285 (5th ed., 1998). A variation on the utilitarian theme is the wealth maximization view, which holds that "...the criterion for judging whether acts and institutions are just or good is whether they maximize the wealth of society." Richard A. Posner, The Economics of Justice 115 (1983).

[5] That is the fatal flaw in the utilitarian philosophy. For more on this point, see Robert W. McGee, The Fatal Flaw in the Methodology of Law and Economics, Commentaries on Law & Economics 1: 209-223 (1997); Robert W. McGee, The Fatal Flaw in NAFTA, GATT and All Other Trade Agreements, Northwestern Journal of International Law & Business 14: 549-565 (1994).

[6] I am not advocating that there should be labeling laws, but am merely using labeling laws as an example. Free speech advocates would be quick to point out that forcing companies to disclose the contents or ingredients of their products violates their right to free speech, or the right to refrain from speech. In cases where pharmaceutical companies must reveal the contents of their drug, there is also a possibility that their property rights are being violated, since they have a property right -- a patent -- for the products they produce.

[7] For more on the value added tax, see Adrian Ogley, Principles of Value Added Tax: A European Perspective, London: Interfisc Publishing, 1998; Alan A. Tait, Value Added Tax: International Practice and Problems, Washington, DC: International Monetary Fund, 1988; Murray L. Weidenbaum, David G. Raboy and Ernest S. Christian, Jr., editors, The Value Added Tax: Orthodoxy and New Thinking, Center for the Study of American Business, Norwell, MA, Lancaster, UK and Dordrecht, The Netherlands: Kluwer Academic Publishers, 1989; Charles E. McLure, Jr., The Value-Added Tax: Key to Deficit Reduction? Washington, DC: American Enterprise Institute, 1987; Graham Bannock, VAT and Small Business: European Experience and Implications for North America, London: Graham Bannock & Partners Ltd., 1986.

PART FOUR

ATTRIBUTES AND TYPES OF TAXATION

Chapter 21

TAX ATTRIBUTES

INTRODUCTION

All governments need money in order to pay for the cost of operations. There are a number of ways that they can obtain the funds they need. Some revenue raising methods are "better" than others. Some are more "fair" than others. When one speaks in terms of "better" tax systems or "fairness," one leaves the realm of value-free economic analysis[1] and enters the field of philosophy, since value judgments are required to answer questions involving bestness or fairness. So constructing a tax system involves more than just economic engineering. Philosophical issues must be discussed and decided.

TAX CHARACTERISTICS AND ATTRIBUTES

This chapter discusses the main characteristics and attributes of the various forms of taxation. Tax systems (more properly, systems of public finance) may be based on coercion or voluntary exchange. They may charge high or low rates. They may be based on the ability to pay principle or the cost-benefit principle. Rates may be uniform -- the same rate for everyone -- or discriminatory. The system may be easy or difficult to administer. Taxes may be hidden or visible. They may be easy or difficult to collect. Collections may go into the general fund or may be earmarked for specific uses. Collections may produce a steady flow of cash or a sporadic and unpredictable flow. The system chosen may produce minor or major distortions to the economy. The system chosen will inevitably have some effect on competitiveness and economic growth. Rules may be either simple or complex, clear or vague. And the rules may be stable over time or may change frequently. The tax base chosen may be either wide or narrow. And the system may result in major or minor effects on behavior and incentives and social harmony. The system may have high or low administrative costs. And the amount of revenue raised from a specific tax may, at times, be less than the cost of administering the costs of collection.

These characteristics and attributes are not mutually exclusive. Indeed, many of them coexist in the tax systems of all modern Western democracies. This chapter discusses these characteristics and attributes and, at times, attempts to determine which attributes are to be preferred over others.

Voluntary or Coercive

The next few paragraphs discuss the distinction between what is coercive and what is voluntary. In a liberal democracy,[2] one goal is to maximize individual liberty and minimize the amount of encroachment on that liberty by the state. This philosophy can be applied to the means government uses to raise revenue. Government can raise revenue in one of two ways, either through coercion or voluntary exchange. Income, property, estate and gift taxes are examples of coercive forms of taxation because those paying have no choice about it. They must pay or face possible punishment. Voluntary forms of revenue raising include lotteries and user fees because coercion is absent.

It might be argued that taxation is not really coercive because voters, somewhere along the line, have consented to be taxed. But there are a number of flaws in this line of reasoning, which we have discussed elsewhere in this book.

In a society where freedom and private property are valued, voluntary forms of revenue raising are superior to coercive forms. If government is viewed as the servant rather than the master of the people, then coercion is to be minimized and the possibilities for voluntary exchange maximized. Forms of revenue raising (like lotteries and user fees) that do not depend on coercion are to be preferred to forms of revenue raising that rely on coercion. And tax laws that expire after some period of time are to be preferred to tax laws that remain on the books until repealed, because of the consent factor.

Tax laws should be subject to review after a few years, and the legislature should be required to decide, periodically, whether the tax laws should be renewed. While this requirement would not solve the consent problem completely, it at least would be a step in the right direction, since the degree of consent that any law enjoys declines with each passing day, as a portion of the citizenry dies and new citizens are born.

One argument that has been made against voluntarism in the area of government finance is that the government cannot raise all the funds it needs through voluntarism. Coercion is necessary for the state to function. While it would take a book to explore this issue, a few points can be made here. For one thing, this line of reasoning is pragmatic rather than philosophical or ethical. This pragmatic view basically holds that coercion is necessary to raise the necessary funds, therefore coercion must be used. Fairness, equity and property rights are totally absent from this line of reasoning.

Even if one concedes the point that coercion is needed to raise the "necessary" funds, one must still ask "how much is necessary?" If the goal of a free society is to minimize coercion and allow maximum room for individual choice, then government expenditures must be kept at a minimum, so that the amount of coercion needed to raise funds is minimized. Thus, the role of government must be minimized.

High or Low Rates

A tax system may impose either high or low tax rates. High tax rates are a major disincentive to production, savings and wealth accumulation. For example, if a painter in the 90% tax bracket[3] is offered a commission to paint a portrait for $20,000, she will only be able to keep $2,000 for her efforts if she accepts the work. In effect, she has the option of working for below market prices or not working at all.[4] It is reasonable to expect that, in some cases, she will decide not to take the work. So the painting will never come into existence. Or perhaps she will take the commission but not declare the income, which increases the amount of tax evasion in the economy and decreases respect for the law.

High tax rates in the area of estate taxes discourage savings and investment. If 90% of one's assets are confiscated by the government at death, there will be a tendency to spend it all now and not leave much for the heirs. Capital accumulation suffers as a result, which has a negative effect on economic growth and the standard of living. Of course, one might give it to the children and grandchildren before death, but this route may not be possible if a gift tax takes a large chunk of the gift.

From a taxpayer standpoint, low rates are superior to high rates. From the government's point of view, high rates may be more attractive than low rates because more revenue can be collected from high rates than from low rates. But while this may be true over a certain range of rates, it is not true in all cases. If rates are too high, people will change their behavior, and the total revenue generated may actually decline.

If the marginal individual income tax rate rises to 100%, for example, individuals will quit working second jobs and will refuse to work overtime, even if they would receive premium pay. And there will be tremendous incentives not to report all income, thus increasing the extent of tax evasion. If the rate is only 90%, the same behavior will occur to a somewhat lesser degree. If the top rate is 5%, people will be willing to work harder and longer because they will be able to keep most of the fruits of their labor. But if the top rate is only 5%, the state may not be able to collect all the revenue it needs to pay its expenses. Somewhere between 0% and 100% there is an optimum rate that will maximize tax collections.[5]

While there is a relationship between tax rates and the amount of taxes collected, there are a number of problems with this "optimum tax rate" approach. For one thing, there is no way to measure precisely what the optimum rate will be. Individuals have different preferences, and their preferences change from time to time. Some people would continue to work if 95% of their income were taxed away, and some would not. Some would work for a few extra hours and some would work for more than a few. Their preferences are not known and cannot be measured. Arriving at an optimal tax rate is almost pure guesswork.

Another, perhaps larger problem also exists with this search for an optimum tax rate. It involves the philosophical question of whether it is even proper for a government to attempt to extract the maximum amount of taxes from the citizenry. If government is the servant rather than the master, then it would seem that attempting to extract the maximum tribute from taxpayers is an illegitimate goal.

The rate of tax also has effects on the economy. Money taken out of the private sector cannot be used to invest in business expansion, cannot be saved, or spent on consumption items. A number of studies have concluded that high tax rates retard economic growth and that low rates encourage it.[6] Economic growth cannot come from raising taxes. All that raising taxes does is redistribute previously created wealth. So if maximizing economic growth is a goal, minimizing taxes must be part of the way to achieve that goal. Thus, it follows that lower rates are better than higher rates.

There is also a relationship between economic efficiency and the tax rate. If rates are high, businesses will stand to lose less if they make a bad investment decision because they can deduct the loss on their tax return. So there is a tendency to be less careful about making investments. And when the tax system has both high rates and complexity, as was the case in the USA before the 1986 Tax Reform Act,[7] there tends to be a number of "tax shelters" -- investments that make no economic sense but make good tax sense. For example, under a tax shelter scheme that has a 5-to-1 write-off, every $100 investment results in a $500 tax deduction. So if the tax rate is 50%, an investor can reduce his taxes by $250 (50% of $500) by making a $100 investment, which is a better return than could be had from most legitimate investments that would create real economic wealth.

It has been argued that raising tax rates can have a beneficial effect on the economy at times when the economy is nearing full employment and becoming "overheated." Keynes[8] and others[9] have argued that fiscal policy -- raising taxes -- can be used to reduce this overheating and ease inflationary pressures. This view is based on the theory that inflation is caused either by excess demand or by increasing costs. Economists call these two causes of inflation "demand-pull" and "cost-push."[10]

But this view has been discredited for a number of years.[11] It is possible to have both unemployment and inflation at the same time.[12] There is much evidence to suggest that inflation -- a general increase in the price level -- is caused by an increase in the quantity of money, not by excess employment or tax rates that are too low.[13] So those who argue that high tax rates may be justified for reasons of economic growth are standing on shaky ground.

Low tax rates are to be preferred to high rates for a number of reasons. Low rates result in less distortion to the economy because less money is being taken from producers and redistributed to tax consumers. Resources are not being squandered on tax shelters that make no economic sense. Low rates aid in economic growth because more money is available for investment. Low rates are fairer than high rates because low rates involve less confiscation of personal property.

Ability to Pay or Cost-Benefit

There are two basic and diametrically opposed views of taxation. Those who favor the ability to pay approach view the state as a master, who extracts tribute from its subjects on the basis of how much they are able to pay. Those who take this first approach often also view the state as a benevolent father figure, who distributes tax benefits on the basis of need. In Karl Marx's words, "From each according to his abilities; to each according to his needs."[14]

Those who take the cost-benefit approach view the state as the servant of the people. Government provides services and taxpayers pay for the services. Those who benefit the most from the services should pay the most. And those who do not use a particular government service should not be forced to pay for it.[15] This topic is discussed in more detail elsewhere in the book.

Uniform or Discriminatory Rates

A tax system can be structured to have either uniform or discriminatory rates. There are basically three options. A tax that has discriminatory rates will take a larger percentage from some groups than others. An example of a discriminatory system would be a graduated personal income tax, which takes a larger percentage of marginal income from those who earn more, and a lesser percentage from those who earn less. For example, a graduated system might take 10% of taxable income between $0 and $10,000; 15% of taxable income between $10,001 and $20,000; 25% of taxable income between $20,001 and $35,000; and 40% of taxable income over $35,000. Such a system can be complex, with 10 or more different rates, depending on income level; or it can be relatively simple, with just two or three rates.

A graduated system discriminates against those who earn more. Such a system is based on the ability to pay philosophy rather than the cost-benefit principle. As was mentioned above, the cost-benefit principle is to be preferred to the ability to pay principle, so a graduated tax is less desirable than one that has the same rate for everyone. This is so not only because of fundamental fairness, but also because it is simpler, and simplicity is to be preferred to complexity.

Economists have given a number of utilitarian reasons against the graduated income tax as well.[16] For one thing, it destroys the incentive of the most productive people. And since it is primarily the most productive people who save, invest and create jobs, a graduated tax will retard economic growth by reducing the amount of capital available for investment.

The second option is a tax that has uniform rates. An example of a tax having a uniform rate would be the flat rate income tax.[17] One advantage of the flat tax is that it is very simple to compute. It has only one rate, not several. Everyone pays the same rate. If the flat rate is 10%, then someone with $10,000 in taxable income will pay $1,000 and someone with $1,000,000 in taxable income will pay $100,000. Thus, the rich will pay more in total than the poor, although they will pay the same percentage.

Another advantage of having a single, flat rate is that it does not penalize those who are more productive,[18] so it does not have as much of an adverse effect on incentives and capital formation (especially if the rate is low). It also does not have as much of an adverse effect on social harmony, since it does not pit one class against another -- the rich against the poor.

A third option would be a tax that charges everyone the same amount. An example would be a poll tax or a head tax.[19] For example, if the total cost of providing government services in a particular community is $1,000,000 and there are 10,000 people in the community, then every individual would be assessed a tax of $100. This form of tax is in keeping with the cost-benefit principle. Assuming everyone benefits equally from government services, then everyone should pay the same amount without regard to income. Otherwise, there are free riders and parasites.

This form of tax is the closest approximation to a market system. For example, if you go into the store to purchase a loaf of bread, the person behind the counter does not ask you what your income is before quoting a price for the bread. The price you pay for the bread is not based on a percentage of your income. The price is the same for everyone regardless of income level. And so it is with the poll tax. But the poll tax is not neutral because some people benefit from government services more than others. And if everyone received $100 worth of services in exchange for a $100 poll tax, why have a tax in the first place? Why not just abolish taxation and eliminate the middle man (government) by letting individuals pay for the services directly?

While a poll tax may be the fairest of the three options, historically, trying to impose a poll tax has resulted in problems. Margaret Thatcher tried to impose a poll tax in England and triggered vehement public reaction. Those who would have to pay more under a poll tax scheme protested loudly (and sometimes violently). Part of the problem was that the poll tax is a direct tax, and it is visible, not hidden, so people knew exactly what they were paying. When the total cost of the tax is hidden, people do not realize what they are really paying, so there is less of a probability that they will protest. So there appears to be an irreconcilable conflict between fairness and feasibility when it comes to implementing a poll tax, especially if some people (such as the poor, unemployed or retired) cannot afford to pay it.

Easy or Difficult to Administer

A tax may be either easy or difficult to administer. Needless to say, a tax that is easy to administer is preferable to one that is difficult to administer. And while such an answer might seem obvious, in practice, many of the taxes now being imposed in the so-called advanced Western democracies are difficult, rather than easy to administer. For some reason, complexities have crept into the system, which make tax administration much more difficult than need be. Emerging economies should be aware of this fact, so that they can avoid similar problems when they construct their own tax systems.

Which leads to another point. The finance ministries of emerging economies should not blindly follow the advice of Western tax experts. It is these very experts who constructed the overly complex systems that now burden the West. This possibility is a very real danger. In Poland and some other emerging economies, the Internal Revenue Service of the USA has been called upon to provide instruction to the local economists and tax collectors about the intricacies of the US tax system.[20] To many people who are familiar with the needless complexity of the tax system in the USA, the thought of such instruction triggers responses ranging from hilarity to worry, fear and disgust.

Visible or Hidden

A tax can be either visible or hidden. The two possibilities seem to be diametrically opposed to each other. Which possibility is better? That depends on the goals of the individual making the determination. If the goal is to raise as much revenue as possible with a minimum of protest, then a hidden tax is to be preferred to a visible tax. If the goal is to restrain the amount of tax the government takes, or to let taxpayers know exactly what they have to pay for government services, then a visible tax is more likely to help achieve that goal.

From a strictly moral or ethical point of view, a visible tax is to be preferred to a hidden tax. Disclosure should be as full and complete as possible. Disclosure is required on corporate financial statements so investors will know something about the stock they are buying. Product labeling laws force manufacturers to disclose the contents of the package.[21] Bankers are required by law to reveal the full interest charges on the loans they make. And people should know the full cost of what they have to pay for government. If they don't, they will not be able to make intelligent decisions at election time, when they are called upon to decide who their political leaders will be.

An example of a hidden tax would be the value added tax. The value added tax is hidden because the people who ultimately pay it -- consumers -- do not know what portion of their purchase is for the product and what portion is for the tax. As a result, they may tend to blame the company that makes or sells the product for the high price, when in fact a significant portion of the price represents a tax.

Excise taxes on alcohol, tobacco and gasoline could be used for examples of hidden taxes. Although the tax may be stated on the package or gas pump, consumers seldom read these things. The tax they pay is part of the stated price.

An example of a visible tax would be a user fee. If people have to pay $4 to enter a national park, they are made aware immediately of the cost of that particular government service. It is not hidden. But if admission is free, the real cost is hidden. Someone has to pay to maintain the park, to pay the salaries of the employees who work there, and so forth. If the cost of maintaining the park is funded through general tax revenues, those who use the park for free are being subsidized at the expense of everyone else. The result is overuse of the park. If individuals had to pay the full cost of using the facility, fewer of them would use it, which would have beneficial effects on the environment, which is being harmed by overuse of government-owned recreational facilities.

Some taxes are partly visible and partly hidden. For example, the personal income tax in the USA is collected by having the employer take the tax directly from employee paychecks before they even receive their pay. The amount of the tax taken is disclosed on their pay stub, but they do not feel the full "bite" of the tax because they never actually saw the money. The tax would be more visible if the employer did not take it out of their checks, since they would then have to write out a check to the government for the amount they owe. Such a requirement would place more pressure on politicians to keep taxes low, since taxpayers would have a better feel for what they are actually paying for government services.

But it would also increase collection problems, since not everyone would pay the tax when it is supposed to be paid. But where there is a tradeoff between disclosure and efficiency, the only ethical choice would be disclosure. If the government is the servant of the people, then the people should know exactly how much their servant costs. The full cost should not be hidden, even if the tax collection process would run more smoothly without disclosure. In the long-run, a full disclosure system would probably result in lower taxes, since taxpayers who are aware of the full cost of government will have a tendency to put pressure on their representatives to keep taxes low.

Easy or Difficult to Collect

A tax may be either easy or difficult to collect. From the collector's point of view, easy is better than difficult. The ease with which a tax may be collected should definitely be kept in mind by those who are trying to devise a tax system. In most Western democracies, corporate income taxes and individual income taxes that are withheld by the employer are relatively easy to collect because corporations and noncorporate employers do the collecting, and they merely turn over the proceeds to the government. The same is true of sales taxes.

Tax liabilities that are generated from participants in the underground economy are much more difficult to collect. Low taxes are generally easier to collect than high taxes because there is less resistance to low taxes than to high taxes. If those who devise a country's tax system choose to impose a tax that is difficult to collect, they must budget large sums of money for tax administration and enforcement, which leads to inefficiency and could have a detrimental effect on civil liberties.

General Fund or Earmarked

Taxes can either go into the general fund or be earmarked -- set aside -- for particular purposes. Income taxes are generally deposited into the general fund, to be used for a variety of purposes. Gasoline taxes are often used to maintain highways. They are set aside for a particular purpose. Some people are presently advocating that a portion of the tax on cigarettes be used for cancer research.

Whether revenues from a particular tax are placed into the general fund or earmarked for special purposes depends on a number of factors. Oftentimes, a tax increase will be more acceptable to the general population if it is earmarked for a particular purpose that is widely accepted.[22] Lottery proceeds that are used for education is an example. Social Security taxes that are set aside for taxpayers' retirement is another.[23]

Segregating tax revenue for specific purposes reduces the possibility that the money will be squandered on pork barrel projects. That is one of the advantages of earmarking tax collections, and it is one of the disadvantages of dumping tax revenues into one big pot. Earmarking tax dollars is a good control device that enhances the chances that the money will actually be spent for its intended purpose. But it is not a device that can be used for every kind of government expenditure. Dumping everything into a common pot gives the government more flexibility to shift spending to where it is needed. So there is a trade-off.

Steady Flow or Sporadic and Unpredictable Flow

Taxes that produce a steady, predictable flow of revenue are to be preferred (by tax collectors) to taxes that produce sporadic and unpredictable flows. Income tax collections provide a steady and somewhat predictable flow of revenue, although collections can drop during recessions. Lottery revenues can be sporadic and unpredictable, although they are more equitable because they rely on voluntary exchange instead of coercion. If the number of people participating in a lottery drops unpredictably, the amount of revenue collected will fall below projections. Relying on sporadic and unpredictable revenue flows makes it more difficult to run a government. Revenue raising methods that depend on choice rather than force are not as controllable or predictable. That is part of the price of freedom.

Minor or Major Distortion to the Economy

From an economic perspective, the best tax is a neutral tax -- a tax that does not divert the operation of the market from the lines it would take in the absence of taxation.[24] The less distortion to the economy, the better the tax, all other things being equal. Economic resources are allocated most efficiently if they are allowed to gravitate to their most highly valued uses. Anything that causes economic resources to be diverted from their optimum use increases inefficiency and retards economic growth. Economic disruptions cause a number of problems, many of which are unforeseen. The best tax is a tax that causes no distortion. However, there is no such thing as a neutral tax,[25] so we must settle for something less than perfect.

Distortion results when resources are taken away from their best and highest use and poured into uses that are less productive. High tax rates produce more distortion than low rates, not only because high rates cause more funds to shift into relatively inefficient paths, but also because high rates cause individuals and businesses to shift their resources into areas that produce tax benefits rather than wealth. When the USA had relatively high tax rates, before the Tax Reform Act of 1986, high-income taxpayers resorted to numerous tax shelters in order to shield their income from the high tax rates. After rates dropped, much of this money was shifted into taxable investments that produced wealth rather than tax deductions.

The 1986 Tax Reform Act also had other, less positive effects on the economy. The 1986 TRA has been cited as a major reason why the real estate industry in the USA went into a depression.[26] "In constructing the Tax Reform Act of 1986 (TRA86) legislators could not have done a better job of destroying this [real estate] market if they had consciously set out to do so."[27] The 86 TRA made three tax law changes that, taken together, deflated the real estate industry practically overnight. The law eliminated the capital gains tax rate differential and the passive loss limitation rules and lengthened the tax write-off period for real property, thus eliminating much of the incentive to invest in real estate. Housing starts have dropped every year since. All housing starts dropped by 36% for the 1986-1990 period, and multifamily housing starts dropped by 71%, sending a ripple effect throughout the economy and sending thousands of housing construction workers to the unemployment lines.

Another adverse effect of the 86TRA's real estate tax changes is the effect the changes have had on the savings and loan industry, which is also in a highly depressed state.[28] Savings & loans, by law, are required to invest a certain percentage of their assets in mortgages. With the depression in the real estate market that resulted from the passage of the 86TRA, the value of these assets declined markedly, sending many savings & loans into a condition of technical insolvency, since the market value of their assets became less than the present value of their liabilities.

Even those S&Ls that did not become technically insolvent have seen their balance sheet position greatly weakened. And to further complicate matters, the government insurance fund that was established to protect investors from losing money in the event of an S&L bankruptcy (FSLIC) does not have enough funds to cover all the losses, so taxpayers are expected to pick up the tab for the difference. And since the savings & loan industry and banking industry have overlapping markets, the 86TRA is having an adverse effect on the banking industry as well.

The Institute for Policy Innovation has estimated that the 86TRA had the following effects on real estate:[29]

- The 86TRA reduced the value of commercial real estate by 17%.
- The value of home ownership fell by more than 9%.
- $35.6 billion of the estimated $150 billion S&L bailout cost is attributable to the 86TRA.
- The capital gains changes in the 86TRA reduced the value of commercial real estate by 9%.
- Rental costs increased 17.5% because of the 86TRA's impact on commercial real estate.
- Changes in the capital gains tax treatment, when combined with lower marginal tax rates, decreased the value of an owner-occupied home worth more than $150,000 by between 5% and 6.5%.[30]
- The changes in the treatment of capital gains reduced the value of owner-occupied housing by about $125 billion.
- About $21 billion of the $35.6 billion in S&L bailout costs are due to the tax changes affecting capital gains and passive losses.

Most or all of these consequences were unintended, although some economists predicted that the 86TRA would have some of these effects. But those in Congress who made the policy change either were not aware of the effect the policy change would have, or did not give it much thought.

The lesson to be learned from these examples is that tax policy has consequences. There is no such thing as a neutral tax, and policymakers should carefully consider what effects a particular tax policy will have on all segments of the economy.

Effect on Competitiveness and Economic Growth

Another attribute of tax policy is the effect it has on competitiveness and economic growth. This aspect of tax policy is especially important to emerging economies, since the transformation from a centrally planned economy to a market economy entails major shocks to the economic system. As a general rule, it can fairly be stated that emerging economies have difficulty competing with more developed market economies, either because they do not make the products that developed economies want, or because the quality is too low and/or the price is too high.

These difficulties can be greatly relieved by knocking down trade barriers and importing modern technology. Many of the emerging economies have skilled workforces that are willing to work at competitive wages, if only the system would allow them to use their skills and energies.[31] It is important that these emerging economies adopt tax rules that make it easier for them to compete rather than more difficult. The tax system they adopt should promote rather than retard economic growth and development.[32]

Which tax policies would foster economic growth and development? The tax system should encourage investment, both foreign and domestic. That means that foreign companies should not be penalized for investing in the local country and domestic companies should not find their own country's tax system more burdensome than those of other countries.

There are a number of factors that make a tax system attractive or burdensome. Companies would rather invest in a country that has low tax rates than high ones. A number of studies have shown that high tax rates retard economic growth.[33] For example, one study concluded that the tax increase President Bush signed into law in 1990 retarded economic growth by 0.7%, destroyed 400,000 jobs, caused the unemployment rate to be 0.45 percentage points higher than it otherwise would have been, and caused stock prices to drop by 15%.

It estimated that each 1.0% increase in the federal tax burden leads to a 1.8% reduction in economic growth.[34] Another study of the U.S. tax system estimates that modifying payroll deductions, adopting neutral cost recovery, eliminating capital gains taxation, eliminating the tax on corporate dividends and eliminating the taxation and deductibility of interest would add 1.1 percentage points to the economy's growth rate; increase gross domestic product by nearly $6.2 trillion dollars between 1992 and 2000, which translates into a roughly 13% increase in the standard of living; create nearly 4 million jobs between 1992 and 2000; increase the stock of capital by $10.4 trillion between 1992 and 2000.[35]

In a model of the U.S. economy that took federal, state and local taxes into account, researchers estimated that for every dollar of extra revenue raised, production declined by $0.332.[36] A World Bank study of 20 countries found that those with lower tax rates had a more rapid expansion of investment, productivity, employment, and government services, and had better growth rates than countries that had higher rates.[37]

But one does not need to refer to studies to reach this conclusion. It is a conclusion that can be reached a priori. It just makes sense that economic growth will be retarded if a large portion of a company's profits are siphoned off in taxes. The more money that is taken as taxes, the less that will be available for further investment. And if tax rates are high, companies will be less careful about how they spend their money, since whatever they buy they get at a large discount.

For example, if the corporate tax rate is 60%, the after-tax cost of a $100 business lunch becomes $40. But if the tax rate is only 10%, the after-tax cost is $90. So tax rates have an effect on behavior. There tends to be less waste -- and more efficiency -- when tax rates are low because companies are more hesitant to squander money under a low rate regime because a large percentage of what they squander comes out of their own pocket.

The tax system should make it easy rather than difficult to accumulate capital. Ideally, there should be no tax on capital or capital gains. Or if there is one, it should be very low. The higher the tax on capital and capital gains, the more economic growth will tend to be retarded. Countries that have no or low capital gains taxes tend to have higher growth rates than those that have high capital gains tax rates.[38]

Simple or Complex Rules

A tax system can have simple or extremely complex rules. Simple rules are to be preferred to complex rules, all other things being equal. While this conclusion comes as no surprise, and may even seem not worthy of mention, it should be noted that many modern western democracies have rules that are far more complex than needed to raise the amount of revenue that is raised.[39] Any emerging economy that looks to a western tax system for guidance should keep this fact in mind.

In the USA, for example, the Internal Revenue Code and Regulations run to many thousands of pages, often in small print. The regulations for many tax code sections run to more than 100 pages. But the guidance does not end there. Tax practitioners and taxpayers who want to dig to the bottom of some tax issues must also consult with the thousands of tax cases that have been decided in three different federal court systems,[40] plus Internal Revenue Service publications and privately published tax treatises. And even then, the answers are not always readily apparent, so they have to guess at what the correct answer might be. And to make matters even more unpredictable, when IRS issues a tax regulation, it sometimes does so retroactively, so a tax rule that is issued in 1993 might take effect as of 1981.[41]

Tax rules in the USA are so complex that even IRS agents do not understand what the law says. A General Accounting Office report found that 44% of the penalties that IRS agents assessed under the payroll tax rules were wrong. And the payroll tax rules are so complex that one-third of all U.S. employers are assessed penalties each year.[42] But complexity is not limited to the payroll tax rules. Many other areas of the tax code are also overly complex. IRS assessed 29 million penalties in 1990, many of which were later abated.[43]

Emerging economies must be very careful that they do not fall into this quagmire of complex and uncertain regulations. Any tax system adopted should have built-in safeguards that protect against unnecessary complexity. The Swiss method might be used as an example. In Switzerland, the number of words that can be used is limited. Emerging economies must also guard against a proliferation of rules and regulations. It would not be too difficult to construct a tax code that is less than 50 pages in length. And there is no need to have three different and often contradictory court systems to settle tax cases. And any tax system that is adopted should have a provision that makes regulations prospective only, to reduce the amount of unfairness in the system and increase the predictability.

Clear or Vague Rules

Laws and regulations can be written in clear, easy to understand language. Or they can be written in language that is extremely vague and obscure. If laws are too vague and indecipherable, a court may rule that the law is void for vagueness.[44] But in other cases, the law may be held to be valid even though it has a high degree of vagueness or obscurity. Obviously, clearly written laws are to be preferred to vaguely written ones. And while this conclusion might seem obvious, in practice, the laws are often vague, especially in the area of taxation. this topic is discussed in more detail elsewhere in this book.

Stable or Frequently Changing Rules

Governments may enact tax rules that remain on the books for decades. Or they may make rules that change constantly. While it is always a good idea to change a law that is bad, or to improve one where possible, many times, governments go beyond mere improvement and engage in fine tuning. In the USA, for example, Congress enacted major changes in the tax laws practically every year during the 1980s, which made many tax practitioners go practically crazy because they couldn't keep up with all the changes. Some tax practitioners actually decided to either retire early or go into another line of work because of all the changes. Congress continues to tinker with the tax code, although the extent of the annual changes in recent years has not been as much as those of the 1980s.

Few tax practitioners would argue that the changes Congress makes have made the tax law either better or easier to comprehend. The tax rules have, in many cases, become more complex and obscure over time. And the constant changes -- sometimes retroactive changes -- have made it difficult for tax planners to plan. The business decisions that businesses must make are often influenced by the tax laws, and when the laws change frequently, they must make their plans with a higher degree of uncertainty.

Frequent changes also increase compliance costs. Tax practitioners and business owners must spend time and money to learn the new rules. And businesses must adjust their practices to comply with new rules. The cost of complying with the tax legislation that was enacted in 1987 is estimated to be $6.2 billion for 1988 alone.[45] The cost of complying with the 1989 tax law changes is estimated to be $0.1 billion for 1989 and $5.6 billion for 1990.[46] Compliance costs for the 1990 Budget Accord were estimated to be $23.2 billion in 1991 and $10 billion in 1992.[47] And few practitioners would take the position that these tax law changes made compliance any easier. The point is, compliance costs must be taken into account when a government is thinking about enacting a new piece of tax legislation.

Another problem with frequent changes in the tax laws that has an especially devastating effect on newly emerging economies is the effect that frequent changes have on foreign investment. It is difficult enough trying to convince foreign investors to invest in a new, unproven country, without making investment returns even more uncertain by frequently changing the tax laws. Russia is only one of several examples that could be given here to illustrate the point. Until recently, the tax situation in Russia was both rapidly changing and uncertain. Not even Russian government officials always know what the tax laws were, or how they should be applied. President Putin tried to remedy the situation by instituting a low flat tax. The result was a rapid increase in foreign domestic investment and a decline in capital outflows. People started placing more confidence in the Russian system and started finding it a more attractive place to invest.

Major or Minor Effect on Behavior and Incentives

Another factor to consider when constructing any tax scheme is the effect that a provision will have on behavior and incentives. If an individual tax rate is close to 100%, it is reasonable to expect that marginal income will not expand, and may even decrease. People will tend to work less overtime and not seek out second, part-time jobs. People will tend to spend their money rather than save and invest it. Investors will seek investments in a country that has lower tax rates. If there is a perception that individuals are not able to keep the fruits of their labor, then they will produce less fruit. And if the measure in question is perceived to be unfair, they will have more of a tendency to cheat and evade the tax, where possible.

Ideally, from a tax collector's perspective, a tax should have both high rates and no negative effect on incentives or behavior. But such a tax exists only in a dream world. There is an inverse relationship between the tax rate and the incentive taxpayers have to create wealth, and that relationship must be taken into account when decisionmakers are constructing or altering their tax system. If the goal is to increase wealth, then one thing decisionmakers can do is reduce taxes. If the goal is to increase revenue, then perhaps (but not necessarily) rates should be raised. But in the real world, government planners usually want to raise more revenue and increase wealth at the same time, so some tradeoffs have to be made between raising revenue and economic growth.

Major or Minor Effect on Social Harmony

The effect that a particular tax law will have on social harmony should be taken into account. Some tax laws anger the general populace, like the poll tax did in England. Other tax laws, like the graduated income tax, pit one class against another, in this case, the high income earners against the low income earners. A graduated income tax is divisive in the sense that it forces high income earners to pay what might be perceived to be more than their "fair share." And it exacerbates the envy that the lower income earners already have toward high income earners.[48] The graduated income tax is based on the ability to pay principle rather than the cost benefit principle and, like all such tax measures, causes resentment, since those who have to pay more feel that they are being exploited by those who do not work as hard and earn as much money.

Another example of a tax policy that reduces social harmony is the current pension law in the USA. The pension law is so complex and the penalties so potentially burdensome and threatening that many employers have terminated their pension plans rather than comply. This decision has adversely affected hundreds of thousands of employees over the years, many of whom really need coverage.

In the area of defined benefit pension plan terminations alone, the effect of the law has been devastating. During the early 1980s, between 4,000 and 5,000 employers were terminating their plans each year. By 1985, the number had increased to more than 12,000, and by 1989, the number of plans terminated annually had jumped to more than

16,000.[49] More recent evidence shows that the situation may be getting worse.[50] Between October, 1991 and September, 1992, 19,390 employers filed termination application letters with the Internal Revenue Service. These termination applications would terminate various types of pension and profit sharing plans for 960,876 employees. And since Social Security will not provide them with much of a pension, these employees will have to find some other way to provide for their retirement.

Most of these employers are terminating their pension plans because the cost of compliance is too high, and the risk of inadvertently running afoul of the many potential penalties is too great. Yet IRS and Treasury Department bureaucrats in Washington continue to write pension laws and regulations that have the opposite effect of what was intended when Congress passed the Employee Retirement Income Security Act of 1974 (ERISA), namely, to provide security for employees.

Emerging economies must be very careful that the tax laws they enact do not have a similar effect. Good intentions are not enough. The result of a well-intentioned tax policy can be devastating on a segment of the population or on the economy in general, and it is not always easy to reverse a bad tax policy, as is seen by the case of the ERISA law in the USA. Policymakers refuse to admit that they have made a mistake, so rather than repeal the law, they make constant attempts to amend it, which only makes the situation worse.

Another social harmony factor that should be considered by those who make tax policy is the effect a particular policy will have on employment. Money that is taken in taxes cannot be used for investment. Some tax increases also increase the administrative burden of business, which also has harmful effects. Productivity can be reduced if private sector employees have to be used to administer a tax law rather than engage in some activity that produces wealth. In the state of Colorado, for example, one study found that a 1% increase in the state sales tax would destroy as many as 75,000 jobs.[51] Another study estimated that 72,000 jobs were lost because of a change in the law requiring restaurants to collect and report the income of employees for Social Security purposes.[52]

Another factor that can reduce social harmony is the methods the tax collection agency uses to collect taxes. In the United States, the Internal Revenue Service conducts more than one million audits of income tax returns each year.[53] While many of the audits IRS conducts are low-key, polite and nonthreatening, such is not always the case. IRS agents sometimes resort to harassment, verbal abuse and the improper confiscation of property. In at least one case, IRS errors drove a taxpayer to suicide. His wife then used the life insurance proceeds to beat the IRS in court.[54]

In many other cases, IRS resorts to illegal methods to collect taxes that are not owed.[55] Property is confiscated without a court order and sold for a fraction of its worth, taxpayers are sometimes assaulted and battered, witnesses are harassed and threatened, all in the name of tax collection. This kind of abuse by government reduces social harmony and exacerbates the tension that exists between the government and the people.

A good tax collection system will incorporate safeguards that minimize the possibility that government bureaucrats will abuse their power. At the very least, government officials should not be able to confiscate property until after some legitimate court has declared that the tax is owed. Such is not now the case in the USA, where IRS can confiscate property without a court order and without any hearing of any kind.

And the burden of proof should be on the government to prove that the tax is owed. At present, the burden is on the taxpayer to show that the tax is not owed. In cases where abuse has taken place, taxpayers should be able to receive compensation for their loss. At present, the amount of compensation they can receive is limited to reimbursement of some court costs, and even then, they can only recover in certain cases. If the government seizes property worth $100,000 and sells it for $10,000, the taxpayer's recovery is limited to $10,000 if it turns out that the tax was not owed in the first place.

Furthermore, IRS employees are immune from prosecution, which means that they can get away with assaulting and battering taxpayers, confiscating their assets without a court order, harassing witnesses and forcing them to change their testimony without fear of personal consequences. A tax system that is constructed on the basis of equity and fairness would provide safeguards against such abuses.[56]

High or Low Administrative Costs

A tax system can be structured so that administrative costs are low. Or one can be structured so that administrative costs are quite high. When one is measuring the administrative cost of a particular tax policy, or of a tax system as a whole, not only the administrative costs to government should be considered. The cost to the taxpaying community must also be taken into account.[57] In the case of the tax system in the USA, for example, the cost of administering the tax law falls more than 99% on the private sector. The budgets of the Internal Revenue Service and the parts of the Treasury and Justice Departments that administer the tax laws was about $6 billion in 1990, whereas the costs of administration that fell to the private sector for the same period were estimated to be $618 billion,[58] which represents about 65% of the tax collected.

A study by Arthur D. Little,[59] a consulting firm, estimated that it took businesses and individuals 3.614 billion hours and 1.813 billion hours, respectively, to comply with federal tax rules in 1985. When this combined total, 5.427 billion hours, is translated into whole persons, the statistic takes on more meaning. If the average work year per employee is 1,844 hours, then it would take 2.943 million people, working full-time, to comply with the tax laws (Just the federal tax laws. State compliance costs are extra.).

That means practically every man, woman and child in a city the size of Chicago -- the USA's third largest city -- would have to work full-time to comply with the USA's federal tax laws.[60] If these individuals charged an average cost of $28.31 per hour, which was the average of the wage cost for Arthur Andersen employees ($35.47) and IRS employees ($21.14) in 1985,[61] then the cost of complying with the federal tax laws in 1985 would have been almost $154 billion, which is about the same as the gross national product for Belgium.[62] This figure excludes the cost of hiring professional assistance, which, in 1985, would have added another $5.8 billion to the cost, which, combined with the $154 billion figure, amounts to 24.43% of the tax revenues collected.[63]

A number of other studies have also estimated the costs that taxpayers incur in complying with various portions of the U.S. tax law. One pension actuary estimated that the cost to employers of complying with just the employee benefit provisions of the Unemployment Compensation Amendments Act of 1992[64] might exceed $4 billion over the first five years, which is more than twice the amount of revenue that is expected to be raised from the law.[65] He estimated that the cost of compliance for a benefit plan would be about $1,500 and the annual administrative costs would be about $1,000 per plan just to fill out the paperwork and comply with the law's requirements.

Since there are about 600,000 defined contribution plans and 100,000 defined benefit plans that fall within the ambit of this law, the total start-up cost of complying would be about $1.05 billion and the annual administration cost would be $0.7 billion, which amounts to $4.55 billion over the first five years. The government expects to raise about $2.147 billion in revenue over the same period of time. And even this revenue estimate might be optimistic. Small employers, who are the least able to pay such costs, might decide to terminate their plans rather than incur the high compliance costs.

It has been estimated that the cost to employers of complying with the payroll tax rules in the USA was more than $59 billion for the five-year period ending in 1992.[66] Another study estimated that it took 2 billion taxpayer hours plus $3 billion in professional assistance to fill out federal and state income tax returns in 1982.[67] Tax law changes since then, plus inflation, would push the cost of compliance to over $30 billion annually, assuming the average taxpayer expends time that is worth $12 or $15 an hour.[68]

A General Accounting Office study estimated that it took 1.815 billion hours for taxpayers to complete the necessary tax return paperwork for fiscal year 1988, although that estimate may be low.[69] A U.S. Office of Management and Budget report estimated that the Treasury Department spent 4.27 billion hours in respondent time collection information in fiscal year 1989.[70]

Another factor that must be considered is the cost of administration from the government's perspective. In the case of the USA, for example, a tax that is collected locally, such as a property tax, can be used almost completely to pay for services. Perhaps only 5%-15% of what is collected is spent on administration. For taxes collected at the state level, the percentage of collections used in administration is somewhat higher, perhaps 20%-30%. Taxes collected at the federal level sometimes involve an even higher administration cost. For some federal programs, the amount spent on administration far exceeds the amount that is available to the population intended to be served. The point is, the farther the distance between the collector and the proceeds recipient, the greater the administrative charge.

Tax policymakers should consider the deadweight loss that a particular tax policy will generate. There will always be some gap between the funds that are collected and the amount that is available for spending on programs because of the administrative charge. Funds can be used most efficiently where this deadweight loss is minimized. In the USA case, there is some resentment because citizens of the individual states do not feel that they are getting their moneysworth out of federal government services. They perceive that they pay more money to Washington than what they get back in benefits. And there is some truth to this perception. Daniel Moynihan, a New York State senator, says that New York State residents paid $838 more, per capita, to the federal government than what they received back in benefits. Over a recent 15 year period, Moynihan reports that New Yorkers have been "cheated" out of $136 billion.[71]

Cost and Benefit

Another factor to consider when constructing a tax scheme is the relative cost and benefit, from the tax collector's point of view. The tax collected should exceed the cost of administration. But the cost-benefit comparison should not be limited to just easily traceable, tax-related administrative costs, because the cost of administering a tax system sends ripple effects throughout the economy. These indirect, ripple-effect costs should also be considered.[72]

The tax law should also result in more tax being collected rather than less. While this seems obvious and hardly worthy of mention, the luxury tax rules in the USA provide an example[73] of where such is not the case.[74] In the early 1990s, the tax code started to place an excise tax on "luxury" automobiles -- automobiles that cost over $30,000.[75] Ever since this rule was passed, auto dealers that sell high priced cars have been complaining because people aren't buying their cars anymore. They are losing business, their profit margins have shrunk, and some auto dealers have had to go out of business. The employees who were employed by these dealers are no longer paying taxes but are collecting unemployment insurance or welfare. The auto dealers are paying less taxes because they make less profit. The amount of taxes lost by this rule has exceeded the amount of tax the government would have collected from the rule.[76] Yet Congress has not yet repealed the tax because of inertia.

The same is true for the excise taxes that have been imposed on boats, airplanes, jewelry and furs. Many boat manufacturers have been driven out of business by the excise tax, as have a few small airplane manufacturers. Rather than raise tax revenues, the imposition of these excise taxes has reduced total tax revenues because the small amounts collected for excise taxes have been more than offset by the lower amounts of income taxes that have been collected. Yet these taxes were not immediately repealed because many members of Congress perceived that repealing luxury taxes would make it appear that they are coddling the rich. In fact, they are destroying working class jobs.

NOTES

[1] Commentators over the years have debated whether economics is a value-free science. Ludwig von Mises clears up this issue in Human Action, third revised edition, Chicago: Henry Regnery, 1966, pp. 882-85. If the goal is to go from point A to point B, policy #4 will be considered a good policy if it achieves the goal and a bad policy if it does not. But the fact that an economist might say that policy #4 is good or bad does not mean that the economist is forming any value judgments, but only that the policy under consideration either measures up to a stated policy goal or not. Value judgments enter into the picture when one asks whether policy #4 is a worthy goal in the first place. It is at this point that the discussion leaves the realm of economics and enters the realm of philosophy.

[2] The term "liberal" has become twisted over time, at least in the USA. In Europe, the term means something much different. One might loosely define a liberal (in the U.S. sense of the term) as someone who wants government to interfere in the economy but not in personal issues. Conservatives want government to regulate personal conduct but not the economy. Authoritarians want to regulate both the economy and personal conduct, while libertarians do not want government to regulate anything. Libertarians would limit government action to the defense of life, liberty and property. Liberals (in the U.S.) would advocate protectionism, tariffs, quotas, wage and price controls, and so forth, whereas conservatives would be against these policies. Liberals would repeal sex legislation for consenting adults whereas conservatives would advocate laws prohibiting homosexual conduct, nude dancing, and so forth. For more on this approach to the classification of the political spectrum, contact Advocates for Self-Government, Inc., 5533 East Swift, Fresno, CA 93727.

Thomas Jefferson, in his first inaugural address, gave perhaps the best definition of liberal democracy in the European (and nineteenth century American) sense of the term. "...a wise and frugal government, which shall restrain men from injuring one another, shall leave them otherwise free to regulate their own pursuits of industry and improvement, and shall not take from the mouth of labor the bread it has earned. This is the sum of good government..." This speech is reprinted in many places, including Lewis Copeland, editor, The World's Great Speeches, Garden City, NY: Garden City Publishing Co., 1942, pp. 259-62, at 261.

[3] Marginal tax rates in the USA and other places (like England) have been as high as 90% or more at times. In some cases, rates have exceeded 100%, as where someone in the 93% bracket is assessed a 10% surcharge.

[4] Mark Skousen has a similar example in Economics on Trial, Homewood, IL: Business One Irwin, 1991, p. 159.

[5] This relationship between tax rates and tax revenues is called the Laffer Curve, named after Arthur Laffer, an economist who spoke about this relationship. The Laffer Curve is discussed in many places, including Campbell R. McConnell and Stanley L. Brue, Economics, 11th edition 389-91 (1990).
[6] Alan Reynolds, International Comparisons of Taxes and Government Spending, in Stephen T. Easton and Michael A. Walker, editors, Rating Global Economic Freedom, Vancouver: Fraser Institute, 1992, p. 366. Reynolds refers to the following studies: Alan Reynolds, Some International Comparisons of Supply-Side Tax Policy, Cato Journal 5: 543-69 (Fall, 1985); Alvin Rabushka and Bruce Bartlett, Tax Policy and Economic Growth in Developing Nations, U.S. Agency for International Development, 1986; Jude Wanniski, The Way the World Works (1978; 1983; 1989). Other studies that reach the same conclusion include Keith Marsden, Links between Taxes and Economic Growth: Some Empirical Evidence, World Bank Staff Working Papers No. 605 (1983); Gary and Aldona Robbins, Promoting Growth Through Tax Policy, Report No. 115, Institute for Policy Innovation, Lewisville, TX, March, 1992.
[7] Pub. L. No. 99-514 (1986). For a technical exposition of this law, see A Complete Guide to the Tax Reform Act of 1986, Prentice Hall, 1986. The Tax Reform Act of 1986 did not reduce complexity. It might be fair to say that the Act actually increased complexity, at least in some areas of the tax code. But it also reduced tax rates, which reduced the incentive to invest in tax shelters, since investing in tax shelters makes no sense when tax rates are low.
[8] John Maynard Keynes, The General Theory of Employment, Interest and Money, New York: Harcourt Brace, 1936.
[9] At least one economist has gone so far as to say that "taxes are needed not to provide governments with money but to take money away from the public." See Richard M. Bird, Tax Policy & Economic Development, Baltimore and London: Johns Hopkins University Press, 1992, p. 4. This statement seems a bit extreme, even for a Keynesian.
[10] For an exposition of this view, see any economic textbook.
[11] For example, see W.H. Hutt, The Keynesian Episode: A Reassessment, Indianapolis: Liberty Press, 1979; W.H. Hutt, Keynesianism: Retrospect and Prospect, Chicago: Henry Regnery Co., 1963; Henry Hazlitt, The Failure of the "New Economics," Princeton, Toronto and London: D. Van Nostrand Co., 1959; Henry Hazlitt, editor, The Critics of Keynesian Economics, Princeton, Toronto, London and New York: D. Van Nostrand Co., 1960; Mark, Skousen, editor, Dissent on Keynes: A Critical Appraisal of Keynesian Economics, New York, Westport and London: Praeger, 1992.
[12] The evidence from the 1970s in the USA provides ample proof of this relationship. The Phillips Curve, which shows a negative relationship between unemployment and inflation, has been discredited. See Milton Friedman, Unemployment versus Inflation? An Evaluation of the Phillips Curve, Occasional Paper 44 (1975); Milton Friedman, Inflation and Unemployment: The New Dimension of Politics, Occasional Paper 51 (1977); Jeffrey M. Herbener, The Fallacy of the Phillips Curve, in Dissent on Keynes: A Critical Appraisal of Keynesian Economics 51-71 (Mark Skousen, ed. 1992),.
[13] The view that inflation is caused by an increase in the supply of money is called the monetarist view or the quantity theory, as opposed to the Keynesian view. The monetarist view is not new. It has been in existence for hundreds of years and provides a better explanation for the cause of inflation than have other theories. Milton Friedman is one of its strongest exponents. See Milton Friedman, A Program for Monetary Stability, New York: Fordham University Press, 1960; Milton Friedman, Essays in Positive Economics, Chicago: University of Chicago Press, 1953; Hans F. Sennholz, Age of Inflation (1979).
[14] Karl Marx, Critique of the Gotha Program (1875). The original wording was "Jeder nach seinen Fähigkeiten, jedem nach seinen Bedürfnissen." Louis Blanc, the French socialist, said basically the same thing in 1848. George Seldes, The Great Thoughts, New York: Ballantine Books, 1985, p. 274.
[15] There are problems with both of these approaches. There is no way to objectively determine what someone's ability to pay is, so it must be decided arbitrarily. And there is

no way to determine how much benefit someone receives from government services that are made available even if few people want them, since the price of such services is determined by bureaucratic fiat rather than through voluntary exchange.

[16] For examples, see Walter J. Blum and Harry Kalven, Jr., The Uneasy Case for Progressive Taxation, Chicago: University of Chicago Press, 1953; F.A. Hayek, The Case Against Progressive Income Taxes, The Freeman 229-32 (December 28, 1953).

[17] Robert E. Hall and Alvin Rabushka, The Flat Tax, Stanford: Hoover Institution Press, 1985. Since no tax is neutral, any change in tax policy will have winners and losers. For a discussion of this point as applied to the flat tax, see Murray N. Rothbard, The Case Against the Flat Tax, Llewellyn H. Rockwell, editor, The Free Market Reader (1988), pp. 342-62.

[18] This statement is not quite accurate. It would be more precise to say that the rich are not penalized any more, percentagewise, than the poor. But all groups who earn income are penalized in the sense that a portion of their income is taken from them.

[19] J.G. Cullis, P. R. Jones and O. Morrissey, Public Choice Perspectives on the Poll Tax, Economic Journal 101: 600-614 (1991).

[20] Officials Outline IRS Help in Setting Up Polish Tax System, Daily Tax Report (BNA), April 6, 1992, at G-1).

[21] I am not advocating that there should be labeling laws, but am merely using labeling laws as an example. Free speech advocates would be quick to point out that forcing companies to disclose the contents or ingredients of their products violates their right to free speech, or the right to refrain from speech. In cases where pharmaceutical companies must reveal the contents of their drug, there is also a possibility that their property rights are being violated, since they have a property right -- a patent -- for the products they produce.

[22] James M. Buchanan, The Economics of Earmarked Taxes, Journal of Political Economy 457-69 (October, 1963), at 457. Buchanan also discusses earmarking in Public Finance in Democratic Process, Chapel Hill: University of North Carolina Press, 1967, pp. 72-87.

[23] The Social Security taxes that are collected in the USA are not really set aside for the taxpayers' retirement. Those who work pay into the system and those who are retired draw from it, so the Social Security Trust Fund is not a true trust fund.

[24] Ludwig von Mises, Human Action, third edition, Chicago: Henry Regnery Co., 1966, p. 737.

[25] Murray N. Rothbard, The Myth of Neutral Taxation, Cato Journal 1: 519-64 (Fall, 1981).

[26] Destroying Real Estate Through the Tax Code, Policy Bulletin No. 48, Institute for Research on the Economics of Taxation, Washington, DC, February 12, 1991.

[27] Id., at 1.

[28] Aldona and Gary Robbins, How Tax Policy Compounded the S&L Crisis, Policy Report No. 109, The Institute for Policy Innovation, Lewisville, TX, February, 1991.

[29] Id.

[30] It should be pointed out that the reduction in individual tax rates also had some beneficial effects in other sectors of the economy, such as freeing up more money for investment and consumption, and enhancing the incentives to work and produce wealth.

[31] There are exceptions, of course. Some of the skills these people have acquired are of little or no use to a market economy. And living under generations of central planning, where jobs are guaranteed for life without regard to performance, has dampened the work ethic in some cases.

[32] A number of commentators have examined the U.S. tax system and have pointed to some policies that stifle growth and reduce competitiveness. For examples, see Martin Neil Baily and Robert Z. Lawrence, Tax Policies for Innovation and Competitiveness (1987); Anthony Baldo, Killing the Goose: How Myopic IRS Tax Policies Are Crippling U.S. Competitiveness Abroad, Finance World 158: 16-17 (August 22, 1989); A Comparison of Japanese and American Taxation of Capital Gains, 14 Hastings International and Comparative Law Review 719-747 (1991); Raymond Haas, U.S. Tax Policies Hurt U.S. Multinationals, CPA Journal 58: 62-73 (October, 1988); Bill Modahl,

How U.S. Corporate Taxes Hurt Competitiveness, Financier 15: 42-48 (November, 1991).
[33] Alan Reynolds, International Comparisons of Taxes and Government Spending, in Stephen T. Easton and Michael Walker, editors, Rating Global Economic Freedom, Vancouver: Fraser Institute, 1992, p. 366. Reynolds refers to the following studies: Alan Reynolds, Some International Comparisons of Supply-Side Tax Policy, Cato Journal 5: 543-69 (Fall, 1985); Alvin Rabushka and Bruce Bartlett, Tax Policy and Economic Growth in Developing Nations, U.S. Agency for International Development, 1986; Jude Wanniski, The Way the World Works (1978; 1983; 1989).
[34] William C. Dunkelberg and John Skorburg, How Rising Tax Burdens Can Produce Recession, Policy Analysis No. 148, Cato Institute, February 21, 1991.
[35] Gary and Aldona Robbins, Promoting Growth Through Tax Policy, Policy Report No. 115, Lewisville, TX: The Institute for Policy Innovation, March, 1992.
[36] The study was conducted by Charles Ballard, John Shoven and John Whalley and was cited by James L. Payne in Unhappy Returns: The $600-Billion Tax Ripoff, Policy Review (Winter, 1992), at 21. Payne points out that, using this average 33.2% figure, the tax system in the USA caused production to be $315.6 billion lower than it otherwise would have been in 1990.
[37] Keith Marsden, Links between Taxes and Economic Growth: Some Empirical Evidence, World Bank Staff Working Papers No. 605 (1983).
[38] Mark Skousen, Economics on Trial 170-71 (1991).
[39] James S. Eustice, Tax Complexity and the Tax Practitioner, 45 Tax Law Review 7-24 (Fall, 1989).
[40] Taxpayers who want to take their case to court have three choices. They can take their case to the federal District Court, the Claims Court or the Tax Court. If they don't like the decision there, they can appeal to the federal appellate court, and again to the U.S. Supreme Court. Which route they choose depends on a number of often complex factors, which is complicated by the fact that the three court systems sometimes take different positions on similar or identical tax issues. And different federal district courts may also take conflicting positions on a tax issue, as may the Tax Court, in some circumstances.
[41] D.W. Ball, Retroactive Application of Treasury Rules and Regulations, New Mexico Law Review 17: 139-163 (Winter, 1987); J.S. Bryant, Retroactive Taxation: A Constitutional Analysis of the Minimum Tax on IDCs, Oklahoma Law Review 36:107-118 (Winter, 1983); The Retroactivity of Treasury Regulations: Paths To Finding Abuse of Discretion, Virginia Tax Review 7: 509-533 (Winter, 1988); T. Robinson, Retroactivity: The Case for Better Regulation of Federal Tax Regulators, Ohio State Law Journal 48: 773-813 (1987); To What Extent Can Taxpayers Rely on IRS Regulations and Rulings to Predict Future IRS Conduct? Gonzaga Law Review 25: 281-298 (1989/90).
[42] James L. Payne, Unhappy Returns: The $600-Billion Tax Ripoff, Policy Review 21 (Winter, 1992).
[43] Id, at 21-22.
[44] For some discussions of what distinguishes a merely obscure law from one that is void for vagueness, see Note, Due Process Requirements of Definiteness in Statutes, Harvard Law Review 62: 77 (1948); Note, The Lawson Decision: A Broadening of the Vagueness Doctrine, Stetson Law Review 13: 412 ff. (1984); Note, Recent Development, Void-for-Vagueness -- Judicial Responses to Allegedly Vague Statutes, Washington Law Review 56: 131. (1980).
[45] Robert Genetski, The True Cost of Government, Wall Street Journal, February 19, 1992, at A14.
[46] Id.
[47] Id.
[48] For more on this point, see Helmut Schoeck, Envy: A Theory of Social Behaviour, New York: Harcourt Brace & World, 1966, pp. 194, 217, 221; Robert Sheaffer, Resentment Against Achievement: Understanding the Assault Upon Ability, Buffalo: Prometheus Books, 1988, pp. 177, 186.
[49] Preliminary Report, Results of the American Academy of Actuaries Survey of Defined Benefit Plan Terminations, June 24, 1992.

[50] Internal Revenue Service Statistics on Employee Plan Determination Letters, October 1991 -- September 1992, Daily Tax Rep. (BNA), November 19, 1992, at L-1.
[51] The study was conducted by The Independence Institute of Golden, Colorado. Reported in Daily Tax Rep. (BNA), October 9, 1992, at H-2.
[52] The study was conducted by the Employee Policies Institute. Reported in Daily Tax Rep. (BNA), March 9, 1992, at H-2).
[53] James L. Payne, Unhappy Returns: The $600-Billion Tax Ripoff, Policy Review 21 (Winter, 1992).
[54] James L. Payne, at 21.
[55] One member of Congress wrote a book that documents some of the many IRS abuses. See George Hansen, To Harass Our People: The IRS and Government Abuse of Power, Washington, DC: Positive Publications, 1984. Also see David Burnham, A Law Unto Itself: Power, Politics and the IRS, New York: Random House, 1989.
[56] It should be pointed out that many of the abuses IRS now gets away with could be eliminated by abolishing the individual income tax, or replacing the present, complicated tax with a flat-rate tax.
[57] Joel Slemrod and Nikki Sorum, The Compliance Cost of the U.S. Individual Income Tax System, National Tax Journal 37: 461-474 (December, 1984).
[58] James L. Payne.
[59] This study is summarized in Payne at 19.
[60] The population of Chicago in 1988 was 2,977,520, according to The World Almanac and Book of Facts 1991 (1990), at 557.
[61] Payne makes this comparison at 19.
[62] The World Almanac and Book of Facts 1991 (1990), at 690 lists Belgium's 1988 gross national product at $153 billion. Note that the estimated $154 billion in compliance cost is in 1985 dollars. If 1988 dollars were used instead, this figure would be slightly higher. This cost also does not include the cost of complying with state and local tax laws.
[63] Payne at 20.
[64] PL 102-318.
[65] Withholding, Direct Transfer Amendments Seen Costing Employers Over $4 Billion, Daily Tax Rep. (BNA), August 4, 1992, at G-4.
[66] Robert Genetski, The True Cost of Government, Wall Street Journal, February 19, 1992, at A14.
[67] Joel Slemrod and Nikki Sorum, The Compliance Cost of the U.S. Individual Income Tax System, National Tax Journal 37: 461-474 (1984).
[68] This estimate is conservative, for several reasons. For one thing, the more an individual makes, the more time he is likely to spend preparing a tax return, so the $12 to $15 hourly estimate is a bit low. And there are many million more taxpayers now than there were in 1982, so the total number of taxpayer hours required to file tax returns is probably much more than 2 billion now. And the tax laws have become more complicated since 1982, so taxpayers probably spend more time in preparation now than then, and probably spend more for professional assistance, too.
[69] U.S. General Accounting Office, Paperwork Reduction: Little Real Burden Change in Recent Years, GAO/PEMD-89-19FS.
[70] U.S. Office of Management and Budget, Report to the Congress: Federal Procurement Paperwork Burden, January, 1990, as cited by Thomas D. Hopkins, Cost of Regulation, A Rochester Institute of Technology Public Policy Working Paper, December, 1991.
[71] Taxes Paid Versus Federal Funds Received, Daily Tax Report (BNA), August 7, 1992, at H-4. These statistics are based on the 16th annual edition of New York State and the Federal Fisc, Who Cheated NY of $136 Billion?, published in association with the Taubman Center for State and Local Government, John F. Kennedy School of Government, Harvard University.
[72] Murray L. Weidenbaum and Robert DeFina, The Cost of Federal Regulation of Economic Activity (1978).
[73] The law under discussion is the Omnibus Budget Reconciliation Act of 1990, which

took effect January 1, 1991.

[74] Some of the effects of this law are examined in U.S. General Accounting Office, Tax Policy and Administration: Luxury Excise Tax Issues and Estimated Effects, GAO/GGD-92-9, February, 1992.

[75] It should be pointed out that this law also acts as a protectionist tool to keep out foreign-made autos, since many of the cars that cost more than $30,000 are imported into the USA.

[76] The law has probably had negative effects on health, too. Since luxury cars tend to be big cars, and since increasing the luxury tax will cause some consumers to substitute smaller, less safe cars for larger cars, it might be that the number of fatal accidents has increased as a result of the luxury tax, since large cars are better able to withstand impact in an accident than are smaller cars. The number of auto fatalities caused by the luxury tax on autos is difficult to estimate, but would be a good topic for further research.

Chapter 22

THE INDIVIDUAL INCOME TAX

The individual income tax is one of the major forms of taxation in most western democracies. As a general rule, it can be said that any tax on individual income is "bad" in the sense that it dampens incentives[1] to produce and takes property without the owner's consent. The individual income tax also causes economic distortions, because it causes resources to shift as part of the redistribution process.

If one must have an individual income tax,[2] there are a number of options to choose from. Some income tax systems are worse than others. Systems with high rates will dampen incentive more than systems with low rates. And as incentives are dampened, economic growth is stifled. Studies of the individual income tax system in the USA have estimated that for every $1 of individual income taxes raised, between $0.24 and $0.47 is lost in production.[3]

A system based on the cost-benefit principle is more equitable than one based on the ability to pay principle because a system based on cost-benefit attempts to employ some form of rough justice, whereas an ability to pay system is based on exploitation A system with uniform rates is more equitable and simpler than one that has graduated rates. Interestingly, Karl Marx advocated a heavy, progressive income tax as a way to destroy capitalism.[4] This fact should be kept in mind when constructing a tax system that includes an income tax.

There are a number of other problems with the concept of a progressive income tax.[5] Some theorists have advocated a progressive income tax as a way to equalize utilities between and among individuals. But, as Hayek and others[6] have pointed out, there is no way to objectively compare the utilities of different individuals.[7] And even if it were possible, it is questionable whether equalizing utilities is a legitimate goal or function of government. Isn't the goal of government supposed to be to provide services to its citizens?

Is it ethical to take a portion of someone's property just because they have more than someone else? Does it make any difference whether the taker is a single individual or a group of individuals (some government)? Yet redistribution is the concept upon which the progressive income tax is based, a concept that some writers regard as unethical.[8] Progressive taxation is also an abuse of the concept of majority rule, because under it, the majority (lower and middle income people) is forcing a minority (upper income individuals) to pay more for government than what they receive in benefits. The majority is forcing a minority to pay for some of its benefits.

Applying the theory of decreasing marginal utility to income taxation leads to some rather interesting conclusions. According to the theory of decreasing marginal utility, it takes more to stimulate a rich man to produce than it does to stimulate a poor man. And since the rich tend to produce more than the poor, it is the rich rather than the poor who should be stimulated by giving them lower tax rates if the goal is to stimulate production and create wealth. Thus, applying the marginal utility theory to taxation leads to the conclusion that tax rates should be regressive rather than progressive. I am not saying that income tax rates should be regressive, but only that those who advocate progressive rates on marginal utility grounds are standing on a shaky theoretical foundation.

The effect that the income tax has on capital accumulation must also be considered. If rich people save and invest more than middle and lower income people, and if the goal is to increase saving and investment,[9] and thus economic growth, then the tax system should encourage (or at least not discourage) capital accumulation. While any form of income taxation has a negative effect on capital accumulation, progressive taxation has a more adverse effect than would a flat tax because a progressive tax takes more money from the segment of the population that is more likely and able to invest.

If a government must resort to an income tax, a flat-rate tax at least would avoid some of the problems that are inherent in a progressive tax system.[10] A flat-tax is also more equitable because it is based, more or less, on the cost-benefit principle rather than ability to pay. A major advantage of a flat tax is that it can be made very simple. Much of the complexity of the U.S. tax code is due to the fact that the system is progressive and attempts to affect behavior by granting deductions and tax credits for a plethora of activities.

A simple, flat tax would eliminate the need for a good percentage of the U.S. tax code[11] and eliminate the need for millions of taxpayers to hire professional assistance to compute their tax liability. Much of the effort that is now being expended in the private sector to comply with the law, keep the necessary records, and do tax planning could then be freed up to do something more productive. The administrative costs saved by businesses could either be plowed back into the business or passed on to customers in the form of lower prices.

Another advantage of the flat tax is that it is more equitable horizontally. In other words, people who earn the same amount of income pay about the same amount in taxes. Under the present system in the USA, people who earn, say, $50,000 in wages might pay more than someone who earns $50,000 in investment income, or someone who owns a home might pay less than someone who rents an apartment, because of the incentives, deductions and credits that are built into the system.

A flat tax would eliminate all of those differences by basing the tax on the amount of income earned, not the sources from which it came or what a taxpayer decides to do with disposable income. Thus, a flat tax would not cause as much distortion in the economy because tax incentives would not induce people to make decisions that result in the misallocation of resources solely to save taxes.

A flat tax would eliminate "bracket creep," the tendency of taxpayers to go into higher tax brackets because of inflation,[12] because everyone would pay the same rate. And it would eliminate the "marriage" tax penalty, since the present system taxes single individuals and married individuals at different rates.[13]

Another problem with the use of any individual income tax, whether progressive or flat-rate, especially in emerging economies, is that it is difficult to collect. Even if a system is in place to collect individual income taxes from the salaries and wages of workers, it is only the workers in the official sector of the economy whose taxes will be collected.[14] Those in the informal sector will escape the tax. So if one of the goals of tax policy is to have a wide tax base, the individual income tax might fall short of the goal if there is a large informal economy.

NOTES

1 Russell Shannon, Incentives and Income Taxes, Freeman 653-656 (November, 1981).

2 Some commentators have advocated replacing the income tax with a value added or consumption tax. We will discuss both of these alternatives below.

3 A 1981 study by Jerry Hausman estimated the loss to be $0.287. A 1984 study by Charles Stuart estimated the loss to be $0.244. A 1987 study by Edgar Browning estimated the cost to be between $0.318 and $0.469. These studies were mentioned in James L. Payne.

4 Karl Marx, The Communist Manifesto (1848).

5 The classic study is by Walter J. Blum and Harry Kalven, Jr., The Uneasy Case for Progressive Taxation (1953).

6 Murray N. Rothbard, Man, Economy and State 260-68 (1970).

7 F.A. Hayek, The Case Against Progressive Income Taxes, The Freeman, 229 (December 28, 1953).

8 For perhaps the most thorough treatise on this point, see Bertrand de Jouvenel, The Ethics of Redistribution (1952;1989).

9 It is questionable whether encouraging people to invest rather than consume is a legitimate function of government, since it is really no business of government telling people what they should do with their money.

10 For a commentary that advocates a flat tax, see Robert E. Hall and Alvin Rabushka, The Flat Tax (1985).

11 The exact percentage of the tax code that could be eliminated by adopting a flat tax depends on what other changes Congress would make to the system. Eliminating excise, estate and gift taxes and the corporate income tax would be feasible under a flat tax system, but whether Congress would choose to do so is another question.

12 Paul Gary Wyckoff, Flat Taxes and the Limits to Reform, Economic Commentary, Federal Reserve Bank of Cleveland, October 22, 1984, at 2.

13 For a treatise on horizontal equity and the taxation of family units, see Rudolph G. Penner, editor, Taxing the Family, Washington, DC and London: American Enterprise Institute, 1983.

14 Richard M. Bird makes this point in Tax Policy & Economic Development (1992), at 15.

Chapter 23

THE CORPORATE INCOME TAX

Much of what was said about the individual income tax can also be said of the corporate income tax. But there are some differences. Whereas individuals can vote, corporations cannot, so politicians encounter less resistance when they advocate raising the corporate tax. But ultimately, only individuals pay taxes,[1] so the corporate tax is a hidden tax, in the sense that those who ultimately pay it do not know that they are paying it. In that sense, then, taxing corporations is dishonest. It also seems unfair to assess a tax on persons who cannot vote, since they are being taxed without representation.

Another aspect of corporate taxes that seems unfair is the double tax effect. For example, if a corporation has taxable income of $100 and it has to pay 40% of its profits in taxes, it will have only $60 left to reinvest or pay dividends. If it decided to pay the $60 as dividends to an individual who is in the 40% tax bracket, the individual will have to pay a $24 tax, which leaves only $36. So the total tax will be $64 ($40 + $24), or 64%, and the corporation's owner receives only $36 after-tax.[2] Yet it is the shareholder who has made all the investment and taken all the risk. The government merely skims two-thirds of the profit and does nothing to earn it. It is for this reason that some economists favor making dividends tax-free, since taxing dividends results in double taxation of the same income.

Another attribute of the corporate income tax is that it is coercive rather than voluntary, which makes it a less favored way of raising revenue. The corporate tax is based on the ability to pay principle rather than cost benefit, which also makes it a less desirable form of taxation.

In the USA, the corporate income tax is progressive. Corporations that earn over a certain amount pay a higher percentage of their income in taxes than corporations that earn a low taxable income. Corporations that suffer losses do not pay any income tax, even though they may receive some government benefits. It is probably fair to say that the vast majority of corporations that pay taxes are not getting an equivalent payback in government services, since the government tends to be more of a hindrance to business than a help.

The present corporate tax structure in the USA makes administration difficult for the private sector. The largest corporations must retain the services of dozens, or even hundreds, of personnel to keep tax records and compute the corporation's tax liability. IRS must employ thousands of individuals to administer the system.[3] Many fewer individuals would have to be employed both by the government and by the private sector if the rules were simpler and clearer and if rates were lower.

The corporate income tax also has a detrimental effect on economic growth. Every dollar that is siphoned off in the form of taxes in not available for investment. The corporate tax also makes American business less competitive in world markets. A Brookings Institution study conducted by Roger Gordon and Burton Malkiel in 1981 estimated that for each dollar raised by the corporate income tax, the country lost $1.39 in production.[4] A 1989 study by Jane Gravelle and Laurence Kotlikoff of the National Bureau of Economic Research estimated that production dropped by between $0.84 and $1.51 for each dollar of taxes raised.[5] One economist has estimated that the value of the efficiency lost by the corporate income tax may be as much as half of the revenue raised by the tax.[6]

While the corporate income tax is "bad," in the sense that it violates the right to property (is coercive), is hidden and retards economic growth, some corporate income taxes are worse than others. If policymakers see the need for a corporate tax, it should adopt one with certain attributes.

Rates should be low. A uniform rate that is easy to compute is better than a myriad of rates and complicated rules that require dozens or hundreds of professionals to interpret. The cost of administration -- both by the tax collector and the private sector -- should be considered when contemplating whether to implement a corporate tax. U.S. companies devote more than 500 million hours a year just to filling out corporate tax forms.[7] If the average salary of the person filling out the form is $20 an hour, then just filling out the forms costs corporations $10 billion a year. And the cost of filling out the forms is only a small percentage of the total cost of tax compliance.[8]

Another criticism of the U.S. corporate income tax is the financial distortions that it causes.[9] The law favors noncorporate enterprises over corporations, encourages debt financing over equity financing, and favors retained earnings over paying dividends.[10] Corporations can take a tax deduction for the interest they pay but cannot deduct dividend payments. They can avoid the tax at the shareholder level if they retain their earnings rather than pay dividends but, in the case of small, closely held corporations, may subject the corporation to an accumulated earnings tax if it does not pay a dividend. Business entities can avoid the corporate tax quagmire by doing business as a partnership, but the partnership form exposes the owners to unlimited liability and makes it more difficult to raise capital, and thus grow.

A tax system that encourages some things and discourages others provides incentives and sanctions for corporate executives to make decisions based on tax avoidance rather than sound business practice. As a result, resources are allocated in a way that is different from what allocation would be in the absence of incentives and sanctions. And inefficient allocation of resources retards economic growth. At least one study has concluded that the corporate income tax is the least efficient of the major taxes.[11] A Treasury Department study concluded that integrating business and income taxes would shift capital to the corporate sector, reduce corporate borrowing, increase dividend payments, and increase Gross Domestic Product by between $3 billion and $30 billion.[12]

These studies provide important information for policymakers in emerging democracies because they point out the potential pitfalls that lurk beneath the surface of a corporate income tax. The best course is not to establish a corporate income tax in the first place, since it is not the corporation that ultimately pays the tax. And corporate taxes have an adverse effect on economic growth, not only because of the distortions to the economic system that they cause, but also because of the disincentives they provide for foreign investors who might otherwise supply badly-needed capital to the emerging democracy.[13]

If policymakers determine that a corporate income tax is needed, in spite of all the evidence of the negative effects of such a tax, they should adopt a set of rules that encourages rather than discourages investment. That means rates should be low, the system should be simple to understand and administer, and the law should not discourage investment, either by foreigners or domestic investors.

NOTES

[1] If the corporation is able to pass on the tax in the form of higher prices, then the individuals who pay for the corporation's products or services ultimately pay the tax. If the tax cannot be passed on, then the individuals who own the corporation's stock have to settle for a lower rate of return on their investment, since the government siphons off a large chunk of the corporation's pretax profits. Either way, individuals ultimately pay the corporation's tax.

[2] At some times in U.S. history, the situation has been much worse. There have been times when the top corporate rate was more than 50% and the top individual rate was more than 90%. With rates as high as these, the high bracket shareholder who received a dividend actually got to keep about 5% of the corporation's pre-tax income.

[3] The IRS has more than 120,000 employees, some of whom are employed in the corporate tax area.

[4] This study was cited by James L. Payne, at 20.

[5] Id. The study Payne referred to was Jane G. Gravelle and Laurence J. Kotlikoff, Corporate Taxation and the Efficiency Gains of the 1986 Tax Reform Act, Working Paper 3142, National Bureau of Economic Research, October, 1989.

[6] J. Gregory Ballentine, Equity, Efficiency, and the U.S. Corporation Income Tax (1980).

[7] Jeffrey J. Hallman and Joseph G. Haubrich, Integrating Business and Personal Income Taxes, Economic Commentary, Federal Reserve Bank of Cleveland, October 1, 1992, at 2.

[8] A Coopers & Lybrand study of corporations having sales of $25 million or more found that the average company assigns 7.4 people to the state and local tax area and 9.3 to the federal tax area. Coopers & Lybrand, State and Local Taxes: The Burden Grows (1992), at 5.

[9] Hallman and Haubrich, at 2. These authors evaluated five proposals to reform the corporate tax system to reduce tax avoidance costs and financial distortions caused by the present corporate tax system.

[10] Although this chapter emphasizes the U.S. corporate tax, many of the same arguments can be made regarding the various European corporate tax systems. For a discussion that

incorporates examples from the European experience, see John Chown, The Corporation Tax -- a Closer Look, London: Institute of Economic Affairs, 1965.

[11] J. Gregory Ballentine, Equity, Efficiency, and the U.S. Corporation Income Tax, Washington, DC: American Enterprise Institute, 1980.

[12] Hallman and Haubrich point this out at 3. The study they referred to was the U.S. Treasury Department's Report to Congress, titled Integration and Individual and Corporate Tax Systems: Taxing Business Income Once, January, 1992.

[13] The U.S. tax system has been criticized for the adverse effect it has on foreign investment. For discussions on this point, see Gary Clyde Hufbauer, U.S. Taxation of International Income: Blueprint for Reform, Washington, DC: Institute for International Economics, 1992; U.S. Foreign Tax Policy and the Global Economy: New Directions for the 1990s, Institute for Research on the Economics of Taxation, 1989.

Chapter 24

THE VALUE ADDED TAX

The value added tax (VAT) suffers from the same major deficiency as most other forms of taxation in that it is coercive. It involves the taking of property without the owner's consent. But if one believes that some forms of takings are better than others, one might ask whether the VAT is a viable alternative to the income tax. For years, some commentators have been calling for the replacement of the income tax with some form of VAT because the income tax discourages production and encourages consumption and leisure, whereas the VAT encourages thrift and enterprise.[1] Certainly, if this is so, it is a form of taxation that should be of interest to an emerging economy, where economic growth is especially important.[2]

In recent years, some commentators in the USA have advocated a VAT not as a replacement for the income tax but as a supplement, because they think that raising more funds via an income tax is not feasible.[3] According to one view, "...consumption taxes alone cannot achieve the ability to pay principle and accordingly could not entirely replace an income tax."[4] But, as has been discussed elsewhere, the ability to pay principle is not a legitimate principle of taxation.

In a sense, they are right. If income tax rates are raised beyond a certain point, it will trigger a reaction among taxpayers and some politicians might get voted out of office in the next election. It would be easier to raise revenue if, instead of raising income tax rates, a form of value added tax were used to make up the difference. The reason for this solution is that the value added tax is a hidden form of taxation, in the sense that the people who ultimately pay[5] it do not know precisely what they are paying.

In a sense, then, the VAT is an unethical way to raise revenue because the tax is hidden. From an ethical standpoint, visible taxes are to be preferred to hidden taxes. The fact that it is hidden makes it easier for the government to raise the tax without the knowledge of the taxpayers, so there is little resistance to increasing the tax. At least one study has pointed out that governments have not been able to resist raising the tax rate once a VAT is in place, which might account for the fact that those OECD countries that have a VAT also have much higher tax ratios than those that do not have one.[6]

In a sense, then, the VAT is a dishonest way to raise revenue because of the lack of full disclosure. The U.S. government[7] is putting increasing pressure on publicly traded corporations to have full disclosure on their financial statements. The Federal Trade Commission pressures banks to fully disclose loan charges. The Food and Drug Administration pressures companies to disclose the content of the cans of food they produce. Yet when some government makes use of a value added tax, there seems to be no need for any disclosure. The amount of the tax is hidden, in the sense that the ultimate payer does not know how much the tax is. The blame for the tax may even be shifted onto the corporations that sell the products. When consumers see that corporations charge high prices for their products, they may blame the corporations, when in fact a large portion of the purchase price is attributable to the VAT.

Another drawback of the VAT is the high bureaucratic cost of administration.[8] On the government's side, it would take thousands of bureaucrats to administer it. And for the businesses that have to pay it, it would take many hours of valuable time to keep the appropriate records and file the proper tax returns.[9] If there were no VAT, these many thousands of individuals could spend their time creating wealth instead of shuffling papers.[10]

But the same argument could be made for abolishing the income tax, which has become increasingly complex with each passing year.[11] All other things being equal, a simple, and easily administered VAT might be preferred to a complex, obscure and burdensome income tax. So simplicity, clarity and administrative burden are issues that must be considered regardless of which form of taxation is chosen.

One advantage of the VAT is that an enormous amount of revenue can be raised while keeping rates relatively low, compared to income tax rates. That is because the tax base for a VAT is much wider. The VAT tax base consists basically of the economy's total output of goods and services, plus imports minus exports.[12] So a 3.5% VAT could raise as much as a 34% corporate income tax, and a 16% VAT could raise as much as an individual income tax that is assessed at the U.S. rates of 15% and 28%.[13] But the revenue-raising aspect of a VAT is a double-edged sword. Those who advocate low taxes see the VAT as a threat because the VAT makes it easy for the government to raise revenue -- to take wealth out of the private sector. "Conservatives fear that instituting a VAT or a retail sales tax would be as risky as turning over the wine cellar key to an alcoholic."[14]

Computing the correct tax might prove to be a problem. Basically, the tax is assessed on the value added, the difference between the value of the product as it comes in the door and the value as it goes out. But in practice, the computation would not be that simple. Certain items would probably be exempt, such as food.[15] And policymakers will be tempted to assess different rates for different products and services, so there would be classification problems.[16] And there would be pressure to exempt governmental units and nonprofit organizations, or perhaps to charge them lower rates. Producers who are engaged in both exempt and taxable activities would have to resort to apportionment, which could get quite complicated.[17]

Proponents of a VAT contend that the VAT offers several additional advantages over other forms of taxation. For example, they say that it is "neutral" because it is levied at a uniform rate over the whole consumption base.[18] Thus, the method of production chosen is not affected by the tax system and producers can shift to more profitable methods of production without affecting their tax burden. There is no penalty for being efficient with a VAT, whereas with an income tax, companies that are more efficient, and that therefore have a higher profit, get hit with a higher income tax. And a VAT does not subsidize waste, whereas an income tax does, in the sense that costs are deductible and reduce the amount of income upon which the income tax is assessed. But a study of several countries has concluded that, in practice, the VAT is far from neutral in most cases.[19]

Those who oppose the VAT give several reasons. For one, it is viewed as regressive, in the sense that those least able to pay will wind up paying a higher percentage of their income in VAT taxes than those who are in the higher income brackets.[20] Some relief could be granted to these groups by exempting certain items, like food and medicine, but doing so would make the system more complicated and difficult to administer. The adverse effect on economic growth must also be considered. One econometric study predicted that the U.S. economy would grow 1% more slowly for each 1% VAT and inflation would be one and a half to two percentage points higher during the initial adjustment period.[21]

A study of European VAT systems found that the VAT is regressive in another way as well. The cost of compliance and administration fall more heavily on small firms than on large ones.[22] This point should be of special interest to emerging democracies, since most economic growth is expected to come from small enterprises rather than large ones. A VAT could choke off growth before it starts in the case of many small businesses.

Another factor that must be considered, especially in an emerging economy, is collection. As is true of an income tax, the VAT will likely be collected only in the formal sector of the economy. Evasion will be widespread in the informal sector. This very fact will encourage enterprises to do their business informally rather than join the formal sector.

CONCLUDING COMMENTS

There are several ethical problems with the value added tax. The main ethical problem, which is shared by just about every form of public finance other than lotteries and user fees, is coercion. In order to collect the tax it is first necessary to take property that rightfully belongs to others. In the case of the VAT, there are other ethical problems as well. For example, the tax is hidden. Those who ultimately pay the tax are not fully aware that they are paying or what they are paying. It is impossible to accurately trace the amount of the tax that is paid by the ultimate consumer or at each stage of production. Worse yet, there is no attempt at disclosure on the part of the government. Hidden taxes are unethical forms of public finance and the VAT is a hidden form of tax.

From a utilitarian ethical point of view, the tax is unethical because it is inefficient. Utilitarian ethics includes the premise that what is efficient is ethical and what is inefficient is unethical.[23] This view may be correct or incorrect, but it violates utilitarian ethics in any event.

NOTES

1 Murray L. Weidenbaum and Ernest S. Christian, Jr., The Allure of Value-Added Taxes: Examining the Pros and Cons 1 (1989).

2 A subtle issue is involved here, whether the tax system should encourage or discourage certain kinds of activity. Those who favor the VAT over the income tax often do so because they think that government should encourage savings over consumption. But is the influencing of taxpayer behavior a legitimate function of government? If government is the servant and taxpayers the masters, should a servant really care what the master does with his own money?

3 Charles E. McLure, Jr., The Value-Added Tax: Key To Deficit Reduction? Washington, DC: American Enterprise Institute, 1987, p. 175. For a study that considers the relative merits of a VAT as an additional revenue source by comparing it to an income surtax on individuals and corporations, see Effects of Adopting a Value-Added Tax (Washington: Congressional Budget Office, February, 1992).

4 Organization for Economic Cooperation and Development, Taxing Consumption, Paris: OECD, 1988, p. 32.

5 The question of who ultimately pays a VAT or other consumption tax is a major one, and economists cannot agree on who ultimately pays the tax. For a discussion of this point, see David G. Raboy and Cliff Massa, III, Who Bears the Burden of Consumption Taxes? in The Value Added Tax: Orthodoxy and New Thinking (Murray L. Weidenbaum, David G. Raboy and Ernest S. Christian, Jr eds., 1989), at 39-68.

6 Graham Bannock, VAT and Small Business: European Experience and Implications for North America, London: Graham Bannock & Partners Ltd., 1986, p. 8.

7 Specifically, the Securities and Exchange Commission and Congress.

8 The Japanese Consumption Tax: Value-Added Model or Administrative Nightmare? American University Law Review 40: 1265-1306 (Spring, 1991). Also see J. Gregory Ballentine, The Administrability of a Value Added Tax, in Charls E. Walker and Mark Bloomfield, editors, New Directions in Federal Tax Policy for the 1980s, Cambridge, MA: Ballinger Publishing Co., 1983; John Blundell, Britain's Nightmare Value Added Tax, Heritage Foundation International Briefing, Washington, DC: Heritage Foundation, June 13, 1988.

9 In England, small businesses complained about the complexity of the British VAT. Their complaints subsided somewhat when the VAT tax forms were simplified. A. R. Prest, Value Added Taxation: The Experience of the United Kingdom, Washington and London: American Enterprise Institute, 1980, p. 38.

10 And where the VAT is used as a supplement to the income tax rather than as a replacement, two sets of bureaucrats and private sector accountants would be required, one to administer the VAT and another to administer the income tax requirements.

11 Nelson Hultberg, Why We Must Abolish the Income Tax and the IRS: A Special Report on the National Sales Tax, Dallas: AFR Publishers, 1997; Bernard Curry, Principles of Taxation of a Libertarian Society, Glendale, CA: BC Publishing Co., 1982; Murray Sabrin,

Tax Free 2000: The Rebirth of American Liberty, Lafayette, LA: Prescott Press, 1994; Frank Champagne, Cancel April 15: The Plan for Painless Taxation, Mt. Vernon, WA: Nookachamps Publishers, 1994; Jack Anderson and Tom Schatz, The Coming Tax Rebellion: How You Can End the Income Tax, Washington, DC: Citizens Against Government Waste, n.d.; Sheldon Richman, Your Money or Your Life: Why We Must Abolish the Income Tax, Fairfax, VA: Future of Freedom Foundation, 1999.

[12] Weidenbaum and Christian, supra, at 4.

[13] Id. These comparisons are based on the tax system in the USA in 1987.

[14] Charles E. McLure, Jr., The Value-Added Tax: Key To Deficit Reduction? 176 (1987).

[15] The author found a very easy way to evade the VAT at a McDonald's in Paris. A VAT is charged on food that is consumed on the premises but not on food that is taken away. All one need do to evade the VAT is to declare that you are taking the food away at the time of purchase, then change your mind and sit down at a table after you have the food in-hand. Enforcement would require the hamburger police to be stationed at every McDonald's.

[16] Is an antidandruff shampoo, for example, a medicine, and therefore exempt, or a cosmetic, and therefore taxable. French tax officials engaged in an extensive debate over this issue, as is pointed out in Weidenbaum and Christian, supra, at 5.

[17] A. R. Prest, Value Added Taxation: The Experience of the United Kingdom 26 (1980).

[18] In fact, it is not neutral, but it is not easy to predict where distortion will occur. The tax is paid by producers, but may be passed on to consumers in the form of higher prices. If it cannot be passed on, then profit margins suffer, shareholders must be content with a lower return on investment, and employment expands less rapidly. And a VAT may adversely affect some lines of business more than others. Any tax also has an adverse effect on economic growth, so it cannot truly be said that a VAT is neutral.

[19] Graham Bannock, supra, at 8.

[20] This view takes for granted that the ability to pay principle is to be preferred over the cost-benefit principle, which is questionable, at best. The ability to pay principle is discussed elsewhere in this book.

[21] Weidenbaum and Christian, supra, at 10. The study they cite is Joel L. Prakken, The Macroeconomics of Tax Reform, in The Consumption Tax: A Better Alternative? (Charls E. Walker and Mark A. Bloomfield eds.1987), at 117-166.

[22] Graham Bannock, supra, at 24-25.

[23] Richard A. Posner, Economic Analysis of Law 284-285 (5th ed. 1998).

Chapter 25

THE RETAIL CONSUMPTION TAX

INTRODUCTION

Retail consumption taxes may be levied at the national, state or local level. In the USA, a retail sales tax is levied on the sale of products (but not services) in nearly all the states. So far, the national government has not seen fit to assess a similar tax at the national level, although there has been talk of instituting such a national tax as a supplement to or as a replacement for the income tax.

UTILITARIAN ARGUMENTS IN FAVOR OF THE TAX

One advantage of a sales tax over a value added tax is that the sales tax would be levied only on the end user.[1] It would only be assessed at the final stage of production rather than along every step of the way, so the amount of bureaucracy and paper shuffling would be much less, compared to the VAT.[2] The cost of administering a national sales tax would be much lower than that required to administer a VAT, especially in jurisdictions that already have a sales tax, since the administrative mechanism would already be in place.

Another relative advantage of a sales tax, at any level -- national, state or local -- is that it is visible, so those who pay it can see that they are paying it. Unlike the VAT, which is hidden, they can see how much they are paying for a purchase because the tax is assessed on every purchase. And where the tax is visible, there is resistance, so there is a built-in restraint on tax increases. Those who have to pay the tax will offer a certain amount of resistance, so politicians will be less likely to raise the tax because their efforts will become known immediately to the taxpayers.

Another phenomenon is present when a sales tax is assessed at the state or local level -- tax competition.[3] If neighboring localities or states each assess a sales tax, there is a tendency for residents who live near the border to go shopping in the place that has the lower tax rate. For example, if New Hampshire has no sales tax and Massachusetts has a high sales tax, Massachusetts residents who live near the New Hampshire border will have a tendency to do their shopping in New Hampshire rather than Massachusetts.

If New Jersey does not assess a sales tax on clothes and New York assesses a high sales tax on clothes, there will be a tendency for New York residents to shop for clothes in New Jersey, even if they have to pay a few dollars to come to New Jersey. The competition for shoppers between New York and New Jersey has become so upsetting to New York tax officials that they are spending time stalking the shopping malls in New Jersey and taking down auto license plate numbers in an attempt to identify New York shoppers who cross the Hudson River to shop in New Jersey.[4]

The law requires that people who purchase merchandise in another state pay a use tax to New York state that is equal to the difference between the tax they paid on the out-of-state purchase and the tax they would have owed if they had made the purchase in New York. But the use tax rules are almost universally ignored by New York residents, who shop in New Jersey with the express intent of evading the New York tax.

While most shoppers don't spend more than a few hundred dollars on clothing at any one time, the effect on tax collections can be much greater for large purchases. For example, a New York resident could save hundreds of dollars by purchasing a $10,000 fur coat in New Jersey rather than New York. This fact has a depressing effect on the fur business in New York, and the New York sales tax leads to increased business for New Jersey furriers. There is also a ripple effect on other industries in the low tax state. Those who purchase furs may also decide to buy lunch or go to a movie while they are in New Jersey.

The competition effect places pressure on the local politicians not to raise taxes. The local residents may tend not to vote for any politician who raises their sales taxes. And local businesses, who stand to lose business if the sales tax is increased, may threaten not to make campaign contributions to any politicians who vote to raise the sales tax. If taxes are high enough, some businesses may decide to close up shop and move to the low tax state. That is precisely what is happening in New York, not just because of the relatively high New York state and City sales tax, but because taxes in New York are generally higher than in the surrounding states.

Another aspect of sales taxes is the fact that everyone pays the same rate. Rates are not graduated based on income,[5] so the tax system does not increase class conflict by assessing higher rates on the rich than on the poor. But anyone can avoid the sales tax simply by not buying. And since the rich tend to spend more than the poor, the rich will end up paying more in sales taxes than the poor anyway. Economists call this result horizontal and vertical equity because equal taxpayers are treated equally and taxpayers who earn more money pay higher taxes because they spend more.[6]

Taxing sales rather than income may also have a positive effect on the savings rate. If people are not taxed until they buy something, there may be more of a tendency to save rather than consume. If savings increase relative to income, the supply of funds available for investment will increase, which will lead to lower interest rates, lower cost of capital, and more investment, which will increase economic growth and create jobs.

This effect is not present with an income tax, since income and investment are both taxed. Where there is an income tax, there is more of a tendency to consume, since the return on investment, after tax, is lower than if no tax were assessed. Studies have estimated that the tax rate on a national sales tax in the USA would have to be about 12% to 15% in order to raise the same amount of revenue that is now being raised by the individual and corporate income tax.[7]

If a national sales tax replaced the income tax in the USA,[8] a number of other beneficial effects would result. Since a sales tax is much simpler and easier to assess than an income tax, there would no longer be a need for individuals or businesses to file income tax returns. Thus, hundreds of millions of hours would be freed up for other uses, such as creating wealth or increasing leisure (which would be beneficial for the leisure industries).

The U.S. tax code,[9] which now consists of thousands of pages of law and regulations, could be almost entirely scrapped. The thousands of cases (from three federal court systems)[10] and thousands of revenue rulings, revenue procedures and other IRS pronouncements could be ignored because they would become irrelevant. The hundreds of thousands of people who administer the tax system at the national level[11] and the many corporate accountants who must keep tax records for their companies could put their time and effort into more productive pursuits.

Replacing the income tax with a sales tax would also greatly reduce the extent of intrusion that government makes into the private lives of its citizens. The government would have no reason to audit the tax returns of millions of individuals[12] and invade their privacy. Replacing the income tax with a sales tax would thus increase individual freedom and reduce official corruption and the use of arbitrary power.[13]

The Internal Revenue Service has at times confiscated property without due process[14] and sold the property for 10 cents on the dollar, only to later discover that the taxpayer owed no tax. Under present law, IRS is only obligated to refund the proceeds it received from selling the taxpayer's property, not the value of the property it seized.

The major criticism of the sales tax is that it is "regressive," in the sense that poor people pay a larger portion of their income in sales taxes than do rich people. This view makes the assumption that poor people have a higher propensity to consume and rich people have a higher propensity to save. But there are many problems with the propensity to consume theory, not the least of which is that the empirical evidence does not consistently support the view that the rich save a higher percentage of their income than the poor.[15] One study found that savings, as a percentage of income, declined for seven years out of the eleven years under study.[16] Another study concluded that savings, as a percentage of income, remains constant over time.[17]

Another problem with the regressivity view is that those who advocate it generally hold the view that taxes should be progressive, that is, they should take a higher percentage of income from the rich than from the poor. They take the Marxist "ability to pay" approach rather than the more equitable benefits received approach. This view, aside from being inequitable, also exacerbates class conflict and reduces social harmony, because it pits one class against another. With a sales tax, the rich pay more than the poor in absolute terms because they spend more. And the rich also receive more benefit from government than do the poor, since they have more property in need of protection. So the sales tax works a rough justice of sorts. The rich receive more benefit from government services (protection of property) than do the poor, and they pay more for it.

SOME ETHICAL PROBLEMS

From the perspective of utilitarian ethics the retail consumption tax has several advantages over the income tax. It is more efficient and results in less distortion to the economy and has fewer adverse effects on incentives to produce. However, the retail consumption tax presents some ethical problems that utilitarian ethics does not address.

Perhaps the main ethical problem is that the tax is coercive. Property rights must necessarily be violated because an individual's property is taken by force or the threat of force every time a transaction occurs. Individuals have the right to contract, to trade what they have for what they want. But when they exercise this right they must pay a tax. Voluntary means of raising revenue, such as user fees and lotteries, are to be preferred to coercive forms of public finance. Thus, a retail consumption tax, even though it is more efficient than an income tax from the perspective of utilitarian ethics, suffers from a defect in that it requires coercion.

Another defect, especially during the transition from an income tax to the retail consumption tax, is that the same income is being taxed twice. First the income was earned. Then a portion of it was taxed by the income tax. Later, when the remainder is spent it is taxed again by the retail consumption tax. This double taxation effect is inherently unfair and there does not seem to be any way around it. One could grant exemptions or exclusions to deal with this problem but that would make the law much more complicated. Simplicity, one of the major advantages of the tax, would be reduced or eliminated.

The retail consumption tax has a tendency to raise prices. According to some ethical perspectives, any tax that raises prices is inherently unfair. Writing from the Islamic perspective, Ahmad states that "the adoption of any methods that create an artificial rise in the prices is strictly forbidden."[18] He goes on to say:

> The term *maks* is used for sales-tax. The Prophet (peace be on him) had repeatedly said: "He who levies *maks* shall not enter Paradise." Since the imposition of sales-tax (or, for that matter, of octroi and excise duties) results in raising the prices unjustly, therefore, Islam does not approve of it. The Caliph 'Umar ibn 'Abd al-'Aziz had abolished *maks*, interpreting it as *bakhs* (diminution in what is due to others) which is expressly prohibited by the Qur'an.[19]

CONCLUDING COMMENTS

A retail consumption tax is superior to an income tax from the perspective of utilitarian ethics because it is simpler and more efficient. The retail consumption tax is also less intrusive. If it replaced the income tax, IRS abuses would be greatly reduced.

However, the retail consumption tax also presents some problems. If it merely supplements the income tax rather than replaces it, as some members of Congress advocate, the overall tax burden would be increased and the economy would work less efficiently. When resources are transferred from the private sector to the public sector, the economy works less efficiently because the private sector can do just about everything more efficiently than the public sector.[20]

Another problem with the retail consumption tax is that is relies on coercion for collection. In a free society, coercion is to be minimized. The retail consumption tax does nothing to minimize coercion and actually increases it, although not by as much as the income tax. So the retail consumption tax is a step in the right direction because it reduces coercion and the possibility of IRS abuse, and because it is more efficient than the income tax, but it is not as good a solution as reduced government spending and massive privatization, which would result in an even more efficient economy and even less coercion.

NOTES

[1] Organization for Economic Cooperation and Development, Taxing Consumption 68-69 (1988).

[2] Id., at 99-101.

[3] This phenomenon is discussed in Timothy Brown, Interjurisdictional Tax Competition: An Economic Perspective, Nebraska Law Review 68: 652-71 (1989). Secession is a related way to restrain governments from raising taxes to excessive levels. For more on the use of secession as a restraint on taxes, see Robert W. McGee, Secession as a Tool for Limiting the Growth of State and Municipal Governments and Making It

More Responsive: A Constitutional Proposal, Western State University Law Review 21: 499-513 (Spring, 1994).

[4] Thomas Moran, N.Y. Tax Collectors Staking Out Malls: Want Payback on N.J. Shopping Deals, The (Bergen County, NJ) Record, December 10, 1992, at A1.

[5] Some people still cling to the outmoded belief that graduated tax rates are desirable. For discussions on the graduated income tax, see Walter J. Blum and Harry Kalven, Jr., The Uneasy Case for Progressive Taxation, Chicago: University of Chicago Press, 1953; F.A. Hayek, The Case Against Progressive Income Taxes, The Freeman 229-232 (1953).

[6] Mark Skousen makes this point at 168 in Economics on Trial, Homewood, IL: Business One Irwin, 1991.

[7] Mark Skousen, Economics on Trial 169 (1991).

[8] The USA is being used as an example here, but the same rules apply to any country that has an income tax.

[9] Title 26, U.S.C.

[10] Three different federal court systems hear tax cases in the USA. Cases can be initiated in the Tax Court, the District Court or the Claims Court. Appeals from these courts go to the federal appellate court, and then, perhaps to the Supreme Court. And the various courts sometimes reach diametrically opposed conclusions about similar or identical fact situations, which makes the system more complicated and less certain, not to mention expensive and time-consuming. All this could be eliminated if the income tax were abolished.

[11] IRS has more than 120,000 employees.

[12] IRS audits about 1 million tax returns a year, or slightly less than 1% of the income tax returns filed in the USA.

[13] For a treatise on IRS abuse, see David Burnham, A Law Unto Itself: Power, Politics and the IRS, New York: Random House, 1989)

[14] James Bovard gives some examples in Shakedown: How the Government Screws You from A to Z , New York: Penguin, 1995, pp. 63-66.

[15] For more on this point, see Henry Hazlitt, The Failure of the "New Economics", Princeton: Van Nostrand, 1959, pp. 98-134, especially 113-15.

[16] Id, at 113.

[17] Alvin H. Hansen, A Guide to Keynes, New York: McGraw Hill, 1953, p. 75.

18 Mushtaq Ahmad, Business Ethics in Islam 123 (1995).

19 Id. The ethics of tax evasion according to Islam is discussed in Athar Murtuza and S.M. Ghazanfar, Taxation as a Form of Worship: Exploring the Nature of Zakat, in The Ethics of Tax Evasion 190-212 (Robert W. McGee, editor 1998) and also in this book.

20 The numerous books on privatization that have been published in the last few decades provide hundreds of examples of how the private sector can do just about everything cheaper and better than government. Perhaps the best single source of information on privatization is the Reason Foundation, [www.privatization.org].

Chapter 26

EXCISE TAXES

INTRODUCTION

Some of the content of this chapter is based on Chapter 1 of Shughart's book on excise taxes.[1] Shughart's book is one of the few books that takes a critical look at the nonrevenue raising aspects of excise taxes. Thus, it is a good starting point for a discussion of how excise taxes have gone astray from their revenue raising function.

THE ECONOMICS OF THE NANNY STATE

Excise taxes are no longer imposed just to raise revenue. In fact, it is becoming increasingly likely that those who advocate imposing or raising excise taxes only pay lip service to the revenue raising aspect. The real goal is often to further some politically correct agenda. That certainly seems to be the case for taxes on alcohol, tobacco and firearms. The government's fiscal function has come to devote increased resources to punishing or regulating behavior rather than raising revenue.

Traditionally, those who advocate excise taxes have used three economic justifications.[2] One justification is the so-called *Ramsey Rule*,[3] which advocates taxing commodities based on their elasticities of demand. Commodities like alcohol and tobacco are highly inelastic, meaning that most people who purchase these products will continue to do so regardless of cost. So it becomes feasible to slap on an excise tax since doing so will not result in reducing demand very much. Supposedly, applying this rule results in minimizing the excess burden of taxation and minimizing social cost.

The second rationale is based on the concept of a user fee. User fees are not really taxes, in a sense, since the only people who pay them are the ones who use the service. This tends to be true in the case of the excise tax on gasoline, provided the revenues generated from the tax are used to support highway maintenance and construction. This line of reasoning has recently been extended to alcohol, tobacco and firearms to justify increasing the tax to pay for alcohol abuse treatment centers, cancer research, and so forth.

The third argument that has been put forth for selective excise taxation is to correct something that some politicians, government bureaucrats or special interest group (usually consisting of do-gooders) think needs correcting. In economic language, one might say that excise taxes could be used to internalize externalities,[4] or to push up the cost to the consumer to equal the total social cost in cases where the purchase price of this or that product does not cover the total social cost.[5]

SELECTIVE TAXES AND THE RAMSEY RULE

Excise taxes have been criticized for violating both the vertical equity rule and the horizontal equity rule,[6] which leads one to wonder why they exist.[7] Those who criticize excise taxes for violating vertical equity do so because of the belief that excise taxes fall disproportionately on the poor, whereas they should fall disproportionately on the rich, since the rich are better able to pay.

While not taking the position that excise taxes are equitable, I question whether the fact that if excise taxes are regressive that is necessarily bad,[8] since lower income groups might derive disproportionate benefits from the proceeds collected from excise taxes. If that is the case, it seems that lower income groups should pay more than those in higher income categories, since they derive more benefit from the taxes.

Another problem with the premise that the ability to pay principle should be used to determine whether excise taxes violate vertical equity is the fact that the ability to pay principle is ethically bankrupt. There are only two ways to look at the relationship between government and the people. Either the government is the master and the people are the servants or the government is the servant and the people are the masters. The ability to pay principle has as its premise the view that government is the master and the rich are to be exploited merely because they (supposedly)[9] are better able to pay for the cost of government. The ability to pay principle ignores the basic rule of fairness that taxpayers should receive benefits more or less in proportion to what they pay in taxes.[10]

Another view of fairness within the public finance literature is horizontal equity, the belief that people who make about the same amount of income should pay about the same amount of taxes. The fact is that they often do not. Rich people who do not smoke do not pay any excise taxes on cigarettes, for example.[11] But so what?

Excise taxes are far from neutral. They have at least three effects. They reduce the supply of whatever commodity or service is taxed, they raise its price and they modify its attributes.[12] In the case of cigarettes, for example, excise taxes can influence the color of the wrapper, the length of the cigarette, the blend of tobacco and the amount of tar and nicotine. That is because the amount of excise tax can be different for different characteristics. Those characteristics that receive relatively favorable tax treatment will tend to be supplied.[13] In the case of cigarettes, for example, the excise tax can cause long cigarettes to become more attractive than short cigarettes,[14] which is the exact opposite of what the anti-tobacco do-gooders probably intended.[15]

One reason, perhaps the main one, why cigarettes and alcoholic beverages sold outside the United States tend to be stronger than those sold in the United States is because other countries charge much higher excise taxes on these products.[16] High tax rates have a tendency to increase potency.

Increasing excise taxes also decreases social welfare, since an increase in price causes consumers to shift their purchases to products that previously ranked lower on their list of preferences.

> ...because the tax inserts a "wedge" between the amount paid by the consumer and the after-tax amount received by the producer, a "deadweight" welfare loss is also imposed on society. This loss is called a deadweight loss because its value is transferred away from market participants but is not captured by the government or anyone else. This deadweight welfare loss is also referred to as the "excess burden" of the tax because it represents the amount by which the value of the welfare losses imposed on producers and consumers exceeds the revenue collected by the tax authority.[17]

The *Ramsey Rule* holds that placing excise taxes on products in inverse proportion to their elasticities of demand is the way to minimize the excess tax burden.[18] In other words, governments should charge high excise taxes on products where consumers will not reduce their consumption by much and low excise taxes on products where consumers will reduce their purchases if excise taxes are raised. This rule provides the intellectual justification for placing heavy excise taxes on alcohol and tobacco.[19]

The *Ramsey Rule* has been criticized on at least three counts.[20] For one, there is little evidence to support the belief that government is motivated to maximize the efficiency of the tax code and much evidence to support the belief that efficiency has little or nothing to do with tax policy. Secondly, the rule assumes that government has as its goal the collection of some predetermined amount of tax revenue, whereas the actual goal of most governments seems to be collecting the maximum in taxes. Finally, the government imposes "sin" taxes to reduce consumption, while the *Ramsey Rule* would impose higher taxes because of the belief that consumption is not affected much because of the highly inelastic demand for products like alcohol and tobacco. Thus, the revenue-raising reasons and the regulatory reasons for high excise taxes work at cross purposes.

USER FEES

A user fee, properly applied, is not really a tax, in the sense that coercion is not involved in collecting it. One can avoid paying the fee by not using the service or product. People can avoid paying the user fee that would be charged for admission to a government owned park by not entering the park.[21]

Ideally,[22] the proceeds used from the collection of a user fee are earmarked[23] to pay for the service provided. The excise tax on gasoline is used to maintain and construct highways. The tax on airline tickets is used to maintain airports.[24] Ideally, an excise tax should be charged by public schools so that only the parents of the children attending the school would have to pay for their education.[25]

Unfortunately, the concept of user fees breaks down when it is actually applied. Earmarked taxes are highly fungible. If a state lottery raises funds for education, the state legislature (perhaps) reduces the amount of funding from the general fund without actually reducing tax rates, so the total tax burden increases. The user fee concept also breaks down as the ultimate use of the funds becomes distant from the funding source.

For example, suppose that the tax on alcohol and tobacco is increased to pay for Medicare and Medicaid. Smokers and drinkers benefit from Medicare and Medicaid but so do nonsmokers and nondrinkers. So some segment of the population is being forced to pay for benefits that another segment of the population receives.[26] Furthermore, some smokers and drinkers do not use Medicare or Medicaid, even though they are being forced to pay for these programs. At this point the concept of a user fee no longer applies.

Another criticism of taxes on alcohol and tobacco is that they transfer wealth from the poor to the middle class.

> Federal health care reform was marketed as an entitlement program for the middle class. Yet the consumers of alcohol and tobacco are disproportionately young and poor. As such, proposals for earmarking selective tax revenues to finance government health care programs are political ruses that serve to disguise a transfer of wealth from the lower end of the income distribution to the middle.[27]

INTERNALIZING EXTERNALITIES & CORRECTIVE TAXES

One rationale for increasing certain excise taxes is because of the belief that the price of certain products, like alcohol and tobacco, does not cover the total cost. For example, when someone purchases cigarettes, he pays only for the cost of the cigarettes, not for the cost of curing or treating his cancer, which will not be incurred for a few decades. When someone buys an alcoholic beverage, the price he pays reflects merely the cost of providing the product, including some profit margin. It does not include the cost of providing alcohol abuse facilities. Thus, the total cost is not captured in the selling price, so excise taxes have to be increased to make up the difference. Economists would call this internalizing the externalities. Externalities are costs or benefits that are not reflected in the purchase price.

There are several problems with this rationale for slapping on excise taxes to internalize the negative externalities. The most obvious problem is that not everyone gets cancer from smoking and not all drinkers need the services of an alcohol abuse center. So all smokers are forced to pay for the services that only some smokers receive and all drinkers are forced to pay for services that only some drinkers receive.

Another problem with this rationale is that many people who take advantage of cancer treatment facilities are nonsmokers. It cannot be said that only smokers get cancer because many people who never smoked also get cancer.

Another, less obvious question, is why government should provide cancer treatment or alcohol abuse treatment facilities. These facilities can be provided through the market. Those who need the services can pay for them and those who do not need to use these facilities should not be forced to pay for them. Private insurance can be used to pay for these services, as can private savings. There is no need to for people to pay taxes for something that can be provided better and cheaper by the market.

Those who advocate the use of selective excise taxes to remedy this imbalance between private costs and social costs begin with the premise that there are "social" costs associated with the consumption of tobacco and alcohol products. The problem with this premise is that, upon closer examination, these "social" costs ultimately become private costs.[28]

Productivity losses, for example, are losses incurred by individuals, not society at large. Individuals who are absent from work because of tobacco and alcohol consumption lose pay and receive lower salary increases than would be the case if they did not consume these items. It is individuals who pay the price, not the general public. Those who perform at a substandard level because of consumption of these products tend to lose their jobs. Again, it is individuals, not society, who incur the cost. There is no externality to internalize.[29]

Which brings us to another point. Since there is no externality to internalize, why increase excise taxes? If the purpose of having selective excise taxes is to internalize externalities, it seems like excise taxes are not called for where there are no externalities to internalize.

The argument has been made that nonsmokers are harmed by cigarette smoke in the workplace. Thus, it follows that they should be compensated. However, studies have shown[30] that nonsmokers tend to be compensated more than nonsmokers in terms of long-term salary, so they are already being compensated. Again, costs that were previously labeled as "social" costs have been shown to be individual costs.

Another aspect of the compensation problem, one that has been neglected in the literature, is the beneficial economic effects of smoking and drinking. If smokers and drinkers die sooner than the general population, they will use less Medicare and Medicaid services than the average population. Thus, they will be less of a drain on these systems. They will also take less from the Social Security fund, thus leaving more for others. These are all positive externalities. The logical inference would be that smokers and drinkers should be compensated for these positive externalities, yet no one ever advocates that such policies be implemented. However, it should be pointed out that these costs are individual, not social costs. The rationale for compensating smokers and drinkers is based on the premise that these costs are social costs, when in fact they are not.

CONCLUDING COMMENTS

Some studies that attempt to measure the "social" cost of smoking and drinking conclude that excise taxes are already more than high enough to compensate others for the social costs of smoking and drinking.[31] Thus, even if we begin with the faulty premise that there are social costs associated with smoking and drinking, it appears that there is no need to increase excise taxes, since the present level of taxation is sufficient to pay for these alleged "social" costs. Of course, when one recognizes the fact that most or all of the costs that were called social costs in the past are actually individual costs that are already accounted for, it leads to the conclusion that existing excise taxes on alcohol and tobacco products should be repealed.

Repealing such taxes will not have the effect of increasing consumption, since the demand curves for alcohol and tobacco products are highly inelastic.[32] One beneficial effect of abolishing excise taxes on alcohol and tobacco products would be that their potency would likely decrease, since there is a positive correlation between the level of excise taxes and the potency of the product. Thus, abolishing excise taxes would result in a more healthy population.

Another beneficial effect of abolishing excise taxes is that consumers would have more money in their pockets to spend on other products and services. The deadweight loss that always is present where there are excise taxes would no longer be present. The economy would operate more efficiently and all segments of the market would expand as the demand curves for their products and services shift to the right.

The bottom line is that there is no ethical reason to have excise taxes on alcohol and tobacco products. All costs associated with these products are individual, not social costs. There are no externalities to internalize. It is not a legitimate function of government to punish people for engaging in activities that are none of the government's business, like smoking and drinking. The only legitimate functions of government are to protect the lives and property of the people who pay taxes. It is never a legitimate function of government to protect people from themselves.

NOTES

[1] William F. Shughart, II, editor, Taxing Choice: The Predatory Politics of Fiscal Discrimination. New Brunswick, NJ and London: Transaction Books, 1997.

[2] Shughart, supra, discusses these three justifications at 13-14. On the subject of justification of taxation, see Walter Block, The Justification for Taxation in the Economics Literature, in The Ethics of Tax Evasion 36-88 (Robert W. McGee, ed., 1998). Block reviewed the economics literature and failed to find a single justification for taxation that would stand up to close analysis.

[3] For discussions of the Ramsey Rule, see Harvey S. Rosen, Public Finance 310-314, 318 (5th Ed. 1999); John Cullis and Philip Jones, Public Finance and Public Choice, 376, 380-381 (2nd ed. 1998); Michael L. Marlow, Public Finance: Theory and Practice 455-456 (1995).

[4] For some discussions of internalizing externalities from a Public Choice perspective, see J.M. Buchanan and W.C. Stubblebine, Externality, Economica 29: 371-384 (1962); J.M. Buchanan, External Diseconomies, Corrective Taxes and Market Structure, American Economic Review 59: 174-177 (1969).

[5] There are a number of problems with the concept of "social cost," since all costs are, in reality, individual costs. Space does not permit a full treatment of this concept. For one critique of the concept of social cost, see S.N.S. Cheung, The Myth of Social Cost, Hobart Paper No 82, London: Institute of Economic Affairs, 1978. For the classic discussion on the problem of social cost, see Ronald H. Coase, The Problem of Social Cost, Journal of Law and Economics 3: 1-44 (1960).

[6] For discussions of vertical and horizontal equity, see Harvey S. Rosen, Public Finance 313, 323-326 (5th Ed. 1999); John Cullis and Philip Jones, Public Finance and Public Choice, 9, 398 (2nd ed. 1998); Michael L. Marlow, Public Finance: Theory and Practice 423-425, 561 (1995); David N. Hyman, Public Finance: A Contemporary Application of Theory to Policy 380 (6th ed., 1999).

[7] Shughart, supra, at 14.

[8] Provided there can be such a thing as a good tax. We will leave discussion of that point for another day. Almost all writers in the area of public finance begin with the presumption that there can be such a thing as a good tax. The problem with this view is that all taxes rely on coercion, which violates the nonaggression axiom -- the starting point of moral philosophy. For more on the nonaggression axiom, see Murray N. Rothbard, For a New Liberty 23-26 (Rev. Ed. 1978). Adam Smith discussed good taxes and bad taxes in The Wealth of Nations (1776). Lord Henry Home Kames listed six rules to be observed in taxing in his Sketches on the History of Man (1769). The tax ideas of these two scholars are discussed in Charles Adams, For Good and Evil: The Impact of Taxes on the Course of Civilization 286-287 (1993).

[9] This view relies on the belief that each marginal unit of income is less needed than previous income units. The problem is that it is impossible to measure such things. Even if it were possible to measure the relative pain of taking an additional monetary unit from a rich man versus a poor man, it does not logically follow that it should be done. To logically conclude such an action is to fall prey to a non sequitur.

[10] It is impossible to precisely match benefits received with the amount of taxes paid. The only way to match payments and benefits would be to completely eliminate taxes and let people pay for all services through the market, which could provide just about everything cheaper and more efficiently than government anyway. For more on this point, see Randall Fitzgerald, When Government Goes Private: Successful Alternatives to Public Services (1988); Madsen Pirie, Privatization in Theory and Practice (1985).

Another problem with attempting to measure the cost of government with the benefits received is due to the fact that people are forced to pay for government services, many of which they would not purchase if they had a choice. Who in his right mind, for example, would voluntarily pay for Social Security, when just about every mutual fund that ever existed would provide a better investment vehicle?

[11] That is not to say that rich people who do not smoke do not have their standard of living reduced just because they do not pay excise taxes. Everyone, smoker and nonsmoker alike, has their standard of living reduced because smokers have to pay excise taxes. That is because the money used to pay excise taxes cannot be used to purchase services and products that the market would otherwise provide. A rich, nonsmoking tailor, for example, might not be able to sell a suit to a smoker because the smoker has to pay hundreds of dollars each year in excise taxes, making it impossible to buy the suit due to lack of available funds. The tailor cannot spend the money he does not receive to go on a vacation, which would benefit the waiters at his favorite Miami Beach restaurant, etc. This relationship between what is seen and what is not seen -- direct and indirect effects -- was pointed out by Frederic Bastiat in France in the 1840s. For a more modern treatment, see Henry Hazlitt, Economics in One Lesson, New York: Harper & Brothers, 1946.

[12] Richard E. Wagner, Public Finance: Revenues and Expenditures in a Democratic Society 259 (1983), as cited in Shughart, supra, at 14.

[13] This phenomenon is merely an application of the Alchian and Allen theorem, "which shows how fixed costs can affect the relative prices of low- and high-quality products." Shughart, supra, at 15. For the theorem, see Armen A. Alchian and William R. Allen, University Economics 63-64 (2nd ed., 1967), as cited in Shughart, supra, at 15.

[14] For more detail on this point, see Shughart, supra, at 15.

[15] For an extensive exposé on do-gooders in general and how they are destroying freedom in America, see James T. Bennett and Thomas J. DiLorenzo, The Food and Drink Police: America's Nannies, Busybodies & Petty Tyrants (1999).

[16] Shughart, supra, at 15. It might also be pointed out that our idiotic war on drugs is responsible for increasing the potency of the illegal drugs that are now available. Drugs are easier to find and confiscate if they are bulky. The solution is to deliver a product that is less bulky but just as potent. That is why crack cocaine has replaced powdered cocaine.

[17] Shughart, supra, at 16.

[18] Shughart, supra, at 17.

[19] Shughart, supra, at 17.

[20] Shughart, supra, at 17.

[21] Why government owned parks should exist is another question, since there is much evidence to suggest that the private sector could do a better job of providing this kind of consumer good at a much lower cost. We will save discussion of this point for another day.

[22] For a discussion of optimal user fees, see Harvey S. Rosen, Public Finance 315-318 (5th Ed. 1999). For a detailed discussion of optimal taxation in general, see John Cullis and Philip Jones, Public Finance and Public Choice, 374-409 (2nd ed. 1998).

[23] Knut Wicksell, the economist who had great influence on Nobel Prizewinner James Buchanan, suggested that all taxes be earmarked. See Knut Wicksell, Finanztheoretische Untersuchungen (1896), reprinted as A New Principle of Just Taxation, In Classics in the Theory of Public Finance 72-118 (Richard A. Musgrave and Alan T. Peacock, eds., London and New York: Macmillan, 1958), as cited in Shughart, supra, at 29. The problem with earmarked taxes is that they are often used to supplement taxes from the general fund rather than to replace them. Thus, the total tax burden is increased. Therefore, earmarking taxes is best accomplished when the earmarked taxes are the only taxes used to fund a particular service. Other taxes should be reduced by the amount of funds raised by earmarked taxes. Unfortunately, this approach is seldom taken.

[24] It is questionable why government should be involved in owning or maintaining airports. Several studies by the Reason Foundation point out the fact that the market does a better job of providing service in this area. See www.privatization.org.

[25] For more on the privatization of education, see Robert W. McGee, Brown v. Board of Education: Forty Years of Asking the Wrong Question & the Case for Privatization of Education, St. Louis University Public Law Review 17(1): 141-155 (1997). A number of studies have found that private schools can provide a better education at one-third to one-half the cost of public schools. For more on this point, see Sheldon Richman, Separating School and State: Hot to Liberate America's Families, Fairfax, VA: Future of Freedom Foundation, 1995.

[26] This fact is pointed out in Shughart, supra, at 20.

[27] Shughart, supra, at 20.

[28] For more on this point, see William F. Shughart, II, The Economics of the Nanny State, in Taxing Choice: The Predatory Politics of Fiscal Discrimination 13-29 (William F. Shughart, II, ed. 1997), at 20-24; Richard E. Wagner, The Taxation of Alcohol and the Control of Social Costs, in Taxing Choice: The Predatory Politics of Fiscal Discrimination 227-246 (William F. Shughart, II, ed. 1997); Paula A. Gant and Robert B. Ekelund, Jr., Excise Taxes, Social Costs, and the Consumption of Wine, In Taxing Choice: The Predatory Politics of Fiscal Discrimination 247-269 (William F. Shughart, II, ed. 1997).

[29] Shughart, supra, discusses these points at 21-24.

[30] Some of these studies are cited in Shughart, supra, at 22.

[31] Some of these studies are cited in Shughart, supra, at 24.

[32] Even if consumption did increase, it is no concern of government, since it is not a legitimate function of government to regulate individual non-rights-violating behavior.

Chapter 27

ESTATE, GIFT AND INHERITANCE TAXES

Estate, inheritance and gift taxes are minor forms of raising revenue.[1] They are related, since they all deal with the taking of accumulated wealth. Estate taxes are levied on the estate of a deceased person.[2] Inheritance taxes are levied by most states on those who receive the property of a deceased person. And gift taxes are levied either on the donor or donee for property that is transferred before death. All three are based on the ability to pay principle, which is morally bankrupt. It would be difficult to argue that these taxes are justified on a cost-benefit basis, since dead people derive no benefit from government.

Karl Marx advocated a 100% inheritance tax as a means of destroying capitalism.[3] And with good reason. These taxes are an effective way to confiscate wealth.[4] If the goal is to reduce inequality of wealth or make capital vanish, these taxes will help to achieve that goal.[5] These forms of taxation do not raise much revenue and government coffers would not be much less full if these taxes were abolished completely, because there are many ways to avoid paying these taxes.[6] So why have them?

There seem to be no clear benefits to implementing any of these taxes, but there are some drawbacks. Wealth tends to leave the country that has such taxes. People who have managed to accumulate wealth do not want to have it confiscated, so they tend to put it in places where it will not be confiscated. Or they will not make an effort to save and accumulate wealth in the first place, since there is no reason for doing so if it will only be confiscated anyway.[7] A number of studies have shown that the right to inherit plays an important role in motivating savings. One study suggests that as much as two-thirds of all capital accumulation is due to inheritances.[8]

So savings, investment and wealth accumulation suffer because it removes the incentive to accumulate wealth. Economic growth must suffer as a result. Emerging economies are least able to afford this dissipation of resources. In fact, they might consider becoming tax havens, places where people can feel safe sending their accumulated wealth to protect it from confiscation in other countries. Such a policy would provide much needed capital at little cost. In the USA, the state of Florida has been able to attract the accumulated wealth of retirement-age people because it does not have an inheritance tax. When people retire, they move to Florida and bring their lifetime savings with them, causing a mini-boom in the trust and wealth management industries. Emerging economies could learn a lesson from such a policy.

Another problem with estate and gift tax law, at least those in the USA, is that they are extremely complicated. Even tax planners cannot always be certain that they are shielding their clients from tax liability, and thousands of court cases involving estate and gift taxes have been heard over the years. The resources that are spent administering these tax laws could be better spent elsewhere.[9]

As strong as all these arguments against estate, inheritance and gift taxes may be, they are all utilitarian-based. In effect, these arguments all take the position that these taxes are bad because they are inefficient. The moral dimension is totally absent. Thus, the utilitarian arguments that have been put forth over the years that call for the abolition of these taxes are incomplete. Several moral arguments can be made for their immediate abolition.

For one thing, estate, inheritance and gift taxes are all forms of double taxation. The income that was earned and retained in order to accumulate this wealth was already taxed. Taxing these assets again when the owner dies or gifts the property to someone else is a second tax.

But the real moral argument involves the underlying purpose of government. Any form of taxation is on shaky moral ground to begin with because it involves the taking of property without the owner's consent. So any tax, to be even theoretically justified, must in some way benefit those who pay. But those who pay estate, inheritance and gift taxes do not benefit as a result of the tax.

There are only two basic forms of government. The first exists where the government is master and the people are servants, to be exploited as the government wishes. As Karl Marx said: "From each according to his ability, to each according to his needs." The second exists where the people are the masters and the government is the servant. In effect, the government's role is to provide services to the people. The first form is inherently immoral because it depends on exploitation. The second form can be moral, at least in cases where the people don't mind being taxed to pay for government services.

Estate, gift and inheritance taxes are all based on the Marxist principle of ability to pay. Thus, they are immoral on their face. In the case of the estate tax, those who pay cannot possibly benefit because they are dead. They cannot receive any government services, yet they have to pay for them. Many people give large gifts in order to avoid the estate tax. The gift tax is a way the government has found to squeeze money out of those who avoid the estate tax. The inheritance tax is just like the estate tax except that it is the recipient rather than the owner of the estate who pays.

All three of these taxes are exploitative, and thus are morally bankrupt. The only solution is to abolish them, the sooner the better.

NOTES

[1] The federal estate and gift tax collections for fiscal 1998 represented less than 2% of federal revenue. Office of Management and Budget, 1998 Fiscal Year Budget, as cited in James W. Pratt and William N. Kulsrud, Individual Taxation, 1998 Edition, Houston: Dame Publications, Inc., 1997, at 1-10.

[2] The top rate at one point was over 90%. The top rate in 1997 was 39.6%. Pratt & Kulsrud, supra, at page before the back cover.
[3] Karl Marx, The Communist Manifesto (1848).
[4] "Historically, the primary function of wealth transfer taxes has been to hinder the accumulation of wealth by family units. Thus, the goal of wealth redistribution generally underlies the design of estate and gift tax systems." Pratt & Kulsrud, supra, at 1-10.
[5] I am not saying that equalizing income is a legitimate goal of government, because it is not. For a detailed discussion of this point, see Bertrand de Jouvenel, The Ethics of Redistribution (1952; 1989).
[6] Some commentators even go so far as to say that these taxes are "voluntary," since they are paid only by those who are too stupid to plan for their death. G. Cooper, A Voluntary Tax? New Perspectives on Sophisticated Estate Tax Avoidance (1979), as cited by Joseph E. Stiglitz, Economics of the Public Sector, second edition (1988), at 559.
[7] Joseph E. Stiglitz, at 558.
[8] Laurence Kotlikoff and Lawrence Summers, The Role of Intergenerational Transfers in Aggregate Capital Accumulation, Journal of Political Economy 89: 706-32 (1981).
[9] For a good example that illustrates the complexity of just one estate tax provision, see Clayton Estate v. Commissioner (5th Cir. 1992).

Chapter 28

CAPITAL GAINS TAXES

The capital gains tax is assessed when certain assets[1] are sold at a "profit." For example, let's say that an individual (or corporation) bought 100 shares of stock in 1975 for $1,000 and sold the stock in 1993 for $1,500. The "profit" on the sale is $500. If the capital gains tax is 30%,[2] then the tax liability is $150 (30% of $500). But has there really been a gain? If inflation between 1975 and 1993 has been 300%, then the purchasing power of $1,000 in 1975 dollars would be the equivalent of $3,000 in 1993 dollars. So, in fact, the owner of the stock incurred a real loss of $1,500 on the sale of the stock -- the difference between the $3,000 purchasing power equivalent in 1993 dollars and the $1,500 received on the sale. But although there has been a real loss of $1,500 on the sale -- the difference between the $3,000 purchasing power equivalent and the $1,500 proceeds from the sale -- the shareholder has to pay a tax.

A number of commentators over the years have pointed out that this result is grossly unfair. In effect, the taxpayer loses twice, once when he has to sell the shares at a loss (in terms of purchasing power) and again when he has to pay a tax on a gain that he never realized. At the very least, the capital gains tax should take inflation into account. A study by the National Bureau of Economic Research found that, if the tax on capital gains in the USA were abolished, the government would actually realize slightly more revenue than if there were a tax because of the Laffer Curve effect.[3]

Another point also needs to be made. Most industrial countries either exempt capital gains from taxation completely or have a very low capital gains tax rate. And the countries with high economic growth rates,[4] such as Germany, Japan, the Netherlands and Italy, all have low or nonexistent capital gains tax rates, while high tax rate countries like Great Britain, Canada and the USA all have low rates of economic growth.[5] The argument has been made more than once that high capital gains tax rates retard economic growth. This argument makes sense, since capital that is not taxed is available for further investment, which leads to industrial expansion and job creation. There is no need to conduct empirical studies on this point. A priori reasoning will lead to the same conclusion in much less time.

Another problem with taxing capital gains is the administrative costs that would be involved, both in the public and private sectors. While indexing capital gains would be less unfair than not indexing, it would also increase the administrative burden. And the amount of revenue raised by a capital gains tax is not all that much, compared to what is raised by an income or value-added tax. To remain competitive and enhance economic growth, which is especially important in an emerging economy, it would probably be a good idea not to have any taxes on capital.

Whether the capital gains tax is an ethical tax may be viewed from the perspective of utilitarian philosophy, among others. Is the tax efficient? Are there more winners than losers? Does it result in the greatest good for the greatest number? If so, then it is ethical according to utilitarian ethics.

From a utilitarian perspective, then, the capital gains tax is unethical because it is inefficient. The utilitarian philosophy, which is the philosophy espoused by the vast majority of economists, holds that an act or policy is ethical if it is efficient. Otherwise, it is unethical. Some utilitarians would say that an act or policy is ethical only if it is the most efficient. All other acts or policies are inefficient and therefore unethical.

The capital gains tax is also unethical from a property rights perspective because it violates property rights. The argument could be made that the capital gains tax is voluntary because we voted for the representatives who are imposing it on us. But this argument soon falls apart upon analysis. First of all, only some of us voted for the representatives who are now imposing the tax on us. Furthermore, it cannot be said that our representatives act in our own interest, since the Public Choice literature of the last 30 years or so has proven conclusively that they act in their own interest, often to the detriment of the general public.

One might also argue that the capital gains tax is unfair, at least in part, since it taxes phantom gains. For example, if you sell stock that has doubled in price, you do not really take a gain if inflation has caused a general rise in prices of 300%. Yet you are taxed on the phantom gain. But in effect you are being taxed on a loss. Alternatively, one might say that you are taxed more than 100%, since the tax exceeds the "real" gain. No one owes the government more than 100%. Therefore, it is not unethical to evade the capital gains tax, at least in cases where phantom gains are taxed or where the real rate is more than 100%.

NOTES

[1] We will not get into a discussion of offsets, short-term versus long-term capital gains, phase-in rules, the different treatment of Section 1231 assets, and so forth, because doing so would take us too far afield of the main topic. I hope the tax techies who read this chapter will forgive me for not making the analysis as complicated as possible.

[2] We will not try to use "real" tax rates here because the rates for capital gains taxes change too frequently. Besides, using current rates would add nothing to the analysis.

3 This study was conducted in 1983 by Roger Gordon and Joel Slemrod and was cited by James L. Payne, Unhappy Returns: The $600-Billion Tax Ripoff, Policy Review 21 (Winter, 1992), at 20-21.

4 The growth rates of some of these countries have declined in recent years, but not because of the rate of tax they charge on capital gains.

5 Mark Skousen points this out in Economics on Trial (1991) at 170-71.

Chapter 29

TARIFFS AS A FORM OF TAXATION

INTRODUCTION

Before the income tax was instituted in the United States and other countries, tariffs were one of the primary methods used to raise revenue for government. In recent decades, tariffs have been used more to protect domestic industry from foreign competition than to raise revenue. It might not be inaccurate to say that the public interest would better be served by abolishing all tariffs, since in the aggregate, the vast majority of people stand to gain much more than they would lose by doing away with tariffs.

One supposed goal of the World Trade Organization (WTO), the Free Trade Area of the Americas (FTAA), the North American Free Trade Agreement (NAFTA) and the various other regional trade agreements is to either reduce or abolish tariffs and quotas because such policies are negative-sum, since the losers exceed the winners. I say "supposed" because some trade agreements, like the WTO and NAFTA agreements, actually perpetuate tariffs and quotas rather than abolish them. They allow existing tariffs to continue in existence and they liberalize some quotas at such a slow pace that one can hardly see any difference from year to year.

In the case of Korean sweater imports, for example, the quota is "liberalized" by one percent a year, which means that if Korean sweater manufacturers were allowed to sell 10,000 sweaters in the United States last year, they will be able to sell 10,100 sweaters in the United States this year.

Actually, tariffs have been used as a means of protectionism in the United States ever since its founding. Alexander Hamilton, the first U.S. Treasury Secretary was strongly in favor of them.[1] President Lincoln, supposedly a man of the people, was actually a man of the special interests on this issue.[2] One reason for the start of the American Civil War (1861-1865) was because the Southern states wanted to secede because of the perception that the Northern manufacturing interests and their high tariffs were strangling the South economically.[3] Southerners felt exploited by the Northern manufacturing interests and they wanted out of the union.[4]

One of the main problems with tariffs is that they raise the price that consumers must pay for imported products, which causes living standards to decline. Various estimates have placed the cost of trade protectionism in the USA at perhaps $65 to $80 billion a year or more. And protectionism destroys more jobs than it creates, which is especially harmful to an emerging democracy that is trying to expand employment.[5]

Protectionism also enhances tension between different groups. It pits consumers against producers, since producers want government protection from foreign competition and consumers want low prices and higher quality. And it pits domestic industries against each other. The steel industry calls for government help in stemming the flow of cheap foreign steel, but the auto industry wants to buy cheap foreign steel to keep its own costs low, so it will be able to compete with foreign auto producers.[6]

Tariffs are a form of sales or excise taxation in the sense that they force people to pay more for a product than would be the case in a free market. Just as one can avoid a sales tax by not making a purchase, one may avoid a tariff by not purchasing the product on which the tariff is placed. However, there may be ways to purchase a product and avoid the tariff. In such cases, is evasion unethical? This chapter explores this question from several economic, ethical and religious perspectives.

SPECIAL INTERESTS AND THE ETHICS OF TARIFFS

No one thinks of tariffs as a way to raise revenue any more. Tariffs are now seen for what they are: tools of protectionism.[7] The Smoot-Hawley Tariff of the 1930s practically cut off all foreign trade. U.S. tariffs were prohibitively high and foreign countries retaliated by erecting high tariff barriers of their own. The Smoot-Hawley Tariff deepened and lengthened the Great Depression of the 1930s.[8]

Even where the tariff is not so prohibitively high as to totally cut off foreign trade, there are several adverse effects. For one thing, consumers have to pay more for the products they buy. If they buy foreign products, the price they pay includes the tariff. If they buy a domestic product, the price is likely to be higher than could be possible in the absence of tariffs because domestic producers do not face the same pressure to keep prices low that would exist in a free market. If the government slaps a 20 percent tariff on some Japanese product, for example, domestic producers of similar products can probably get away with raising prices by 10 or 15 percent without losing many sales and may even gain sales because the Japanese products are no longer as price competitive as was the case before the tariff was added to the price of the Japanese product.

Government is legitimate to the extent that it provides for the general welfare.[9] From a utilitarian point of view, one might say that a government policy is good if the good outweighs the bad, or if the majority benefit. The greatest good for the greatest number is another phrase that is often used in connection with utilitarian ethics.[10] There are some flaws in this form of reasoning, however. For example, any law that violates individual rights is prima facie a bad law, even if the majority might benefit. But utilitarianism might be used as a starting point for determining whether a law is legitimate. The final determination, however, depends on whether the law violates anyone's rights. If rights are violated, the law is illegitimate, regardless of majorities.

How can one distinguish a good law from a bad law? Frederic Bastiat, the nineteenth century French philosopher and economist, formulated the following rule for determining whether a particular law was legitimate:

> See if the law takes from some persons what belongs to them, and gives it to other persons to whom it does not belong. See if the law benefits one citizen at the expense of another by doing what the citizen himself cannot do without committing a crime. Then abolish this law without delay, for it is not only an evil itself, but also it is a fertile source for further evils because it invites reprisals. It such a law -- which may be an isolated case -- is not abolished immediately, it will spread, multiply, and develop into a system.[11]

Tariffs fit the definition of a bad law. Tariffs benefit special interests at the expense of the general public. They take from consumers and give to producers.

IS A TARIFF REALLY A TAX?

Crowe defines a tax as follows:

> A tax is a compulsory contribution to the government, imposed in the common interest of all, for the purpose of defraying the expenses incurred in carrying out the public functions, or imposed for the purpose of regulation, without reference to the special benefits conferred on the one making the payment.[12]

In a sense, a tariff is not a tax according to Crowe's definition, since it is not imposed in the common interest of all. The problem is that many members of Congress might actually think that a tariff is good for America, given the mentality of most members of Congress. So there is a dichotomy between what the legislators think to be true and reality. The better view is that a tariff is the equivalent of a redistributive tax, since it takes property from some (consumers) and gives it to others.[13]

According to Crowe, there are three criteria for a just tax. A tax is just only if it is imposed by legitimate legislative authority;[14] for a just cause;[15] and where there is just distribution of the tax burden.[16] Thus, it appears that tariffs are not just taxes, since they are not for a just cause. Taxes raise the price that consumers must pay for foreign (and domestic) products and they feather the nests of special interests (domestic producers) at the expense of the general public. It is difficult to imagine a scenario where such a practice can be labeled a just cause.

That being the case, the next question to ask is whether it is unethical to evade an unjust tax. The obvious answer is no, but some authors would disagree.[17] The Muslim position on this point is of particular interest.

The Islamic system of taxation is a voluntary one, at least partially, although Islamic literature makes it clear that a government is justified in forcing people to pay taxes if the amount raised by zakat[18] is insufficient to cover all the legitimate costs of government. However, "This right of interference with the individual's personal property will be limited to the extent required by the general welfare of the society."[19]

In other words, there is no right of interference with an individual's personal property to pay for things that do not benefit the general welfare. Tariffs do not further the general welfare. They are protectionist and amount to no more than special interest legislation. Thus, a government may not legitimately raise money by imposing tariffs.

This conclusion was arrived at by logical reasoning. One may challenge whether such an interpretation reflects the Muslim view, since logic is not always appropriate where religion is concerned.[20] However, the Muslim literature supports this conclusion.

Ahmad[21] cites Yusuf's *Economic Justice in Islam*,[22] which provides a list of practices that would be immoral for an Islamic state to engage in. Two of these practices are of particular interest.

> There is no room in Islam for custom barriers, restrictive tariffs or exchange control. The Islamic state, therefore, must not resort to them.[23]
>
> It is illegitimate and unlawful for the state to tax directly or indirectly the general body of consumers and to give "protection" to the interests of a class of producers in the name of industrialization.[24]

From these passages it seems clear that customs barriers and tariffs have no place in an Islamic state and there is no ethical reason why a Muslim should recognize their existence. Ahmad elaborates on some of the points made by Yusuf. Protectionism is condemned because it amounts to a direct or indirect tax placed upon consumers by the state. The general public must pay higher prices because the favored few (domestic producers) are being enriched. Traders and consumers are not morally bound to pay the increased price, whether the price increase is the result of protectionism or price fixing.[25]

According to Ahmad, "the adoption of any methods that create an artificial rise in the prices is strictly forbidden."[26] Price fixing and protectionism are only two actions that cause prices to artificially rise. Other causes mentioned by Ahmad include the sales tax and the excise tax, both of which have the same effect as a tariff as far as the price consumers pay is concerned.

> The term *maks* is used for sales-tax. The Prophet (peace be on him) had reportedly said: 'He who levies *maks* shall not enter Paradise'. Since the imposition of a sales-tax (or, for that matter, of octroi and excise duties) results in raising the prices unjustly, therefore, Islam does not approve of it. The Caliph 'Umar ibn Abd al-' Aziz had abolished *maks*, interpreting it as *bakhs* (diminution in what is due to others) which is expressly prohibited by the Qur'an.[27]

Thus, it is clear that under Islam, there is no moral duty to pay a tariff. Under Islam, any and all kinds of trade protectionism are morally bankrupt, and there is no ethical duty to comply with any kind of protectionist legislation. Under Islam, all price fluctuations are the work of Allah and no human agency should interfere with the operation of the law of supply and demand, which is considered part of the natural law.[28]

> Protection is disapproved, writes Abu Yusuf, because it provides affluence to the favoured ones at the expense of the general public.[29]

> Ibn al-Qayyim regards protectionism as the worst form of injustice and predation. He declares it harmful to both the protector and the protected on the ground that they restrict the freedom of trade granted by Allah.[30]

> The customs duties are all outlawed. The Muslims and the *dhimmis* have the fundamental right to free import.[31]

> ... protectionism initiates a process of robbing Peter to pay Paul; Peter is the general body of consumers and Paul the protected industrialist.[32]

CONCLUDING COMMENTS

The Muslim position is quite clear. There is no ethical duty to pay a tariff. Thus, there is nothing unethical about evading payment of a tariff.[33]

Secularists could also advance strong arguments to arrive at the same conclusion. If the only legitimate actions of government are to do things for the general welfare,[34] tariffs are not a legitimate function of government, since they protect and enrich special interests at the expense of the general public. As a general rule, there is no ethical duty to obey a law or regulation that the government has no legitimate authority to make. Such laws include systematically killing Jews, sending U.S. citizens of Japanese ancestry to concentration camps and any kind of special interest legislation, including tariffs. Thus, there is nothing unethical about evading a tariff.

NOTES

1 Alexander Hamilton, Report on Manufactures, 1791, reproduced in A.H. Cole, editor, Industrial and Commercial Correspondence of Alexander Hamilton. New York: Kelley, 1968.

2 Mark E. Neely, Jr., The Fate of Liberty: Abraham Lincoln and Civil Liberties. New York and Oxford: Oxford University Press, 1991; Thomas J. DiLorenzo, The Real Lincoln: A New Look at Abraham Lincoln, His Agenda, and an Unnecessary War. Roseville, CA: Prima Publishing (Random House), 2002.

3 Charles Adams. When in the Course of Human Events: Arguing the Case for Southern Secession. Lanham, MD and Oxford: Rowman & Littlefield, 2000; John Remington Graham, A Constitutional History of Secession. Gretna: Pelican Publishing Cop., 2002.

4 For more on the theory of secession, including how the theory applied to the Southern U.S. secession and some other places, see Robert W. McGee, A Third Liberal Theory of Secession, Liverpool Law Review 14(1): 45-66 (1992); Robert W. McGee, The Theory of Secession and Emerging Democracies: A Constitutional Solution, Stanford Journal of International Law 28(2): 451-476 (1992);Robert W. McGee, Secession and Emerging Democracies: The Kendall and Louw Solution. Journal of International Law & Practice 2(2): 321-335; Robert W. McGee, Secession Reconsidered," Journal of Libertarian Studies 11(1): 11-33 (1994), Translated into Spanish and published as "La secesión reconsiderada" in Libertas No. 33 (Octubre 2000) by the Escuela Superior de Economía y Administración de Empresas (ESEADE) in Argentina and also published at http://www.eseade.edu.ar/revista/N33McGee.html; Robert W. McGee and Danny Kin Kong Lam, Hong Kong's Option To Secede, Harvard International Law Journal 33(2): 427-440 (1992).

5 Gary Clyde Hufbauer, Diane T. Berliner and Kimberly Ann Elliott, Trade Protection in the United States: 31 Case Studies. Washington, DC: Institute for International Economics, 1986.

6 I.M. Destler and John S. Odell, Anti-Protection: Changing Forces in United States Trade Politics. Washington, DC: Institute for International Economics, 1987.

7 For discussions of trade protectionism, see Robert W. McGee, A Trade Policy for Free Societies: The Case Against Protectionism, Westport, CT and London: Quorum Books, 1994; Robert W. McGee, The Cost of Protectionism, The Asian Economic Review 32(3): 347-364 (December, 1990); Robert W. McGee, The Cost of Protectionism: Should the Law Favor Producers or Consumers?" Georgia Journal of International and Comparative Law 23(3): 529-557; Robert W. McGee, An Economic Analysis of Protectionism in the United States with Implications for International Trade in Europe, The George Washington

Journal of International Law and Economics 26(3): 539-573 (1993); Robert W. McGee and Yeomin Yoon, Trade Protectionism of the United States Toward Japan and Korea, International Journal of Korean Studies 2: 45-74 (1995); Robert W. McGee and Walter Block, Must Protectionism Always Violate Rights? International Journal of Social Economics 24(4): 393-407 (1997); Robert W. McGee, The USA's Assault on Trade With the People's Republic of China: Antidumping Laws as Weapons of Protectionism, in Trade and Investment in Asia, edited by Edward B. Flowers, Thomas P. Chen and Ibrahim Badawi, New York: Center for Global Education, St. John's University, 1997, pp. 187-198; Robert W. McGee, The Protectionist Mentality: An Accounting and Philosophical Analysis -- Part I, The Mid-Atlantic Journal of Business 25(7): 63-83 (1989); Robert W. McGee, The Protectionist Mentality: An Accounting and Philosophical Analysis -- Part II, The Mid-Atlantic Journal of Business 26(1): 81-104 (1989); Robert W. McGee, Legal Ethics, Business Ethics and International Trade: Some Neglected Issues, Cardozo Journal of International and Comparative Law 10(1): 109-216 (2002).

[8] The Smoot-Hawley Tariff Act of 1930, Pub. L. No. 71-361, 46 Stat. 590, 19 U.S.C. §§ 1671-77g, 19 U.S.C.A. §§ 1673-73I (1980 & 1992 Supp.); Murray N. Rothbard, America's Great Depression 213-215, Los Angeles: Nash Publishing, 1963; Hans F. Sennholz, Age of Inflation 52, 128, New Rochelle, NY: Arlington House, 1979; Christian Saint-Etienne, The Great Depression 1929-1938: Lessons for the 1980s 29 (1984).

[9] There are problems with this position but we will concede the point for now and leave further discussion for another day.

[10] There are a number of problems with utilitarian ethics. We will not get into them now because that would take us too far afield of the present discussion. Utilitarian ethics is mentioned in this article because that is the ethical system the vast majority of economists subscribe to. The main problems with utilitarian ethics are that it is impossible to measure gains and losses and utilitarian ethics totally ignores rights. For a discussion of utilitarian ethics from a pro-utilitarian perspective, see William H. Shaw, Contemporary Ethics: Taking Account of Utilitarianism, Oxford: Blackwell Publishers, 1999. For criticisms of utilitarian ethics, see Robert W. McGee, The Fatal Flaw in the Methodology of Law & Economics, Commentaries on Law & Economics 1: 209-223 (1997); Robert W. McGee, The Fatal Flaw in NAFTA, GATT and All Other Trade Agreements, Northwestern Journal of International Law & Business 14: 549-565 (1994).

[11] Frederic Bastiat, The Law, Irvington-on-Hudson: Foundation for Economic Education, 1968, p. 21.

[12] Martin T. Crowe, The Moral Obligation of Paying Just Taxes, The Catholic University of America Studies in Sacred Theology No. 84 (1944), at 14-15. This definition has been criticized, but the criticisms are not relevant for purposes of this article. For a discussion of the weaknesses of this definition, see Robert W. McGee, When is Tax Evasion Unethical? in Robert W. McGee, editor, The Ethics of Tax Evasion, Dumont, NJ: The Dumont Institute for Public Policy Research, 1998, pp. 9-10.

[13] The "others" in this case might be either the government or domestic producers. Government receives the proceeds of the tariff, but since domestic producers can both increase sales because of reduced foreign competition and charge higher prices because of reduced price competition, some property flows out of consumer pockets and into the pockets of domestic producers as well. For a discussion on the ethics of redistribution, see Bertrand DeJouvenel, The Ethics of Redistribution, Cambridge: Cambridge University Press, 1952.

[14] Crowe, supra, at 22-23.

[15] Id., at 23-24.

[16] Id., at 24-26.

[17] For discussions of the view that all taxes must be paid, even if they are unjust, see Meir Tamari, Ethical Issues in Tax Evasion: A Jewish Perspective, Journal of Accounting, Ethics & Public Policy 1: 121-132 (Spring 1998), also published in The Ethics of Tax Evasion 168-178 (Robert W. McGee, ed. 1998); Gordon Cohn, The Ethics of Tax Evasion: A Jewish Perspective, Journal of Accounting, Ethics & Public Policy 1: 109-120 (Spring 1998), also published in The Ethics of Tax Evasion 180-189 (Robert W. McGee, ed.

1998); Sheldon R. Smith and Kevin C. Kimball, Tax Evasion and Ethics: A Perspective from Members of The Church of Jesus Christ of Latter-day Saints, Journal of Accounting, Ethics & Public Policy 1: 337-448 (Summer 1998), also published in The Ethics of Tax Evasion 220-229 (Robert W. McGee, ed. 1998); Wig DeMoville, The Ethics of Tax Evasion: A Baha'i Perspective, Journal of Accounting, Ethics & Public Policy 1:356-368 (Summer 1998), also published in The Ethics of Tax Evasion 230-240 (Robert W. McGee, ed. 1998).

[18] Zakat is the tenet of Islam that requires Muslims to give part of their property for charitable causes.

[19] Mushtaq Ahmad, Business Ethics in Islam 134 (1995).

[20] One common trait of all religions is that faith supercedes logic.

[21] Ahmad, supra, at 135-136.

[22] S.M. Yusuf, Economic Justice in Islam (1971).

[23] Yusuf, supra, at 68, 101.

[24] Yusuf, supra, at 9-10.

[25] Ahmad, supra, at 122.

[26] Id., at 123.

[27] Id.

[28] Id., at 122.

[29] Id.

[30] Id., at 123.

[31] Yusuf, supra, at 68.

[32] Id., at 100.

[33] The Jewish, Mormon and Baha'i views would seemingly disagree with the Muslim view, since these latter views, if correctly represented by the authors cited elsewhere in this book, state that all laws must be obeyed, even if they are bad laws.

[34] I have never heard a good argument advocating the position that government acts legitimately when it advances the policies of special interests at the expense of the general public.

Chapter 30

THE PROPERTY TAX

In the United States, property taxes are assessed mostly by state and local governments. Real and personal property taxes account for about 37% of state and local government's total tax receipts.[1] Much of what is collected, especially from real estate taxes, is used to pay for local services. The tax on real property has long been thought of as the most inequitable form of taxation by many people. Yet it is still a major form of financing local government.[2]

Property taxation has some of the same attributes of income taxation. Both are coercive rather than voluntary. Both take property from owners without their consent. Both cause economic distortions. But there are some differences as well.

One difference is the competitive effect. In the case of the federal individual income tax, for example, individuals have the option of either paying the tax or moving to another country.[3] But avoiding property taxes is easier. Individuals who feel that they are paying too high a property tax can often get a tax break by moving a few miles down the road, to another community that has lower tax rates. This competitive tax effect also occurs for other kinds of taxes, such as the state individual and corporate income tax. In fact, one of the main reasons why individuals and businesses are moving out of New York and into New Jersey, which is just across the Hudson River, is because of the lower tax rates in New Jersey.

One positive attribute of the competitive effect, from the taxpayer's perspective, is the restraint it places on government expenditures.[4] As is the case with any monopoly, costs tend to be higher and the quality of services tends to be lower then where there is competition. One reason for this tendency is because there is no incentive to improve the quality of service or cut costs because consumers have no place else to go. And since governments all have monopolies over a certain geographic territory, their behavior conforms to general monopoly theory.

However, with the competitive tax effect, the monopolies must compete with each other. The government that has a monopoly over the geographic territory of New York must compete with the neighboring monopoly across the river in New Jersey. If citizens and businesses in one state think they can get a better deal in another state, they will have a tendency to move, thereby depleting the tax base of the state that offers a less desirable package of services, and providing its bureaucrats with an incentive to spend less tax dollars more wisely.

Of course, not everyone moves from one community to another in order to avoid high taxes. Sometimes, people are willing to move to a community that has higher taxes if they think that they can improve their situation by the move. For example, it is not uncommon in the USA for parents to move to a new community to take advantage of the local schools, which are financed heavily by local property taxes.

There are a number of injustices associated with the property tax. For example, all homeowners have to pay the tax, even if they do not have any children. In effect, they are being forced to pay for the education of other people's children. And if they have children of their own that they would rather send to a private school, they must incur the additional expense of private school tuition.

Another problem with financing education through the property tax is that the tax is hidden, in a sense, because the people who use the services do not know how much it costs to educate their children. Education is "free" in the public schools, so they do not realize that it costs perhaps $6,000 or $8,000 or more for each of their children. And because they do not know the true cost of the service, there is less of an incentive to place restraints on educational spending.

Even those parents who do not own homes are paying the tax, ultimately, because their landlord tacks on the property tax to their monthly rental bill, if possible. If, for some reason, the property tax cannot be passed on to tenants in that fashion, then they wind up paying somehow anyway. If landlords cannot pass on the property tax to the tenants, they must absorb it themselves, which means they will have less money available to invest in other apartments. And since the supply of available housing is thus crimped, the cost -- rent -- will increase. And if the profit margins of landlords are squeezed because of the inability to pass on the property tax to their tenants, they will try to cut costs by deferring maintenance, reducing heat in the building, and so forth. So the tenants wind up paying the tax anyway, by not getting their full moneysworth.

NOTES

[1] Coopers & Lybrand, State and Local Taxes: The Burden Grows (1992), at 3. State and local governments get their tax revenues from the following sources: real property taxes, 22%; personal property taxes, 15%; sales and use taxes, 16%; corporate income taxes, 38%; capital-based franchise taxes, 9%.

[2] For a series of papers suggesting ways in which the property tax can be reformed, see George E. Paterson, editor, Property Tax Reform, Washington, DC: The Urban Institute, 1973.

[3] Actually, they must do more than just move to another country to avoid paying the U.S. individual income tax. The United States is one of the few countries that taxes its citizens even if they live outside the United States. So to avoid the tax, they must not only move but also give up their citizenship. But even then they are not safe from the tax collector. Congress, in its wisdom, has passed a law that requires people to continue to pay taxes to the United States for 10 years after they renounce their citizenship. They made this law because a number of billionaires and other super rich people who did not

want to have a large portion of their assets confiscated by the U.S. estate tax decided to renounce their U.S. citizenship and spend their remaining days living in a foreign country.

[4] Some of these points are discussed in Timothy Brown, Interjurisdictional Tax Competition: An Economic Perspective, Nebraska Law Review 68: 652-71 (1989).

Chapter 31

USER FEES

INTRODUCTION

User fees are fairer than some other forms of taxation because they link cost to benefit. Those who use the service pay for it and those who don't use the service are not forced to subsidize someone else's use of it. Examples of user fees include government-owned electric, gas and water company charges,[1] subway and bus fares, garbage collection fees, admission fees to public zoos, parks and museums, turnpike tolls,[2] and gasoline taxes. Another aspect of user fees, from a human rights perspective, is that they are not as coercive as most other forms of taxation because they do not force some people to pay for other people's benefits.

One major area where user fees could be applied but are not is in the financing of public schools. Under the present system in the USA, property owners are forced to pay for the education of other people's children. The public school system is free (in the sense that those who use the service do not have to directly pay for it), and the cost is borne by residents in the community who own real estate and, to a lesser extent, taxpayers who earn income.

It would be especially beneficial for emerging economies to adopt a user fee approach to education, since their school systems in the past have often been used for indoctrination as much as for education. Privatizing their school system would make it impossible for some future government to use the schools for this purpose.

User fees can be used to provide a number of services often thought to be in the sole domain of government, including fire prevention and, in some cases, even police protection. In the case of fire protection, individuals in some communities in the USA can subscribe with a local provider for fire protection so that if their house catches fire, they can call the fire prevention agency and have the fire put out free of charge. And they can get protection even if they don't subscribe to the service, although if they ask for assistance without being subscribers, they are assessed a premium. Fire prevention services in these communities have proven to be more efficient and less costly than similar services provided by government. Homeowners in communities that offer this approach to fire prevention have found that the fire insurance premiums they pay are lower in cases where the services is provided privately rather than by government.[3]

Even parts of the civil and criminal justice system can be set up on a user fee basis.[4] In the USA, the American Arbitration Association and other groups are available to settle disputes and can do so much faster and cheaper than the government court system. Some commentators have advocated the establishment of competing private police forces that consumers could subscribe to just as they now do for private fire protection.[5] In fact, some police forces are already privatized, such as in cases where companies hire private security guards to protect their property. In fact, more than half of all police protection is already private in the United States, since there are more security guards than government police officers.

SOME POSSIBLE ECONOMIC AND ETHICAL PROBLEMS

There are a few economic and ethical problems with user fees, or rather with calling something a user fee when it is not in fact a user fee. One problem is that the amount collected as a user fee might not be equal to 100 percent of the cost of the service. If the user fee collects less than 100 percent of the cost of providing the service, some form of coercive taxation has to help subsidize the activity, which is not only unfair to those who must be forced to pay for someone else's benefit, but also is distortive, since the price system cannot function efficiently where subsidies exist.[6]

Another problem with user fees exists when the proceeds raised are used for things other than to pay for the service. If user fees are charged to pay for subways but are used to build bridges, those who use the subways are forced to subsidize people who use bridges, which is morally bankrupt. If user fees are collected on gasoline to pay for highway maintenance but some of the proceeds are used to pay for government schools, those who use the highways are forced to subsidize the education of other people's children, which is both economically distortive and unethical.

Another user fee that has been abused is the Airport and Airway Trust Fund, which raises revenue by imposing an excise tax on airline tickets. The fund was originally set up to pay for the costs of maintaining airports. The problem is that the fund collects much more than is needed for maintenance. In some years the amount collected was twice the amount spent. Rather than reducing the excise tax, Congress decided to continue collecting the tax at the current rate and using the surplus to reduce the federal deficit.[7]

Another problem with user fees is that some "user fees" are not really user fees at all, but are more akin to excise taxes in the worst sense of the term. For example, various levels of government slap a heavy excise tax on tobacco products for a variety of reasons that have nothing to do with raising revenue. The do-gooders who lobbied the various legislatures to impose heavy excise taxes on tobacco products did so not to raise revenue but to reduce use of tobacco products. This "sin tax" is really nothing more than social engineering, which government has no business getting involved in. The purpose of government is to protect basic rights. Nothing more. When it goes beyond the protection of basic rights it goes beyond the scope of its legitimate authority.

Part of the excise tax collected on cigarettes is used to fund cancer research. Part is used to treat cancer. On the surface, such uses appear to be good and legitimate, but when one digs beneath the surface, a different picture emerges. For example, many people who smoke never get cancer, yet they are being forced to subsidize those who do get cancer.

Also, cigarette smoking is not the only cause of cancer. There are other causes as well. Yet all cigarette smokers are forced to subsidize cancer treatment, which means that nonsmokers who get cancer are being subsidized by cigarette smokers, most of whom never get cancer. One group pays and another group benefits, which is inherently unfair. Where one group pays and another group benefits, there is a basic problem with calling the collection mechanism a user fee, since those who use the service are not those who pay. Yet politicians resort to this terminology, either out of ignorance or for the more sinister purpose of hiding the true situation from the public.

Another problem with user fees is that they are often assessed on services that the government should not be involved in in the first place. The private sector can do just about everything more efficiently than the government,[8] which raises the very basic question of why the government is providing the service in the first place, especially if one starts with the premise that the only legitimate functions of government are to protect rights. Historically that is why governments were formed. They were not formed to provide services. The provision of services is a relatively recent phenomenon, although the Roman Empire (before its collapse) provided its citizens with bread and circuses.

CONCLUDING COMMENTS

The main advantage of user fees over most other forms of public finance is that they are voluntary. Coercion is not required to collect them. This is important in a society that places a high value on individual freedom and property rights, since the more government takes by force, the less freedom there is. A major problem with user fees is that they are assessed to provide services that government probably has no business providing, both because the private sector can do a better job at lower cost and because providing services other than the protection of rights goes beyond the legitimate scope of government.

Another, more serious problem with user fees is that some user fees are not really user fees at all. They are more like excise taxes. The people who use the service are not necessarily the ones who pay for it.

Thus, there is an ethical problem of redistribution because some people are being forced to pay for the services that other people receive.[9]

There is also an economic issue. Where the charge is a true user fee, there is minimum distortion in the economy, since a true user fee is akin to a market price, or at least a shadow market price. The fee charged should be sufficient to cover the full cost of the service. Of course, where government is involved it is not a true market price, but at least the price charged might approximate a market price.

In some cases, the price charged does not approximate the market price. Where the price charged is either less than the market price or more than the market price, the result is distortion in the economy, resulting in inefficiencies and a reduced standard of living, not to mention reduced employment.

Thus, although user fees offer some advantages over other forms of public finance, such as the lack of coercion, there are also some inherent problems in the use of user fees to raise funds for government services. The only way to solve these structural problems that all user fees face is to get the government out of the areas where it has no business.

NOTES

1 It is questionable whether the government should be involved in these activities because the market -- private companies -- can do a better job at a lower price, but that is another issue. For examples of cases where the private sector can provide services more efficiently and at lower cost than government, see Robert W. Poole, Jr., Cutting Back City Hall (1980); Randall Fitzgerald, When Government Goes Private: Successful Alternatives to Public Services (1988); James T. Bennett and Manuel H. Johnson, Better Government at Half the Price: Private Production of Public Services (1981); Walter Block, Free Market Transportation: Denationalizing the Roads, Journal of Libertarian Studies 3: 209-238 (Summer 1979).

2 G.J. Roth, A Self-Financing Road System (1966).

3 For more on the private provision of fire protection, see Randall Fitzgerald, When Government Goes Private 71-80 (1988); E.S. Savas, Privatizing the Public Sector 95-96 (1982); Robert W. Poole, Jr., Cutting Back City Hall 62-78 (1980). These books also cite examples of where police protection has been provided privately.

4 See Robert W. Poole, Jr., supra, at 51-61; Randall Fitzgerald, supra, at 93-119; Bruce L Benson, The Enterprise of Law: Justice Without the State, San Francisco: Pacific Research Institute, 1990; Gustav de Molinari, The Production of Security, New York: Center for Libertarian Studies, 1977; Hans-Hermann Hoppe, The Economics and Ethics of Private Property, Boston, Dordrecht and London: Kluwer Academic Publishers, 1993.

5 Murray N. Rothbard, Power and Market: Government and the Economy, Menlo Park, CA: Institute for Humane Studies, 1970, p. 123.

6 Most public finance and principles of economics texts discuss this point.

7 Randall G. Holcombe, Selective Excise Taxation from an Interest-Group Perspective, in Taxing Choice: The Predatory Politics of Fiscal Discrimination 81-103 (William F. Shughart, II, ed. 1997), at 87-89.

8 For case studies that support this view, contact the Local Government Center, c/o Reason Foundation, 3415 South Sepulveda Boulevard, Suite 400, Los Angeles, CA

90034 or [www.privatization.org]. Municipal solid waste disposal costs 61% to 71% more when done by government. See E.E. Savas, Privatizing the Public Sector 93 (1982).

Another study found that contracting out waste collection to the private sector saved between 22% and 30%. See Barbara J. Stevens, Solid Waste Management 215-243, in Privatization for New York: Competing for a Better Future, A Report of the New York State Senate Advisory Commission on Privatization, January 1992. It takes 68% more federal government employees to remove 21% as much railroad track as private sector employees over the same period of time and under similar conditions. See Randall Fitzgerald, When Government Goes Private: Successful Alternatives to Public Services 17 (1988).

A study of 121 cities in the Los Angeles county area found that contracting out street cleaning to the private sector saves an average of 43%. The savings in other areas are also substantial: 73% for janitorial services, 42% for refuse collection, 56% for traffic signal maintenance, 96% for asphalt overlay construction, 40% for grass maintenance and 37% for street maintenance. See John C. Goodman, Privatization 119 (1985).

9 For more on the ethical problems associated with redistribution, see Bertrand DeJouvenel, The Ethics of Redistribution (1952).

Chapter 32

LOTTERIES

From a human rights perspective, a lottery is the best kind of tax because it involves absolutely no coercion. No one's property is confiscated. No one is forced to pay for someone else's benefits. Lotteries involve no parasitism. Several states in the USA use a lottery to raise revenue. Florida's lottery raises more than $2 billion a year.[1] Other state lotteries also raise large sums. In an emerging economy that limits spending and privatizes wherever possible, it might be possible to raise all the funds that are needed to run government by using just a lottery and user fees, thus doing away with the need for coercive taxation.

Lotteries can be relatively easy and inexpensive to administer, and can provide employment in the private sector, if store owners are permitted to sell lottery tickets. However, some people do not favor the use of lotteries to raise government revenue. One reason often given is that gambling is a sin, and the government should discourage, rather than encourage sin. Emerging economies that have a population with strong religious beliefs in this regard might run into problems with a lottery.

NOTES

[1] Record-Breaking Lottery, Daily Tax Report (BNA), January 19, 1990, at H-2.

PART FIVE

THE TAX SYSTEM OF A FREE SOCIETY

Chapter 33

THE TAX SYSTEM OF A FREE SOCIETY

> "...government has proved incompetent at solving social problems. Virtually every success we have scored has been achieved by nonprofits."[1] Peter Drucker

INTRODUCTION

Since the private sector can do just about anything better and cheaper than the government sector, it makes sense to minimize government action to the things that it can do better than the private sector. Whatever things that might be I do not know, but perhaps it can do something better. Economic efficiency will be maximized if resources are permitted to flow to their highest uses, and that means that people should be able to keep as much of their money as possible, since only they know where their money should be spent. It is condescending and an insult to take the position that some politician or unelected bureaucrat who might live thousands of miles away knows how to spend your money better than you do. Yet that is one of the arguments used to fund the federal government.

If government is needed at all, it must be kept on a short leash, lest it grow and encroach on our freedoms. The tendency of government is to expand, at the expense of individual liberty. Government starts out being the servant of the people but usually winds up being the master. Any government that taxes away and spends 30 or 40 percent or more of gross domestic product (GDP) is both bloated and dangerous. Such governments have no place in a free society. How free can you be if you have to work two days a week to pay your taxes? Such people are 40 percent slave.

Government has no money of its own. Whatever it gets it must first take from someone. It is an inconvenient fact that politicians who make promises at election time would prefer that we forget.

Taxation is theft, since it involves the taking of property without the owner's consent. It cannot be said that we have given our consent just because we elect the people who take our money from us. Many people who vote, vote for losing candidates, which means that perhaps 49% of the people who vote get fleeced by someone not of their own choosing. Since less than 50% of the eligible voters actually vote in most elections, that means that the politicians who do get elected actually receive only 25% or less of the votes of all eligible voters [50% x 50%]. People vote for politicians who promise not to raise taxes, then turn around and raise taxes after they get elected.

Since the private sector is more efficient, cheaper and better than the government sector, and since the private sector relies on voluntary exchange, whereas all governments rely on force or the threat of force, it seems logical that the government should not be trusted to do much of anything. However, if for some reason people insist on having governments perform some services, those services must be paid for. The question then becomes How do we pay for the cost of government? This is one of the classic questions of public finance, and many people have come up with many different and conflicting answers over the years.[2]

The only two methods of raising funds that do not violate property rights are lotteries and user fees. Where the government is small, these forms of public finance may be sufficient to cover the costs of government. A third option, voluntary contributions is also a possibility. This third option may seem strange, or even utopian. However, governments do get some of their funding through voluntary contributions. Kirk Kirkorian, an extremely rich person of Armenian descent, offered to give the Armenian government sufficient funds to pave the streets of Yerevan, the capital of Armenia, which had pot hole problems. Of course, in a totally free economy, all roads would be private,[3] but we do not yet live in such a world. So private contributions would be one way to fund government services. Some people who now give to charity might decide to give something to some government if it is deemed worthy.

This concept of having rich people give money to support government functions is not new. It goes back to the ancient Greeks, who called it *liturgy*. The Athenian government was partially supported for a number of years by just such contributions. Rich Athenians supported various activities such as religious festivals and also contributed toward the support and maintenance of bridges, gymnasia and, occasionally, the military.[4]

PLACING RESTRAINTS ON GOVERNMENT

If government needs more money than what is provided by user fees, lotteries and voluntary contributions, restraints must be placed on government so that it is not able to grow too large. The more money government takes, the less money that will be left in the private sector, which is the more efficient of the two sectors. As funds are siphoned from the private sector, economic efficiency decreases, perhaps to the point where the economy is in a permanent state of stagnation. That is what has happened to some of the bloated welfare states of Western Europe. We should learn from that experience.

There are some other ways to restrain the growth of government. Some have been more successful than others. Putting rules into the constitution might help,[5] but constitutions are only as good as the people who enforce their provisions. The constitution of the United States is a case in point.

The U.S. constitution grants only limited powers to the federal government. [6] It lists the things that the federal government can do. Anything that is not on the list is something the federal government cannot do.[7] But over the centuries the federal government has encroached into practically every area of our lives, partly because America's founding fathers made the mistake of including the general welfare clause and the necessary and proper clause in the constitution. Politicians and the courts[8] have used these two clauses to allow the federal government to expand beyond recognition.[9]

The federal constitution says nothing about education. Therefore, the federal government may not engage in or fund education. Yet it does, to the tune of billions of dollars a year. The constitution says nothing about providing welfare or social security. Yet the government spends billions of our tax dollars on these programs every year. The constitution does not say anything about giving money to other countries. Yet politicians vote to give billions of dollars in foreign aid to dozens of countries every year, even though some of those countries are not really our friends. The constitution says that only Congress may declare war, yet the last several wars America has fought have been fought without congressional approval.

The point is that merely putting something into the constitution like a balanced budget amendment may not be enough to restrain government growth. Other things must also be done. Although balanced budget amendments have been fairly successful at the state level,[10] it remains to be seen whether such an amendment would be successful at the federal level.

The budget could get balanced through accounting tricks such as using off balance sheet accounts.[11] Or it could become balanced by raising taxes. Balance just means that the revenues and expenses are the same. If there is a deficit, there are basically just two ways to get rid of it. One can either cut spending or raise taxes. So having a balanced budget amendment might result in giving politicians one more excuse to raise taxes.

Another way to limit spending would be to have some kind of spending limitation built into the constitution. California's Proposition 13 helped to restrain the growth of property taxes, although it did not prevent the amount of property taxes collected from increasing each year.

A line item veto is another means of restraining government spending. In the USA, the legislature often combines several proposals into a single bill, which the president must either sign or veto. As a result, there are sometimes attempts by certain members of Congress to insert some otherwise unacceptable provision into an acceptable piece of legislation. The president will often sign such a bill into law, even though there may be some provisions of which he disapproves. If the president had a line-item veto, he would be able to cross out the provisions he does not want to pass, providing him with an opportunity to exercise some spending restraint in cases where the legislature is not willing or able to do so. A line-item veto thus acts as a spending restraint.

Hawks has come out with a proposal that would take bits and pieces from several of these spending limitation proposals. The Hawks proposal would give the president the authority to use a line item veto only in cases where Congress failed to balance the prior year's budget. This proposal would have to be enshrined in the Constitution, since the U.S. Supreme Court has previously held that a legislative line item veto was unconstitutional. In substance, his proposal might not be much different than a mere line item veto that is enshrined in the Constitution, since Congress has been unable to balance the budget practically every year.[12]

Another restraint that could be placed on government would be to abolish the law that requires employers to withhold taxes from employees' paychecks. If employees had to write out a check to the government every month, they would be able to see precisely what government costs, and politicians might feel more constrained about raising taxes.[13]

Sunset laws are another way to keep government under control. A sunset law merely says that some piece of legislation will have a limited life. It will cease to be the law after some period of time. If such a provision were incorporated into the constitution, it would help keep government in check.

It is easier to pass a law than to repeal one, so even though a law may be a bad law, and even though politicians and the general population know that the law is a bad law, it is difficult to repeal such laws. Having a sunset law imbedded into the constitution would alleviate some of the damage done by bad laws by giving them a limited life span.

What about the bad laws that are already on the books? What can we do about them? We could incorporate language into the constitutional amendment that establishes the sunset provision that all existing laws would become null and void within some time period, perhaps five years, after the sunset provision becomes part of the constitution. Five years would give the legislature sufficient time to study which laws should be retained on the books and which ones should be allowed to lapse. It would be interesting to see whether the income tax and the social security tax would be able to survive a sunset provision.

Another constraint on government excesses would be a supermajority requirement. If 60 percent or two-thirds or three-fourths of the legislators present, or of total members of the legislature would have to vote in favor of any tax increase, it would be more difficult to pass tax increases. Another possibility would be to have a referendum,[14] meaning that the voters themselves would have to vote on any proposed tax increase. There could be a supermajority requirement for referendums as well, so that it would take more than a simple majority to pass a tax initiative.

Establishing a weighted voting system would also serve to restrain government taxing and spending. Rather than having one vote per person, each person would be entitled to one vote for every dollar of taxes paid since the last election. Corporations have a similar system. The more shares a shareholder has, the more votes he can cast. It is a fair system, since the people who contribute or invest the most should be entitled to a bigger voice in the governance of the corporation.

For federal elections, voters would have one vote for every dollar of federal taxes paid since the last election. That would include both federal income tax and social security tax. For local elections, voters would be entitled to cast one vote for every dollar of property taxes paid. Homeowners and landlords would get to vote but tenants would not. That seems fair, since tenants in some communities put pressure on the local politicians to pass rent control laws, which are actually nothing more than a redistribution scheme that transfers wealth from landlords to tenants. Were such a voting scheme to be adopted, it is likely that rent control laws would soon go out of existence, which well they should.

Another benefit of having a weighted voting system is that people on welfare would not be able to vote themselves increases in benefits. Since people on welfare don't pay taxes, they would not be able to vote for politicians who promise to increase their benefits, and politicians would be less likely to make such promises, since the people they would be making the promises to would not be able to vote for them and the people who would have to pay for the welfare schemes would likely vote against them. Politicians would no longer be able to bribe people to vote for them by promising to redistribute other people's money to them in the form of welfare.

The largest expenditure in the federal budget, after national defense, is interest on the debt. If that debt could be wiped out once every generation, the size of the federal budget would shrink dramatically. There is a way to wipe out this large debt. Simply announce that at some point in time, say ten years after the date of the announcement, any federal debt outstanding will become worthless. Furthermore, the federal government will not be permitted to borrow money again for an additional year. That provision would prevent the politicians and bureaucrats from rolling over the debt, and thus perpetuating it. This process could be repeated once every generation.

This solution to the national debt problem may seem harsh and even unfair, but actually it is quite fair and ethical. The present generation should not have to be saddled with the debts from the last generation. Implementing this suggestion would prevent the last generation's debts from being a burden on the current generation. Thomas Jefferson has the following to say in this regard:

> It is a wise rule and should be fundamental in a government disposed to cherish its credit, and at the same time to restrain the use of it within the limits of its faculties, "never to borrow a dollar without laying a tax in the same instant for paying the interest annually, and the principal within a given term; ..." But what limits, it will be asked, does this

> prescribe to their powers? What is to hinder them from creating a perpetual debt? The laws of nature, I answer. The earth belongs to the living, not to the dead. The will and the power of man expire with his life, by nature's law...We may consider each generation as a distinct nation, with a right, by the will of its majority, to bind themselves, but none to bind the succeeding generation, more than the inhabitants of another country.[15]

Jefferson goes on to says that 19 years after the contract is entered into, the majority of the contractors are dead, and their contract with them. He based his estimate on the life expectancy at the time. The point is that one generation should not have to pay the debts incurred by another generation. It is inherently unfair. Having a provision that automatically cancels any outstanding debt of the prior generation would make it more difficult for government to fund its spending programs by borrowing money, but it would not make it impossible to resort to borrowing in time of emergency. Such a provision would act as an additional restraint on government excesses.

Podolsky has made a proposal that, while not limiting spending, would allow taxpayers to have more say in how their tax money is spent.[16] His proposal would include a menu of spending categories as part of the tax return. Taxpayers could choose what percentage of their taxes would be spent on a variety of categories such as public safety, public health, charity, agriculture, transportation, education, information gathering and dissemination, intergovernmental relations, regulation of commerce, labor benefits, science, technology and energy, peace, legislation, resource protection and utilization and discretionary items.

One advantage of such a proposal is that the people who actually pay the bills would have more say in how their money is spent. Politicians, bureaucrats and lobbyists would have their wings clipped to a certain extent. Politicians would be less able to buy people's votes by making promises to give the various special interest groups whatever it is that they want. Special interests would have less incentive to make contributions to politicians because the politicians would not have as much discretionary authority to influence legislation.

One criticism that could be made of his proposal would be that it would inject more instability into the planning process, since the people who make government budgets would not be able to make five-year spending plans because they do not know that far in advance how much money they will be able to spend in each category. But since so much money is wasted by governments at all levels, this instability factor is more than offset by giving those who pay more control over how their money is spent.

One enhancement to the Podolsky proposal would be to include a category either for overall spending reduction or for reducing the national debt. That would give taxpayers who do not approve of the government's spending projects an opportunity to have their money used for other purposes.

Another proposal that would place restraints on politicians who want to spend other people's money would be to pass a law making it legal to kill any politician who promises not to raise taxes and then votes to raise them. This solution might seem severe, but actually it is basically the same as saying that telling such a lie (breaking such a contract) becomes a capital crime and that anyone may perform the execution.

George Bush the elder comes to mind. During his bid for election to the presidency he promised not to raise taxes. He repeated his pledge several times. People voted for him based on that pledge. Then, after he was elected, he raised taxes anyway. What can people do when politicians lie to them, costing them thousands of dollars in extra taxes? What they did to George Bush the elder was to elect his opponent in the next election. But the tax increase he signed remained on the books and President Clinton, his successor, increased taxes further.

Politicians might try to get around such a strict rule by not disclosing who voted for the tax increase, but that possibility could be dealt with by having a law stating that any tax increases passed by a secret vote was null and void.

A less severe restraint, short of execution, would be to have a law stating that any politician who has promised not to increase taxes and who later votes to increase them anyway is automatically considered to have resigned from office. Such a provision would probably serve to restrain lying politicians nearly as well as the execution proposal. However, in this latter case, it might take a lawsuit to yank the politician from office, whereas with the execution option, the matter would be settled once and for all and taxpayers would not be forced to pay any court costs.

It might not even be necessary to have such a law if politicians who take the no tax pledge would also sign a resignation letter that is conditional upon their breaking the pledge. The problem with this variation is that many politicians would not sign such a letter.

Another variation on the theme of holding elected officials responsible if they lie about raising taxes would be to pass a law that would make it legal to confiscate their multimillion dollar congressional pension and use the proceeds to pay for some of the programs that they voted to pass. That way, members of Congress who resign or who don't get re-elected would not be able to take their excessive pensions with them. It is a kind of rough justice, since politicians who lie about raising taxes are not entitled to pensions that are paid for out of taxpayer funds. The main problem with this solution would be to pass such a law, since the very individuals likely to be targeted in the future would be the ones who would have to vote for the law.

CONCLUDING REMARKS

If the proposals recommended in this book were implemented, taxes would be very low indeed. Property taxes would be cut by more than half if parents paid for the education of their own children rather than forcing the rest of us to do it. If everything that could be privatized were privatized, the services we now receive from government could be obtained at a fraction of the present cost. Perhaps property taxes, income taxes and sales taxes could be abolished completely.

Most people now pay more taxes for social security than they do in federal income taxes. If social security were privatized, their tax bills would be cut by more than 50 percent and they would be able to have a nice fat nest egg at retirement, which they could will to their heirs. If the national debt could be wiped out once every generation, the largest nondefense expense in the federal budget would be eliminated, thus greatly reducing the need for an income tax. If only half of the restraints on government that are proposed in this book were adopted and implemented, the growth of federal spending would be greatly restrained, to the benefit of all taxpayers.

NOTES

[1] Peter Drucker, Wall Street Journal, December 19, 1991, as quoted in Murray Sabrin, Tax Free 2000: The Rebirth of American Liberty, Lafayette, LA: Prescott Press, 1994, p. 174.

[2] Some of the classic documents on this question have been reprinted in Richard A. Musgrave and Alan T. Peacock, editors, Classics in the Theory of Public Finance, New York and London: Macmillan, 1958. Chapters of special interest include Lorenz von Stein, On Taxation, pp. 28-36; Arnold Jacob Cohen Stuart, On Progressive Taxation, pp. 48-71; Knut Wicksell, A New Principle of Just Taxation, pp. 72-118; Francis Ysidro Edgeworth, The Pure Theory of Taxation, pp. 119-136; Giovanni Montemartini, The Fundamental Principles of a Pure Theory of Public Finance, pp. 137-151; Paul Leroy-Beaulieu, On Taxation in General, pp. 152-164; Erik Lindahl, Just Taxation -- A Positive Solution, pp. 168-176; Emil Sax, The Valuation Theory of Taxation, pp. 177-189; Rudolf Goldscheid, A Sociological Approach to Problems of Public Finance, pp. 202-213; Erik Lindahl, Some Controversial Questions in the Theory of Taxation, pp. 214-232. For a more modern discussion of some of these dame classic issues that are given from two diametrically points of view, see James M. Buchanan and Richard A. Musgrave, Public Finance and Public Choice: Two Contrasting Visions on the State, Cambridge, MA and London: MIT Press, 1999.

[3] Walter Block, A Free Market in Roads, in Tibor R. Machan, editor, The Libertarian Reader, Totowa, NJ: Rowman and Allanheld, 1982, pp. 164-183, reprinted from Journal of Libertarian Studies 3(2): 209-238 (Summer 1979) under the title Free Market Transportation: Denationalizing the Roads.

[4] Sabrin, pp. 51-52; Charles Adams, Fight, Flight and Fraud: The Story of Taxation, Curaçao: Euro-Dutch Publishers, 1982, pp. 49-51.

[5] For some discussions on constitutional solutions, see Richard E. Wagner, Robert D. Tollison, Alvin Rabushka and John T. Noonan, Jr., Balanced Budgets, Fiscal Responsibility, and the Constitution, Washington, DC: Cato Institute 1982; Alvin Rabushka, A Compelling Case for a Constitutional Amendment to Balance the Budget and Limit Taxes, 2nd edition, Washington, DC: Taxpayers' Foundation, 1984; Lewis K. Uhler, Constitutional Control of Government: Setting Limits, Washington, DC: Regnery Gateway, 1989; W.S. Moore and Rudolph G. Penner, editors, The Constitution and the Budget: Are Constitutional Limits on Tax, Spending, and Budget Powers Desirable at the Federal Level, Washington, DC and London: American

Enterprise Institute, 1980; Aaron Wildavsky, How to Limit Government Spending, Berkeley, Los Angeles and London: University of California Press, 1980.

[6] The U.S. Constitution was intended to place restraints on government. America's founding fathers believed that there are limits to what governments should do. For other treatises on this point, see Wilhelm von Humboldt, The Limits of State Action, J.W. Burrow, editor, Cambridge: Cambridge University Press, 1969; Joseph F. Johnson, Jr., The Limits of Government, Chicago: Regnery Gateway, 1984.

[7] Randy E. Barnett, editor, The Rights Retained by the People: The History and Meaning of the Ninth Amendment, Fairfax, VA: George Mason University Press, 1989.

[8] For more on this point, see Alan M. Dershowitz, Taking Liberties: A Decade of Hard Cases, Bad Laws and Bum Raps, Chicago and New York: Contemporary Books, 1988; Gary L. McDowell, Curbing the Courts: The Constitution and the Limits of Judicial Power, Baton Rouge and London: Louisiana State University Press, 1988.

[9] Ron Paul, Freedom Under Siege: The U.S. Constitution After 200 Years, Lake Jackson, TX: Foundation for Rational Economics and Education, 1987.

[10] David Merriman, The Control of Municipal Budgets: Toward the Effective Design of Tax and Expenditure Limitations, New York, Westport and London: Quorum Books, 1987.

[11] Joseph J. DioGuardi, Unaccountable Congress: It Doesn't Add Up, Washington, DC: Regnery Gateway, 1992; James T. Bennett and Thomas J. DiLorenzo, Underground Government: The Off-Budget Public Sector, Washington, DC: Cato Institute, 1983.

[12] Anthony W. Hawkes, The Balanced Budget Veto: A New Mechanism to Limit Federal Spending, Policy Analysis 487, Washington, DC: Cato Institute, September 4, 2003.

[13] For a brief history of the payroll withholding provision and the effects that it has, see Mark Schmidt, Income Tax Withholding: Why "First Dibs" for Uncle Sam Leaves Taxpayers Finishing Last. NTU Policy Paper #106. Washington, DC: National Taxpayers Union, July 2002.

[14] David Butler and Austin Ranney, editors, Referendums: A Comparative Study of Practice and Theory, Washington, DC: American Enterprise Institute, 1978; Austin Ranney, The Referendum Device, Washington, DC and London: American Enterprise Institute, 1981.

[15] Letter of Thomas Jefferson to John Wayles Eppes, June 24, 1813, reprinted in Thomas Jefferson: Writings, New York: The Library of America, 1984, at p. 1280.

[16] Robert E. Podolsky, Titania: The Practical Alternative to Government. Boca Raton, FL: The Titania Group, Inc., 2002, pp. 131-132.

REFERENCES

Aaron, Henry J., Barry P. Bosworth and Gary Burtless. 1989. Can America Afford to Grow Old? Paying for Social Security, Washington, DC: The Brookings Institution.

Abdu'l-Baha, Selections from the Writings of Abdu'l-Baha 293 (1978), as cited in DeMoville (1998), at 234.

Adams, Charles. 2000. When in the Course of Human Events: Arguing the Case for Southern Secession. Lanham, MD and Oxford: Rowman & Littlefield.

Adams, Charles. 1993. For Good and Evil: The Impact of Taxes on the Course of Civilization, Madison Books.

Adams, Charles. 1982. Fight, Flight and Fraud: The Story of Taxation, Curaçao: Euro-Dutch Publishers.

Adie, Douglas K. 1989. Monopoly Mail: Privatizing the U.S. Postal Service. New Brunswick, NJ and Oxford: Transaction Publishers.

Adler, Jonathan H. 1996. Property Rights, Regulatory Takings, and Environmental Protection. Washington, DC: Competitive Enterprise Institute.

Ahmad, Mushtaq. 1995. Business Ethics in Islam. Islamabad, Pakistan: The International Institute of Islamic Thought and the International Institute of Islamic Economics.

Albon, Robert. 1991. The Future of Postal Services. London: Institute of Economic Affairs.

Albon, Robert and Greg Lindsay, editors. 1984. Occupational Regulation and the Public Interest: Competition or Monopoly? St. Leonard's, Australia: The Centre for Independent Studies.

Alchian, Armen A. and William R. Allen. 1967. University Economics, 2nd edition, Wadsworth Publishing Co.

Anderson, Jack and Tom Schatz. n.d. The Coming Tax Rebellion: How You Can End the Income Tax, Washington, DC: Citizens Against Government Waste.

Anderson, Terry L. and P.J. Hill. 1979. An American Experiment in Anarcho-Capitalism: The Not So Wild, Wild West, Journal of Libertarian Studies 3: 9-29.

Armentano, Dominick T. 1999. Antitrust: The Case for Repeal, 2nd revised edition. Auburn: The Ludwig von Mises Institute.

Armentano, Dominick T. 1990. Antitrust and Monopoly: Anatomy of a Policy Failure, 2nd edition. New York and London: Holmes & Meier.

Article III Problems in Enforcing the Balanced Budget Amendment, Columbia Law Review 83: 1065-1107 (1983).

Atkins v. Crosland, 417 S.W.2d 150 (Tex. 1967).

Baden, John A. and Donald Leal, editors, 1990. The Yellowstone Primer. San Francisco: Pacific Research Institute for Public Policy Research.

Baha'u'llah, Tablets of Baha'u'llah 22-23 (1978), cited in DeMoville (1998) at 233.

Baily, Martin Neil and Robert Z. Lawrence. 1987. Tax Policies for Innovation and Competitiveness.

Baim, Dean. 1987. Private Ownership Incentives in Professional Sports Facilities, in Calvin A. Kent, editor, Entrepreneurship and the Privatization of Government. New York, Westport and London: Quorum Books, pp. 109-121.

Baldo, Anthony. 1989. Killing the Goose: How Myopic IRS Tax Policies Are Crippling U.S. Competitiveness Abroad, Finance World 158: 16-17 (August 22).

Ball, D.W. 1987. Retroactive Application of Treasury Rules and Regulations, New Mexico Law Review 17: 139ff.

Ballas, Apostolos A. and Haridimos Tsoukas. 1998. Consequences of Distrust: The Vicious Cycle of Tax Evasion in Greece, in Robert W. McGee, editor, The Ethics of Tax Evasion, Dumont, NJ: The Dumont Institute for Public Policy Research, 1998, pp.284-304.

Ballentine, J. Gregory. 1983. The Administrability of a Value Added Tax, in Charls E. Walker and Mark Bloomfield, editors, New Directions in Federal Tax Policy for the 1980s, Cambridge, MA: Ballinger Publishing Co.

Ballentine, J. Gregory. 1980. Equity, Efficiency, and the U.S. Corporation Income Tax. Washington, DC: American Enterprise Institute.

Bancroft v. Indemnity Insurance Co. of North America, 203 F.Supp. 49 (W.D. La. 1962), aff'd mem., 309 F.2d 959 (5th Cir. 1963).

Bannock, Graham. 1986. VAT and Small Business: European Experience and Implications for North America, London: Graham Bannock & Partners Ltd.

Barbarick, Richard. 1996. Government Highways: Unsafe at any Speed, in Lawrence W. Reed, editor, Private Cures for Public Ills: The Promise of Privatization, Irvington-on-Hudson, NY: Foundation for Economic Education, pp. 78-83.

Barker, Dan. 1992. Losing Faith in Faith: From Preacher to Atheist, Madison, WI: Freedom from Religion Foundation.

Barnett, Randy E., editor. 1989. The Rights Retained by the People: The History and Meaning of the Ninth Amendment, Fairfax, VA: George Mason University Press.

Bartkus, Viva Ona 1999. The Dynamic of Secession, Cambridge University Press.

Bastiat, Frederic. 1968. The Law, Irvington-on-Hudson: Foundation for Economic Education.

Becker, Elizabeth and Cotton M. Lindsey. 1994. Does the Government Free Ride? Journal of Law and Economics 37: 277-296 (April).

Behn, Robert D. 1977. The False Dawn of the Sunset Laws, Public Interest, 103-18 (Fall).

Beia. 1591. Responsiones Casuum Conscientiae, cas. 13, 53ff., cited in Crowe (1944), p. 32.

Bennett, James T. and Thomas J. DiLorenzo. 1999. The Food and Drink Police: America's Nannies, Busybodies & Petty Tyrants, New Brunswick, NJ: Transaction Publishers.

Bennett, James T. and Thomas J. DiLorenzo. 1983. Underground Government: The Off-Budget Public Sector, Washington, DC: Cato Institute.

Bennett, James T. and Manuel H. Johnson. 1981. Better Government: Private Production of Public Services. Ottawa, IL and Ossining, NY: Caroline House Publishers.

Benson, Bruce L. 1990. The Enterprise of Law: Justice Without the State, San Francisco: Pacific Research Institute.

Benson, Bruce L. 1989. Enforcement of Private Property Rights in Primitive Societies: Law without Government, Journal of Libertarian Studies 9: 1-26.

Benson, Bruce L. and David W. Rasmussen. 1997. Predatory Public Finance and the Origins of the War on Drugs: 1984-1989, in William F. Shughart, II., editor, Taxing Choice: The Predatory Politics of Fiscal Discrimination 197-225.

Bentham, Jeremy. 1988. The Principles of Morals and Legislation. Amherst, NY: Prometheus Books.

Bentham, Jeremy. 1962. A Fragment on Government, in The Works of Jeremy Bentham, vol. 1 (J. Bowring, ed. 1962).

Bethell, Tom. 1998. The Noblest Triumph: Property and Prosperity Through the Ages, New York: St. Martin's Press.

Bible, 2 Kings 23:35; Matthew 22:17, 21; Romans 13:7.

Bick v. Peat Marwick and Main, 799 P.2d 94 (Kan. App. 1990).

Biffle, Christopher and Julius J. Jackson. 1992. A Guided Tour of John Stuart Mill's Utilitarianism. New York: McGraw-Hill.

Billings Clinic v. Peat Marwick Main & Co., 797 P.2d 899 (Mont. 1990).

Binswanger, Harry, editor. 1986. The Ayn Rand Lexicon: Objectivism from A to Z. New York: New American Library.

Bird, Richard M. 1992. Tax Policy & Economic Development, Baltimore and London: Johns Hopkins University Press.

Blahous, Charles P., III. 2000. Reforming Social Security, Westport, CT: Praeger.

Block, Walter. 1993. The Justification for Taxation in the Economics Literature, Canadian Public Administration/Administration Publique du Canada 36(2): 225-262 (Summer/Été), reprinted in Robert W. McGee, editor, The Ethics of Tax Evasion, Dumont, NJ: The Dumont Institute for Public Policy Research, 1998, 36-88.

Block, Walter. 1982. A Free Market in Roads, in Tibor R. Machan, editor, The Libertarian Reader, Totowa, NJ: Rowman and Allanheld, pp. 164-183, reprinted from Journal of Libertarian Studies 3(2): 209-238 (Summer 1979) under the title Free Market Transportation: Denationalizing the Roads.

Block, Walter, William Kordsmeier and Joseph Horton. 1999. The Failure of Public Finance, Journal of Accounting, Ethics & Public Policy 2(1): 42-69.

Blum, Walter J. and Harry Kalven, Jr.. 1953. The Uneasy Case for Progressive Taxation. Chicago: University of Chicago Press.

Blumenfeld, Samuel L. 1988. The New Illiterates. Boise, ID: The Paradigm Company.

Blumenfeld, Samuel L. 1985. Is Public Education Necessary? Boise, ID: The Paradigm Company.

Blundell, John. 1988. Britain's Nightmare Value Added Tax, Heritage Foundation International Briefing, Washington, DC: Heritage Foundation, June 13.

Boaz, David. 1997. The Separation of Art and State, Cato Institute, August 14.

Boaz, David, editor. 1991. Liberating Schools: Education in the Inner City, Washington, DC: Cato Institute.

Bolick, Clint. 1996. Public Lands and Private Incentives, in Lawrence W. Reed, editor, Private Cures for Public Ills: The Promise of Privatization, Irvington-on-Hudson, NY: Foundation for Economic Education, pp. 95-101.

Bonacina. 1687. De Morali Theologia, Tractatus de Restitutione, disp. II, q. IX, n. 5 (1687), II, p. 449, as quoted in Crowe (1944).

Borg, Mary O. and Paul M. Mason. 1988. The Budgetary Incidence of a Lottery to Support Education, National Tax Journal 41: 75-85.

Bovard, James. 1999. Freedom in Chains: The Rise of the State and the Demise of the Citizen, Palgrave Macmillan.

Bovard, James. 1995. Lost Rights: The Destruction of American Liberty, New York: St. Martin's Press.

Bovard, James. 1995. Shakedown: How the Government Screws You from A to Z, New York: Penguin.

Bovard, James. 1991. The Fair Trade Fraud, New York: St. Martin's Press.

Bowring, J. editor. 1962. The Works of Jeremy Bentham. Thoemmes Press.

Bowsher, Jack E. 1989. Educating America: Lessons Learned in the Nation's Corporations, New York: John Wiley & Sons, Inc.

Bradshaw, Bill and Helen Lawton Smith, editors. 2000. Privatization and Deregulation of Transport, Palgrave Macmillan.

Brandt, Richard B. 1992. Morality, Utilitarianism, and Rights. Cambridge and New York: Cambridge University Press.

Brandt, Richard B. 1979. A Theory of the Good and the Right. Buffalo: Prometheus Books.

Brown, Timothy. 1989. Interjurisdictional Tax Competition: An Economic Perspective, Nebraska Law Review 68: 652-71.

Bryant, J.S. 1983. Retroactive Taxation: A Constitutional Analysis of the Minimum Tax on IDCs, Oklahoma Law Review 36:107-118.

Buchanan, Allen. 1991. Secession: The Morality of Political Divorce from Fort Sumter to Lithuania and Quebec, Boulder, CO and Oxford: Westview Press, 1991.

Buchanan, James M. 1986. Liberty, Market and State: Political Economy in the 1980s, New York: New York University Press.

Buchanan, James M. 1983. Social Security Survival: A Public-Choice Perspective. Cato Journal 3(2): 339-353.

Buchanan, James M. 1969. External Diseconomies, Corrective Taxes and Market Structure, American Economic Review 59: 174-177.

Buchanan, James M. 1967. Public Finance in Democratic Process: Fiscal Institutions and Individual Choice. Chapel Hill: University of North Carolina Press.

Buchanan, James M. 1963. The Economics of Earmarked Taxes, Journal of Political Economy. 457-69 (October), pp. 457ff.

Buchanan, James M. and Marilyn R. Flowers. 1975. The Public Finances, 4th edition. Homewood, IL: Richard D. Irwin.

Buchanan, James M. and Richard A. Musgrave. 1999. Public Finance and Public Choice: Two Contrasting Visions on the State, Cambridge, MA and London: MIT Press.

Buchanan, James M. and W.C. Stubblebine. 1962. Externality, Economica 29: 371-384.

Buchheit, Lee C. 1978. Secession: The Legitimacy of Self-Determination, New Haven and London: Yale University Press, 1978.

Bird, Richard M. 1992. Tax Policy & Economic Development, Baltimore and London: The Johns Hopkins University Press.

Burnham, David. 1989. A Law Unto Itself: Power, Politics and the IRS, New York: Random House.

Burr, William Henry. 1860. Self-Contradictions of the Bible, New York: A.J. Davis & Company, reprinted by Prometheus Books, Buffalo, 1987.

Butler, David and Austin Ranney, editors. 1978. Referendums: A Comparative Study of Practice and Theory, Washington, DC: American Enterprise Institute.

Butler, Stuart and Peter Gremanis. 1983. Achieving Social Security Reform: A "Leninist" Strategy. Cato Journal 3(2): 547-556.

Cameron v. Montgomery, 225 N.W.2d 154 (Iowa 1975).

Camp, Brian T. 1988. The Retroactivity of Treasury Regulations: Paths to Find Abuse of Discretion, Virginia Taxation Review 7:509ff.

Campanile, Carl. 2003. Billionaire Gives $51M to City Schools. New York Post, September 18, p. 2.

Cantwell v. Connecticut, 310 U.S. 296, 308 (1940).

Caplin, Joan 1998. 6 Mistakes Even the Tax Pros Make, MONEY 104-106 (March).

Cassirer, Ernst. 1981. Kant's Life and Thought. New Haven and London: Yale University Press.

Castro. 1571. De Potestate Legis Poenalis I, c. IX, col. 1613 (1571), cited in Crowe (1944), p. 88.

Cato Handbook for Congress: Policy Recommendations for the 106th Congress 65 (1999)

Causey, Denzil Y., Jr. and Sandra A. Causey. 1995. Duties and Liabilities of Public Accountants, 5th edition, Accountants Press.

Champagne, Frank. 1994. Cancel April 15: The Plan for Painless Taxation, Mt. Vernon, WA: Nookachamps Publishers.

Charter of the United Nations, G.A. Res. 2625, Annex, 25 U. N. GAOR, Supp. 28, at 121, U.N. Doc. A/5217 (1970).

Cheung, S.N.S. 1978. The Myth of Social Cost, Hobart Paper No 82, London: Institute of Economic Affairs.

Chown, John. 1965. The Corporation Tax -- a Closer Look, London: Institute of Economic Affairs.

Clayton Estate v. Commissioner (5th Cir. 1992).

Coase, Ronald H. 1960. The Problem of Social Cost, Journal of Law and Economics 3: 1-44.

Cohn, Gordon. 1998. The Jewish View on Paying Taxes, Journal of Accounting, Ethics & Public Policy, 1(2): 109-120, reprinted in slightly different form under the title The Ethics of Tax Evasion: A Jewish Perspective, in Robert W. McGee, editor, The Ethics of Tax Evasion, Dumont, NJ: The Dumont Institute for Public Policy Research, 1998, 180-189.

Collins, Marva and Civia Tamarkin. 1982. Marva Collins Way, Los Angeles: Jeremy P. Tarcher, Inc.

Colten v. Kentucky, 407 U.S. 104, 110 (1972).

Comment, Reconciliation of Conflicting Void-for-Vagueness Theories by the Supreme Court, Houston Law Review 9: 82 (1971).

A Comparison of Japanese and American Taxation of Capital Gains, 14 Hastings International and Comparative Law Review 719-747 (1991).

A Compilation of State Sunset Statutes with Background Information on State Sunset Laws, A Staff Report prepared for the Committee on Rules, U.S. House of Representatives, by the Subcommittee on the Legislative Process, October, 1983.

A Complete Guide to the Tax Reform Act of 1986, Prentice Hall, 1986.

Concina. 1774. Theologia Christiana Dogmatico-moralis, VI, 309, cited in Crowe (1944), p. 55.

Congressional Budget Office. 1992. Effects of Adopting a Value-Added Tax. Washington: Congressional Budget Office, February.

Connally v. General Construction Co., 269 U.S. 385, 391 (1926).

Consolidated Management Services, Inc. v. Halligan, 368 S.E.2d 148 (Ga. App. 1988), affirmed, Halligan v. Consolidated Management Services, Inc., 369 S.E.2d 745 (Ga. 1988).

Constitutional Law -- The Governor's Item Veto Power, Missouri Law Review 39: 105-110 (1974).

The Constitutionality of a Line-Item Veto: A Comparison With Other Exercises of Executive Discretion Not To Spend, Golden Gate University Law Review 19: 305-345 (1989).

Cooley, Thomas. 1883. Constitutional Limitations, 5th ed. The Lawbook Exchange Ltd.

Coons, John E. and Stephen D. Sugarman (1978). Education by Choice: The Case for Family Control. Berkeley: University of California Press.

Cooper, George. 1979. A Voluntary Tax? New Perspectives on Sophisticated Estate Tax Avoidance. Washington, DC: Brookings Institution.

Coopers & Lybrand. 1992. State and Local Taxes: The Burden Grows.

Copeland, Lewis, editor. 1942. The World's Great Speeches, Garden City, NY: Garden City Publishing Co.

Cox, Wendell and Jean Love. 1992. Bus Service, in E.S. Savas, editor, Privatization for New York: Competing for a Better Future, A Report of the New York State Senate Advisory Commission on Privatization, January, pp. 154-185.

Crisp, Roger. 1997. Mill on Utilitarianism. London and New York: Routledge.

Crolly. 1877. Disputationes Theologicae de Justitia et Jure III, pp. 1001 ff.

Crowe, Martin T. 1944. The Moral Obligation of Paying Just Taxes. Catholic University of America Studies in Sacred Theology No. 84. Doctoral Dissertation.

Cullis, J.G., P. R. Jones and O. Morrissey. 1991. Public Choice Perspectives on the Poll Tax, Economic Journal 101: 600-614.

Cullis, John and Philip Jones. 1998. Public Finance and Public Choice, second edition, Oxford: Oxford University Press.

Curry, Bernard. 1982. Principles of Taxation of a Libertarian Society, Glendale, CA: BC Publishing Co.

Dasgupta, Parta. 1999. Utilitarianism, Information and Rights, in Amartya Sen and Bernard Williams, editors, Utilitarianism and Beyond. Cambridge: Cambridge University Press, pp. 199-218.

David, Anna. 1996. Disestablishing Public Education, in Lawrence W. Reed, editor, Private Cures for Public Ills: The Promise of Privatization, Irvington-on-Hudson, NY: Foundation for Economic Education, pp. 152-157.

Davis, H. 1938. Moral and Pastoral Theology, as quoted in Crowe (1944) at 40.

Davis, Jefferson. 1958. The Rise and Fall of the Confederate Government, cited in H. Newcomb Morse, The Foundations and Meaning of Secession, Stetson Law Review 15: 419-433 (1986) at 424.

DeJouvenel, Bertrand. 1952. The Ethics of Redistribution, Cambridge: Cambridge University Press. Reprinted by The Liberty Fund, Indianapolis, 1990.

Deloitte Haskins & Sells v. Green, 403 S.E.2d 818 (Ga. App. 1991).

DeMoville, Wig. 1998. The Ethics of Tax Evasion: A Baha'i Perspective, Journal of Accounting, Ethics & Public Policy 1:356-368, also published in Robert W. McGee, editor, The Ethics of Tax Evasion, Dumont, NJ: The Dumont Institute, 1998, pp. 230-240.

Dershowitz, Alan M. 1988. Taking Liberties: A Decade of Hard Cases, Bad Laws and Bum Raps, Chicago and New York: Contemporary Books.

Derthick, Martha. 1990. Agency under Stress: The Social Security Administration in American Government, Washington, DC: Brookings Institution.

Destler, I.M. and John S. Odell. 1987. Anti-Protection: Changing Forces in United States Trade Politics. Washington, DC: Institute for International Economics.

Destroying Real Estate Through the Tax Code, Policy Bulletin No. 48, Institute for Research on the Economics of Taxation, Washington, DC, February 12, 1991.

Dial v. Adamson, 570 N.E.2d 1167 (Ill. App. 1991).

Dietze, Gottfried. 1960. The Federalist: A Classic of Federalism and Free Government, Baltimore: Johns Hopkins University Press.

DiLorenzo, Thomas J. 2002. The Real Lincoln: A New Look at Abraham Lincoln, His Agenda, and an Unnecessary War. Roseville, CA: Prima Publishing (Random House).

DiLorenzo, Thomas J. 1983. A Constitutional Approach to Social Security Reform. 1983. Cato Journal 3(2): 443-459.

DioGuardi, Joseph J. 1992. Unaccountable Congress: It Doesn't Add Up, Washington, DC: Regnery Gateway.

Dreier, David and William Craig Stubblebine. 1983. The Balanced Budget/Tax Limitation Amendment, Hastings Constitutional Law Quarterly 10: 809-819.

Dunkelberg, William C. and John Skorburg. 1991. How Rising Tax Burdens Can Produce Recession, Policy Analysis No. 148, Cato Institute, February 21.

Edgeworth, Francis Ysidro. 1897. The Pure Theory of Taxation, reprinted in Richard A. Musgrave and Alan T. Peacock, editors, Classics in the Theory of Public Finance, New York and London: Macmillan, 1958, pp. 119-136.

Editorial, Shackle Congress, Free Taxpayers, Investor's Business Daily, April 21, 1998, cited in National Center for Policy Analysis, Tax Limitation Amendment [www.ncpa.org/congress/apr98b.html].

Edwards, Chris and Veronique de Rugy. 2002. International Tax Competition: A 21st-Century Restraint on Government, Policy Analysis No. 431, Washington, DC: Cato Institute, April 12, at p. 3. [www.cato.org].

Edwards, James Rolph. 1998. Regulation, the Constitution, and the Economy. Lanham, MD, New York and London: University Press of America.

Effendi, Shoghi. 1982. The Light of Divine Guidance 1: 54-55, cited in DeMoville (1998) at 234-235.

Elliott, E. Donald. 1985. Constitutional Conventions and the Deficit, Duke Law Journal 1077-1110.

Ellis, Larry V. 1987. The Privatization of Money: A Survey of the Issues, in Calvin A. Kent, editor, Entrepreneurship and the Privatization of Government. New York, Westport and London: Quorum Books, pp. 135-144.

Elving, Ronald D. 1990. Congress Braces for Fallout From State Measures, Congressional Quarterly 3144-6 (September 29).

Emerson, Rupert. 1967. From Empire to Nation: The Rise of Self-Assertion of Asian and African Peoples. Cambridge, MA: Harvard University Press.

Epstein, Richard A. 1998. Principles for a Free Society: Reconciling Individual Liberty with the Common Good. Perseus Books.

Epstein, Richard A. 1997. Mortal Peril: Our Inalienable Right to Health Care? Perseus Publishing

Epstein, Richard A. 1995. Simple Rules for a Complex World Cambridge, MA. Harvard University Press.

Epstein, Richard A. 1985. Takings: Private Property and the Power of Eminent Domain. Cambridge, MA: Harvard University Press.

Eustice, James S. 1989. Tax Complexity and the Tax Practitioner, Tax Law Review 45: 7-24.

Evans, Jeffrey Merle. 1980. Void-for-Vagueness – Judicial Response to Allegedly Vague Statutes – State v. Zuanich, 92 Un. 2d 61, 593 P.2d 1314 (1979), Washington Law Review 56: 131ff.

Everhart, Robert B., editor (1982). The Public School Monopoly. San Francisco: Pacific Institute for Public Policy Research.

Feldman v. Granger, 257 A.2d 421 (Md. 1969).

Ferrara, Peter J., editor. 1990. Free the Mail: Ending the Postal Monopoly. Washington, DC: Cato Institute.

Ferrara, Peter J., editor, 1985. Social Security: Prospects for Real Reform. Washington, DC: Cato Institute.

Ferrara, Peter J. 1983. The Prospect of Real Reform. Cato Journal 3(2): 609-621.

Ferrara, Peter J. 1980. Social Security: The Inherent Contradiction. Washington, DC: Cato Institute.

Feulner, Edwin. 1998. Welfare for Artists. Views, The Heritage Foundation, June 16 [www.heritage.org].

Fisher, Louis and Neal Devins. 1986. How Successfully Can the States' Item Veto be Transferred to the President? Georgia Law Journal 75: 159-197.

Fitzgerald, Randall. 1988. When Government Goes Private: Successful Alternatives to Public Services. New York: Universe Books, pp. 149-181.

Fitzgerald, Randall and Gerald Lipson. 1984. Pork Barrel: The Unexpurgated Grace Commission Story of Congressional Profligacy, Washington, DC: Cato Institute.

Folsom, Burton W., Jr. 1996. Private Industry Puts Michigan Railroads Back on Track, in Lawrence W. Reed, editor, Private Cures for Public Ills: The Promise of Privatization, Irvington-on-Hudson, NY: Foundation for Economic Education, pp. 65-67.

Fox, Joel. 1997. (Howard Jarvis Taxpayers Association), Making Taxes Harder, Wall Street Journal, April 15.

Frassinetti. 1866. Compendio della Teologia Morale I.

Frey, R.G., editor. 1984. Utility and Rights. Minneapolis: University of Minnesota Press.

Friedman, Milton. 1977. Inflation and Unemployment: The New Dimension of Politics, Occasional Paper 51.

Friedman, Milton. 1975. Unemployment versus Inflation? An Evaluation of the Phillips Curve, Occasional Paper 44.

Friedman, Milton. 1970. The Social Responsibility of Business, The New York Times Magazine, September 13, pp. 33, 122-126, reprinted in many places, including Kurt R. Leube, editor, The Essence of Friedman, Stanford: Hoover Institution Press, 1987, pp. 36-42.

Friedman, Milton. 1962. Capitalism & Freedom. Chicago: University of Chicago Press.

Friedman, Milton. 1960. A Program for Monetary Stability, New York: Fordham University Press.

Friedman, Milton. 1953. Essays in Positive Economics, Chicago: University of Chicago Press.

Friedman, Milton and Rose. 1979; 1980.Free to Choose. New York and London: Harcourt Brace Jovanovich.

Fund, John H. 1990. Term Limitation: An Idea Whose Time Has Come, 141 Policy Analysis (Cato, Oct. 30).

Gant, Paula A. and Robert B. Ekelund, Jr.. 1997. Excise Taxes, Social Costs, and the Consumption of Wine, in William F. Shughart, editor, Taxing Choice: The Predatory Politics of Fiscal Discrimination, New Brunswick, NJ and London: Transaction Publishers, pp. 247-269.

Garrison, Roger W. 1983. Misdirection of Labor and Capital under Social Security. 1983. Cato Journal 3(2): 513-529.

Gatto, John Taylor 1992. Dumbing Us Down: The Hidden Curriculum of Compulsory Schooling. Philadelphia: New Society Publishers.

Gattuso, James L. 1988. Amending the Constitution by the Convention Method, State Backgrounder (Heritage Foundation April 19).

Genetski, Robert. 1992. The True Cost of Government, Wall Street Journal, February 19, at A14, col. 3.

Genicot-Salsmans, Institutiones Theologiae Moralis I (1927).

Gifford, Adam, Jr. 1997. Whiskey, Margarine, and Newspapers: A Tale of Three Taxes, William F. Shughart, editor, Taxing Choice: The Predatory Politics of Fiscal Discrimination, New Brunswick, NJ and London: Transaction Publishers, pp. 57-77.

Goldberg, Arthur J. 1983. The Proposed Constitutional Convention, Hastings Constitutional Law Quarterly 11: 1-4.

Goldscheid, Rudolf. 1925. A Sociological Approach to Problems of Public Finance, reprinted in Richard A. Musgrave and Alan T. Peacock, editors, Classics in the Theory of Public Finance, New York and London: Macmillan, 1958, pp. 202-213.

Goodin, Robert E. 1995. Utilitarianism as a Public Philosophy. Cambridge: Cambridge University Press.

Goodman, John C., editor. 1985. Privatization. Dallas: National Center for Policy Analysis.

Goodman, John C. 1983. Private Alternatives to Social Security: The Experience of Other Countries. Cato Journal 3(2): 563-573.

Gorbachev's bolshie republics, The Economist, Jan. 13, 1990, at 13-4.

Gorbachev's turbulent south, The Economist, Jan. 13, 1990, at 45.

Gordon, David, editor. 1998. Secession, State & Liberty, New Brunswick, NJ and London: Transaction Publishers.

Gousset, S.E. le Card. 1869. Théologie Morale I, cited in Crowe (1944).

Grace, J. Peter. 1984. Burning Money: The Waste of Your Tax Dollars. New York: Macmillan.

Graham, John Remington. 2002. A Constitutional History of Secession. Gretna: Pelican Publishing Co.

Gravelle, Jane G. and Laurence J. Kotlikoff. 1989. Corporate Taxation and the Efficiency Gains of the 1986 Tax Reform Act, Working Paper 3142, National Bureau of Economic Research, October.

Gray, Wayne B. 1987. The Cost of Regulation: OSHA, EPA and the Productivity Slowdown. American Economic Review 77: 998-1006.

Grayned v. City of Rockford, 408 U.S. 104, 108-09 (1972).

Green, Ruth Hurmence. 1999. The Born Again Skeptic's Guide to the Bible, Freedom from Religion Foundation.

Gressman, Eugene. 1986. Is the Item Veto Constitutional? North Carolina Law Review 64: 819-23.

Gronbacher, Gregory M.A. 1998. Taxation: Catholic Social Thought and Classical Liberalism, Journal of Accounting, Ethics & Public Policy 1: 91-100, reprinted in Robert W. McGee, editor, The Ethics of Tax Evasion. South Orange, NJ: The Dumont Institute for Public Policy Research, 1998: 158-167.

Gross, Martin L. 1992. The Government Racket: Washington Waste from A to Z, New York: Bantam Books.

Gury, Compendium Theologiae Moralis (1850), cited in Crowe (1944), p. 61.

H & R Block v. Testerman, 338 A.2d 48 (Md. App. 1975).

Haarmeyer, David and Elizabeth Larson. 1996. Zoo, Inc., in Lawrence W. Reed, editor, Private Cures for Public Ills: The Promise of Privatization, Irvington-on-Hudson, NY: Foundation for Economic Education, pp. 121-125.

Haas, Raymond. 1988. U.S. Tax Policies Hurt U.S. Multinationals, CPA Journal 58: 62-73 (October).

Haley, John W. 1977. Alleged Discrepancies of the Bible, Grand Rapids, MI: Baker Book House.

Hall, Robert E. and Alvin Rabushka. 1985. The Flat Tax, Stanford: Hoover Institution Press.

Hallman, Jeffrey J. and Joseph G. Haubrich. 1992. Integrating Business and Personal Income Taxes, Economic Commentary, Federal Reserve Bank of Cleveland, October 1, 1992, p. 2.

Hamilton, Alexander. 1791. Report on Manufactures, reproduced in A.H. Cole, editor, Industrial and Commercial Correspondence of Alexander Hamilton. New York: Kelley, 1968.

Hansen, Alvin H. 1953. A Guide to Keynes, New York: McGraw Hill.

Hansen, George. 1984. To Harass Our People: The IRS and Government Abuse of Power, Washington, DC: Positive Publications.

Hardy, Dorcas R. and C. Colburn Hardy. 1991. Social Insecurity: The Crisis in America's Social Security System and How to Plan Now for Your Own Financial Survival, New York: Villard Books (Random House).

Harrington, Arthur J. 1977. The Propriety of the Negative -- The Governor's Partial Veto Authority, Marquette Law Review 60: 865-89.

Harvey, Richard J. 1990. The Right of the People of the Whole of Ireland to Self-Determination, Unity, Sovereignty and Independence, New York Law School Journal of International and Comparative Law 11: 167-206.

Hawkes, Anthony W. 2003. The Balanced Budget Veto: A New Mechanism to Limit Federal Spending, Policy Analysis 487, Washington, DC: Cato Institute, September 4.

Hawthorne, Christopher. 2001. Breaking Up Is Hard To Do, Architecture 90(3): 64-66.

Hayek, F.A. 1990. Denationalisation of Money -- The Argument Refined, 3rd edition. London: Institute of Economic Affairs.

Hayek, F.A. Hayek. 1953. The Case Against Progressive Income Taxes, The Freeman 229-32 (December 28).

Hayek, F.A. 1944. The Road to Serfdom. Chicago: University of Chicago Press.

Hazlitt, Henry, editor. 1960. The Critics of Keynesian Economics, Princeton, Toronto, London and New York: D. Van Nostrand Co.

Hazlitt, Henry. 1959. The Failure of the "New Economics", Princeton: Van Nostrand.

Hazlitt, Henry. 1946. Economics in One Lesson, New York: Harper & Brothers.

Heller, Francis H. 1982. Limiting a Constitutional Convention: The State Precedents, Cardozo Law Review 3: 563-79.

Herbener, Jeffrey M. 1992. The Fallacy of the Phillips Curve, in Dissent on Keynes: A Critical Appraisal of Keynesian Economics 51-71 (Mark Skousen, editor).

Higgs, Robert, editor. 1995. Hazardous to Our Health? FDA Regulation of Health Care Products, Independent Institute.

Hilke, John. 1993. Cost Savings from Privatization: A Compilation of Findings, How-to Guide No. 6, Reason Public Policy Institute, March [www.privatization.org].

Hobbes, Thomas. Leviathan. 1651.

Hodge, Scott, William Beach, John Barry, Mark Wilson and Joe Cobb. 1996. Is There a "Clinton Crunch"? How the 1993 Budget Plan Affected the Economy, Backgrounder No. 1078, Heritage Foundation, May 1.

Holcombe, Randall G. 1997. Selective Excise Taxation from an Interest-Group Perspective, in William F. Shughart, II., editor, Taxing Choice: The Predatory Politics of Fiscal Discrimination 81-103.

Honigman, David and George Leef. 1996. It's Time to Privatize Unemployment Insurance, in Lawrence W. Reed, editor, Private Cures for Public Ills: The Promise of Privatization, Irvington-on-Hudson, NY: Foundation for Economic Education, pp. 146-151.

Hook, Janet. 1990. New Drive to Limit Tenure Revives an Old Proposal, Congressional Quarterly 567-9 (February 24).

Hopkins, Thomas D. 1991. Cost of Regulation. An RIT Public Policy Working Paper, Rochester Institute of Technology.

Hoppe, Hans-Hermann. 1993. The Economics and Ethics of Private Property, Boston, Dordrecht and London: Kluwer Academic Publishers.

Horne v. Peckham, 158 Cal.Rptr. 714 (Cal. App. 1979).

Howard, Philip K. 1994. The Death of Common Sense: How Law Is Suffocating America. New York: Random House.

Hudgins, Edward Lee, editor. 2001. Mail at the Millennium: Will the Postal Service Go Private? Washington, DC: Cato Institute.

Hufbauer, Gary Clyde. 1992. U.S. Taxation of International Income: Blueprint for Reform, Washington, DC: Institute for International Economics.

Hufbauer, Gary Clyde, Diane T. Berliner and Kimberly Ann Elliott. 1986. Trade Protection in the United States: 31 Case Studies. Washington, DC: Institute for International Economics.

Hultberg, Nelson. 1997. Why We Must Abolish the Income Tax and the IRS: A Special Report on the National Sales Tax, Dallas: AFR Publishers.

Humboldt, Wilhelm von. 1969. The Limits of State Action, J.W. Burrow, editor, Cambridge: Cambridge University Press.

Hunt, Albert R. 1990. Congress's Terms: Just Fine As They Are, The Wall Street Journal, Apr. 24, at A-18, col. 3.

Hutt, W.H. 1979. The Keynesian Episode: A Reassessment, Indianapolis: Liberty Press.

Hutt, W.H. 1963. Keynesianism: Retrospect and Prospect, Chicago: Henry Regnery Co.

Hyman, David N. 1999. Public Finance: A Contemporary Application of Theory to Policy, 6th edition. Orlando: Dryden Press.

Ingersoll, Robert G. 1986. Some Mistakes of Moses, Buffalo: Prometheus Books.

Internal Revenue Service Statistics on Employee Plan Determination Letters, October 1991 -- September 1992, Daily Tax Rep. (BNA), November 19, 1992, at L-1.

Isaacson, Stolper & Co. v. Artisan's Savings Bank, 320 A.2d 130 (Del. 1974).

The Item Veto Power in Washington, Washington Law Review 64: 891-912 (1989).

James, Michael, editor. 1987. Restraining Leviathan: Small Government in Practice. St. Leonard's, Australia: The Centre for Independent Studies.

Jarvik, Laurence. 1997. Ten Good Reasons to Eliminate Funding for the National Endowment for the Arts, Roe Backgrounder No. 1110, The Heritage Foundation, April 29.

Jefferson, Thomas. 1813. Letter of Thomas Jefferson to John Wayles Eppes, June 24, 1813, reprinted in Thomas Jefferson: Writings, New York: The Library of America, 1984, at p. 1280-81.

Jefferson, Thomas. 1789. Letter of Thomas Jefferson to James Madison, Paris, September 6, 1789, reprinted in Thomas Jefferson: Writings, New York: The Library of America, 1984, pp. 959-64.

Jerry Clark Equipment, Inc. v. Hibbits, d/b/a AAA Bookkeeping Service, 612 N.E.2d 858 (Ill. App. 1993).

Johnson, Bryan T., Kim R. Holmes and Melanie Kirkpatrick, 1999 Index of Economic Freedom, The Heritage Foundation and the Wall Street Journal, 1999.

Johnson, Joseph F., Jr. 1984. The Limits of Government, Chicago: Regnery Gateway.

Johnson, Robin A., John McCormally and Adrian T. Moore. 2002. Long-Term Contracting for Water and Wastewater Services, How-to Guide No. 19, Reason Public Policy Institute, May [www.privatization.org].

Jung, Leo. 1987. Business Ethics in Jewish Law. Hebrew Publishing Company.

Kahn, Alfred E. Kahn. 1989. The Economics of Regulation: Principles and Institutions, 2 volumes, Cambridge, MA and London: MIT Press.

Kahn, Joseph. 2002. Valley Girls (and Guys) Push to Secede from Los Angeles, The New York Times, April 20.

Kames, Lord Henry Home. 1769. Sketches on the History of Man.

Kant, Immanuel. 1983. Ethical Philosophy, James W. Ellington, translator, Indianapolis and Cambridge: Hackett Publishing Company.

Kant, Immanuel. 1952. The Critique of Pure Reason. Great Books of the Western World, Vol. 42. Chicago: Encyclopedia Britannica, pp. 1-250.

Kant, Immanuel. 1952. Fundamental Principles of the Metaphysics of Morals, Great Books of the Western World, Vol. 42. Chicago: Encyclopedia Britannica, pp. 251-287.

Kant, Immanuel. 1952. The Critique of Practical Reason. Great Books of the Western World, Vol. 42. Chicago: Encyclopedia Britannica, pp. 289-361.

Kant, Immanuel 1952. Preface and Introduction to the Metaphysical Elements of Ethics, Great Books of the Western World, Vol. 42. Chicago: Encyclopedia Britannica, pp. 363-379.

Kant, Immanuel. 1952. General Introduction to the Metaphysics of Morals, Great Books of the Western World, Vol. 42. Chicago: Encyclopedia Britannica, pp. 381-394.

Kant, Immanuel Kant, The Critique of Judgment, Great Books of the Western World, Vol. 42. Chicago: Encyclopedia Britannica, pp.459-613.

Kauffman, Bill. 1990. Subsidies to the Arts: Cultivating Mediocrity, Policy Analysis No. 137, Cato Institute, August 8.

Kean, Thomas H. 1986. A Constitutional Convention Would Threaten the Rights We Have Cherished for 200 Years, Detroit College of Law Review 4: 1087-91.

Keller, Bill. 1990. Can Gorbachev Stay On if Lithuania Chooses to Leave? The New York Times, Jan. 14, at E-3, col. 1.

Kendall, Frances and Leon Louw. 1987. After Apartheid: The Solution for South Africa, San Francisco: ICS Press.

Kesler, Charles R. 1990. Bad Housekeeping: The Case Against Congressional Term Limitations, Policy. Review 20-25 (Summer).

Keynes, John Maynard. 1936. The General Theory of Employment, Interest and Money, New York: Harcourt Brace.

King, R.G. 1983. On the Economics of Private Money. Journal of Monetary Economics 12: 127-158.

Kirkpatrick, David W. 1990. Choice in Schooling: A Case for Tuition Vouchers. Chicago: Loyola University Press.

Kohr, Leopold. 1957 & 1986. The Breakdown of Nations, London and New York: Routledge & Kegan Paul.

Kolbert, Elizabeth. 1990. Staten Island Is Voting, but It's Only a Sitcom Secession, The New York Times, March 11, 1990, at 22E, col. 1.

Kolko, Gabriel. 1965. Railroads and Regulation 1877-1916. Princeton: Princeton University Press.

Kolko, Gabriel. 1963. The Triumph of Conservatism: A Reinterpretation of American History, 1900-1916. Glencoe: The Free Press.

Kotlikoff, Laurence and Lawrence Summers. 1981. The Role of Intergenerational Transfers in Aggregate Capital Accumulation, Journal of Political Economy 89: 706-32.

L.B. Laboratories v. Mitchell, 244 P.2d 385 (Cal. 1952).

Laffer, William G. III. 1992. George Bush's Hidden Tax: The Explosion in Regulation, Backgrounder No. 905, The Heritage Foundation, July 10.

Latvia Is an Independent, Democratic Republic, The Wall Street Journal, May 5, 1990, at A-14, col. 3.

LeCard, S.E. 1869. Gousset, Theologie Morale I, as quoted in Crowe (1944) at 59.

Ledbetter, Cal, Jr. 1975. The Constitutional Convention of 1975 And Some Remaining Constitutional Problems, Arkansas Law Review 29: 199-214.

Lee, Dwight R. 1997. Overcoming Taxpayer Resistance by Taxing Choice and Earmarking Revenues, in William F. Shughart, editor, Taxing Choice: The Predatory Politics of Fiscal Discrimination 105-116.

Lee, Dwight R. 1991. Environmental Economics and the Social Cost of Smoking, Contemporary Policy Issues 9: 83-92 (January).

Lee, Dwight. 1986. The Political Economy of Educational Vouchers, The Freeman, July, 244-248.

Lehmkuhl. 1902. Theologia Moralis I, n. 981, as cited in Crowe (1944), p. 76.

Leonhart v. Atkinson, 289 A.2d 1 (Md. App. 1972).

Leroy-Beaulieu, Paul. 1906. On Taxation in General, reprinted in Richard A. Musgrave and Alan T. Peacock, editors, Classics in the Theory of Public Finance, New York and London: Macmillan, 1958, pp. 152-164.

Leube, Kurt R., editor. 1987. The Essence of Friedman, Stanford: Hoover Institution Press.

Lewis, Joseph. 1926. The Bible Unmasked, New York: The Freethought Press Association.

Lieberman, Myron. 1989. Privatization and Educational Choice, New York: St. Martin's Press.

Lien v. McGladrey & Pullen, 509 N.W.2d 421 (S.D. 1993).

Linck v. Barokas & Martin, 667 P.2d 171 (Alaska 1983).

Lindahl, Erik. 1928. Some Controversial Questions in the Theory of Taxation, reprinted in Richard A. Musgrave and Alan T. Peacock, editors, Classics in the Theory of Public Finance, New York and London: Macmillan, 1958, pp. 214-232.

Lindahl, Erik. 1919. Just Taxation -- A Positive Solution, reprinted in Richard A. Musgrave and Alan T. Peacock, editors, Classics in the Theory of Public Finance, New York and London: Macmillan, 1958, pp. 168-176.

Lithuania on brink of leaving U.S.S.R.: It's only a question of how and when, The (Bergen County, New Jersey) Record, Feb. 25, 1990, at A-20, col. 1.

Locke, John. 1689. Two Treatises on Government.

Logan, Charles H. 1996. Competition in the Prison Business, in Lawrence W. Reed, editor, Private Cures for Public Ills: The Promise of Privatization, Irvington-on-Hudson, NY: Foundation for Economic Education, pp. 136-145.

Logan, Charles H. 1990. Private Prisons: Cons & Pros. New York and Oxford: Oxford University Press.

Long, Douglas G. 1976. Bentham on Liberty: Jeremy Bentham's Idea of Liberty in Relation to His Utilitarianism. Toronto: University of Toronto.

Los Angeles Police Protective League, White Paper On Secession, July, 2002, available at [www.lapd.com].

Lott, John R., Jr. and W. Robert Reed. 1989. Shirking and Sorting in a Political Market With Finite-Lived Politicians, Public Choice 61: 75-96.

Louw, Leon and Frances Kendall. 1986. South Africa: The Solution, Ciskei: Agami Publishers.

MacDonnell, Lawrence J. 1989. Government Mandated Costs: The regulatory burden of environmental, health and safety standards, Resources Policy 15(1): 75-100. March 1.

Machan, Tibor R. 1998. Generosity: Virtue in Civil Society. Washington, DC: Cato Institute.

Manne, Henry G. and Henry C. Wallich. 1972. The Modern Corporation and Social Responsibility, Washington, DC: American Enterprise Institute.

Marlow, Michael L. 1995. Public Finance: Theory and Practice. Orlando: The Dryden Press.

Marsden, Keith. 1983. Links between Taxes and Economic Growth: Some Empirical Evidence, World Bank Staff Working Papers No. 605.

Martin, Michael. 1993. The Case against Christianity, Philadelphia: Temple University Press.

Marx, Karl. 1875. Critique of the Gotha Program.

Marx, Karl. 1848. The Communist Manifesto.

Mascaro, Lisa, Beth Barrett and James Nash. 2002. Breakup Leaders Weigh Methods to Sustain Clout, Los Angeles Daily News, November 6.

Mayor's Press Office Statement Regarding Brooklyn Museum of Art's Board of Director's Vote, Release #381-99, September 28, 1999, http://www.ci.nyc.ny.us/html/om/html/99b/pr381-99.html.

McConnell, Campbell R. and Stanley L. Brue. 1990. Economics, 11th edition, New York: McGraw Hill.

McDonald, Forrest. 1985. Novus Ordo Seclorum: The Intellectual Origins of the Constitution, Lawrence, KS: University Press of Kansas.

McDowell, Gary L. 1988. Curbing the Courts: The Constitution and the Limits of Judicial Power, Baton Rouge and London: Louisiana State University Press.

McGee, Robert W. 2002. Legal Ethics, Business Ethics and International Trade: Some Neglected Issues, Cardozo Journal of International and Comparative Law 10(1): 109-216.

McGee, Robert W., editor. 1998. The Ethics of Tax Evasion. Dumont, NJ: The Dumont Institute for Public Policy Research.

McGee, Robert W. 1998. When Is Tax Evasion Unethical? in Robert W. McGee, editor, The Ethics of Tax Evasion, Dumont, NJ: The Dumont Institute for Public Policy Research, pp. 5-35.

McGee, Robert W. 1998. Christian Views on the Ethics of Tax Evasion, Journal of Accounting, Ethics & Public Policy, 1(2): 210-225.

McGee, Robert W. 1997. Taxation and Public Finance: A Philosophical and Ethical Approach, Commentaries on the Law of Accounting & Finance 1: 157-240.

McGee, Robert W. 1997. The USA's Assault on Trade With the People's Republic of China: Antidumping Laws as Weapons of Protectionism, in Trade and Investment in Asia, edited by Edward B. Flowers, Thomas P. Chen and Ibrahim Badawi, New York: Center for Global Education, St. John's University, 1997, pp. 187-198.

McGee, Robert W. 1997. The Fatal Flaw in the Methodology of Law & Economics, Commentaries on Law & Economics 1: 209-223.

McGee, Robert W. 1996. Tax Advice for Latvia and Other Similarly Situated Emerging Economies, International Tax & Business Lawyer 13(2): 223-308.

McGee, Robert W. 1994. Is Tax Evasion Unethical? University of Kansas Law Review 42(2): 411-435.

McGee, Robert W. 1994. A Trade Policy for Free Societies: The Case Against Protectionism. Westport, CT: Quorum Books.

McGee, Robert W. 1994. The Fatal Flaw in NAFTA, GATT and All Other Trade Agreements, Northwestern Journal of International Law & Business 14: 549-565.

McGee, Robert W. 1994. Secession Reconsidered," Journal of Libertarian Studies 11(1): 11-33. Translated into Spanish and published as "La secesión reconsiderada" in Libertas No. 33 (Octubre 2000) by the Escuela Superior de Economía y Administración de Empresas (ESEADE) in Argentina and also published at http://www.eseade.edu.ar/revista/N33McGee.html.

McGee, Robert W. 1993. Principles of Taxation for Emerging Economies: Some Lessons from the U.S. Experience, Dickinson Journal of International Law 12(1): 29-93.

McGee. Robert W. 1993. If Dwarf Tossing Is Outlawed, Only Outlaws Will Toss Dwarfs: Is Dwarf Tossing a Victimless Crime? American Journal of Jurisprudence (38): 335-358.

McGee, Robert W. 1993. The Case to Repeal the Antidumping Laws. Northwestern Journal of International Law & Business 13(3): 491-562.

McGee, Robert W. 1993. The Cost of Protectionism: Should the Law Favor Producers or Consumers?" Georgia Journal of International and Comparative Law 23(3): 529-557.

McGee, Robert W. 1993. An Economic Analysis of Protectionism in the United States with Implications for International Trade in Europe, The George Washington Journal of International Law and Economics 26(3): 539-573.

McGee, Robert W. 1993. Secession and Emerging Democracies: The Kendall and Louw Solution. Journal of International Law & Practice 2(2): 321-335.

McGee, Robert W. editor. 1992. The Market Solution to Economic Development in Eastern Europe, The Edwin Mellen Press.

McGee, Robert W. 1992. A Third Liberal Theory of Secession, Liverpool Law Review 14(1): 45-66.

McGee, Robert W. 1992. The Theory of Secession and Emerging Democracies: A Constitutional Solution, Stanford Journal of International Law 28(2): 451-476.

McGee, Robert W. 1990. The Trade Policy of a Free Society. Capital University Law Review 19: 301-341.

McGee, Robert W. 1990. The Cost of Protectionism, The Asian Economic Review 32(3): 347-364.

McGee, Robert W. 1989. The Protectionist Mentality: An Accounting and Philosophical Analysis -- Part I, The Mid-Atlantic Journal of Business 25(7): 63-83.

McGee, Robert W. 1989. The Protectionist Mentality: An Accounting and Philosophical Analysis-- Part II, The Mid-Atlantic Journal of Business 26(1): 81-104.

McGee, Robert W. and Walter Block. 1997. Must Protectionism Always Violate Rights? International Journal of Social Economics 24(4): 393-407.

McGee, Robert W. and Danny Kin Kong Lam. 1992. Hong Kong's Option To Secede, Harvard International Law Journal 33(2): 427-440.

McGee, Robert W. and Yeomin Yoon. 1995. Trade Protectionism of the United States Toward Japan and Korea, International Journal of Korean Studies 2: 45-74.

McKenzie, Richard B. 1983. Social Security: The Absence of Lasting Reform. Cato Journal 3(2): 467-478.

McKinsey, C. Dennis. 1995. The Encyclopedia of Biblical Errancy, Amherst, NY: Prometheus Books.

McLure, Charles E., Jr.. 1987. The Value-Added Tax: Key to Deficit Reduction? Washington, DC: American Enterprise Institute.

"Measuring Up": Do the Palestinian Homelands Constitute a Valid State Under International Law? Dickinson Journal of International Law 8: 339-48 (Winter 1990).

Mendez, Ruben P. 1992. International Public Finance: A New Perspective on Global Relations. Oxford: Oxford University Press.

Merriman, David. 1987. The Control of Municipal Budgets: Toward the Effective Design of Tax and Expenditure Limitations, New York, Westport and London: Quorum Books.

Mill, John Stuart. 1979. Utilitarianism (G. Sher, ed.). Indianapolis: Hackett Publishing Company.

Mill, John Stuart. 1962. Utilitarianism, On Liberty, Essay on Bentham. New York: New American Library.

Miller, Roger LeRoy. 1994. Economics Today: The Micro View, eighth edition. New York: Harper Collins College Publishers.

Mills v. Garlow, 768 P.2d 554 (Wyo. 1989).

Mises, Ludwig von. 1985. Liberalism, 3rd edition, Irvington-on-Hudson, NY: Foundation for Economic Education and San Francisco: Cobden Press.

Mises, Ludwig von. 1983. Nation, State, and Economy, New York: New York University Press.

Mises, Ludwig von. 1966. Human Action, third revised edition, Chicago: Henry Regnery.

Mises, Ludwig von. 1962. The Free and Prosperous Commonwealth, Princeton, NJ: Van Nostrand. First published in German as Liberalismus (1927).

Mises, Ludwig von. 1919. Nation, Staat, und Wirtschaft.

Mishnah Torah Hilkhot Gezeilah Chap. 5 halakhah 11, cited by Tamari (1998).

Mitchell, Cleta Deatherage. 1990. Insider Tales of an Honorable Ex-Legislator, The Wall Street Journal, Oct. 11, at A-14.

Mitchell, Daniel J. 2001. A Tax Competition Primer: Why Tax Harmonization and Information Exchange Undermine America's Competitive Advantage in the Global Economy, Backgrounder No. 1460, Washington, DC: Heritage Foundation, July 20 [www.heritage.org].

Mitchell, Daniel J. 2000. An OECD Proposal to Eliminate Tax Competition Would Mean Higher Taxes and Less Privacy, Backgrounder No. 1395, Washington, DC: Heritage Foundation, September 18 [www.heritage.org].

Mitchell, Daniel J. 1996. The Historical Lessons of Lower Tax Rates, Backgrounder No. 1086, Heritage Foundation, July 19.

Mitchell, Daniel J. 1996. Taxes, Deficits, and Economic Growth, Heritage Lecture No. 565, Heritage Foundation, May 14.

Modahl, Bill. 1991. How U.S. Corporate Taxes Hurt Competitiveness, Financier 15: 42-48 (November).

Molina. 1611. De Justitia et Iure, III, disp. 674, n. 9, concl. 5, in Gabriel Vasquez, De Restitutione, cap. 6, para. 3, dub. 2, n. 43 (1631), Cited in Crowe (1944).

Molinari, Gustav de. 1977. The Production of Security, New York: Center for Libertarian Studies.

Montemartini, Giovanni. 1900. The Fundamental Principles of a Pure Theory of Public Finance, reprinted in Richard A. Musgrave and Alan T. Peacock, editors, Classics in the Theory of Public Finance, New York and London: Macmillan, 1958, pp. 137-151.

Moore, Adrian T. 2000. Integrating Municipal Utilities into a Competitive Electricity Market, Policy Study 270, Reason Public Policy Institute, June [www.privatization.org].

Moore, Adrian T. 1998. Private Prisons: Quality Corrections at Lower Cost, Policy Study 240, Reason Public Policy Institute, April [www.privatization.org].

Moore, Adrian T., Geoffrey F. Segal and John McCormally. 2000. Infrastructure Outsourcing: Leveraging Concrete, Steel, and Asphalt with Public-Private Partnerships, Policy Study 272, Reason Public Policy Institute, September [www.privatization.org].

Moore, W.S. and Rudolph G. Penner, editors. 1980. The Constitution and the Budget: Are Constitutional Limits on Tax, Spending, and Budget Powers Desirable at the Federal Level, Washington, DC and London: American Enterprise Institute.

Morales, Alfonso. 1998. Income Tax Compliance and Alternative Views of Ethics and Human Nature, in Robert W. McGee, editor, The Ethics of Tax Evasion, Dumont, NJ: The Dumont Institute for Public Policy Research, 1998, pp. 242-258.

Moran, Thomas. 1992. N.Y. Tax Collectors Staking Out Malls: Want Payback on N.J. Shopping Deals, The (Bergen County, NJ) Record, December 10, at A1.

Murphy, Liam and Thomas Nagel. 2002. The Myth of Ownership: Taxes and Justice. Oxford: Oxford University Press.

Murtuza, Athar and S.M. Ghazanfar. 1998. Tax as a Form of Worship: Exploring the Nature of Zakat. Journal of Accounting, Ethics & Public Policy 1(2): 134-161.

Musgrave, Richard A. 1959. The Theory of Public Finance. New York: McGraw-Hill.
Musgrave, Richard A. and Alan T. Peacock, editors. 1958. Classics in the Theory of Public Finance, New York and London: Macmillan.
Musgrave, Richard A. and Peggy B. Musgrave. 1976. Public Finance in Theory and Practice, second edition, New York: McGraw-Hill.
Neely, Mark E., Jr., The Fate of Liberty: Abraham Lincoln and Civil Liberties. New York and Oxford: Oxford University Press, 1991.
New Rules for an Old Faith. 1992. Newsweek, November 30, p. 71
The 1987 Information Please Almanac 308 (1986). Time Publishing Company.
Norton, Gale Ann. 1985. The Limitless Federal Taxing Power, Harvard Journal of Law & Public Policy 8: 591-625.
Note, The Japanese Consumption Tax: Value-Added Model or Administrative Nightmare? American University Law Review 40: 1265-1306 (Spring, 1991).
Note, The Proposed Federal Balanced Budget Amendment: The Lesson from State Experience, Cincinnati Law Review 55: 563-583 (1986).
Note, The Lawson Decision: A Broadening of the Vagueness Doctrine, Stetson Law Review 13: 412 ff. (1984).
Note, The Balanced Budget Amendment: An Inquiry Into Appropriateness, Harvard Law Review 96: 1600-1620 (1983).
Note, "The Monster Approaching the Capital:" The Effort To Write Economic Policy Into the United States Constitution, Akron Law Review 15: 733-751 (1982).
Note, Recent Development, Void-for-Vagueness -- Judicial Responses to Allegedly Vague Statutes, Washington Law Review 56: 131. (1980).
Note, Void for Vagueness: An Escape from Statutory Interpretation, Indiana Law Review 23: 272ff (1948).
Note, Due Process Requirements of Definiteness in Statutes, Harvard Law Review 62: 77 (1948).
Nozick, Robert. 1974. Anarchy, State and Utopia. New York: Basic Books.
OECD, Towards Global Tax Co-operation: Report to the 2000 Ministerial Council Meeting and Recommendations by the Committee on Fiscal Affairs; Progress on Identifying and Eliminating Harmful Tax Practices, Paris: OECD, 2000 [www.oecd.org].
OECD, Harmful Tax Competition: An Emerging Global Issue, Paris: OECD, 1998. [www.oecd.org].
OECD,.1988. Taxing Consumption, Paris: OECD.
Office of Management and Budget, 1998 Fiscal Year Budget.
Officials Outline IRS Help in Setting Up Polish Tax System, Daily Tax Report (BNA), April 6, 1992, at G-1).
Ogley, Adrian. 1998. Principles of Value Added Tax: A European Perspective, London: Interfisc Publishing.
Olasky, Marvin. editor. n.d. Loving Your Neighbor: A Principles Guide to Personal Charity. Washington, DC: Capital Research Center.
Olson, Walter K. 1997. The Excuse Factory: How Employment Law is Paralyzing the American Workplace, Free Press.
Omnibus Budget Reconciliation Act of 1990.
Palmer v. City of Euclid, 402 U.S. 544 (1971).
Papachristou v. City of Jacksonville, 405 U.S. 156, 92 S. Ct. 839 (1972).
Paterson, George E., editor. 1973. Property Tax Reform, Washington, DC: The Urban Institute.
Patuzzi. 1770. Ethica Christiana sive Theologia Moralis I, 90, cited by Crowe (1944), p. 57.
Paul, Ron. 1987. Freedom Under Siege: The U.S. Constitution After 200 Years, Lake Jackson, TX: Foundation for Rational Economics and Education.
Payne, James L. 1992. Unhappy Returns: The $600-Billion Tax Ripoff. Policy Review (Winter): 18-24.
Peirce, Neal R. 1990. Zeroing in on 'Permanent Incumbency,' National Journal, October 6.

Pellechio, Anthony and Gordon Goodfellow. 1983. Individual Gains and Losses from Social Security before and after the 1983 Amendments. Cato Journal 3(2): 417-442.

Penner, Rudolph G., editor. 1983. Taxing the Family, Washington, DC and London: American Enterprise Institute.

Pennock, Robert T. 1998. Death and Taxes: On the Justice of Conscientious War Tax Resistance, Journal of Accounting, Ethics & Public Policy 1: 58-76, reprinted in Robert W. McGee, editor, The Ethics of Tax Evasion. South Orange, NJ: The Dumont Institute for Public Policy Research, 1998: 124-142.

Perry, James H. and Peter Cleary. n.d. Growth, Prosperity and Honest Government: The Case for Constitutional Tax Limitation, Americans for Tax Reform, [www.atr.org/pressreleases/Issues/i0039.htm].

Petracca, Mark P. 1991. The Poison of Professional Politics, 151 Policy Analysis, Cato Institute, May 10.

Pirie, Madsen 1988. Privatization: Theory, Practice and Choice. Hants, UK: Wildwood House.

Plato. The Republic. Various editions.

Podolsky, Robert E. 2002. Titania: The Practical Alternative to Government. Boca Raton, FL: The Titania Group, Inc.

Pollock v. Farmers Loan & Trust Co., 157 U.S. 429; 158 U.S. 601.

Poole, Robert W., Jr. 1995. Privatizing Emergency Medical Services: How Cities Can Cut Costs and Save Lives, How-to Guide No. 14, Reason Public Policy Institute, November [www.privatization.org].

Poole, Robert W., Jr. 1994. Guidelines for Airport Privatization, How-to Guide No. 13, Reason Public Policy Institute, October [www.privatization.org].

Poole, Robert W., Jr. 1993. How to Enable Private Toll Road Development, How-to Guide No. 7, Reason Public Policy Institute, May [www.privatization.org].

Poole, Robert W., Jr.. 1992. Airports, in E.S. Savas, editor, Privatization for New York: Competing for a Better Future, A Report of the New York State Senate Advisory Commission on Privatization, January, pp. 77-105.

Poole, Robert W., Jr. 1980. Cutting Back City Hall. New York: Universe Books, 1980; James T. Bennett and Manuel H. Johnson, Better Government at Half the Price, Ottawa, IL and Ossining, NY: Caroline House Publishers.

Posner, Richard A. 1998. Economic Analysis of Law, 5th edition, New York: Aspen Law & Business.

Posner, Richard A. 1983. The Economics of Justice, Cambridge, MA: Harvard University Press.

Prakken, Joel L. 1987. The Macroeconomics of Tax Reform, in Charls E. Walker and Mark A. Bloomfield, editors, The Consumption Tax: A Better Alternative? at pp. 117-166.

Pratt, James W. and William N. Kulsrud. 1997. Individual Taxation, 1998 Edition, Houston: Dame Publications, Inc.

Preliminary Report, Results of the American Academy of Actuaries Survey of Defined Benefit Plan Terminations, June 24, 1992.

Prest, A.R. 1980. Value Added Taxation: The Experience of the United Kingdom, Washington and London: American Enterprise Institute.

Quigley, J. 1989. Palestine's Declaration of Independence: Self-Determination and the Right of the Palestinians to Statehood, Boston University International Law Journal 7: 1-33.

Raboy, David G. and Cliff Massa, III. 1989. Who Bears the Burden of Consumption Taxes? In Murray L. Weidenbaum, David G. Raboy and Ernest S. Christian, Jr editors, The Value Added Tax: Orthodoxy and New Thinking, Norwell, MA, Lancaster, UK and Dordrecht, The Netherlands: Kluwer Academic Publishers, pp. 39-68.

Rabushka, Alvin. 1984. A Compelling Case for a Constitutional Amendment to Balance the Budget and Limit Taxes, 2nd edition, Washington, DC: Taxpayers' Foundation.

Rabushka, Alvin and Bruce Bartlett. 1986. Tax Policy and Economic Growth in Developing Nations, U.S. Agency for International Development.

Rand, Ayn. 1986. Textbook on Americanism, pamphlet, p. 10, as cited by Harry Binswanger, editor, The Ayn Rand Lexicon: Objectivism from A to Z. New York: New American Library, p. 519.

Rand, Ayn. 1964. The Virtue of Selfishness. New York: New American Library.

Rand, Ayn. 1957. Atlas Shrugged. New York: New American Library.

Ranney, Austin. 1981. The Referendum Device, Washington, DC and London: American Enterprise Institute.

Ranson, David. 1983. Criteria for Reforming Social Security. Cato Journal 3(2): 489-505.

Rassieur v. Charles, 188 S.W.2d 817 (Mo. 1945).

Reed, Lawrence W. 1996. Privatization: Best Hope for a Vanishing Wilderness, in Lawrence W. Reed, editor, Private Cures for Public Ills: The Promise of Privatization, Irvington-on-Hudson, NY: Foundation for Economic Education, pp. 102-111.

Reinhold, Robert. 1990. Voters Propose to Put a Lid on Their Representatives, The New York Times, Apr. 29, at 4E, col. 1.

Remedies of a Proud Outcast: The Legal Probability and Implications of Restructuring the Government and Boundaries of the City of New York, A New York State Senate Finance Committee Staff Report, July, 1983.

The Retroactivity of Treasury Regulations: Paths To Finding Abuse of Discretion, Virginia Tax Review 7: 509-533 (Winter, 1988).

Reynolds, Alan. 1992. International Comparisons of Taxes and Government Spending, in Stephen T. Easton and Michael A. Walker, editors, Rating Global Economic Freedom, Vancouver: Fraser Institute.

Reynolds, Alan. 1985. Some International Comparisons of Supply-Side Tax Policy, Cato Journal 5: 543-69.

Rhoads, Saralee. 1996. Can Private Schools Survive "Privatization?" in Lawrence W. Reed, editor, Private Cures for Public Ills: The Promise of Privatization, Irvington-on-Hudson, NY: Foundation for Economic Education, pp. 158-165.

Rhodes, Robert M. 1973. A Limited Federal Constitutional Convention, University of Florida Law Review 26: 1-18.

Ricardo, David 1817. Principles of Political Economy and Taxation, reprinted Amherst, NY: Prometheus Books, 1996.

Rice, William Craig. 1997. I Hear America Singing: The Arts Will Flower Without the NEA, 82 Policy Review, March-April available at [www.heritage.org].

Richard v. Staehle, 434 N.E.2d 1379 (Ohio App. 1980).

Richman, Jack. 1992. Housing in New York City, in E.S. Savas, editor, Privatization for New York: Competing for a Better Future, A Report of the New York State Senate Advisory Commission on Privatization, January, pp. 244-265.

Richman, Sheldon. 1999. Your Money or Your Life: Why We Must Abolish the Income Tax, Fairfax, VA: Future of Freedom Foundation.

Richman, Sheldon. 1995. Separating School & State: How to Liberate America's Families, Fairfax, VA: The Future of Freedom Foundation.

Roberts, Paul Craig. 1983. Social Security: Myths and Reality. Cato Journal 3(2): 393-401.

Robertson, A. Haeworth. 1983. The National Commission's Failure to Achieve Real Reform. Cato Journal 3(2): 403-416.

Robbins, Aldona and Gary. 1991. How Tax Policy Compounded the S&L Crisis, Policy Report No. 109, The Institute for Policy Innovation, Lewisville, TX, February.

Robbins, Gary and Aldona. 1992. Promoting Growth Through Tax Policy, Policy Report No. 115, Lewisville, TX: The Institute for Policy Innovation, March.

Robinson, Glen O. 1988. Public Choice Speculations on the Item Veto, Virginia Law Review 74: 403-22.

Robinson, T. 1987. Retroactivity: The Case for Better Regulation of Federal Tax Regulators, Ohio State Law Journal 48: 773-813.

Rodino, Peter W., Jr., 1983. The Proposed Balanced Budget/Tax Limitation Constitutional Amendment: No Balance, No Limits, Hastings Constitutional Law Quarterly 10: 785-807.

Rosen, Harvey S. 1999. Public Finance, 5th edition. Irwin/McGraw-Hill.

Rosenau, Pauline, editor. 2000. Public-Private Policy Partnerships, Cambridge, MA: MIT Press.
Roth, G.J. 1966. A Self-Financing Road System. London: Institute of Economic Affairs.
Rothbard. Murray N. 1998. The Ethics of Liberty, New York and London: New York University Press.
Rothbard, Murray N. 1988. The Case Against the Flat Tax, Llewellyn H. Rockwell, editor, The Free Market Reader, Auburn, AL: Mises Institute, pp. 342-62.

Rothbard, Murray N. 1981. The Myth of Neutral Taxation, Cato Journal 1: 519-64.
Rothbard, Murray N. 1978. For a New Liberty, revised edition, New York: Libertarian Review Association.
Rothbard, Murray N. 1970. Man, Economy, and State. Los Angeles: Nash Publishing.
Rothbard, Murray N. 1970. Power and Market: Government and the Economy, Menlo Park, CA: Institute for Humane Studies.
Rothbard, Murray N. 1963. America's Great Depression, Los Angeles: Nash Publishing.
Rottenberg, Simon, editor. 1980. Occupational Licensure and Regulation, Washington, DC: American Enterprise Institute.
Rousseau, Jean Jacques. 1762. The Social Contract.
Rubenstein, Edwin S. 1992. Medicaid, in E.S. Savas, editor, Privatization for New York: Competing for a Better Future, A Report of the New York State Senate Advisory Commission on Privatization, January, pp. 44-76.
Ruwart, Mary J. 1992. Healing Our World, Kalamazoo, MI: Sun Star Press.
Sabrin, Murray. 1994. Tax Free 2000: The Rebirth of American Liberty, Lafayette, LA: Prescott Press.
Saint-Etienne, Christian. 1984. The Great Depression 1929-1938: Lessons for the 1980s. Stanford: Hoover Institution Press.
St. Antoninus. 1571. Summa Sacrae Theologiae II, cited in Crowe (1944), p. 42.
Salisbury, David F. 2003. What Does a Voucher Buy? A Closer Look at the Cost of Private Schools, Policy Analysis No. 486, Washington, DC: Cato Institute, August 28.
Sandburg, Carl, editor. 1939. Abraham Lincoln, The War Years. New York: Harcourt Brace.
Savas, E.S. 1982. Privatizing the Public Sector: How to Shrink Government. Chatham, NJ: Chatham House Publishers.
Sax, Emil. 1924. The Valuation Theory of Taxation, reprinted in Richard A. Musgrave and Alan T. Peacock, editors, Classics in the Theory of Public Finance, New York and London: Macmillan, 1958, pp. 177-189.
Scarlett, Lynn and J.M. Sloan. 1996. Solid Waste Management: A Guide for Competitive Contracting for Collection, How-to Guide No. 16, Reason Public Policy Institute, September [www.privatization.org].
Scarre, Geoffrey 1996. Utilitarianism. London and New York: Routledge.
Schansberg, D. Eric. 1998. The Ethics of Tax Evasion Within Biblical Christianity: Are There Limits to "Rendering Unto Caesar"? Journal of Accounting, Ethics & Public Policy 1: 77-90, reprinted in Robert W. McGee, editor, The Ethics of Tax Evasion. Dumont, NJ: The Dumont Institute for Public Policy Research, 1998: 144-157.
Schmidt, Mark. 2002 Income Tax Withholding: Why "First Dibs" for Uncle Sam Leaves Taxpayers Finishing Last. NTU Policy Paper #106. Washington, DC: National Taxpayers Union, July .
Schoeck, Helmut. 1966. Envy: A Theory of Social Behavior. New York: Harcourt Brace & World.
Schoenbrod, David. 1990. Presidential Lawmaking Powers: Vetoes, Line Item Vetoes, Signing Statements, Executive Orders, and Delegations of Rulemaking Authority, Washington University Law Quarterly 68:533-60.
Scott, Cordia 2001. OECD 'Harmful' Tax Competition May Violate WTO Obligations, Expert Says, Tax Notes International, April 24, reproduced at [www.freedomandprosperity.org].
SEC v. Seaboard Corp., 677 F.2d 1301 (9th Cir. 1982).

Segal, Geoffrey F., Adrian T. Moore and Samuel McCarthy. 2002. Contracting for Road and Highway Maintenance, How-to Guide No. 21, Reason Public Policy Institute, March [www.privatization.org].

Segal, Geoffrey F. and Adrian Moore. 2002. Weighing the Watchman: Evaluating the Costs and Benefits of Outsourcing Correctional Services, Part 2: Reviewing the Literature on Cost and Quality Comparisons, Policy Study 290, Reason Public Policy Institute, January [www.privatization.org].

Segal, Geoffrey and Adrian T. Moore. 2000. Privatizing Landfills: Market Solutions for Solid-waste Disposal, Policy Study 267, Reason Public Policy Institute, May [www.privatization.org].

Segal, Geoffrey F. and Samuel R. Staley. 2002. City of Angels, Valley of Rebels, Cato Policy Report 34(5): September/October.

Seijas, Nancy and Frank Vorhies. 1996. Private Preservation of Wildlife: A Visit to the South African Lowveld, in Lawrence W. Reed, editor, Private Cures for Public Ills: The Promise of Privatization, Irvington-on-Hudson, NY: Foundation for Economic Education, pp. 112-120.

Seldes, George. 1985. The Great Thoughts. New York: Ballantine Books.

Self-Determination: the Case of Palestine, American Society of International L. Proc.: 334-51 (1988).

Seligman, Edwin Robert Anderson. 1931. Essays in Taxation. Augustus M. Kelley Publishers (1969).

Semmens, John. 1996. Highways: Public Problems, Private Solutions, in Lawrence W. Reed, editor, Private Cures for Public Ills: The Promise of Privatization, Irvington-on-Hudson, NY: Foundation for Economic Education, pp. 68-77.

Sen, Amartya. 1982. Utilitarianism and Beyond. Cambridge: Cambridge University Press.

Senese, Donald J. 1996. Privatizing Japan's Railroads, in Lawrence W. Reed, editor, Private Cures for Public Ills: The Promise of Privatization, Irvington-on-Hudson, NY: Foundation for Economic Education, pp. 84-89.

Senior, Ian. 1983. Liberating the Letter: A Proposal to Privatise the Post Office. London: Institute of Economic Affairs.

Senior, Ian. 1970. The Postal Service: Competition or Monopoly? London: Institute of Economic Affairs.

Sennholz, Hans F. 1979. Age of Inflation, New Rochelle, NY: Arlington House.

Shannon, Russell. 1981. Incentives and Income Taxes, Freeman 653-656 (November).

Shaw, William H. 1999. Contemporary Ethics: Taking Account of Utilitarianism, Oxford: Blackwell Publishers.

Sheaffer, Robert. 1988. Resentment Against Achievement: Understanding the Assault Upon Ability. Buffalo: Prometheus Books.

Sheppard, Harrison. 2002. VICA Backs Cityhood, Los Angeles Daily News, September 24.

Shribman, David. 1990. Drive to Restrict Tenure in Congress to 12 Years Is Pressed in Capital and One-Third of the States, The Wall Street Journal, March 12, at A-12, col. 1.

Shughart, William F., II, editor. 1997. Taxing Choice: The Predatory Politics of Fiscal Discrimination. New Brunswick, NJ and London: Transaction Books.

Shughart, William F., II. 1997. The Economics of the Nanny State, in William F. Shughart, II, editor, Taxing Choice: The Predatory Politics of Fiscal Discrimination. New Brunswick, NJ and London: Transaction Books, pp. 13-29.

Sidak, J. Gregory and Thomas A. Smith. 1990. Four Faces of the Item Veto: A Reply To Tribe and Kurland, Northwestern University Law Review 84: 437-79.

Siddiqi, M. Nejatullah. 1996. Role of the State in the Economy: An Islamic Perspective. Leicester, UK: The Islamic Foundation.

Sidgwick, Henry. 1966. The Methods of Ethics. Indianapolis: Hackett Publishing Co.

Sins, Ancient and Modern. 1992. The Economist, November 21, p. 50.

Skousen, Mark, editor. 1992. Dissent on Keynes: A Critical Appraisal of Keynesian Economics, New York, Westport and London: Praeger.

Skousen, Mark. 1991. Economics on Trial, Homewood, IL: Business One Irwin.

Sladky v. Lomax, 538 N.E.2d 1089 (Ohio App. 1988).

Slaughter v. Roddie, 249 So.2d (La. App. 1971).

Slemrod, Joel and Nikki Sorum. 1984. The Compliance Cost of the U.S. Individual Income Tax System, National Tax Journal 37: 461-474.

Smart, J.J.C. and Bernard Williams. 1973. Utilitarianism - For and Against. Cambridge: Cambridge University Press.

Smatrakalev, Gueorgui. 1998. Walking on the Edge: Bulgaria and the Transition to a Market Economy, in Robert W. McGee, editor, The Ethics of Tax Evasion, Dumont, NJ: The Dumont Institute for Public Policy Research, 1998, pp.316-329.

Smith, Adam. 1776; 1937. The Wealth of Nations.

Smith v. Goguen, 415 U.S. 566 (1974).

Smith v. St. Paul Fire & Marine Insurance Co., 366 F.Supp. 1283 (M.D. La. 1973), aff'd per curiam, 500 F.2d 1131 (5th Cir. 1974).

Smith, Sheldon R. and Kevin C. Kimball. 1998. Tax Evasion and Ethics: A Perspective from Members of The Church of Jesus Christ of Latter-day Saints. Journal of Accounting, Ethics & Public Policy 1: 337-348 (Summer), reprinted in Robert W. McGee, editor, The Ethics of Tax Evasion. Dumont, NJ: The Dumont Institute for Public Policy Research, 1998: 220-229.

Smoot-Hawley Tariff Act of 1930, Pub. L. No. 71-361, 46 Stat. 590, 19 U.S.C. §§ 1671-77g, 19 U.S.C.A. §§ 1673-73I (1980 & 1992 Supp.).

Snydergeneral Corporation v. KPMG Peat Marwick, No. 90-14145-K (District Court of Dallas County 1992).

Sorenson v. Fio Rito, 413 N.E.2d 47 (Ill. App. 1980).

Soviet Decolonization, The Wall Street Journal, Jan. 3, 1990, at A-6, col. 1.

The Speeches of Abraham Lincoln (1908).

Spellmire, George, Wayne Baliga and Debra Winiarski. 1990. Accountants' Legal Liability Guide. New York: Harcourt Brace Jovanovich.

Spencer, Herbert. 1970. Social Statics. New York: Robert Schalkenbach Foundation.

Spooner, Lysander. 1870. No Treason: The Constitution of No Authority, originally self-published by Spooner in Boston in 1870, reprinted by Rampart College in 1965, 1966, and 1971, and by Ralph Myles Publisher, Inc., Colorado Springs, Colorado, in 1973.

Spring, Joel. 1983. The Public School Movement vs. the Libertarian Tradition, Journal of Libertarian Studies 7:1, 61-79.

Springer v. U.S., 102 U.S. 586 (1881).

Stansel, Dean. 1998. Supermajority: A Super Idea, Cato Institute, April 15 [www.cato.org].

Steckler, Steve and Lavinia Payson. 1992. Infrastructure, in E.S. Savas, editor, Privatization for New York: Competing for a Better Future, A Report of the New York State Senate Advisory Commission on Privatization, January, pp. 186-214.

Stein, Lorenz von. 1885. On Taxation, reprinted in Richard A. Musgrave and Alan T. Peacock, editors, Classics in the Theory of Public Finance, New York and London: Macmillan, 1958, pp. 28-36.

Stevens, Barbara J. 1992. Solid Waste Management, in E.S. Savas, editor, Privatization for New York: Competing for a Better Future, A Report of the New York State Senate Advisory Commission on Privatization, January, pp. 215-243.

Stiglitz, Joseph E. 1988. Economics of the Public Sector, second edition. New York: W.W. Norton & Company.

Stroup, Richard L. and John C. Goodman. 1989. Making the World Less Safe: The Unhealthy Trend in Health, Safety, and Environmental Regulation. NCPA Policy Report #137, Dallas: National Center for Policy Analysis.

Stuart, Arnold Jacob Cohen. 1889. On Progressive Taxation, reprinted in Richard A. Musgrave and Alan T. Peacock, editors, Classics in the Theory of Public Finance, New York and London: Macmillan, 1958, pp. 48-71.

Sunset Act of 1980: Report of the Committee on Governmental Affairs, United States Senate, to accompany S. 2, To Require Authorizations of New Budget Authority for Government

Programs at Least Every Ten Years, To Provide for Review of Government Programs Every Ten Years, and for Other Purposes, July 24, 1980 (Report No. 96-865).

Supermajority at the State Level, Americans for Tax Reform. The number varies from year to yet. See [www.atr.org] for the latest statistics.

Tait, Alan A. 1988. Value Added Tax: International Practice and Problems, Washington, DC: International Monetary Fund.

Tamari, Meir. 1998. Ethical Issues in Tax Evasion: A Jewish Perspective, Journal of Accounting, Ethics & Public Policy, 1(2): 121-132, reprinted under the same title in Robert W. McGee, editor, The Ethics of Tax Evasion, Dumont, NJ: The Dumont Institute for Public Policy Research, 1998, 168-178.

Tax Foundation. 1991. Tax Freedom Day 1991 Is May 8 -- Latest Date Ever: State Tax Freedom Days Range from April 24 to May 26, 35 Tax Features (April) 1ff.

Taxes and Growth: The London Conference, Critical Issues No. 10, Australian Institute for Public Policy, 14 October 1986.

Taxes Paid Versus Federal Funds Received, Daily Tax Report (BNA), August 7, 1992, at H-4. These statistics are based on the 16th annual edition of New York State and the Federal Fisc, Who Cheated NY of $136 Billion?, published in association with the Taubman Center for State and Local Government, John F. Kennedy School of Government, Harvard University.

Templeton, Charles. 1996. Farewell to God: My reasons for rejecting the Christian faith, Toronto: McClelland & Stewart.

The Term Limit Train, The Wall Street Journal, Oct. 11, 1990, at A-14.

Terms of Limitation, The Wall Street Journal, Dec. 11, 1989, at A-14.

To What Extent Can Taxpayers Rely on IRS Regulations and Rulings to Predict Future IRS Conduct?. Gonzaga Law Review 25: 281-298 (1989/90).

Top-level plea for Soviet unity, The (Bergen County, New Jersey) Record, Jan. 13, 1990, at A-5, col. 4.

Tritch, Teresa. 1993. Tritch, Keep an Eye on Your Tax Pro, MONEY (March), p. 100.

Tritch, Teresa and Deborah Lohse. 1992. Tax Payers, Start Worrying! MONEY (March), p. 90.

Ture, Norman B. 1983. Supply-Side Effects of Social Insurance. Cato Journal 3(2): 537-546.

Uhler, Lewis K. 1989. Constitutional Control of Government: Setting Limits, Washington, DC: Regnery Gateway.

United Nations, World Investment Report 2001, New York: United Nations Conference on Trade and Development (UNCTAD), 2001.

U.S. Declaration of Independence. 1776.

U.S. Foreign Tax Policy and the Global Economy: New Directions for the 1990s, Institute for Research on the Economics of Taxation, 1989.

U.S. v. Helmsley, 733 F.Supp. 600, 941 F.2d 71 (2nd Cir. 1991).

United States v. Simon, 425 F.2d 796 (2d Cir. 1969), cert. denied, 397 U.S. 1006 (1970).

United States General Accounting Office. 1993. Regulatory Burden: Recent Studies, Industry Issues, and Agency Initiatives. GAO/GGD-94-28. December.

U.S. General Accounting Office, Paperwork Reduction: Little Real Burden Change in Recent Years, GAO/PEMD-89-19FS.

U.S. General Accounting Office. 1992. Tax Policy and Administration: Luxury Excise Tax Issues and Estimated Effects, GAO/GGD-92-9, February.

United States General Accounting Office. 1978. The Navy Overhaul Policy -- A Costly Means of Insuring Readiness for Support Ships, Report by Comptroller General of the United States: LCD-78-434, December 27.

United States International Trade Commission. 2002. The Economic Effects of Significant U.S. Import Restraints, Third Update 2002, USITC Pub. 3519 (June), available at [www.usitc.gov].

U.S. Office of Management and Budget, Report to the Congress: Federal Procurement Paperwork Burden, January, 1990, as cited by Thomas D. Hopkins, Cost of Regulation, A Rochester Institute of Technology Public Policy Working Paper, December, 1991.

United States Trade Representative, 2003 National Trade Estimate Report on FOREIGN TRADE BARRIERS (Washington, DC: Superintendent of Documents).

U.S. Treasury Department's Report to Congress, titled Integration and Individual and Corporate Tax Systems: Taxing Business Income Once, January, 1992.

Utt, Ronald. 1991. The Growing Regulatory Burden: At What Cost To America? IPI Policy Report No. 114, Lewisville, TX: Institute for Policy Innovation. November.

Vaguine, Vladimir V. 1998. The "Shadow Economy" and Tax Evasion in Russia, in Robert W. McGee, editor, The Ethics of Tax Evasion, Dumont, NJ: The Dumont Institute for Public Policy Research, 1998, pp.306-314.

Vaubel, R. 1984. The Government's Money Monopoly: Externalities or Natural Monopoly? Kyklos 37: 27-57.

Vedder, Richard K. and Lowell E. Gallaway. 1997. Out of Work: Unemployment and Government in Twentieth-Century America, New York: New York University Press.

Veljanovski, Cento. 1989. Privatization: Monopoly Money or Competition? In Cento Veljanovski, editor, Privatisation & Competition: A Market Prospectus. London: Institute of Economic Affairs, pp. 26-51.

Village of Hoffman Estates v. The Flipside, 455 U.S. 489, 498 (1982).

Voit, E. 1833. Theologia Moralis I, 855, cited in Crowe (1944), p. 57.

Wagner, Richard E. 1997. The Taxation of Alcohol and the Control of Social Costs, in William F. Shughart, II, editor, Taxing Choice: The Predatory Politics of Fiscal Discrimination. New Brunswick, NJ and London: Transaction Books, pp. 227-246.

Wagner, Richard E. 1983. Funded Social Security: Collective and Private Options. Cato Journal 3(2): 581-602.

Wagner, Richard E. 1983. Public Finance: Revenues and Expenditures in a Democratic Society. Little Brown & Co.

Wagner, Richard E., Robert D. Tollison, Alvin Rabushka and John T. Noonan, Jr. 1982. Balanced Budgets, Fiscal Responsibility, and the Constitution, Washington, DC: Cato Institute.

Wanniski, Jude. 1978; 1983; 1989. The Way the World Works. Regnery Publishing Company.

Warmbrodt v. Blanchard, 692 P.2d 1282 (Nev. 1984).

Warren, Chris. 1998. Some Westsiders Want to Follow the Valley to Independence from L.A., Los Angeles Magazine, September.

Washington's Partial Veto Power: Judicial Construction of Article III, Section 12, University of Puget Sound Law Review 10: 699-720 (1987).

Weaver, Carolyn L. 1983. The Economics and Politics of the Emergence of Social Security: Some Implications for Reform. Cato Journal 3(2): 361-379.

Weidenbaum, Murray L., David G. Raboy and Ernest S. Christian, Jr., editors. 1989. The Value Added Tax: Orthodoxy and New Thinking, Center for the Study of American Business, Norwell, MA, Lancaster, UK and Dordrecht, The Netherlands: Kluwer Academic Publishers

Weidenbaum, Murray L. and Ernest S. Christian, Jr. 1989. The Allure of Value-Added Taxes: Examining the Pros and Cons.

Weidenbaum, Murray L. and Robert DeFina. 1978. The Cost of Federal Regulation of Economic Activity. Washington, DC: American Enterprise Institute. May.

West, E.G. 1970. Education and the State, second edition. London: Institute of Economic Affairs.

Wheless, Joseph. 1997. Is It God's Word: An Exposition of the Fables and Mythology of the Bible and the Fallacies of Theology, Montana: Kessinger Publishing Co.

Wheless, Joseph. 1997. Forgery in Christianity: A Documented Record of the Foundations of the Christian Religion, Montana: Kessinger Publishing Co.

Wicksell, Knut. 1896. Finanztheoretische Untersuchungen [A New Principle of Just Taxation], reprinted in Richard A. Musgrave and Alan T. Peacock, editors, Classics in the Theory of Public Finance, New York and London: Macmillan, 1958, pp. 72-118.

Wilborn, Paul 2002. Failed Secession Forces Pressure LA Mayor for Better Services, Associated Press, November 6. [www.sfgate.com].

Wilborn, Paul. 2002. Los Angeles Has Become Too Big, Say Those Who Want to Break It Up, Associated Press, November 2, 2002, available at [www.sfgate.com].

Wilborn, Paul. 2002. Los Angeles Secession Efforts Getting Closer to Winning Spots on the Ballot, Associated Press, May 19 [www.sfgate.com].

Wilcox, Gregory J. 2002. Commerce Back to Business as Usual? Los Angeles Daily News, November 6.

Wildavsky, Aaron. 1980. How to Limit Government Spending, Berkeley, Los Angeles and London: University of California Press, 1980.

Will, George F. 2003. California, Ugly: Recall war headed downhill, New York Post, September 4, p. 27.

Will, George F. 1992. Purring Along the Potomac, Newsweek, November 30, p. 96.

Williams, Walter E. 1999. More Liberty Means Less Government, Stanford: Hoover Institute Press.

Williams, Walter. 1987. All It Takes Is Guts: A Minority View, Washington, DC: Regnery Books.

Winters v. New York, 333 U.S. 507, 515 (1948).

The Wisconsin Partial Veto: Past, Present and Future, Wisconsin Law Review 1395-1432 (1989).

Withholding, Direct Transfer Amendments Seen Costing Employers Over $4 Billion, Daily Tax Rep. (BNA), August 4, 1992, at G-4.

Wood, John R. 1981. Secession: A Comparative Analytical Framework, Canadian Journal of Political Science 14: 107-34.

The World Almanac and Book of Facts 1991 (1990).

World Bank. 1994. Averting the Old Age Crisis,: Policies to Protect the Old and Promote Growth, New York: Oxford University Press.

Wright v. Williams, 121 Cal.Rptr. 194 (Cal. App. 1975).

Wyckoff, Paul Gary. 1984. Flat Taxes and the Limits to Reform, Economic Commentary, Federal Reserve Bank of Cleveland, October 22.

Yandle, Bruce. 1994. Regulatory Takings, Farmers, Ranchers and the Fifth Amendment. Center for Policy Studies, Clemson University.

Young, S. David Young. 1987. The Rule of Experts: Occupational Licensing in America. Washington, DC: Cato Institute.

Yunker, James A. 1986. In Defense of Utilitarianism: An Economist's Viewpoint, Review of Social Economy 44(1): 57-79.

Yusuf, S.M. 1971. Economic Justice in Islam. Lahore: Sh. Muhammad Ashraf.

Zagaris, Bruce. 2001. Application of the OECD Harmful Tax Practices Criteria to the OECD Countries Shows Potential Dangers to the U.S. Sovereignty, April 25, posted at [www.freedomandprosperity.org].

NAME INDEX

SUBJECT INDEX